Home Feelings

CARLETON LIBRARY SERIES

The Carleton Library Series publishes books about Canadian economics, geography, history, politics, public policy, society and culture, and related topics, in the form of leading new scholarship and reprints of classics in these fields. The series is funded by Carleton University, published by McGill-Queen's University Press, and is under the guidance of the Carleton Library Series Editorial Board, which consists of faculty members of Carleton University. Suggestions and proposals for manuscripts and new editions of classic works are welcome and may be directed to the Carleton Library Series Editorial Board c/o the Library, Carleton University, Ottawa K1S 5B6, at cls@carleton.ca, or on the web at www.carleton.ca/cls.

CLS board members: John Clarke, Ross Eaman, Jennifer Henderson, Paul Litt, Laura Macdonald, Jody Mason, Stanley Winer, Barry Wright

233 *W.A. Mackintosh*
    The Life of a Canadian Economist
    Hugh Grant

234 *Green-lite*
    Complexity in Fifty Years of Canadian Environmental Policy, Governance, and Democracy
    G. Bruce Doern, Graeme Auld, and Christopher Stoney

235 *Canadian Expeditionary Force, 1914–1919*
    Official History of the Canadian Army in the First World War
    G.W.L. Nicholson
    Introduction by Mark Osborne Humphries

236 *Trade, Industrial Policy, and International Competition, Second Edition*
    Richard G. Harris
    Introduction by David A. Wolfe

237 *An Undisciplined Economist*
    Robert G. Evans on Health Economics, Health Care Policy, and Population Health
    Edited by Morris L. Barer, Greg L. Stoddart, Kimberlyn M. McGrail, and Chris B. McLeod

238 *Wildlife, Land, and People*
    A Century of Change in Prairie Canada
    Donald G. Wetherell

239 *Filling the Ranks*
    Manpower in the Canadian Expeditionary Force, 1914–1918
    Richard Holt

240 *Tax, Order, and Good Government*
    A New Political History of Canada, 1867–1917
    E.A. Heaman

241 Catharine Parr Traill's *The Female Emigrant's Guide*
    Cooking with a Canadian Classic
    Edited by Nathalie Cooke and Fiona Lucas

242 *Tug of War*
    Surveillance Capitalism, Military Contracting, and the Rise of the Security State
    Jocelyn Wills

243 *The Hand of God*
    Claude Ryan and the Fate of Canadian Liberalism, 1925–1971
    Michael Gauvreau

244 *Report on Social Security for Canada* (New Edition)
    Leonard Marsh

245 *Like Everyone Else but Different*
    The Paradoxical Success of Canadian Jews, Second Edition
    Morton Weinfeld with Randal F. Schnoor and Michelle Shames

246 *Beardmore*
    The Viking Hoax That Rewrote History
    Douglas Hunter

247 *Stanley's Dream*
    The Medical Expedition to Easter Island
    Jacalyn Duffin

248 *Change and Continuity*
    Canadian Political Economy in the New Millennium
    Edited by Mark P. Thomas, Leah F. Vosko, Carlo Fanelli, and Olena Lyubchenko

249 *Home Feelings*
    Liberal Citizenship and the Canadian Reading Camp Movement
    Jody Mason

Home Feelings

Liberal Citizenship and the Canadian Reading Camp Movement

JODY MASON

Carleton Library Series 249

McGill-Queen's University Press
Montreal & Kingston • London • Chicago

© McGill-Queen's University Press 2019

ISBN 978-0-7735-5886-1 (cloth)
ISBN 978-0-7735-5887-8 (paper)
ISBN 978-0-7735-5959-2 (ePDF)
ISBN 978-0-7735-5960-8 (ePUB)

Legal deposit fourth quarter 2019
Bibliothèque nationale du Québec

Printed in Canada on acid-free paper that is 100% ancient forest free (100% post-consumer recycled), processed chlorine free

This book has been published with the help of a grant from the Canadian Federation for the Humanities and Social Sciences, through the Awards to Scholarly Publications Program, using funds provided by the Social Sciences and Humanities Research Council of Canada.

Funded by the Government of Canada | Financé par le gouvernement du Canada | | Canada Council for the Arts | Conseil des arts du Canada

We acknowledge the support of the Canada Council for the Arts.

Nous remercions le Conseil des arts du Canada de son soutien.

Library and Archives Canada Cataloguing in Publication

Title: Home feelings: liberal citizenship and the Canadian reading camp movement / Jody Mason.

Names: Mason, Jody, 1976– author.

Description: Series Statement: Carleton Library Series; 249 | Includes bibliographical references and index.

Identifiers: Canadiana (print) 20190120274 | Canadiana (ebook) 20190120495 | ISBN 9780773558878 (softcover) | ISBN 9780773558861 (hardcover) | ISBN 9780773559592 (ePDF) | ISBN 9780773559608 (ePUB)

Subjects: LCSH: Frontier College—History—20th century. | LCSH: Literacy—Canada—History—20th century. | LCSH: Citizenship—Canada—History—20th century.

Classification: LCC LC154 .M37 2019 | DDC 302.2/2440971—dc23

This book was typeset by Marquis Interscript in 10.5 / 13 Sabon.

Social scientists and historians have seized upon prairie settlement in the early part of the twentieth century as a feature of Canadian society of special interest ... The camps, like the settling of the prairies, have been a characteristic Canadian phenomenon, but they have not drawn comparable attention ... Perhaps it is because social scientists have found it easier to deal with communities on the one hand and migration on the other than with something in between: a social form that has in many of its characteristics been widespread and persistent but that has no fixed location. Perhaps it is because the campmen themselves, often illiterate and always on the move, have not told their story.
Jean Burnet, "Introduction," The Bunkhouse Man

Production thus not only creates an object for the subject, but also a subject for the object.
Karl Marx, Grundrisse

Contents

Tables and Figures ix

Abbreviations xi

Acknowledgments xiii

Preface: Reformers, Literacy, and the Canadian Reading Camp Movement xv

Introduction 3

1 Creating a "Home Feeling": The Uses of Fiction and Poetry, 1899–1905 23

2 Print for "The Immigrant" and the Limits of Liberal Citizenship, 1906–1919 67

3 Using the Pedagogy of Liberal Citizenship, 1920–1929 120

4 "Red" Literacy and Counter-Literacy in Relief Camps for the Unemployed, 1930–1936 171

Conclusion 218

Notes 235

Bibliography 305

Index 337

Tables and Figures

TABLES

3.1 Instructors' results, 1921. MG 28, I 124, vol. 119, "Registers, 1921," FC-LAC. 164

4.1 Instructors' results, 1933. MG 28, I 124, vol. 126, "Registers, 1933," FC-LAC; "Reports, 1933," MG 28, I 124, vol. 108; and "Reports, 1934," MG 28, I 124, vol. 108, FC-LAC. 210

FIGURES

1.1 "Travelling Libraries" circular, 1900. MG 28, I 124, vol. 143, "Clippings," FC-LAC. 35

1.2 Home-like reading room, Canadian Reading Camp Association's early period. "Historical Photographs of Camps in Winter [ca. 1910–80]," R3584-1-2-E, vol. 489, FC [multiple media]-LAC. Image used with permission of Frontier College. 55

2.1 "The Bank." Fitzpatrick, *Handbook for New Canadians*, 105. 108

3.1 "Making Good Canadian Citizens Out of Our Foreign Workmen," *The Toronto Daily Star*. 25 October 1920, 6. 123

3.2 Ethnic composition of Frontier College camps, 1922 and 1929. Data taken from *Coming of Age, Annual Report 1921, The Frontier College, with Twenty-Second Annual Report*, MG 28, I 124, Vol. 107 and *General Report, Frontier College Activities Among Foreign-Born Labourers Throughout*

       Canada, Season 1929, MG 28, I 124, Vol. 109, FC-LAC. 124
- 3.3 Register of "N. McKague," MG 28, I 124, vol. 119, "Instructors' Reports, 1921," FC-LAC. 143
- 3.4 Student Sketch in Register. "Earle W. Carr," MG 28, I 124, vol. 122, "Registers, 1926," FC-LAC. 161
- 4.1 "Fanatical Outbursts," *Relief Camp Worker,* 16 May 1935. 189
- 4.2 Ethnic Composition of Frontier College Camps, 1933. MG 28, I 124, vol. 126, "Registers, 1933," FC-LAC. 195
- 4.3 "Reading Matter for Campmen," MG 28, I 124, vol. 108, "Reports, 1934," FC-LAC. 198

Abbreviations

AFL	American Federation of Labor
CAAE	Canadian Association for Adult Education
CBC	Canadian Broadcasting Corporation
CCCC	Advisory Committee on Cooperation in Canadian Citizenship
CPC	Communist Party of Canada
CPR	Canadian Pacific Railway
CNR	Canadian National Railway
DND	Department of National Defence
IWW	International Workers of the World
NCUC	National Council of Unemployed Councils
NUWA	National Unemployed Workers' Association
NFB	National Film Board
OBU	One Big Union
RCWU	Relief Camp Workers' Union
RCMP	Royal Canadian Mounted Police
SDPC	Social Democratic Party of Canada
TLC	Trades and Labor Congress of Canada
YMCA	Young Men's Christian Association
WCTU	Women's Christian Temperance Union
WEA	Workers' Educational Association
WUL	Workers' Unity League
UNESCO	United Nations Education, Scientific, and Cultural Organization

Acknowledgments

So many people have helped me make this book. For archival assistance, I was lucky to draw on the knowledge of André D'Ulisse (NFB Archives), Aaron Hope (Archives of Ontario), and the always helpful staff in the reference room at Library and Archives Canada, where I spent many long days. Frontier College has helped me with permissions and with the work of tracking down sources; I owe particular thanks to Philip Fernandez, Sandy Kiverago, and James Morrison. I have worked with very committed research assistants: Steve McLeod and Chris Doody put in many hours at Library and Archives Canada and only complained when the cafeteria disappeared. I've benefited from the knowledge of other scholars working on Frontier College, and especially from the archival acuity of Lorne Bruce, who generously shared his work on the Ontario Travelling Library series with me. I have workshopped elements of this project at many conferences since 2013 and thank the Society for the History of Authorship, Reading, and Publishing; the Association for Canadian and Québec Literatures / l'Association des littératures canadienne et québecoise; the TransCanada Institute; and the Society for Textual Scholarship for hosting my work. Part of this book's first chapter was published in *Labour/Le Travail* 76 (Fall 2015). I'm thankful to the editor, Sean Cadigan, and to the peer reviewers who helped me define what the larger project could be. I owe thanks as well to Jonathan Crago and Kathleen Fraser at McGill-Queen's University Press, to Matthew Kudelka for fine copy editing, and to the peer reviewers who read the manuscript and paraphrased its arguments attentively, turning elements I had overlooked into claims that are now important to the book.

I have amazing colleagues. I've received invaluable feedback from the Research Working Group, and especially from my colleagues Brenda Carr Vellino, Sarah Brouillette, Travis DeCook, Jennifer Henderson, Stuart Murray, and Franny Nudelman. Students in my graduate seminars on the history of reading (2015) and on citizenship and cultural forms (2017) were important interlocutors as I developed this project from idea to manuscript. The Faculty of Arts and Social Sciences at Carleton University has provided really valuable material support and teaching release in the form of a Junior Faculty Research Award and a Faculty Research Award.

The work of researching and writing a book relies on those who care for my children while I'm working and travelling. I am very grateful to Tara Gerrie; Pat Armand Schmidt; Linda Jewers; Nina Kirliuk; Nathalie Lehoux; Margaret and Ian MacLaren; Bill and Linda Mason; Mimi Noble; Jacqui Roye and the after-school team; Megan Schmidt; and Emeline Villedary.

In *The Sociology of Literature*, Raymond Williams observes that "the great advantages of writing, with its enormous expansion of newly possible kinds of continuity and access, have been counterpointed, throughout, by the radical disadvantages of its inherent specialization of the faculty of reception." Although I didn't always attribute it to Williams, this contention hovered around all my university work in English; it became relevant in a new way when, in my late twenties, I worked as a volunteer literacy facilitator at Parkdale Project Read, a community-based adult literacy program in Toronto. The people I met there pushed me to think more self-consciously about how we acquire literacy and what we do with it. Project Read confirmed my impression that literacy can mean very different things to different people, depending on their experiences, beliefs, needs, and desires. This book is for Project Read, and for street-corner literacy organizations everywhere, because in these places, despite narrow, top-down definitions of "literacy," people find ways of making literacy matter for them.

PREFACE

Reformers, Literacy, and the Canadian Reading Camp Movement

As an identification of a skill increasingly deemed necessary to society, the term "literacy" and the related term "illiteracy" came to name in the nineteenth century what were perceived as new social problems that required attention. As Raymond Williams points out in his classic account of "keywords" in culture and society, "literacy" emerged in English in the late nineteenth century as a term "to express the achievement and possession of what were increasingly seen as general and necessary skills." Formerly denoted by the word "literature," this meaning required a word of its own once "literature" came to acquire its specialized modern sense as "creative" or "imaginative" work. As Harvey J. Graff's seminal work on literacy demonstrates, the longstanding association of literacy with social and economic progress and its use as a "measure of modernity" constitutes a powerful "literacy myth" in Western societies. This myth, embedded in post-Enlightenment social thought, assumed a shape particular to early twentieth-century Canada in relation to the combined but nonetheless dissensual forces of eighteenth- and nineteenth-century utilitarianism and cultural idealism, which privileged the functional uses of literacy for their ability to engender individual and social progress, on the one hand, and reading as a source of spiritual and aesthetic encounter, on the other.[1]

While the "literacy myth" is pervasive, it is nonetheless true that the attainment of mass literacy in industrializing, nineteenth-century Britain contributed significantly to existing class tensions. Education, the influence of evangelical and utilitarian ideologies, and changes in the book and periodical trades made literacy a mass phenomenon in nineteenth-century Britain; however, as Richard Altick points out in his history of the development of Britain's "mass reading public," the spread of literacy in early-nineteenth-century Britain was enmeshed in the class conflict produced by the emergence of industrial capitalism. As the dominant classes "conceded it was impossible to prevent the lower ranks from reading, they embarked on a long campaign to ensure that through the press the masses of people would be induced to help preserve the status quo and bulwark the security and prosperity of the particular sort of national life that they, its upper- and middle-class rulers, cherished." Books and the ability to read them were championed by evangelicals and utilitarians alike as a means of producing, in the former case, better Christians, and in the latter case, better workers, but both of these groups insisted that the emerging lower middle class should have highly circumscribed and directed engagements with print. Both also agreed that guided education could smother working-class discontent and radicalism. The well-known work of Terry Eagleton on the "rise of English" in nineteenth-century Britain adds another layer to Altick's analysis insofar as it narrows in on the particular ways that middle-class reformers such as Matthew Arnold viewed *literature* in the English vernacular, in particular, as a "humanizing" antidote to "political bigotry and ideological extremism" in the context of religion's declining influence. The prophylactic functions of books, literacy, and, finally, literature, are thus deeply rooted in the emergence of industrial capitalism and the class conflict and consciousness it engendered.[2]

British North Americans were also largely literate by the beginning of the twentieth century. Provisions for public education in both Canada West and Canada East in the decade preceding Confederation led to rising literacy levels (measured by the ability to sign one's name). As measured by the 1861 census in Canada West, urban, anglophone Protestants in Hamilton had one of the highest literacy levels in the western world. By the 1870s, literacy was a "majority phenomenon" in Quebec, and Ontario recorded almost full literacy by the end of the nineteenth century; according to the census, nearly full literacy had been achieved in Canada by 1921.[3] The provision of mass elementary education in Ontario preceded industrialization, which paved the way for a transition to industrialization in the late nineteenth and early twentieth centuries that was relatively peaceful compared with England's. Shaped by the views of Egerton Ryerson, Ontario's public schools promoted "discipline, moral values, and the 'training in being trained' which mattered most in the preparation of a modern industrial workforce." Yet whether or not increased literacy actually engendered social progress, economic growth, or class mobility among the communities it touched is a matter of significant debate. David Vincent and Harvey J. Graff treat the phenomenon of mass literacy carefully, cautioning that it did not necessarily lead to occupational or class mobility for the majority of unskilled and semi-skilled workers in England and Ontario in the latter half of the nineteenth century. As Graff's work demonstrates, literacy's meaning is not autonomous but rather dependent on other factors, including ascribed social characteristics and the institutional contexts in which that meaning is gained. For instance, literacy was not unattached from class; the literacy of an unskilled worker produced different social effects than the literacy of an educated professional. In Graff's view, literacy reinforced existing class identities in nineteenth-century Ontario.[4] Moreover, census data do not tell us much about the immigrant men who worked on Canada's resource frontier in the first decades of the twentieth century and whose itinerant lives likely escaped the census measure on many occasions.[5] Literate or not in their native languages – and contemporary census data suggest that they had high rates of self-reported literacy in these languages – these immigrants were not literate in English, a fact that brought literacy and citizenship – a term that came to mean "Canadianization" during the 1910s – into urgent relation in this period. As we will see, for these workers as for schoolchildren of the mid-nineteenth century, what Graff calls literacy's "perceived contribution to attitudinal and value preparation and socialization" was more central to reformers' efforts than the specific skills it represented.[6]

The organization that began as the Canadian Reading Camp Association in 1899 and later became Frontier College was not the first of its kind, but it has been the most enduring. In Canada, as in Britain and other parts of the English-speaking world, the nineteenth century was a great period for voluntary associations and reform-oriented organizations, and it is in this voluntary realm that the first Canadian experiments in adult workers' education were undertaken. Although industrial capitalism emerged almost a century later in Canada than in Britain, British experiments in workers' education influenced British Canadians, particularly in more urban areas. Variously motivated by liberal ideologies of self-improvement, technological change and its implications for labour, religious mission, the desire to encourage cooperation between labour and capital, and the conviction, as public education advocate Egerton Ryerson put it, that "educated labour is more productive than uneducated labour," those involved in the voluntary adult education efforts of the nineteenth and early twentieth centuries included ministers and lay people, middle-class reformers, and wealthy philanthropists. Their efforts ranged from adult Sunday schools (particularly in Methodist and nonconforming churches) to reading rooms, and from public lectures to minstrel shows. The mechanics' institute movement was perhaps the most broad-ranging attempt by middle-class reformers to address the question of worker's education in the nineteenth century: modelled on their British counterparts, these institutes proliferated throughout British North America in the first half of the nineteenth century.[7] Early libraries and mechanics' institutes in Upper Canada / Canada West benefited from some public support well before Confederation, but a "conscious" and, in many cases, state-sponsored adult education movement did not develop in Canada until after the outbreak of the First World War.[8] Workers, whether skilled urban labourers or rural farmers, developed their own educational organizations in this same period: urban workers had their own friendly societies, sporting fraternities, fire companies, and workingmen's clubs in the late nineteenth century, all run by and for themselves, and farmers undertook collective organization and education through bodies such as the Ontario-based Dominion Grange. These were not, generally speaking, forms of social organization that privileged education and literacy initiatives, though there were exceptions.[9]

An important precursor to the Canadian Reading Camp Association was the Aberdeen Association, founded in Winnipeg in 1890 under the leadership of Lady Aberdeen of Scotland (whose husband became Governor General of Canada in 1893). It sought to alleviate the extreme social and cultural isolation of settlers in Canada, particularly those in the West and Northwest, by collecting print materials in Canadian cities and in Britain for distribution to frontier settlers. In its early years, the Aberdeen Association was dependent on books and magazines supplied from Great Britain, and its primary object was to narrow the vast distances of empire with reading material from the centre of that empire. The story of the association's founding demonstrates its British axis: on an 1890 visit to the Canadian West that had as one of its aims the study of the conditions facing Scottish crofters, Lady Aberdeen noted the "bareness" of the lives of these settlers living at great distances from Great Britain, many of whom had some education but whose homes were now utterly devoid of reading material.¹⁰ She wanted to increase their proximity to their natal culture through the distribution of books from that culture. As a result of her subsequent entreaty, Sir Adolphe Caron, the Postmaster General of Canada between 1892 and 1896, agreed to modify the already generous system of low postal rates for domestic periodicals. For the Aberdeen Association, he agreed to ship donations of new and used books and periodicals (not all of which were produced domestically) free of charge, indicating in 1898 that "it is almost impossible to comprehend how men go forth spreading liberty, spreading the constitutional views of the British Empire all over the world, without some Association like this."¹¹

An important donor to the Aberdeen Association's stock of print was William Thomas Stead, English newspaper editor, founder of modern tabloid journalism, and Christian social purity campaigner. In its 1898 annual report, the Aberdeen Association gratefully acknowledged Stead's continuing monthly donation of 1,200 copies of *Review of Reviews* and "many thousands" of copies of his "Penny Books." Subsequent annual reports similarly noted his frequent contributions.¹² Stead's conception of *Review of Reviews* – essentially an inexpensive compendium of Britain's monthly reviews for a "poor but aspirational readership" – was lofty: its first issue (in January 1890) promised that it would be "to the English-speaking world what the Catholic Church in its prime was to the intelligence of Christendom ... with affiliates ... [and] correspondents in every village, read as men used to read their Bibles."¹³ An even more ambitious undertaking was Stead's Masterpiece Library series, which began as a subscription library service in 1895 and grew to become a tremendously successful reprint enterprise that included "Penny Poets" and "Penny Popular Novels." The "Penny Poets" series, which came first, was deeply informed by late-nineteenth-century reform discourse and its insistence on the possibility of moulding individual character through reading: according to Stead, the series would introduce working-class youth to abridgements of classic verse in order to "inculcate patriotism, to quicken the sense of duty, and to familiarize the mind of youth with the heroism of self[-]sacrifice." The first titles in the series included Macaulay's *Lays of Ancient Rome*; Lord Byron's "Childe Harold's Pilgrimage"; and selections by Walter Scott, James Russell Lowell, John Milton, William Shakespeare, Geoffrey Chaucer, and Alexander Pope. The series was enormously successful (2,000,000 copies of the "Penny Poets" sold in the first seven months), but critics complained that, in attempting to supplant the "penny dreadful" with better literature, Stead's "Penny Steadfuls" presumed to direct the reading preferences of the British masses. Stead defended himself by asserting the value of *all* reading, but the "Penny Poets" and the later "Penny Popular Novels" series were indeed premised on an appeal to the value of the "classics" and their ability to enjoin young people, especially, to a sense of duty linked to empire.[14]

An important aspect of the Aberdeen Association's commitment to preventing "the sort of separation which is dangerous to the unity of the State" was the correspondence work of its various branches, whose volunteers surveyed the reading habits, religious identities, and interests of their subscribers and contacted these readers by letter twice a year.[15] If the association was initially intended to serve British settlers – to limit their errantry from the perceived centre of empire – its local branches soon had to confront the diverse religious and ethnic identities of the nation's western settlers, whom they both accommodated – by inquiring about the native language and religious identity of each subscriber, for example – and attempted to influence.[16] For example, the association monitored the taste and discernment of its far-flung subscribers through Chautauqua-inspired initiatives and a newsletter. The 1898 annual report notes that "competitions, suggestions for family or individual courses of reading with lists of questions provided on the Chautauqua plan, the offer of rewards for prize essays on specified subjects, might all be developed as time goes on, more especially as the personal correspondence which is so essential a part of our system brings the workers to know the circumstances and needs of their recipients more and more closely." This plan never seems to have developed, but beginning in 1903, the association began to publish a quarterly newsletter, *The Aberdeen Visitor*. The newsletter provided a vehicle for regular communication with the "general circle" of the association's readers. It also served as a kind of instructional manual, printing "such matter as shall be in harmony with the general tone and character of literature distributed, and shall afford assistance to those who are reading with a view to the improvement of their minds." The subscriber who might "doubt his or her capacity to judge rightly of books," for instance, was guided with a firm hand to find an "admittedly good book" and make that "your standard."[17] When faced with evidence of subscribers whose cultural and intellectual predilections were doubtful, as in the case of one seventeen-year-old girl who informed the Winnipeg branch that she had "no religion" and preferred "stories of Jesse James, stories of murders," Aberdeen workers were convinced that a "monthly parcel of pure, elevating, educating reading" could have a "salutary and far-reaching effect on the future good of this country."[18] Organizers for the Aberdeen Association clearly felt that instruction and guidance were indispensable companions to the "elevating, educating reading" that could potentially mould individual virtue. In 1905, Lady Aberdeen observed that the demand for the services of the association had fallen off significantly "of late years as the towns of Canada have become more able to supply the remoter parts." After 1905, the Canadian Reading Camp Association, a recipient of books donated by the Aberdeen Association, assumed an important aspect of the older association's work in rural areas, while also developing its goal of soldering the distribution of literature to a program of instruction, and therefore of carefully conceived and monitored character formation.[19]

In many cases, the educational organizations established by business, educational, and political elites in the latter half of the nineteenth century experienced serious challenges from worker-led activism in the early twentieth century. After the fin-de-siècle demise of mechanics' institutes, the field of adult education was increasingly "contested," with elite sponsors and worker-led interests jostling for control. The Workers' Educational Association (WEA), the Antigonish Movement, and the Women's Institute movement all witnessed this sort of internal contest.[20] In the West, agrarian radicals developed grain growers' associations – educational institutions that were distinct from their "uplifting" Victorian predecessors insofar as they openly challenged "the power of railroads, bankers, and grain merchants."[21] Early-twentieth-century worker-led education frequently had ties to specific ethnic communities, as well as to specifically religious, cultural, and/or political interests: urban Jewish communities established synagogues, societies, schools, newspapers, theatres, unions, workers' circles, and benevolent organizations; Winnipeg's Ukrainian immigrants founded reading clubs, socialist circles, libraries, drama societies, choirs, cooperatives, and national homes; and the Finns of Fort William and Port Arthur, Ontario, had their own reading rooms and libraries, discussion groups, lectures, and language classes.[22] The meaning of citizenship – a term that, as we will see, was increasingly tied to workers' education initiatives as the twentieth century unfolded – became a site of considerable contest in these contexts. For example, Tom Mitchell reads the birth of western agrarian radicalism in the 1910s as crucial to the formation of "an unprecedented range of populist visions of a new citizenship in an uncorrupted democracy." Similarly, although workers and the academic leadership of the University of Toronto-based WEA shared, in the late 1910s, a language of "education for citizenship," this language "masked some very significant differences" regarding the meanings of both education and citizenship. Worker critiques of "the limits of education in a class society" and their promotion of the "social and collective purpose" of workers' education gained little traction among academic leaders. Such differences would lead to the association's demise in the early 1950s.[23]

At the same time, reformers' efforts to reach working-class – and especially non-British immigrant – Canadians extended during the early twentieth century into diverse areas of social life. These efforts drew on an older reformist language that associated literacy with progress to conflate English-language acquisition with a vaguely defined project of citizenship education. Libraries and educational programs or groups located in settlement houses (the first of which was established in Toronto in 1902); attached to political, labour, religious, and ethnic associations; sponsored by private companies and benevolent associations; or affiliated with university extension programs, reached countless workers in an era of westward expansion and nation-building.[24] In the first decade of the twentieth century, particularly in the West, night schools for immigrant adults wanting to learn English were established: the Roman Catholic Church in Edmonton set up a night school for Ukrainian girls working in the city in 1901, and Manitoba's Department of Education set up a similar service in north-end Winnipeg in 1907.[25] Private industry often participated in initiatives designed to encourage immigrant workers, in particular, to read and write in English and to adopt British Canadian, Protestant values, especially in rural areas where there were no other educational services for adults. In 1905, for example, railway companies, in cooperation with universities and the federal Department of Agriculture, established their first "school on wheels," a program based in the western provinces and designed to service their remote, largely immigrant populations. In the mid-1920s, the Canadian National and Canadian Pacific Railways (CNR and CPR) undertook a joint project with the Ontario Department of Education that sent railway cars equipped with teachers into the northern parts of the province. These "schools on wheels" were designed to serve the children of the (largely Italian) immigrant railway workers who maintained the tracks north of Sudbury, but they also functioned as mobile night schools and libraries for the workers and their wives. As the government of Ontario encouraged these itinerant teachers to do, they taught adults English reading, writing, and arithmetic, while introducing "the Canadian way of life": "democratic principles" and "national loyalty and good citizenship."[26]

More often, early forms of language and citizenship education were aimed specifically at those non-British immigrant communities that were taking root in Canada's growing cities. For example, the Winnipeg People's Forum, organized by a young J.S. Woodsworth and other labour leaders, was established in 1909 as a means of encouraging Winnipeg's ethnically diverse community to debate civic and social questions in a common setting. Such reform-oriented missionary work was carried out across the country in the late nineteenth and early twentieth centuries, particularly by Methodists, Presbyterians, and the ecumenically minded YMCA, and it generally included language instruction in English.[27] Emerging from this context, Woodsworth's People's Forum shifted its attention away from proselytizing towards the more secular and nationalist work of nurturing citizens. Near the end of the First World War, Woodsworth claimed that the work done for immigrants by the established churches and fraternal organizations in the nineteenth and early twentieth centuries was being supplanted by what Allen Mills describes as the "unifying," "inclusive and public-spirited" efforts of a "vast and growing state apparatus," as well as by newly created private agencies, such as social welfare agencies, social settlements, non-denominational churches, people's forums, consolidated school districts, and community centres.[28]

The organization that became Frontier College was initially known (until 1919) as the Canadian Reading Camp Association ("Canadian" was dropped in 1906). Founded in 1899 or 1900 by Alfred Fitzpatrick, a Presbyterian minister influenced by the values of the Social Gospel movement, the movement inaugurated its work in 1900–1 in four lumber camps near Nairn Centre, Ontario.[29] Its first rooms, in makeshift shacks, were stocked with reading material but were unsupervised. The association grew quickly, and by 1903, there were at least twenty-four reading rooms in shacks, tents, and railcars across Northern Ontario.[30] It continued to expand its work westward with the growth of the railway, mining, and construction industries, which relied on itinerant and increasingly non-British immigrant labour. As the association grew, it altered its methods. The unsupervised reading room gradually ceded place to the librarian-instructor and then, by the end of the association's first decade, to the labourer-teacher – often and later almost exclusively university students who worked on the sleigh haul and steam shovel by day and who conducted classes in English and other basic subjects by night.[31] The growth of the Canadian Reading Camp movement was precarious in these early decades: the association received no government funding at the outset (although it began to receive modest provincial grants during its first decade) and instead relied on donations from churches, individuals, and the companies that benefited from its operations.

This book confines its attention to the early years of the association, focusing on the period prior to the Second World War. My concentration on these years permits me to examine the period of Canada's "Great Transformation," when immigration and industrialization posed acute challenges to a settler nation that was in the process of articulating its cultural and political identity; these years offer a rich site for the analysis of relations among imperialism, settler nationalism, citizenship, non-British immigration, and capitalism.[32] Shaped by the pressures and conflicts of these four decades, the Canadian Reading Camp Association assumed a particular form: throughout this period, the association's focus remained the deployment of labourer-teachers to mining, construction, railway, and lumber camps across Canada; its pedagogy for citizenship was conceived, developed, expanded, and adapted; and it worked to convince provincial and federal governments to assume responsibility for the education of adults. Although there were significant interruptions and digressions from this main work (the diminishment of work camps during the First World War, and the creation of a degree-granting program between 1922 and 1934, for example), the basic character of the association's work did not change in this period. As a means of naming this consistency, the title of this book refers to the work of the association in the first four decades of the twentieth century as the Reading Camp movement. In the wake of the Second World War, "a changing economy, new labour technology, the disappearance of 'remote' work camps, structural unemployment, and new advances in the education environment," coupled with the growing role of organized labour and the federal Technical and Vocational Assistance

Act in worker education, significantly altered the kind of initiatives that Frontier College undertook.³³

Between 1899 and 1939, the Canadian Reading Camp Association and the early Frontier College derived most of its work and much of its *raison d'être* from the non-British immigrant labourers who were filling the nation's work camps. Even in the earliest days, instructors made particular efforts to reach out to foreign-born workers, particularly those who could not speak English. These efforts increased steadily as more and more labourer-teachers went west in the first decade of the twentieth century to work on rail and construction gangs, which were populated overwhelmingly by non–English-speaking workers. The relevance of these efforts to the concept of "citizenship" was articulated in 1912, when the association's annual report indicates its desire to impart "our ideas of citizenship and our ideals of life" to immigrant camp workers.³⁴ As the link between the immigrant and "the Red" was solidified in liberal thought, and as labour conflicts such as the 1919 Winnipeg General Strike generated new liberal anxieties about the stability of the capitalist economy, the work of Frontier College focused almost exclusively on a counter-literacy for liberal citizenship. The publication of the association's *Handbook for New Canadians* in 1919 was the culmination of two decades of fieldwork, and it prepared the ground for the association's future citizenship education efforts, which, as we shall see, were to be augmented considerably during the 1920s. After 1932, the work of Frontier College shifted somewhat. Labourer-teachers were deployed not to regular work camps but to the relief camps for unemployed men that were operated throughout the first half of the 1930s by the Department of National Defence (DND). Although the work of combating radical political organizing that Frontier College undertook in these camps was not new, the task of educating for liberal citizenship was complicated by the fact that citizenship was subject to new kinds of contest in this period.

Home Feelings

Introduction

In 1999, Frontier College, Canada's longest-running movement to teach adults to read and one of the first organizations in the country to undertake the project of citizenship education, celebrated its hundredth anniversary. Frontier College, known until 1919 as the Canadian Reading Camp Association, has long been dependent to some degree on the support of Canada's federal government; in recent decades, it has also been the object of frequent memorialization by the state. Such memorialization serves the state discourse of multiculturalism well, supporting what Eva Mackey identifies as Canada's self-promotion as a tolerant, liberal-pluralistic nation. A commemorative stamp for the hundredth birthday of Frontier College in 1999, for example, narrates the organization's provision of "education for all." The media backgrounder for the 2009 unveiling of a Historic Sites and Monuments Board of Canada plaque at the Frontier College headquarters in Toronto notes that the organization's early twentieth-century labourer-teachers served an "army of camp labourers – many of whom recent immigrants – [who] worked under unpleasant, dangerous conditions for poor pay."[1] This way of casting the meanings of Frontier College has also been adopted in popular historical narratives, such as the "Heritage Minute" produced by Historica Canada, a not-for-profit organization dedicated to increasing awareness of Canadian history and citizenship. Such remembering offers an alternative collective memory that occludes the racism that guided Canadian immigration policy in the early decades of the twentieth century. For instance, it helps to reorient the remembering of a history of immigration policy that used a head-tax mechanism (1885–1923) and, later, outright exclusion (1923–47), to prevent Chinese immigration. Complementing the state's commemoration of Frontier College is the persistent assumption in the history of Canadian adult education that there is a tradition of "communitarianism" (often contrasted with American individualism) that might explain the nation's long-standing devotion to "the imaginative training for citizenship" and, it is implied, its development of a tolerant liberal politics of multiculturalism.[2] In a broader sense, the suturing of citizenship to the values of liberal multiculturalism is crucial to the federal government's ongoing narration of the former as a sign of the nation's open doors and egalitarian social system. For instance, the current citizenship guide, *Discover Canada*, observes that "Canada is often referred to as a *land of immigrants* because, over the past 200 years, millions of newcomers have helped to build and defend our way of life." As is typical of liberal pluralism, the "our" of this narrative is deliberately ambiguous: it is at once a sign of everyone – Canada is an egalitarian land where each can participate in this collective pronoun – and a select group – those who identify with the groups from which "Canadian society stems," the "English-speaking and French-speaking Christian civilizations brought here from Europe by settlers." Historical instances of racism, such as the 1923 Chinese Immigration Act, are represented as exceptional rather than constitutive. *Discover Canada* implies that an ideology of "unity in diversity" has inspired the social shape of Canada since at least the interwar period.[3]

Using Frontier College as its principal case study and offering the first sustained analysis of this organization and its archive, this study offers an alternative to liberal state narratives that have cast the nation's pre–Second World War history of adult education in the light of liberal tolerance and anticipatory multiculturalism. This book analyzes the production, use, and consumption of a print culture of liberal citizenship through a critical history of the early-twentieth-century Reading Camp Movement, employing an interdisciplinary approach that draws on social history, the history of reading, literary and cultural studies, and the sociology of culture in order to show how contests among non-state actors were important in shaping ideas about citizenship that may seem to be simply effects of postwar state policy. Eschewing the nation's more frequently studied urban centres, the better-known state literacy and citizenship initiatives of the postwar period, and evolutionary narratives of social citizenship, I argue that literature, literacy, and citizenship were being brought into new relation and were subject to new kinds of meaning and contestation in early-twentieth-century Canada, particularly in the frontier work camps where Frontier College focused the efforts of its Reading Camp Movement. As the British Canadian settler majority sought to define itself in relation to an expanding non-British immigrant population and as capital's need for non-British immigrant labour produced important social and political tensions, an early pedagogy for citizenship emerged that drew on the affective dimensions of citizenship ("home feelings") as a means of engaging a principal adversary and interlocutor – socialist and communist print cultures and the non-British immigrant communities with which these were associated.

More broadly, the arguments of the book explore what Corrinne Harrol and Mark Simpson call "literary/liberal entanglement": both emerging in the late seventeenth century, these paradigms share a "history of entanglement," one "foundational to politics and culture across English-speaking liberal modernity."[4] If state legal mechanisms for monitoring and controlling immigration proliferated during the decades under examination here, my interest is in how the Reading Camp Movement combined the cultural mechanisms of literature, literacy, and citizenship to encourage apparently benevolent forms of liberal selfhood, particularly among non-British immigrants. In the context of Frontier College's early-twentieth-century work, older ideas about literacy and literature came to shape conceptions of citizenship and ideas about its cultivation: post-Enlightenment beliefs in literacy-as-progress and the particularly Victorian commitment to the prophylactic functions of books, literacy, and literature in the context of industrial capitalism, which I discuss in more detail in the Preface, came to lend authority and purpose to emergent citizenship education efforts. Both literacy and citizenship served as important instruments of social distinction, differentiating those who could "give" them from those who – be they British or French Canadian workers, as in the earliest camps, or non-British immigrant workers, as was increasingly the case by the early 1910s – lacked them.

The Reading Camp Movement emerged at the beginning of the twentieth century from a social reform tradition deeply shaped by both the literacy-as-progress and literature-as-prophylactic arguments; it was also influenced, however, by a maternal-feminist ideology that privileged the family as the ideal site for the cultivation of the citizen. All of these forces coalesced in the association's emphasis on literacy and the private consumption of books as tools of individual improvement, yet the association departed from the traditions of the reform-oriented workers' education movement in its privileging of popular fiction and poetry, which Frontier College founder Alfred Fitzpatrick viewed as necessary proxies for the homes and families rendered absent by the needs of the labour-camp economy. As the organization came into contact with a state reluctant to support the use of these tools among adults and with an increasingly non-British immigrant and non-English speaking population of camp workers, it adapted its conception of literacy and moral citizenship to a pedagogy for "Canadianization," an assimilative vision of citizenship that worked to consolidate settler prerogatives and to cultivate the individualism and autonomy of liberal selfhood. Literary forms retained an important place in this emergent pedagogy for citizenship, assuming the function of introducing the immigrant and his family to the interventions of the state. However, in the relief camps for the unemployed where Frontier College deployed its services during the 1930s, instructors turned from the language of citizenship – a term increasingly appropriated by the unemployed movement – towards poetry as a means of cultivating individual moral reflection and of encouraging individual responsibility to the family over commitments to collective organizing.

Importantly, all of these various interlacements of literary culture, literacy, and citizenship demonstrate the affective dimensions of liberal citizenship that are occluded in Habermasian analyses of the liberal public sphere and its "bourgeois reading public." Attending consistently to the important role that women and family – and the more general affective dimensions of citizenship that I call "home feelings" – played in an emergent pedagogy for liberal citizenship, particularly as these informed the uses of literary culture as a counter to leftist political print, the chapters that follow reorient the analysis of Canadian citizenship away from the public sphere–focused approaches that have typified evolutionary liberal narratives of citizenship.[5] While the pedagogy for liberal citizenship that Frontier College deployed in frontier camps was far from stable – the respective values of literature, literacy, and citizenship shifted in response to the ethnic and class relations of each period – the individualism that it promoted consistently endorsed the worker's intimate relation to home and family as a crucial aspect of citizenship.

Those Frontier College commitments that produced a less receptive state response in the 1910s and 1920s – the critique of labour camp conditions, the dismantling of hierarchies of manual and mental labour, the democratization of access to public universities – were abandoned in the name of survival. More amenable to state interests was an argument, increasingly adopted by Frontier College, that proffered literacy and citizenship as remedies for a political threat that was identified with the non-British immigrant labour force, while attenuating focus on the exploitative labour relations of the industries that depended on the work camp. If these early elaborations of the meanings of literacy, culture, and citizenship were important to the formation of state institutions in the postwar period, they were subject to significant contest in the first three decades of the twentieth century as Frontier College confronted various state bureaucracies and as it attempted to engage camp workers who interrogated or, more often, chose not to avail themselves of its versions of literacy or citizenship.

LIBERAL CITIZENSHIP

Citizenship was not a legal category in Canada until 1947; prior to the passage of the Citizenship Act in that year, those born in Canada and Britain were subjects, not citizens, and naturalization was the process that rendered (qualifying) non-British immigrants Canadians.[6] Although, according to Janine Brodie, there was a "decided absence of citizenship discourse" at the level of the state until after the Second World War, a discourse of citizenship did emerge earlier in relation to the various reform movements of the late nineteenth and early twentieth centuries, as well as in the context of the class struggles of the interwar period. It is this earlier emergence, and its relation to more familiar postwar conceptions of citizenship, that interests me here.[7] Despite citizenship's lack of legal meaning in Canada prior to 1947, a common narrative of citizenship in this country emplots an evolution from classic liberalism's negative rights to the positive rights of a "new" liberalism, or, depending on the interpreter, a liberalism remade by various left-of-centre political forces.[8] According to this narrative, the liberal paradigm of citizenship prevailed in nineteenth-century Canada. Citizenship as understood in this paradigm is less an activity than a legal status, and the privileged unit is the individual who uses his (seldom her) rights to promote his self-interest, and whose freedom is limited only by the necessity of respecting the rights of others.[9] According to Robert Menzies, Dorothy Chunn, and Robert

Adamoski, the liberal paradigm was "hegemonic in Canada until ... progressivism, welfarism, and scientific governance began to emerge" in the early to mid-1900s, eventually arriving at the level of the state after the Second World War.[10] Jane Jenson argues that Canada's postwar "citizenship regime" was a "central pillar of the country's postwar model of development of permeable Fordism, in which the state's relationship to markets was active and pan-Canadian social programs replaced provincial and private provision."[11] Influenced by British sociologist and architect of postwar reconstruction T.H. Marshall, this regime of social citizenship attempted to compensate for the inequalities of the capitalist economy by adding social entitlements to the civil and political aspects of citizenship.[12] This conception of citizenship in Canada traces important shifts – the shift in emphasis away from individual towards social rights in the postwar period, for instance. However, it runs the risk of obscuring the genealogy of the national citizenship regime that was eventually institutionalized in the 1947 Citizenship Act. On the one hand, its evolutionary tendencies tend to elide the significant conflict and negotiation that attended early-twentieth-century elaborations of the meanings of citizenship –both of which require us to dislodge conceptions of social citizenship rights as generated exclusively by the state or as dealing exclusively with public-sphere activities, identities, and attitudes. On the other hand, it underemphasizes the "tentative and uneven" quality of the social citizenship rights now commonly associated not only with Canadian citizenship but also with Canadian identity in a more general sense.[13]

By returning to the period of citizenship's emergence, I thus aim to complicate the evolutionary periodicity of the history of citizenship. Throughout the book, I use the term "liberal citizenship" to name the complex ways in which British Canadian reformers affiliated with Frontier College imagined their task of working for both individual and social improvement while simultaneously defining their own settler claims to national space through a pedagogy and practice of national citizenship that served primarily to distinguish them from the non-British immigrant settler population. This early-twentieth-century form of citizenship education was forged in close relation to imaginative literature and drew deeply on the liberal reformist and idealist conceptions of the literary that emerged in Victorian Britain, a fact that has not been acknowledged in histories of citizenship in Canada.

Part of a more general tendency in Canadian historiography to emplot the past according to a liberal narrative of progress and expansion, the evolutionary conception of citizenship might be rethought through what historian Ian McKay has described as a "liberal-order strategy of reconnaissance." Urging scholars to work at the intersections rather than the dividing line between social/cultural and political, legal, and intellectual history, McKay posits a historiographical paradigm that analyzes how liberal principles, such as the epistemological and ontological primacy of the individual, whose "freedom should be limited only by obligations to others or to God, and by the rules necessary to obtain the equal freedom of other individuals," became hegemonic in Canada between about 1840 and 1940. The "liberal order" that McKay outlines is both an "*extensive* projection of liberal rule across a large territory and an *intensive* process of subjectification, whereby liberal assumptions are internalized and normalized within the dominion's subjects." At the same time, the liberal order framework attends to the "momentous and complex enterprise" that was the slow and uneven installation of liberal common sense in Canada, as well as to the forms of resistance these processes engendered. Citizenship forms part of this process, but its history, as McKay notes, remains largely unwritten.[14] This book interprets the emergence of citizenship as a key element of the liberal order's early-twentieth-century consolidation, focusing on its utility for what McKay calls "intensive" processes of subjectification; I am particularly interested in the uses of literary print culture in these processes. If the significant body of historical scholarship that has addressed the difficulty with which an emerging liberal order grappled with the influx of immigrant workers and other illiberal groups after the turn of the century provides crucial groundwork for this project, my attention to the contests generated by literacy, literature, and citizenship is unique.[15] The work that has touched on the enmeshment of liberalism, citizenship, and culture in nineteenth- and early-twentieth-century Canada tends to be structured by Foucauldian governmentality studies; this study is more sympathetic to McKay's Gramscian analysis of subjectification and to Gramsci's theorization of hegemony as rule by consent, which casts education as a key activity in realizing "spontaneous assent" in civil society. The "how" of this process is crucial, as Gramsci notes: "But how will each single individual succeed in incorporating himself into the collective man, and how will educative pressure be applied to single individuals so as to obtain their consent and their collaboration, turning necessity and coercion into 'freedom'?"[16]

Questioning the evolutionary narrative of citizenship, this analysis of the early-twentieth-century emergence of citizenship also contributes to the literature that explores how contests among non-state actors were important in shaping ideas about citizenship that may seem to be simply effects of a bureaucratizing state but are actually far from being a simple effect of (postwar or other) state policy.[17] Key to the emergence of ideas of about citizenship in Canada were labour and leftist organizations and the various reform movements of the late nineteenth and early twentieth centuries. The relationship of the latter to the work of Frontier College is fruitfully understood in relation to the liberal order framework, but some careful distinctions are required. While I draw on McKay's framework, I also take seriously Bruce Curtis's challenge to McKay, which reminds us that many of liberalism's projects – public education, national citizenship – are "communal" in nature. As a result, "the historical contrast is not, then ... between liberal individualism and Aboriginal or Catholic or socialist collectivism, but rather between competing or antagonistic forms of collectivism and of individuality." Though liberal projects such as citizenship can "serve as vehicles for forms of domination," Curtis reminds us that liberal discourse nonetheless retains its claims to universality.[18] Like so many of his early-twentieth-century contemporaries in the Social Gospel, maternal feminist, and welfare advocacy movements, Alfred Fitzpatrick was deeply shaped by what Nancy Christie calls the private-public "maternalist welfare state," which sought to soften the effects of (but not do away with) liberal individualism and industrial capitalism.[19] As McKay notes, the first wave feminist movement's illiberal emphasis on collectivities (the collective identity of women, the family) strained liberal definitions of the individual, yet this movement employed rhetoric that was "deeply marked by the liberalism [it] both implicitly and explicitly questioned."[20] Reformers associated with the early-twentieth-century Social Gospel movement, such as Alfred Fitzpatrick, articulated collectivist ideas regarding literacy, education, and social policy that led to their eventual promotion of Canadianization or citizenship education. While this later citizenship work was collectively oriented – it was meant to extend education to a population of immigrant adult workers who lacked access to public schooling, and it was meant to provide a new collective identity – and even, as we will see, occasionally radical, it was at the same time deeply individualistic: it privileged citizenship as an *individual* identity that entailed self-government, hard work, thrift, property acquisition, and lawful behaviour.

I also attempt to challenge elements of the evolutionary narrative of social citizenship that cast it in exclusive relation to public-sphere activities, identities, or attitudes. Influenced in a general way by Gramsci's insistence that "civil society" is "the 'State' too, indeed, is the State itself," and drawing on affect theory, particularly as it has been taken up in theorizations of citizenship, the chapters explore, in a general sense, the ways that affect-oriented thinking can destabilize the public/private binary of liberal citizenship by analyzing how interests, beliefs, and values cannot be bracketed to a "private holding, 'internal' to any given agent." Instead, as Michael Feola, drawing on Lauren Berlant, Sarah Ahmed, Brian Massumi, and others, puts it, such affect is "bound up with transpersonal economies of value, perception, and desire that exceed and implicate the subject." The chapters that follow attend consistently to the important role that "home feelings," or affective conceptions of citizenship, played in emergent early-twentieth-century ideas about citizenship, particularly as these informed the uses of literary culture in the camps. In making these arguments, I draw on the work of feminist scholars, and in particular on Carol Johnson's study of the "affective underpinnings" of citizenship in Western liberal democracies. Johnson employs the phrase "affective citizenship" to explore "which intimate emotional relationships between citizens are endorsed and recognized by governments in personal life" and how "citizens are also encouraged to feel about others and themselves in broader, more public domains." Building on scholarship in feminist settler colonial studies, Johnson shows how, particularly in settler colonies since the late nineteenth century, the household, intimate relationships, and marriage have been crucial to formulations of citizenship as an identity, a set of entitlements, and a practice. In the final chapter of the book, I turn to other forms of affect that were important to Frontier College's pedagogy for citizenship in the relief camps for the unemployed during the 1930s – those tied more closely to what Lauren Berlant theorizes as "intimate publics," those publics that, in contradistinction to Jürgen Habermas's "intimate sphere" of modernity, "render citizenship as a condition of social membership produced by personal acts and values." Such intimate publics, as Berlant demonstrates in *The Female Complaint: On the Unfinished Business of Sentimentality in American*

Culture, have their origins in the eighteenth- and early-nineteenth-century vogue for sentimentality, which leveraged sentimentality as a politically ambivalent form of critique.[21] In the chapters that follow, I consider how print culture – and imaginative literature in particular – was used as a means of cultivating, in different ways in the periods examined, citizenship's affective "home feelings."

The history of adult education is the scholarly field that has grappled most extensively with Frontier College and organizations like it. Although a handful of recent essays on Frontier College draw new attention to the association's imbrication in questions social and labour historians have long been probing, Michael Welton's (admittedly now dated) assertion that the history of Canadian adult education is largely written by "insiders" remains very true of Frontier College, in particular.[22] Moreover, within the larger field of the history of education, early Frontier College work with immigration and citizenship tends to be presented in the context of liberal narratives regarding "two founding nations and an increasingly multicultural society" and in terms of an apparently national predilection for "communitarian" initiatives of the kind that came to be associated with postwar state and civil society efforts to build "imaginative training for citizenship."[23] As McKay points out, one of liberalism's most powerful narratives is the one that plots the nation's progress from "nineteenth-century dominion" to "multicultural liberal democratic nation state" – a narrative that is crucial to the evolutionary conception of national citizenship, as well: "Canada simply glided, slowly and surely, down Arthur Lower's Most Famous Stream of liberal democracy. More and more people were brought aboard the good ship, and the unsightly detritus of the past vanished into the distance." The liberal-order approach, McKay suggests, "would undoubtedly offer a much bumpier and less pleasant ride."[24]

Forged out of the contradictions of liberalism, the liberal citizenship I explore in this book was universal in theory and exclusive in practice. The exclusion of particular immigrant groups – particularly non-white immigrants and those with communist political affiliations – and of Indigenous peoples from this period's emergent conceptions of national citizenship signal its limits. The power to exclude, or rather to effect what Étienne Balibar calls "internal exclusion," to produce the non-citizen, is one that has had particular effect in the Canadian context, where Indigenous peoples were denied both personhood and citizenship until the 1950s.[25] In establishing its terms, its mode of invitation, and its boundaries, settler British Canadians naturalized their identity as *the* identity of the Canadian citizen. Settler colonial studies tends to theorize this process in Foucauldian terms: for example, analyzing the unique demographic triangularity – a settler population (British and French), an exogenous (non-British, non-French immigrant) population, and an Indigenous population – that came to characterize Canada, particularly in the wake of the significant non-British and non-French immigration of the first decades of the twentieth century, Lorenzo Veracini observes the settler population's heightened perception of the need to manage its "population economy." Veracini's term refers to recurrent settler anxiety regarding the need to "biopolitically manage their respective domestic domains," a capacity that is crucial to "settler substantive sovereignty" vis-à-vis the metropole. Similarly, in his discussion of settler or "intraverted" colonialism, Ato Quayson notes the importance of "the deployment of devices for the management and control of populations, especially when such populations are considered heterogeneous and require placing under the 'empty' signifier of the nation-state in the process of nation-building." Citizenship, in this context, becomes an important strategy for granting legitimacy to settler claims and, more abstractly, to settler conceptions of identity. As Veracini points out, settler colonies often generate an "ongoing settler need to pit indigenising settlers against exogenous (often racialised) alterities," but if exogenous Others actually confirm the indigenization of the settler population, Indigenous groups pose an ongoing challenge to the "basic legitimacy of the settler entity."[26] In this contested field, emergent citizenship regimes work to establish settler authenticity, rendering exogenous and Indigenous claims to citizenship a matter of settler prerogative. This Foucauldian reading is helpful, but it does not attend adequately to the ways that the needs of British Canadian settler society were implicated in the emergence of industrial capitalism, particularly in the early twentieth century's "Great Transformation." By the early part of the twentieth century, the presence of significant numbers of non-British immigrant workers in Canadian work camps, coupled with the increasing anxiety of governments and employers alike regarding the political sympathies of those immigrants and the havoc that radicalism could wreak, prompted Frontier College to turn its conception of citizenship away from individual Canadian- and British-born men and towards those deemed a threat to capitalist relations of production.

WORKER READERS AND THE REFLEXIVE SOCIOLOGY OF LITERATURE

If we know very little about the mutual implication of liberalism, culture, and citizenship in early-twentieth-century Canada, we know even less, as Yvonne Hébert and Lori Wilkinson point out, about how state and other institutions of settler culture encourage "social and civic participation." In other words, we know little, particularly in relation to the period prior to the Second World War, about how institutions and groups cultivated attitudes or practices of citizenship.[27] Still more difficult to study are the responses of those who were the intended subjects of such cultivation.

Drawing on the liberal order framework, I recognize, as R.W. Sandwell does, its "potential to disrupt and de-naturalize" the "persistent master narrative" of liberalism – its ability to make visible "those forms of behavior and belief that preceded and coexisted with it." For Sandwell, these other behaviours and beliefs belong to an "a-liberal past" peopled by "those who, throughout the nineteenth and even twentieth centuries, constituted an ever-shrinking portion of the population who, for a variety of reasons, had less exposure to, or were slower to take up, the new forms of knowledge, identity, and power that distinguished the liberal order from other ways of being, and being in society." As much of Sandwell's scholarship has shown, the nation's rural communities are a crucial element of this "a-liberal past." Moreover, although historiography has tended to emphasize the importance of urbanization in the first decades of the twentieth century, scholars such as Sandwell insist that the particularly rural character of Canadian society persisted until at least the Second World War. The predominantly frontier spaces that Frontier College engaged in the early twentieth century were undoubtedly rural, and part of the work this book undertakes is to understand the often illiberal cultural and social practices of frontier workers.[28]

To this end, I analyze the ways the association failed to engage the men it worked among. The chapters that follow certainly demonstrate how this organization worked to secure what Gramsci calls the "spontaneous assent" of the ruled – its attempts to encourage workers to view the nation's "legal order" as "freedom, and not simply the result of coercion."[29] However, these efforts were often met by workers who, for diverse reasons, found the association's mission difficult to understand or simply rejected it *tout court*. There are definite methodological and theoretical challenges to narrating this history from the point of view of the workers themselves; not least among them is the fact that my access to the workers in question is always mediated by a document produced within the institutional framing of Frontier College, most commonly an instructor's report. Nevertheless, it is clear that the association experienced great difficulty in establishing meaningful contact with the workers it so earnestly attempted to address. This difficulty was not always due, *pace* Ian McKay, to the counterpoint provided by what he calls the "people's enlightenment" – diverse forms of leftist resistance to the governing project. To be sure, the liberal self-improvement and individual progress that labourer-teachers promoted in the camps, most obviously through the pedagogy for citizenship that was developed in the 1910s, faced significant challenges in contexts such as the relief camps for the unemployed where Frontier College took up its work in the 1930s. However, there are also more mundane matters to consider. As Ian Radforth contends in his work on early-twentieth-century logging camps in Northern Ontario, the association's goals were limited by the practical fact that its efforts were largely confined to the summer months.[30] Yet the organization's difficulties might also be attributed to the many obstacles that confronted its work from the outset and that labourer-teachers frequently witnessed in their reports: workers were exhausted; they were intimidated; they were mistrustful; they felt patronized; or they preferred to play cards, read independently, or talk politics in their bunkies.

Thinking through workers' engagement of the forms of print culture mediated by the institution of Frontier College, my method is sociological and historical. I sparingly employ qualitative measures to assess workers' attendance at formal classes; I complement this limited method with a wider qualitative analysis of Frontier College as an institution that mediated textual engagements. Following Elizabeth Long and others, who seek "the infrastructure of literacy and the social or institutional determinants of what is available to read, what is 'worth reading,' and how to read it," I try to understand not the reading practices of an exceptional individual, but the whole social process that shaped the reading culture associated with the

Frontier College project in the first part of the twentieth century.[31] While reading and educational and cultural initiatives have formed a part of Canadian labour history and the history of immigrant communities in Canada, this book is an attempt to understand illiberal social practices and print cultures *in relation to* an institution that was earnestly attempting to install liberal citizenship in workers through print culture and pedagogy. As Jonathan Rose notes, historians of labour and the left have frequently derided initiatives to educate workers as instruments of middle-class ideological coercion and liberal identity-making. This book argues that isolating worker-led initiatives from middle-class efforts ignores their mutual implication.[32]

Tying archival research to the "new literacy studies," qualitative histories of reading, the sociology of culture, and Gramscian cultural studies, all of which eschew the enumeration of literacy as a technical capacity in favour of the study of literacy as a highly mediated social practice, *Home Feelings* aims to expand the ways in which the relationship between citizenship and print culture (and particularly imaginative literature) has been studied in Canada, moving beyond approaches that focus on the *representation* of citizenship to analyze the production, use, and consumption of a print culture of liberal citizenship.[33] Scholars influenced by cultural studies, book history, and the sociology of literature are urging Canadianists to, in Heather Murray's words, "account for the ways in which varieties of print production, from a multiplicity of cultures, were imported, accessed, assessed, and understood" in order to write the history of literatures in Canada.[34] Such work will help us understand not just the literary preferences of the postwar critics who shaped what has become the early canon of Canadian literatures; it will also aid us in answering questions such as who read, what were they reading, in what social and political contexts were they reading, and how and why they were reading, or, just as importantly, why they were choosing not to read.

Moreover, approaching such questions through Raymond Williams's later work on the sociology of culture, I aim to understand cultural practices associated with literacy and citizenship not simply as "derived from an otherwise constituted social order" but as "themselves major elements" in the constitution of that social order. As Williams notes in his formulation of a "sociology of culture," the "fundamental principle" of such a method is to avoid the isolation of discrete elements in favour of analysis of the "complex unity of the elements" at play:

As so often, the two dominant tendencies of bourgeois cultural studies – the sociology of the reduced but explicit "society" and the aesthetics of the excluded social remade as a specialized "art" – support and ratify each other in a significant division of labour. Everything can be known about a reading public, back to the economics of printing and publishing and the effects of an educational system, but what is read by that public is the neutralized abstraction "books," or at best its catalogued categories. Meanwhile, but elsewhere, everything can be known about the books, back to their authors, to traditions and influences, and to periods, but these are finished objects before they go out into the dimension where "sociology" is thought to be relevant: the reading public, the history of publishing. It is this division, now ratified by confident disciplines, which a sociology of culture has to overcome and supersede, insisting on what is always a whole and connected social material process. This is of course difficult, but great energy is now expended, and is often in effect trapped, in maintaining the abstract divisions and separations. Meanwhile in cultural practice and among cultural producers, before these received abstractions get to work, the process is inevitably known, if often indistinctly and unevenly, as whole and connected.

According to Williams, this is at once a "sociology" and an "aesthetics." A sociology of culture, says Williams, must be a historical sociology, disdaining any "universal or general explanatory scheme," concerning itself not only with institutions, formations, means of production, and texts as signifying systems, but also with the "processes of social and cultural 'reproduction,'" such as education. A form of cultural reproduction that "can be linked with that more general reproduction of existing social relations which is assured by existing and self-prolonging property and other economic relations, institutions of state and other political power, religious and family forms," Williams's conception of education shares much with Pierre Bourdieu's "reflexive" sociology of literature and the analysis of education as a form of power in Gramsci's theorization of hegemony, both of which have shaped my method of understanding pedagogical practices and the habits of print consumption they attempt to engender.[35] Gramscian hegemony theory has been particularly useful to a cultural studies approach that balances "structure" and "agency": as John Storey puts it, such an approach examines "the commodities people consume within the field of the economic conditions of their existence," while also analyzing "important questions of audience and use" as a means of treating the cultural as "a serious terrain for agency, struggle, and study."[36] It seems to me that such an approach is most fruitfully undertaken in contexts such as the one this book examines, contexts in which the common sense of the liberal-capitalist order was far from being perfectly sealed.

How did what Long calls the "infrastructure of literacy" that Frontier College developed imagine reading as a practice? In what ways did Frontier College and the workers whom it addressed make meaning from the texts that circulated as part of the Reading Camp movement's literacy and Canadianization efforts? What processes of resistance and incorporation attended Frontier College's practices of individuation and subjectification through liberal print culture? Like historians of literacy such as Harvey J. Graff, historians of reading in modern Western nations have frequently noted the connections among Enlightenment values, liberalism, and reading. Robert Darnton sums up the Enlightenment ideal of reading as follows: "The eighteenth century imagined the Republic of Letters as a realm with no police, no boundaries, and no inequalities other than those determined by talent. Anyone could join it by exercising the two main attributes of citizenship, writing and reading. Writers formulated ideas, and readers judged them. Thanks to the power of the printed word, the judgements spread in widening circles, and the strongest arguments won." The privileging of writing and reading as conduits to enlightenment framed literacy as a means of becoming progressively autonomous in one's thought and action, which was understood to lead to a fuller, improved human life. As Darnton notes, the Republic of Letters was "democratic only in principle"; in a settler colonial nation like Canada, the limits of this ideal came to be shaped in the early twentieth century by the ethnic and class tensions produced by capital's insatiable need for non-British immigrant labour in this period.[37]

At the same time, however, the emergence in the nineteenth century in Canada, as in Britain and in many British colonies, of what Gauri Viswanathan calls the "bureaucratic rational state" entailed the redefinition of education away from older, aristocratic ideals of character formation and towards the use of writing and reading as means of aiding the state in absorbing citizens and colonial subjects: "While such absorption is admittedly uneven and disproportionate across class and gender, the presumably noncoercive nature of education to enact that state's desires allows for assimilation by consent. When the focus of instruction shifts from individual regeneration to self-consciousness as national subjects, morality can no longer be a matter of individual will and conscience, but rather merges with national loyalty and public affirmation." As scholars like Bruce Curtis have amply demonstrated, such redefinition was occurring in the nineteenth century in British North America, but, as this study aims to show, it unfolded at a slower pace in relation to the adult population, for whom a state bureaucracy of education was deemed to be less pressing.[38] In early-twentieth-century Canada, residual Enlightenment values – especially as these were transmitted through the Scottish Enlightenment – and liberal conceptions of individual freedom met and merged with the ideals of the Social Gospel movement and cultural idealism and found themselves determined by the specific settler colonial politics and class relations of the period. In the first camps where Frontier College undertook its work, which were mostly populated by British and French Canadian workers, literary reading was cast as a conduit to moral citizenship that did not require much institutional intervention; however, as we will see, strong guidance did exist in the association's efforts to choose reading materials that could introduce the individual to his role as a national citizen, while nourishing the particular affective attachments that camp life sundered but that were deemed crucial to citizenship. This attitude shifted across the 1910s and 1920s as the proportion of non-British immigrants in the camps grew. While literary materials and strategies retained a place in the association's conceptions of literacy and reading, these were now organized into a formal, institutionally authored pedagogy that, as I discuss above, elaborated a liberal citizenship that granted centrality and legitimacy to settler prerogative. This formal pedagogy for liberal citizenship faced new challenges in the relief camps of the 1930s, where unemployed men were effectively disenfranchised; it gave way to a renewed emphasis on direct contact with literary forms. The association favoured poetry, in particular, as a form that could promote introspection, transcendence, liberty, individual responsibility, and sentimental community in contexts where collective action was both proscribed and feared.

Admittedly, the study of reading or participation in cultural and civic education is challenging, particularly when the participants in question belong to barely literate, working-class, often immigrant communities. The Frontier College archive offers rich material for the study of reading, but, as I have already noted, this material must be approached with some caution. In an article that appeared in *Journal of Adult Education* in 1939, then-president of Frontier College, Edmund Bradwin, claims: "The constituency of Frontier College lies with the 80,000 to 110,000 camp men who are found annually in frontier works across Canada: in bush operations, at hydro developments, with mining camps, and on railway gangs. These camp workers are not effusive, but each year there come hundreds of letters and notes of approval from camp men, giving thanks for the help that they have received from labourer-teachers and expressing kindly esteem for this new type of educator who has come among them."[39] Despite what Bradwin characterizes as the ready availability of workers' responses to the Frontier College undertaking, contemporary historians of adult education in Canada continue to point to the lacunae this issue presents. In his 1998 chronology to the history of adult education in Canada, James Draper observes that he and his colleagues must "often infer the kind of learning which occurred historically for average people (the masses)" because "such persons seldom recorded their thoughts or living conditions, partly because their main preoccupation was survival and also because few were literate." Writing several years after Draper and focusing specifically on the history of Frontier College, Pierre Walter asserts that "uncovering and interpretation of the perspectives of immigrant learners" in this period remains "a largely illusive yet keenly important undertaking."[40] It is not that the volumes of correspondence that Frontier College received from workers that Bradwin refers to in his 1939 article no longer exist – they do – but they remain difficult texts to read. They are literally difficult to read because they are handwritten, often on poor quality paper; the English they employ is often halting, formulaic. Yet they remain difficult to read on a more abstract level, as well: this correspondence was most typically reproduced, either in an "appreciation" section appended to instructors' seasonal registers or, in the name of good publicity, in the association's annual reports. As I work through these texts, I attempt to acknowledge the mediated quality of this material and recognize how it might assist in the crucial task of narrating the history of Frontier College from the vantage point of the workers themselves.

FRONTIER COLLEGE AND ITS ARCHIVE

This is not the first history of Frontier College, but it is the first sustained attempt to understand the relationship between the organization and the learners, mostly immigrant men, whom it attempted to reach. Erica Martin writes that the existing historiography of the organization is focused on the biography of its founder, Alfred Fitzpatrick, or narrates the history of the organization from the perspective of people intimately connected to it.[41] As a result, much of the extant historiography remains untouched by social history's commitment to broader narratives of the past.

This book undertakes both a more theoretically informed study of the college and a more thorough examination of the primary documents associated with it. In 1975 and again in 2001, Frontier College was granted a permanent place in what Jacques Derrida describes as the "privileged topology" of the national archive.[42] The Frontier College archive located at Library and Archives Canada has been my principal source. I examined all the annual reports between 1900 and 1939; all instructors' correspondence between 1900 and 1920; all instructors' registers between 1921 and 1929; and instructors' registers for 1933 and 1935. Based on evidence from this research, I decided to further consult specific parts of the fonds relevant to the period this book covers (the following were selectively consulted): Alfred Fitzpatrick's general correspondence; E.W. Bradwin's notes, manuscripts, and diaries; correspondence relating to newspapers and magazines; correspondence with various levels of government; and documents related to the relief camp phase of the association's work. Given my interest in emphasizing the pedagogical and sociological aspects of the association's work, I avoided those elements of the archive that focus specifically on the bureaucratic and financial history of the organization (files on tax information or on instructors' accounts, for example), partly because some of this information already appears in instructors' registers and annual reports. The many hours that I spent with the instructors' registers, in particular, were fruitful: to my knowledge, no other study has brought the contents of these registers to light, and, as I hope to show, they are valuable material records of the complicated relations that existed between labourer-teachers and frontier workers. To complement the limited representation of workers' reading in the Frontier College archive, I turned to other archival sources, such as the catalogues of books contained in the Ontario Travelling Libraries that circulated in work camps during the first two decades of the twentieth century. These catalogues are held in the Archives of Ontario.

Of course, these archival records do not render up the past transparently. The instructors' registers (and, prior to 1920, their correspondence with Fitzpatrick) are reports that determined, to a significant extent, whether or not an instructor was paid (even though this was only a small honorarium in the early years), how much, and whether or not he would receive a reference letter or a job offer in a subsequent year. Such reports are difficult documents to interpret: their formulas determined, to some extent, the responses they elicited, and as these reports grew more detailed and demanded more and more information from the instructor, their reliability did not necessarily increase. I pay attention to the genre of the instructor's register throughout the book, noting, in particular, how changes to the format of the report altered instructors' responses.

In addition to the published sources on Frontier College noted above, I have also relied to a significant extent on editorials, articles, and book reviews from contemporary newspapers and magazines (especially periodicals related to industry, such as *The Canada Lumberman*). Alfred Fitzpatrick found a particularly supportive audience for his work at *The Globe*, and this has proved to be an excellent source for editorials and other articles related to the earliest phases of the association's work.

The chapters that follow proceed more or less chronologically, moving from the association's earliest work in the camps of central and Northern Ontario, to its period of development and westward expansion in the 1910s and 1920s, and, finally, to its work in the context of the relief camps run by the DND during the early 1930s. In the conclusion of the book, I take up more carefully an argument that I follow throughout the chapters: Frontier College, a non-governmental organization that continues its work with adult learners to this day, exerted an important influence on emergent state conceptions of citizenship that later came to be crucial to the postwar order.

1

Creating a "Home Feeling": The Uses of Fiction and Poetry, 1899–1905

This chapter focuses on the brief but crucial period of the association's birth and argues that the forces that shaped it – its founder's schooling in the values of the Scottish Enlightenment, but also his engagement of the Social Gospel movement and the maternal feminist movement, and more particularly with these movements' attempts to grapple with the crises of late-nineteenth-century capitalism – encouraged a particularly affective conception of citizenship that was focused on the reforming of individual character through the reading of fiction and poetry, both of which were imagined to function as proxies for absent homes and families.

Fiction and poetry played a crucial role in the early years of the Canadian Reading Camp Association's work, not least because Alfred Fitzpatrick, the association's founder, was interested in supplying workers with the kind of reading matter they were asking for – popular fiction, and, in particular, adventure stories. Although literature was prominent in nineteenth-century British workers' education, Fitzpatrick's early-twentieth-century promotion of literacy via fiction for frontier labourers signalled a new acceptance in Canada of the notion that individual workers might actually be *improved* through fiction. This acceptance is partly explained by the fact that, in its earliest years, the Canadian Reading Camp Association was quite responsive to the cultural tastes of camp workers: Fitzpatrick, who paid frequent visits to the camps, sought to understand and respond to workers' reading preferences. Most remarkably, he took seriously their preference for popular adventure fiction and attempted to shape camp libraries to appeal to their tastes. Though he was willing to cater to popular taste, an idealist conception of literature amenable to the liberal values he espoused was central to this initial reading project.[1] Moreover, it is abundantly clear that workers preferred self-directed reading over guided instruction.

Although shaped by workers' preferences, the conditions of existence for Fitzpatrick's uses of popular fiction and poetry were also provided by the structures of the labour-camp economy: concerned about the moral health of workers who were subject to long periods away from home and family, Fitzpatrick turned to literature as a remedy. Although he regularly appealed in this period to the imperilled *citizenship* of camp workers, he was invoking a particularly moral rather than political concept that was much more firmly attached to the home than to the state. In Fitzpatrick's view, camp workers were responding to their poor working conditions by succumbing to moral diseases that left them incapable of governing themselves rationally. Such threats to individual moral character could have dire consequences for the emergent settler nation and, in this early period, for the empire. The response offered by the Canadian Reading Camp Association to the particular social relations required by capitalist resource extraction focused less on structural aspects of the labour economy and more on individual camp workers, whose lack of family attachment was identified as the source of their imperilment. Thus, like the labourer-teacher who was charged with bringing literacy to frontier camps, the fiction and poetry that the Canadian Reading Camp Association provided was imagined as a kind of surrogate for the absent family – and for the absent wife and mother, in particular. As Fitzpatrick negotiated his own nascent conception of the relation between education and citizenship, he drew liberally on the contemporary maternal feminist argument that viewed the family as the key site of individual moral formation and thus of the making of the citizen. The association's earliest address to the state, therefore, called primarily for the provision of a travelling library service – for books that could provide the moral influence that women offered in normal conditions. From the beginning, Fitzpatrick understood his initiative in frontier camps as one that could benefit from state intervention and support; however, this remained a nascent idea in the first half-decade of the association's work. As we will see, it is one that developed quickly after 1905.

When Alfred Fitzpatrick arrived in the 1890s as a travelling missionary for a Presbyterian church in the Georgian Bay region, he was confronted with the men who populated the numerous lumber camps of the area and immediately ascertained that poor working conditions left these largely Canadian-born men unable to exercise the rights proper to them as individuals. In the first two decades of the twentieth century, the Canadian Shield developed "as a new resource hinterland," one that attracted the attention of investors from Toronto, Montreal, Britain, and the United States. Mineral discoveries on the Shield in the first decade of the twentieth century (e.g., silver at Cobalt in 1903; gold in the Porcupine–Kirkland Lake area between 1909 and 1912), and the development of the "Nickel Belt" in that same period, led to "heavily capitalized hard-rock mining" in the region. Service centres such as Sudbury grew out of this development, and other towns, such as Sault Ste. Marie, became important processing centres of steel for the branch railway lines being built across the Shield and the Prairies after the turn of the century. A boom in the pulp and paper industry commenced on the Shield after 1900, when the Ontario government and (subsequently) the Quebec government limited the export of pulpwood (thereby preventing the American companies that controlled much of this sector on the Canadian Shield from exporting pulpwood for processing). The primary sector of the pulp and paper industry remained "primitive" for the first half of the twentieth century, meaning that the logging was done in winter camps by seasonally employed wage earners – that is, by seasonally unemployed general labourers, agriculturalists working for winter wages, and professional bushworkers, who often laboured in the secondary (manufacturing) sector of the logging industry during the summer months. All of these industries required seasonal labour forces that had to absorb, in an era prior to federal unemployment insurance, periods of no work. As Ian Radforth observes, this winter joblessness was not new – it structured the "pre-industrial economy of the first half of the nineteenth century," creating an annual crisis for "thousands of labourers thrown out of their jobs on the farms, wharves, and transportation projects of British North America." Yet rapid industrialization in post-Confederation Ontario did not spell an end to this seasonal unemployment, largely because frontier camps remained essential sites of unskilled work in the primary sectors.[2] Moreover, the geographical isolation of frontier labour camps created a host of difficult working conditions: camps were difficult to reach, and workers were generally obliged to pay the costs of transportation to and from camp; supplies needed in the camp were usually provided by the employer at very high prices; and wage agreements were frequently misrepresented, yet workers with grievances could not easily leave camp for other employment.[3]

In his first annual report for the Canadian Reading Camp Association, Fitzpatrick estimates that there were "at least" five hundred such camps in Northern Ontario with "an average of seventy men at work in mid-winter"; Radforth, for his part, contends that in almost every winter prior to 1945 (except during the Depression), Ontario lumber camp operators offered jobs to two or three hundred thousand men.[4] During the first five years of the twentieth century, this workforce was dominated by labourers belonging to the settler population (Canadian-born, of British or French ancestry). Although that workforce included some non-British immigrants, it was not until after 1904–5, when the association began its work in Prairie rail construction camps, that Fitzpatrick's organization encountered camps populated almost entirely by such immigrants.[5]

The men who were employed in these Northern Ontario work camps were housed in the fashion of all frontier workers in this period – in log cabins fitted out with straw-lined bunks. Although generally warm, these bunkhouses were home to vermin-infested camp blankets, had inadequate ventilation, and were poorly lit. Typically, a sixty-by-thirty-foot bunkhouse had only two small windows; consequently, as one early labourer-teacher reported, it was "impossible to read or write in such domiciles except in a limited space under the lights." These poor living conditions, the remote situation of the camps, the low wages, and the fees charged for board and supplies and by labour agents, encouraged the habit popularly known in the period as "jumping" camp – what Radforth describes as "a form of labour protest in which bushworkers engaged whenever employment conditions permitted."[6] This habit was abhorrent to Fitzpatrick, who attributed it not to a lack of commitment on the part of the workers but to the "isolation, and consequent moral degradation," as well as the "dangers and great privations," of camp life. In Fitzpatrick's estimation, "jumping" was not simply a labour problem for employers and a symptom of workers' illiberal behavior; it was a crisis for the state: in shirking its responsibility for camp workers, whom it had failed to protect through legislation, the state was nurturing the "nursing beds of the tramp, the drunkard, licentious and insane," men who were a "menace to any state."[7]

To stave off this crisis, Fitzpatrick engaged in a vigorous print campaign that was meant to attract the attention of reform organizations, churches, employers, and provincial and federal governments. In this campaign, he generally rejected what Richard Allen, in his study of Canada's Social Gospel movement, calls the conservative focus on "personal ethical issues" and individual sin. In challenging the efficacy of missionary work, in particular, Fitzpatrick was aligning himself with the more progressive elements of the movement and the "secular city" they anticipated, while remaining aloof from what Ian McKay calls the Social Gospel movement's "revolutionary left."[8] For instance, when smallpox epidemics broke out repeatedly in the camps during the first half decade of the association's work, Fitzpatrick generally refused to equate the epidemic with the moral laxity of camp workers. Indeed, to do so would have been to imperil the existence of his first reading rooms: the outbreak fed the prejudice that camp men were inherently unclean and threatened to undermine Fitzpatrick's claim that they could be bettered by books.[9] One clerk's comments during the epidemic, cited in a 1901 article in *The Canadian Magazine*, offer an example of the kind of thinking Fitzpatrick was attempting to counter:

> Calling [the foreman's] attention to the fact that this spring must be polluted from the cook camp, stables, etc., I suggested that he should have a drain dug to carry off the poisonous soakage. I even offered to assist in doing so, and had almost won when the clerk, a clever young fellow, but no expert in sanitary science, turned the scales by saying that do what you would dysentery was a disease that always followed camps. This is a similar argument to that another tried to convince me with, that because two men had been killed within a month by logs rolling off a skidd-way, unhappily no uncommon occurrence, the camp at which it happened was a very unlucky one.

Fitzpatrick thus unabashedly criticized employers for the "unsanitary conditions of the camps" that aggravated such outbreaks. In his estimation, the unchecked festering of such literal disease allowed metaphorical diseases to prosper, and these latter were a threat not only to employers but also to the vigour of the young nation: "Can we expect to be healthful and safe from contagion while any section of the community is neglected? The world is a unit, and no part of it lives unto itself. Disease germs bred and nourished out in the fringes of civilization, come to us in hundreds of ways."[10] Despite Fitzpatrick's emphasis on the problems that ensued from employer negligence and poor conditions in the camps, he did not wholly avoid referencing the question of workers' morality. As Mariana Valverde points out, the "attempts to humanize and/or Christianize the political economy of urban-industrial capitalism" that characterized even the progressive end of the Social Gospel movement were often intertwined with the "sexual and moral" – that is, "personal ethical" – concerns of what she calls the social purity movement. Even the most progressive reform language of the era drew upon a discourse of individual character that had been established in the previous century. The influence of this emphasis on individual moral character and responsibility is perhaps most visible in Fitzpatrick's deployment of metaphors of "moral diseases" to describe the degradation of camp labourers.[11] Fitzpatrick was also deeply concerned that poor treatment of camp workers discouraged habits central to the governance of one's self-conduct: thrift, sobriety, and respect for the terms of an agreement. A reading camp could help men to "improve their spare moments," to "quit the demoralizing habit of 'jumping'" and of frequenting the saloons on payday.[12] Fitzpatrick further apprehended individual character formation as crucial to the health of the larger society: "An enlightened and healthy citizenship is a better asset than ignorant and filthy slaves. Camp Schools are cheaper than soldiers, paupers, drunkards and criminals."[13] In a period when collectivist, worker-led education initiatives were beginning to emerge in Canada, Fitzpatrick's association and others like it prized individual self-governance via education as the most potent medicine for the sicknesses that festered in frontier camps.[14]

As Nancy Christie points out, the term "citizenship" in the context of the reform movements of late-nineteenth- and early-twentieth-century Canada, particularly among Social Gospellers and maternal feminists, denoted less a political identity and more a conception of "individual spiritual responsibility, upon which modern society was thought to depend."[15] Fitzpatrick's gesturing to this contemporary language of reform is not surprising, given his energetic promotion of the project among middle-class women's organizations that focused on "personal ethical issues," such as the Women's Christian Temperance Union (WCTU), which lent its support to the Canadian Reading Camp

Association. The durable affiliations that existed between Protestant leaders and the many extra-denominational Protestant organizations, such as the WCTU, established by maternal feminists in this period certainly influenced Fitzpatrick's mission. Christie's work demonstrates the important differences between these early-twentieth-century reformers and their nineteenth-century liberal counterparts, such as Egerton Ryerson: if the latter believed that public educational institutions had the responsibility to inculcate "national character and political citizenship," the former tended to privilege the family as the ideal locus for developing "self-reliant Christian citizens."[16] Moreover, this feminist privileging of the family had important class and "race" dimensions: settler colonies produced particularly powerful sites for production of the intimate (white, heterosexual) couple and nuclear family as forms of liberal power, a fact that gave white, middle-class women new and specific forms of authority in late-nineteenth- and early-twentieth-century Canada. What Carol Johnson calls "affective citizenship" – the long-standing Western construction of citizen identity and entitlements vis-à-vis conceptions of the "intimate affective couple and familial relationships" – thus came to assume particular importance in this context, particularly given that intimate family bonds were threatened by the needs of capitalist resource extraction.[17]

In fact, Fitzpatrick echoed both classic liberal thinking and nineteenth-century British and Canadian reformers' ideas about the work that education should do. Adam Smith's *An Inquiry into the Nature and Causes of the Wealth of Nations* (1789) argues that the state ought to bear some of the expense of education, particularly for labourers who had been degraded by the monotony of specialized industrial work. Such men were "not only incapable of relishing or bearing a part in any rational conversation, but of conceiving any generous, noble, or tender sentiment, and consequently of forming any just judgment concerning many even of the ordinary duties of private life. Of the great and extensive interests of his country he is altogether incapable of judging."[18] The remedies proposed by the Canadian Reading Camp Association drew on liberal ideas about education and the social good, while insisting on the importance of the family to the cultivation of the citizen – a crucial function not to be usurped by the state. The association's earliest work thus emphasized the important roles of the instructor and of fiction, both of which were understood to function as surrogate "families" for the displaced worker. This emphasis on culture as a proxy for family emerged out of the specific social relations that capitalist resource extraction engendered – seasonal unemployment and labour mobility. The Canadian Reading Camp's remedy focused not on structural change at the level of the economy or the labour force – although Fitzpatrick, as we will see, did undertake some efforts in this direction – but rather on the task of restoring the absent family through compensatory forms of literary encounter.

In the first half-decade of its work, the Canadian Reading Camp Association began to develop an appeal to the state that demonstrated Fitzpatrick's growing apprehension of the role government might play in both improving camp conditions and educating camp workers for citizenship. Fitzpatrick's early efforts to provoke legislative change are a good example of the former; they also indicate the difficult position he was negotiating. He desired the financial support and goodwill of employers, and by 1903–4, he had organized a board on which sat some of the most influential owners of lumber, railway, and mining enterprises, such as J.R. Booth (the first honorary president and a lumber and railway baron), J.T. Charlton (president and owner of the lumber company J. and T. Charlton), and E.W. Rathbun (second vice-president and owner of lumbering and manufacturing enterprises).[19] Nevertheless, Fitzpatrick was also willing, in these early years, to criticize camp conditions, to call for state intervention in these ungoverned spaces, and to decry the utter absence of workers' social rights. In the winter of 1901, he sent a report to the provincial legislature that "ventured to characterize the neglect to provide sanitary regulations and Government inspection of the camps as criminal." The Ontario government subsequently passed An Act Respecting Sanitary Regulations on Unorganized Territories (1901), but in the first decade of the twentieth century, lumbermen were too powerful to permit much strict enforcement of this legislation. In his fourth annual report, Fitzpatrick further advocates the state's duty to ensure the rule of law in the name of the common good: "To give employers and contractors a free hand in determining their relation to their employees is to grant a licence of them to compel men to work overtime and on Sundays, to live in small and unsanitary quarters, and is nothing short of criminal."[20]

Yet the line of argument that brought Fitzpatrick the most success with government, and the one he consequently pursued most actively, was the one that emphasized education and culture as remedies for camp life. Between 1899 and 1905, the association worked to convince provincial governments, in particular, to contribute to the education of the isolated frontier workers who had powered the economic growth of the Dominion. In the association's second annual report, Fitzpatrick notes the good work of the German government in providing night school for labourers but calls for a more modest arrangement for Canada's frontier workers: "Why should not the Public Libraries Act be so amended as to aid in supplying books, papers, and magazines, and in the provision for evening classes in the reading camps and clubhouses? This would encourage employers to engage teachers, and it would encourage teachers to go to the camps, and relieve the congestion of the teaching profession in the older parts of the province."[21] Aiming his efforts at a specific mechanism of provincial government – the Ontario Public Libraries Act – Fitzpatrick urged the state to assume some responsibility for the social rights of adult workers, while emphasizing the important function of employers (who might hire teachers) and, more generally, the simple presence of reading materials in the camps.

To demonstrate what kind of educational work could be done in the camps, Fitzpatrick developed a model that included reading rooms, books and periodicals, and, eventually, labourer-teachers. His remedy should not surprise us: his methods of social amelioration drew on his heritage as a Presbyterian Scots Canadian. Presbyterianism's insistence on literate parishioners influenced Fitzpatrick, as did the eighteenth-century Scottish Enlightenment's privileging of democracy and practicality in education. This Enlightenment included not just educating well beyond the aristocracy but also emphasis on subjects such as science, agriculture, mathematics, and moral philosophy (from which the study of vernacular literature emerged in the eighteenth century).[22] Fitzpatrick was shaped by the "democratic" influence that Scottish immigrants to British North America wielded over the formation of nineteenth-century educational institutions, an influence that is constantly cited in the historiography of Canadian education.[23] A key North American inheritor of the Scottish Enlightenment was the Reverend Thomas McCulloch, who established Nova Scotia's Pictou Academy in 1816 as a means of contesting both the elitist restrictions of the Church of England's King's College School and its classical language curriculum.[24] Like many of his Scots Canadian contemporaries, McCulloch championed the teaching of rhetoric and the "power of communication," a preference that Sarah Phillips Casteel links to the context of post-Union Scotland and educated

Scots' desire to promote the economic and political status of their people within a larger Britain.[25] It was to Pictou Academy that Alfred Fitzpatrick, the youngest of a family of eleven children, went in 1876, at the age of fourteen. Significantly, the principal of Pictou Academy at that time, Alexander H. MacKay, was committed to democracy in education ("opening the doors to all") and to the belief that "knowledge should be made available beyond the walls of the classroom."[26] At Pictou Academy, Fitzpatrick would also have encountered the evangelical liberalism that was beginning in this period to transform Canadian Presbyterianism. According to Michel Gauvreau, Thomas McCulloch's "balancing of Calvinist and evangelical outlooks was a vital determinant of the Presbyterian intellectual tradition in Canada."[27]

Fitzpatrick followed his Pictou Academy formation with six years at Queen's College (now University), where he studied for the Arts with an emphasis on theology, received a prize for his work in both spoken and written English, and subsequently obtained his theology degree. His final years at Queen's (1888–90) coincided with the arrival of the college's new English specialist, James Cappon, a recently arrived Scot who was "well prepared to use literature to counter any arguments for utility and materialism" and to harness it as a quasi-religious form of cultural idealism.[28] Thus the utilitarian bent of Fitzpatrick's education at Pictou later came into contact with the Arnoldian idealism that became dominant in Anglo-Canadian universities during the 1880s. Yet these philosophies were not as discrete as they might seem, as Phillips Casteel acknowledges: just as Scots in early- and mid-nineteenth-century Canada, such as Thomas McCulloch, saw the economic benefit to be derived by Scots immigrants from rhetorical study, so those Scots Canadian educators who followed them apprehended the self-serving value of "staking their claim to the English cultural legacy" in the context of an empire that might grant Canada a leading role.[29] Queen's was also the first university in the country to offer extension education courses to extramural students, a commitment that would later shape Fitzpatrick's philosophy of education.[30]

Another important influence on Fitzpatrick at Queen's was principal George Monro Grant, a fellow alumnus of Pictou Academy who was Fitzpatrick's mentor. He was also a leader in Canada's first experiments in university extension and in the nation's emerging Social Gospel movement. Grant's gospel of "active social service" drew on the idealism that had inspired the evangelical liberalism of the Free Church movement among Scotland's Presbyterians and, by the late 1880s, their Canadian counterparts. Grant's sympathy with the theological liberalism that was spreading throughout the Protestant churches in this period (and particularly his Presbyterian church) included a belief in the "application of ethics to economics," but he was an "outspoken opponent" of the socialist ideas of men like T. Phillips Thompson, preferring instead to view the diffusion of education as linked to inexorable human progress. Grant's Social Gospel beliefs were also central to his political commitment to imperialism: he believed that ecumenical cooperation was necessary to realize Christ's work on earth and that imperial unity was one form it took. As we shall see in this chapter's discussion of W.H. Drummond, Fitzpatrick's thinking amply reflected Grant's influence.[31]

After nine years of service in small, remote parishes, Fitzpatrick commenced his work as a travelling missionary in the Georgian Bay area. Soon after beginning this work in 1899, he left his duties in the church to focus exclusively on the region's frontier camps. As he notes in a 1922 reflection on this decision,

> [t]wenty-two years ago I was on the point of giving my life to an endeavor to better conditions generally in Frontier camps and to organize labor in these camps, and decided then that as labour was represented by abler men, its ends would be accomplished in due course and that I could do more effective work along educational and welfare lines. I therefore sought to prepare the worker by utilising the time already at his disposal to be ready to take advantage of more leisure and better conditions as soon as these should be obtained.[32]

Thus began Fitzpatrick's transition from ministry to bibliostry. In addition to offering medical and religious services to lumber camp workers in the Georgian Bay area, he handed out books, "popular literature" that he hoped would "replace the sensational dime novels that the men usually read."[33] In the summer of 1900, he reached out to the state for first time, seeking support from the Ontario Department of Education for a plan to develop reading camps in Northern Ontario; he was ignored. The following autumn, he turned to the Little Current Free Library as well as to lumber camp managers in the area around Georgian Bay, asking them to support the interim organization of camp library clubs until the Ontario government developed a travelling library service (see figure 1.1). This appeal was successful, and Fitzpatrick organized four camps in makeshift shacks in the fall of 1900; three of these received their books from a local library, and one obtained a case of ten books from McGill University's travelling library service. The camps also received book and periodical donations from various church and philanthropic organizations, including the local chapters of the Imperial Order Daughters of the Empire and the Aberdeen Association, an organization that collected and distributed magazines, technical, agricultural, and scientific journals, and "standard works of history, biography, travel, and fiction" to settlers in Canada.[34] In early 1901, Richard Harcourt, the Minister of Education, bowed to Fitzpatrick's entreaties and announced his intention to create travelling libraries for Northern Ontario's work camps. The government subsequently made good on its promise, supplying eight cases of books to camps during the 1901–2 season; by 1904, thirty-seven travelling libraries had been prepared and sent out by the Department of Education.[35] While the Ontario government thus came to accept its role as a provider of library services to remote communities, it consistently declined to assume responsibility for the project at the heart of the Reading Camp Association's enterprise – the education of adults on the frontier.

UTILITARIAN LEGACIES AND LIBERAL HUMANISM: WHAT SHOULD WORKERS READ?

In 1901, Fitzpatrick began publishing annual reports as a means to publicize his project and garner financial and other support. In these reports, he explicitly links the association's practical tasks – the distribution of books and other reading material to frontier camps, the creation of reading rooms, and the possible development of camp instruction – to the idealist thinking that had such an important influence on both the rise of evangelical liberalism in Canadian Presbyterianism and the Social Gospel movement. According to Fitzpatrick, the "Association aims to dignify isolated manual labor and to free it from sordid and degrading conditions." Labour "thus ennobled and made intelligent will become what Carlyle foresaw it would become, 'the grand sole miracle of man' and the key to the industrial, social and religious problems of our time."[36] The ideas of Victorian cultural critic Thomas Carlyle exercised an enormous

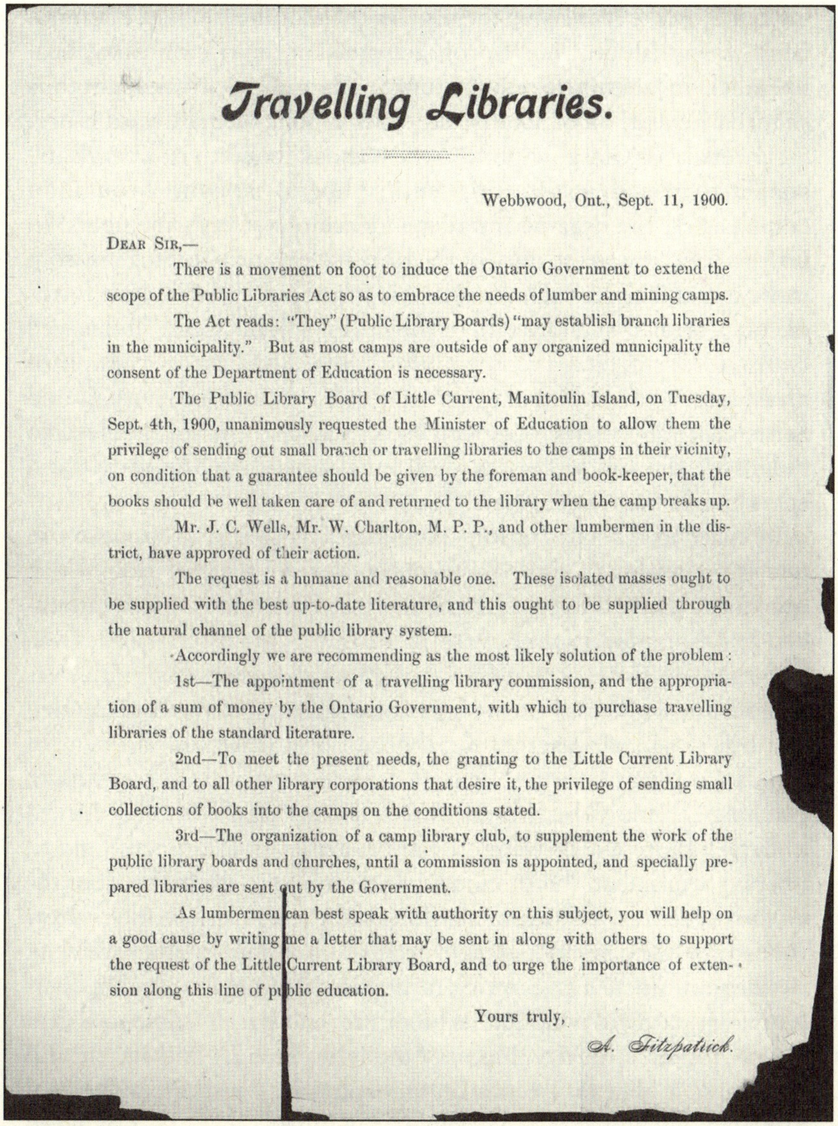

Travelling Libraries.

Webbwood, Ont., Sept. 11, 1900.

Dear Sir,—

There is a movement on foot to induce the Ontario Government to extend the scope of the Public Libraries Act so as to embrace the needs of lumber and mining camps.

The Act reads: "They" (Public Library Boards) "may establish branch libraries in the municipality." But as most camps are outside of any organized municipality the consent of the Department of Education is necessary.

The Public Library Board of Little Current, Manitoulin Island, on Tuesday, Sept. 4th, 1900, unanimously requested the Minister of Education to allow them the privilege of sending out small branch or travelling libraries to the camps in their vicinity, on condition that a guarantee should be given by the foreman and book-keeper, that the books should be well taken care of and returned to the library when the camp breaks up.

Mr. J. C. Wells, Mr. W. Charlton, M. P. P., and other lumbermen in the district, have approved of their action.

The request is a humane and reasonable one. These isolated masses ought to be supplied with the best up-to-date literature, and this ought to be supplied through the natural channel of the public library system.

Accordingly we are recommending as the most likely solution of the problem :

1st—The appointment of a travelling library commission, and the appropriation of a sum of money by the Ontario Government, with which to purchase travelling libraries of the standard literature.

2nd—To meet the present needs, the granting to the Little Current Library Board, and to all other library corporations that desire it, the privilege of sending small collections of books into the camps on the conditions stated.

3rd—The organization of a camp library club, to supplement the work of the public library boards and churches, until a commission is appointed, and specially prepared libraries are sent out by the Government.

As lumbermen can best speak with authority on this subject, you will help on a good cause by writing me a letter that may be sent in along with others to support the request of the Little Current Library Board, and to urge the importance of extension along this line of public education.

Yours truly,

A. Fitzpatrick.

Figure 1.1 "Travelling Libraries" circular, 1900

influence on the increasing idealism in the moral philosophy component of Scottish university programs and on the rise of evangelical liberalism in late-nineteenth-century Scotland. Carlyle's thought thus shaped a generation of Scottish students, among them Edward Caird, a University of Glasgow philosopher whose "collectivist liberalism" sought to remedy eighteenth-century liberal thought through an emphasis on the organic interdependence of society's members. In Caird's view, it was the duty of the state to "emancipate citizens from those forces that denied human development [and to] eliminate forms of competition that allowed the strong to exploit the weak." Influenced by this idealism, Fitzpatrick was also drawing on Caird's example of an engaged life – Caird was active in the University Extension and Settlement movements – as well as on Caird's belief in the need to "elevate" the lower classes without dismantling the social and economic structure of society.[37]

In shaping his association, Fitzpatrick was also drawing more widely on idealist and utilitarian concepts of worker education, which remained tightly intertwined in late-nineteenth and early-twentieth-century Canada, as they were in Britain. This intertwining was important to the role that literary fiction was granted in initiatives to educate workers. For evangelicals, "self-improvement" tended towards the ideal, whereas for those of a more utilitarian bent of mind, Western literary education was understood as a means of teaching the individual to exercise reason, moral will, and critical understanding, which were crucial capacities in the functioning of liberal government.[38] From the mid-nineteenth to the first part of the twentieth century, educational efforts aimed at British workers drew robustly on the conflation of skill acquisition and moral improvement. By the mid-nineteenth century, utilitarians in England, despite their initial antipathy to imaginative literature, had largely come to accept claims for its ethical value, its "didactic power," and its "moral usefulness."[39] The nineteenth-century mechanics' institute movement in Britain aimed to train workers in the fullest sense and privileged imaginative literature for its purported ability to improve the individual, to allay class conflict and otherwise incendiary thinking, and to foster independent and quiet reflection and thus stimulate further self-improvement.[40]

In nineteenth-century Canada, however, the government only very reluctantly accepted fiction in its attempt to regulate reading habits. For example, Bruce Curtis's account of Egerton Ryerson's founding of public libraries in Canada West in the early 1850s reveals that character formation was more commonly linked to "useful knowledge" (natural history, manufactures, "useful" arts, agriculture) in early state initiatives to encourage mass reading. In post-Rebellion Canada West, Ryerson viewed the education to be had from the right kind of reading as a powerful tool for managing social unrest, the "best means to limit the apparently unbridled independence of the mass of the population that had resulted from the breakdown of earlier relations of domination and subordination."[41] These themes continued throughout the century with the growth of the mechanics' institute movement. With its origins in early-nineteenth-century Glasgow and London, this movement was inspired by an amalgam of the seemingly conflicting Victorian ideologies of utilitarianism and evangelicalism, which together produced what Richard Altick calls the "gospel of self-improvement": "The ambitious artisan was to share in the diffusion of useful knowledge, not by following his own inclinations but by systematically reading what he had to learn in order to become a better workman."[42] Both utilitarianism and evangelicalism did much to reinforce certain kinds of reading as means of spiritual, intellectual, and ethical improvement; both also harboured grave concerns about the influence of sensational, imaginative, and politically radical reading material. The concern for the moral life of the mechanic that was present in the discourse of the mechanics' institute movement, therefore, emerged primarily from utilitarianism, but it was often reinforced by the evangelical spirit that left nothing untouched in Victorian England.

The first Canadian mechanics' institute, in St. John's, Newfoundland, was established in 1827; it was followed by institutes in Montreal (1828), Toronto and Quebec City (1830), Halifax (1831), Kingston (1834), and Hamilton (1839). In Upper Canada/Canada West, where the movement flourished most robustly, there were approximately thirty-five by the end of the 1850s.[43] These institutes first operated on a combination of private funds and legislative grants (the earliest state grants for culture in British North America), but the grants ceased at the end of the 1850s, likely because, as the Ontario Minister of Education's 1881 report on mechanics' institutes speculated, these institutes were largely functioning as circulating libraries rather than as providers of technical education.[44] In 1868, in the wake of Confederation, grants were restored by Ontario's new Department of Agriculture, which supplied funds to those institutes that offered evening classes in technical subjects and that established technical libraries.⁴⁵ From the very beginning, then, government intervention in the mechanics' institute movement prioritized the technical training of workers.

If government ministers thus continually insisted on the presence of technical literature (books related to mechanics, engineering, manufacturing, etc.) in institute libraries, the Association of Mechanics' Institutes repeatedly opposed this imposition and requested more latitude in their selection of library titles. The list of acceptable subject areas and genres was expanded at least twice as a result of the association's pleas, and in 1877, the Minister of Agriculture reluctantly acknowledged that novels had a place in the libraries of the province's mechanics' institutes.⁴⁶ Similarly, despite his evident distaste for novel reading (which he likened to "dram drinking," opium eating, and betel nut chewing), Samuel May, the superintendent of the Ontario Department of Education, recommended in 1881 that mechanics' institutes be permitted to supply "light reading" as long it was selected from a list prepared by the Department of Education.⁴⁷ Evidence suggests that it was library users rather than institute executives who were lobbying hardest for fiction. For example, May's survey of Ontario mechanics' institutes concludes that in 1879–80, fiction constituted 20 percent of the holdings of the libraries under study but accounted for 47 percent of circulation.⁴⁸ Slightly earlier, in 1876, the Toronto Mechanics' Institute, which held 2,688 books of fiction and 530 books of "science and art" in its library, lent out more than ten times the number of fiction titles it held but less than twice the number of science and art titles on its shelves during the year in question.⁴⁹ At the Montreal Mechanics' Institute, the executive balked at members' taste for popular fiction but bowed to it throughout the 1850s and '60s in order to keep its doors open.⁵⁰ The Montreal Mechanics' Institute's 1860 library catalogue abundantly reflects the results of this pressure: the largest sections in the catalogue were devoted to novels and tales, voyages and travels, and biography, and these sections dwarfed categories such as chemistry, mathematics, and natural history.⁵¹

As Edward Austin Hardy's 1912 study *The Public Library: Its Place in Our Educational System* suggests, the public purchasing of fiction for the purpose of creating and maintaining a "university of the people" was, by the end of the first decade of the twentieth century, more widely accepted than it had been in the latter half of the nineteenth, although it was still a cause of significant hand-wringing. According to Hardy, the first secretary of the Ontario Library Association (1900–25), Ontario's new public libraries had "informational" and "teaching" functions, but they also had important "recreative" functions:

> What the drama was in the golden age of Elizabeth, fiction is to-day, the natural expression of life in its multitude of phases. Politics, war, finance, high life, the lower strata, school and church, are all portrayed by the skillful pen of the novelist. In his pages one may escape from the routine of daily life and visit far-away lands or move in distant centuries, refreshing the spirit and finding new stimulus for the tasks of the next day. At the same time there comes a heightening of literary standards, an increase in general knowledge, a broader outlook upon men and affairs, and a deeper sympathy with humanity. Scott, Dickens, Thackeray, Stevenson and a host of others are to be counted among the benefactors of the human race.

However, Hardy warns against "inferior fiction," noting that librarians might confidently follow the tastes of the American and Ontario Library Associations in their selection of titles for recreational reading.[52]

Yet even in the early twentieth century, there was residual reticence regarding the use of fiction in worker education. When the long-standing conflation of character formation and manual training became known in Canada as the Macdonald–Robertson movement, for example, fiction did not play a primary role in utilitarian ideas about the education of young people and workers. Advocates of this movement championed manual training in schools as a means of encouraging and equipping young people to stay in declining rural areas and as a method of training a workforce in a rapidly industrializing economy; but, although moral training was a primary goal, fiction was not this movement's favoured tool for achieving that end.[53] Fitzpatrick drew frequently from the lexicon of this manual training movement, but his ideas about the importance of literary texts, and fiction in particular, in the moral training of workers signalled an important difference in his thought. This can be ascribed to his contact with Arnoldian idealism at Queen's College and, more generally, to what Brian McKillop calls the "hegemony of idealism" that emerged in Canadian Protestant thought and practice during the 1890s.[54]

However, Fitzpatrick enthusiastically adopted utilitarian ideas in describing and promoting what eventually came to be a key figure in the association's work – the labourer-teacher. The very first camps in the fall of 1900 were unsupervised, an arrangement that proved immediately unsatisfactory. As Fitzpatrick observes in a 1901 article in *The Canadian Magazine*, the government-sponsored travelling libraries would be a "great boon" to literate lumbermen and miners, but for the estimated 35 percent of men in the camps who were able neither to read nor to write, "the system will require extension" in the form of "specially qualified" instructors.[55] This slight shift of emphasis from "library" to "school" is a crucial one in the history of the Canadian Reading Camp Association. Lacking government funds to pay instructors, Fitzpatrick turned in the 1902–3 season to the solution of the labourer-teacher – instructors who would be "willing to work in the woods during the day, and conduct informal classes at night."[56] He very quickly began to emphasize what he perceived as the reciprocal benefit of the plan; thus, in the fourth annual report, he refers to "neurasthenia" – the "arrested development" of the urban student who works only with his brains and who must, for the sake of his physical and moral health, engage in manual training; and by 1904, Fitzpatrick was insisting on the "benefits to both teacher and taught." As Carl Berger demonstrates, this emphasis on the need to renew urban Canadian masculinity through contact with rural Canada was embedded in the logic of Canadian imperialism, and it was taken up in a variety of contexts around the turn of the century.[57] By 1903–4, Fitzpatrick was readily deploying the imperialist-inflected language of the educational reform of the era, calling his labourer-teacher scheme the complement of the nation's new manual training schools, which were "aimed at the useful and the ethical, the development of character being the chief consideration."[58]

In the first half-decade of the Canadian Reading Camp Association's work, most of the books that arrived in frontier camps were supplied via the government-sponsored Ontario Travelling Libraries. As was the case with Ontario's nineteenth-century mechanics' institutes, there was considerable state anxiety regarding the use of public education funds to promote and enable the reading of popular fiction and a simultaneous desire to see such funds channelled towards the encouragement of what nineteenth-century utilitarianism deemed "useful knowledge," particularly when the education of workers was the goal. In Fitzpatrick's first annual report, Richard Harcourt,

Ontario's Minister of Education, expresses concerns about the titles being selected for libraries, as well as a clear distaste for anything belonging "to that class of books which are known in England as 'shilling shockers.'"[59] A January 1901 article in *The Globe* reports that Harcourt, "would be glad if it were insisted upon that a reasonable percentage of each box of books would be devoted to work on practical agriculture, horticulture, etc." As the Department of Education was preparing its first round of travelling libraries in the spring of 1901, it consulted "the heads of several colleges as well as a number of literary men in Ontario" in order to ensure the quality of the libraries. According to *The Globe* in May of the same year, these men produced libraries that contained not more than 10 percent of "good fiction," the balance constituted by travel, adventure, biography, science, agriculture, domestic science, and so on.[60]

In his second annual report, Fitzpatrick affirms the feasibility of "technical education" for workers in the camps, noting that government-supported efforts to teach mineralogy, geology, and metallurgy in the mining camps had met with great success.[61] In the summer of 1901, when he advised *The Globe* regarding the type of reading material he was seeking for the following season, he prioritized "clean, healthy literature," such as the animal tales of Ernest Thompson Seton and William Alexander Fraser, Booker T. Washington's autobiography *Up From Slavery*, and William Drummond's *The Habitant and Other French-Canadian Poems*.[62] In the first decade of the twentieth century, Seton's *Wild Animals I Have Known* (1898) was being used to implement the "nature study" component of the new "practical education" promoted by the Macdonald–Robertson movement, and Fitzpatrick's choice of the Washington autobiography signals his approval of the latter's program of education for African Americans, which emphasized agricultural and industrial training as a means of self-improvement.[63]

Though he shared with government officials and the reformers of the Macdonald–Robertson movement an enthusiasm for "practical" and "technical" education, Fitzpatrick clearly favoured fiction over the technical and scientific literature they preferred. Meshing his utilitarian convictions with the cultural idealism of his age, he envisioned a new place for fiction in the lives of Canada's workers. He believed that the act of reading imaginative literature could serve as a powerful antidote to the "moral diseases" of bunkhouse life that rendered individuals "reckless of the responsibilities of home."[64]

However, while he shared with idealist Scots Canadian educational leaders of the late nineteenth and early twentieth centuries, such as James De Mille and W.J. Alexander, a conviction that reading could form individual character and broaden sympathy, Fitzpatrick was much less specific than these cultural leaders about the kind of literature that was required for moral influence. The De Milles and Alexanders privileged poetry and the "greats" of English literature, whereas Fitzpatrick – largely because of his first-hand experience with camp labourers – was quick to apprehend the inappropriateness of such works for frontier reading rooms. The literary genre he favoured most – the bildungsroman, or novel of individual development – was particularly appropriate to Fitzpatrick's idealism, which, like the "collectivist liberalism" Brian Fraser associates with Edward Caird and his colleagues at the University of Glasgow in the late nineteenth century, links the self-governance apparently encouraged by reading to a wider vision of legislative reform and state responsibility.[65] An imaginative form that depends on the individual reader's identification with the story of a young person, conventionally a young man finding his place in the world, the bildungsroman is double-faced, focusing on the development of the individual personality with a view to, as Gauri Viswanathan notes, "inserting the mature individual into the accepted social spaces of the modern nation-state."[66]

In the fall of 1901, soon after the first provincial travelling libraries began their rounds, Fitzpatrick wrote to the Minister of Education to suggest that one third of the books in the libraries be "elementary" readers and to ask for books in French; in a letter that followed a month later, Fitzpatrick notes the importance of "up-to-date fiction": "The men ask for stories." "Do you not think," he queried, "the first step is to interest as well as educate and elevate?" According to Fitzpatrick, the men "prefer" books such as William Kirby's *The Golden Dog*, H.S. Merriman's *The Sowers*, Edward Westcott's *David Harum*, Gilbert Parker's *Seats of the Mighty*, Ernest Thompson Seton's *Wild Animals I Have Known*, Ralph Connor's *Black Rock* and *The Sky Pilot*, and W.H. Drummond's *The Habitant*.[67] Fitzpatrick also engaged a librarian for his association who would be sympathetic to this conception of reading. Edward Austin Hardy, secretary of the new Ontario Library Association, agreed to serve in this role, and in the first annual report, he expresses his belief that reading in the camps was both "recreation and uplifting."[68] At the second annual meeting of the Ontario Library Association, both Fitzpatrick and Hardy insisted on the need for "fiction and light reading" in the camps, and Hardy even suggested that as much as 50 percent of the material in the travelling library cases be fiction.[69] Fitzpatrick's favouring of fiction clearly had some effect on the Department of Education, but the department also had proof of workers' preferences in the form of "fingermarks" (or marks of use) on the volumes of fiction they had sent out in their first libraries. By the end of 1901, the department had modified its position and agreed to include more "standard and recent fiction" in its travelling libraries, complemented, of course, by a "sprinkling of biography and general science."[70]

The government's list of books "received and registered" for the libraries for the period 6 September–30 December 1901 reflects this shift: fully 72 percent of the books catalogued in this period were fiction titles, the balance supplied by works of history (including natural history, 11 percent), science (5 percent), travel (4 percent), biography (3 percent), cooking and home economics (1 percent), and so on.[71] Yet this modification was slow, and even in 1904, Fitzpatrick was writing to Harcourt with the complaint that many of the books in the travelling libraries, such as the titles by Scott, Dickens, and Thackeray, were not "elementary enough" for the purpose of teaching workers to read: "I find a good simple story, in words of one syllable, to be the best for adult beginners. They do not like primers, etc. They realize that they are grown up men, and will begin with a story, while they hesitate to work with ordinary readers." He recommended one-syllable versions of titles such as *Kidnapped*, *Gulliver's Travels*, *Black Beauty*, and *Rab and His Friends*, as well as other books he had long been requesting, such as Ralph Connor's *Black Rock*, *The Sky Pilot*, and *The Man from Glengarry* and W.H. Drummond's *The Habitant*.[72] In the 1903–4 annual report (and again in the one that followed and in 1906–7), Fitzpatrick states his preference for the animal stories of Ernest Thompson Seton, William Alexander Fraser, and Charles G.D. Roberts; W.H. Drummond's poetry of the *habitant*; the plays and poems of the liberal and anticlerical French Canadian Louis Fréchette; the masculine, historical, and often imperialist adventures and mysteries of Winston Churchill, Conan Doyle, G.A. Henty, and Stewart White; the travel writing of missionary Edward Thwing; popular illustrated weeklies such as *The Boy's Own*, an immensely successful periodical published by the British Religious Tract Society; and the novels of Ralph Connor.[73] By 1905, Fitzpatrick's pleas were landing on fertile ground: the government's list of books "received and labeled" for 1905 includes an overwhelming proportion of fiction (92 percent) and, significantly, not a single title that might fall into the categories of history or science.[74] Moreover, there is not a single Scott, Dickens, or Thackeray; instead, one finds Gilbert Parker (10 titles), W.A. Fraser (7 titles), W.H. Drummond (6 titles), Stewart White, and Ralph Connor (4 titles each) – authors whom Fitzpatrick had long been requesting.

One interesting thing to note about Fitzpatrick's privileging of the popular fiction and verse of writers such as Ralph Connor and W.H. Drummond is that this literature offers highly romantic and idealized portraits of working people. In his 1923 study *The University in Overalls*, Fitzpatrick points out that such idealizations of work in literature have not redounded to the benefit of workers themselves: "It is a safe assertion that very few Canadians realize the debt which this country owes to the men in the camp. The works of such writers as Doctor Drummond, Stewart Edward White and 'Ralph Connor' have thrown a certain glamor around the life of the lumber-jack and river-driver, but the commercial value of these men to the country is seldom considered." While Fitzpatrick laments that a kind of mythologizing of work on the frontier has not accompanied recognition of the economic importance of frontier labourers to the nation's economy, he stops short of suggesting that such mythologizing is part of the problem – that its reification might occlude the actual social relations that constitute frontier labour. Fittingly, then, he invokes as his solution the idea of rendering visible the idealized worker's importance to the nation: "Just as surely, however, as the foundation of England's trade and commerce was laid by the gallant seamen who served under Hawkins and Drake, so the basis of this country's financial prosperity has been firmly set by those daring sons of the frontier represented by Macdonald Ban [sic] and Johnny Courteau."[75] The "glamour" of the "lumber-jack" and "river-driver" remains fixed, a fact of nature rather than a contingent creation of the social relations of work. Fitzpatrick's thinking on this point is significant, for it shaped his belief that workers in the camps would find representations of their own experiences in the literary texts of authors such as Ralph Connor and W.H. Drummond. Fitzpatrick's mistaking of romance for reality participates in the idealization of the mythologized "lumber-jack," drawing on the discourse that shaped popular conceptions of work and workers in early-twentieth-century Canada. As Carole Gerson argues, in a settler nation where writers anxious about place "shrank from the intimate self-examination practised by Trollope, Thackeray, and Eliot," social realism made almost no impact on the literary field prior to the First World War. The "more painful questions that would be raised by analysing a socio-economic structure which permitted gouging landlords, exploitative factory owners, and prostitution rarely appear in the literature of a country trying to present itself in congruence with the ideals it found in Sir Walter Scott."[76] The Canadian authors who did broach the issue of labour unrest and class conflict in late-nineteenth- and early-twentieth-century Canada – among them Archibald Lampman, Agnes Maule Machar, Albert Carman, and Ralph Connor – tended to do so, as we will see, as social reformers who invoked idealized portraits of labour in order to plead their case with middle-class readers. There were of course emergent exceptions to this rule – in the periodicals *Ontario Workman* (1872–75), the *Palladium of Labor* (1883–86), the *Labor Advocate* (1890–91), and the *Western Clarion* (1903–25), as well as in the verse collected in T. Phillips Thompson's *Labor Reform Songster* (1892).[77] Such texts, which, at their most radical, exhort workers to revolutionary action, never appeared in Fitzpatrick's recommendations. As we will see, the emergence in the first two decades of the twentieth century of a more robust social realist fiction and radical periodical culture eventually led the Canadian Reading Camp Association to develop a counter-literacy that could compete with these print forms in the camps.

THE ANIMAL STORY AND THE RIGHTS-BEARING CREATURE

Fitzpatrick's favouring of the genre of the animal story was consistent during the first five years of the association's work. He frequently identified Seton's *Wild Animals I Have Known* (1898) as a fine example of the genre. Animal stories by Rudyard Kipling, William Alexander Fraser, Charles G.D. Roberts, and Ernest Thompson Seton were popular around the turn of the nineteenth century and bestsellers throughout the English-speaking world, so it is hardly surprising that Fitzpatrick favoured Seton's book as food for camp workers' appetite for entertaining stories. Yet Fitzpatrick seems also to have grasped how the themes of *Wild Animals I Have Known* might be put to work in labour camps. Despite the popularity of Seton's animal tales in the context of utilitarian educational initiatives that sought to bring urban dwellers into closer contact with rural life, such as the Macdonald-Robertson movement, Seton's stories are as much about the animal world as they are about the particular characteristics of humanity that Seton (and Fitzpatrick) wished to promote – justice, mercy, loyalty, obedience, and, above all, reason. Employing "wilds and barrens" as what Glenn Willmott calls "projections of a more general, modern consciousness," Seton's stories allegorize the coming-of-age of the young, modern individual in a world of "instability and risk."[78] Seton's animal tales argue that, as rational beings capable of merciful actions, animals, like humans, possess rights within certain constraints: "Man has nothing that the animals have not at least a vestige of, the animals have nothing that man does not in some degree share. Since, then, the animals are creatures with wants and feelings differing in degree only from our own, they surely have their rights."[79] Seton's mission was thus to demonstrate to his readers how modern individuals, facing complex and mutable life situations, might retain their rationality. Throughout *Wild Animals I Have Known*, he employs the language of liberalism to trace the contours of this argument.

The eight stories of *Wild Animals* are carefully arranged. The first to appear is "Lobo, the King of Currumpaw," which demonstrates the brute strength but also the cunning of a prairie wolf. This capacity for rational, considered choices is then extended in the stories that follow, but so are the animal attributes of mercy and justice, which are conspicuously absent from the opening story. The brute savagery and strength of the animal kingdom that Lobo exemplifies are not the victors of this collection of tales; rather, the stories that follow the first, particularly "Raggylug, The Story of a Cottontail Rabbit," consistently isolate an animal who uses his or (less often) her wits to thwart a physically stronger rival. A precondition for the ability to act with rational intelligence is the capacity for mercy: alongside the animals is a first-person narrator, an authorial persona who has little distance from Seton and whose strong empathy for animal suffering functions as a kind of moral centre in many of the tales, implicitly valorizing this same ability to feel the pain of others when it is exhibited in dogs or foxes. The closing story, "Redruff, The Story of the Don Valley Partridge," amplifies the privileged characteristics, particularly reason. For instance, as he describes a mother partridge and her flock of downy chicks, the narrator stresses that the babies' survival depends on both "instinct, that is, inherited habit" and "reason," which leads the little ones to "keep under the shadow of her tail when the sun was smiting down." From their first day, "reason entered more and more into their expanding lives." Redruff, the exceptional individual of the partridge family, grows into a particularly rational and merciful creature, one who cares for his little family, notwithstanding that "good fathers are rare in the grouse world."[80]

However, as many contemporary critics have noticed, the reason and, consequently, the rights that Seton would extend to animals such as Redruff are paradoxically figured as impossible gifts. That is to say, they are gifts that the pro-conservationist narrator, despite his intense empathy and identification with the animal world, cannot bestow because the animal world is slowly being extinguished by encroaching modernity. Brian Johnson and Manina Jones read this paradox as an allegory for the "dying race" theses that charged settler Canadian representations of Indigeneity in the early twentieth century.[81] Yet this ironically impossible proffering of rights to an ostensibly non-speaking other (animal, Indigenous person) might also be read in the wider context of the liberal anxiety that shaped so much of this period's discourse regarding class, "race," and gender. If the male settler of British heritage was this era's liberal subject par excellence, then those men who failed to take up this subjectivity represented a particularly potent threat to the emerging liberal order.

This threat is especially visible in "Redruff, The Story of the Don Valley Partridge." Redruff and his sympathetic narrator are almost indistinguishable; the story's human foil for the exceptional partridge is Cuddy, a "squatter" who lives in a "wretched shanty" on the banks of Toronto's Don River: "He was what Greek philosophy would have demonstrated to be an ideal existence. He had no wealth, no taxes, no social pretensions, and no property to speak of. His life was made up of no work and a great deal of play, with as much out-of-door life as he chose." Cuddy, who refuses to abide by the laws regulating the hunting of wild game, shoulders the blame for the extinction of the "Don Valley race" of partridges. Yet this is the story's sleight-of-hand, for surely it is the modernity that the author-narrator – a cosmopolitan resident of New York, London, and Paris – represents that is the greatest threat to Redruff's kind. Nevertheless, it is Cuddy, a man without work, property, family, or respect for the rule of law, who is the story's villain, and who functions as a powerfully negative example for the man – and particularly the working-class, single man of the frontier work camp – who would disregard the trappings of liberal selfhood. Who would want to be the man responsible for killing

Redruff's mate, for blowing "poor brave, devoted Brownie into quivering, bloody rags"?[82] Who would want to emulate such a cruel and shiftless individual? Such rhetorical questions had a clear application to the project of the Canadian Reading Camp Association, which sought to bring the largely settler population of the frontier camps into right relation with liberal selfhood. Fitzpatrick's preference for the animal stories that flowed from Ernest Thompson Seton's pen thus should not surprise us. However, while we have little evidence of *how* camp workers engaged Seton's popular text, there is proof of how they responded to the work of two other popular writers whom Fitzpatrick favoured: Charles Gordon and W.H. Drummond.

CREATING A "HOME FEELING": THE BILDUNGSROMAN AND AFFECTIVE CITIZENSHIP

As we have seen, Fitzpatrick was listening closely to reports from the camps regarding book selection so that he could properly fit books to readers, and what he heard was that the workers preferred popular fiction to the technical or scientific materials that were initially favoured by those who were tasked with assembling the Ontario Travelling Libraries. A 1904 account from a lumber company official suggests that the fiction of Ralph Connor and G.A. Henty – an author whose work is very similar to Connor's – was particularly in demand: "a considerable number of the books supplied seem to be rather above the class of men in the camps," but the "men never seem to tire of reading stories by Ralph Connor, Conan Doyle, Thwing, Stuart [sic] White, and Henty."[83]

Unsurprisingly, then, no fiction played as prominent a role in the association's early work as the novels of Ralph Connor. By the turn of the century, Ralph Connor, pseudonym for Charles Gordon, a Presbyterian minister and former missionary in the work camps of the Canadian West, was widely known across the English-speaking world as a bestselling writer of muscular Christian fiction. Fitzpatrick observes in his first annual report that the "majority of the men on the frontier seem prejudiced against the so-called religious literature"; he thus discourages donations of "sectarian literature" and insists that the work of his organization is non-denominational. Although many instructors continued to use the Bible at informal Sunday gatherings, that book ceded place in the everyday work of the association to fiction by authors like Henty and Connor. However, while Catholic priests were often invited to use the association's tents and cabins, and despite the fact that the Department of Education asked Ontario priests to provide lists of suitable reading for the travelling libraries, some commentators were unhappy with Fitzpatrick's promotion of an obviously Protestant author like Ralph Connor, whose novels express "something like a hate for the Catholic people of Ireland."[84] Charles Gordon was an active supporter of the Canadian Reading Camp Association: his letters of encouragement appeared in its first annual reports, he consistently donated money to the association in its early years, and, into the 1920s, he provided words of praise for Frontier College publications that the association used in its promotional efforts.[85] In the association's second and third seasons, Gordon also contributed six copies each of his popular novels: *Black Rock* (1897), *The Sky Pilot* (1899), and *The Man from Glengarry* (1901), all of which draw on his experiences as a missionary in frontier mining and lumber camps in the West. Other donated copies of Ralph Connor's novels arrived in the camps during the association's first few seasons. A clerk at a Rat Portage Lumber Company camp, for instance, reported in 1902 that his manager donated *The Man from Glengarry*, and in the same year, J.B. McWilliams, Superintendent of Woods and Forests, donated a dozen copies of *The Man from Glengarry* to the camps.[86] The catalogue for the Ontario Travelling Library lists eighteen Connor titles for the period 1901 to 1905.[87] In the association's seventh season, labourer-teacher Thomas Hindle wrote from a Saskatchewan camp asking for more books because "the only books I have yet received are those by 'Ralph Connor.'"[88] In December of 1901, Fitzpatrick wrote to Gordon, thanking him for his donations of his novels and for his continuing support: "These books are sure to do good to these lonely men and I am sure the consciousness of this is to you an all sufficient reward. They have already been forwarded to six different reading camps – three to each. Our work is very encouraging and perhaps no one has given us a stronger impetus than yourself."[89]

Significantly, Fitzpatrick was unabashedly modelling his efforts among frontier labourers after the example fictionalized in the Ralph Connor novels. Fitzpatrick drew on Gordon's preface to his first novel, *Black Rock*, in his first annual report: "The men of this book are still there in the mines and lumber camps of the mountains, fighting out that eternal fight for manhood, strong, clean, God-conquered. And, when the west winds blow, to the open ear the sounds of battle come, telling the fortunes of the fight."[90] Moreover, it seems clear that Fitzpatrick's concept of the reading room drew on the representation of the temperance "league" in *Black Rock*. The league comprises a group of hard-living miners in the Selkirk Mountains who are bound together by the spiritual guidance of Mr. Craig, a missionary, and Mrs. Mavor, a miner's widow whose gentleness pervades the "cosy room" in which she hosts the men of the league. Yet to a significant extent, Fitzpatrick secularized Gordon's concept of the league, adapting the proposal of a camp manager in *Black Rock*, who calls for a "comfortable club-room" with "books, magazines, pictures, games, anything, 'dontcheknow, to make the time pass pleasantly.'"[91] In *The Man from Glengarry*, which was published in the wake of Fitzpatrick's earliest reading room experiments in the fall of 1900, Gordon extended this club room idea, drawing on *Black Rock* but also possibly inspired by Fitzpatrick's project in Northern Ontario. *The Man from Glengarry* is a bildungsroman that follows the individual development of Ranald Macdonald, a farm boy with Highlander roots who learns to be both muscular and merciful under the watchful tutelage of the Lowlander Mrs. Murray, the selfless minister's wife. This is a westward-moving allegory of nation-building; it is set in the years following Confederation and places Ranald at the centre of the negotiations that brought British Columbia into the Dominion. The novel may root its protagonist in the collectively oriented, rural life of Glengarry, Ontario, but it is the very clannishness of the "Glengarry" cry that Ranald must shed in order to become a citizen of the nation. Similarly – and here the parallels to the early-twentieth-century transformation of the Canadian Reading Camp Movement are intriguing – Ranald is profoundly shaped by the revivalist religious fervour of Glengarry, but its spirit will assume more secular, liberal, and individualist dimensions as he applies its values to his work in the lumber industry – an industry that will, he predicts, come to play a leading role in the expanding nation's economy. Moreover, a significant demonstration of Ranald's adult strength and goodness is his application of his Christian ideals to the secular contexts of the modern, liberal nation and its economy: his establishment of reading rooms in the western lumber camps he comes to manage reflects his conviction that the economic growth subtending the new nation will be more robust and enduring if it does not depend on what Mrs. Murray calls "unjust and uncharitable dealings."[92]

For Joseph Slaughter, the bildungsroman, a modern narrative form rooted in German idealism and its "elevation of the bourgeois male citizen to the universal class," narrates not simply the modern, individuated self, but that individuation "as an incorporative process of socialization, without which individualism itself would be meaningless." The German idealist theory of the bildungsroman and the literary form it generated takes "the relations between the individual and the society as their problematic" and the solution or resolution of a "perceived conflict between the anarchistic predispositions of the individual and the conformist demands of society and the state" as their goal. As this latter comment indicates, it is the nation-state that typically provides the "social": "Abiding by what we might call the Westphalian narrative unities of nation-time and -space, the traditional *Bildungsroman* provided the dominant novelistic form for depicting and acquiring this new national and historical consciousness, which it emblematized in the individual's emergence in the public sphere as a rights-and-duty bearing citizen – as a person before the law."[93] For Ranald Macdonald, the social meaning of individualism that is carved out in the leap from community to nation is not tortuous; due to his roots in the Highland Scots immigrant community of Glengarry, he is well-versed in such sociality, even if its more brutish and vengeful tendencies must be softened by Mrs. Murray's grace. As the novel implies, it is this that makes him such an ideal allegorical type for the nascent nation. Daniel Coleman reads Ranald as an instance of what he calls the "enterprising Scottish orphan," a type prevalent in nineteenth- and early-twentieth-century Scottish Canadian fiction. According to Coleman, this type functions to insert Scots "at the head of the procession in Canada." By "means of the mediating concept of Britishness," Scots "created the Canadian version of Englishness in their own image." More specifically, characters such as Ranald Macdonald must negotiate with and ultimately overtake not just their inferior Irish and French Catholic counterparts but also "a corrupt English hierarchy" in the process of "emerging as the allegorical figure for the nascent Canadian nation."[94]

Yet the bildungsroman's principle poles – the local community and home, identified with Mrs. Murray, and the nation, identified with male-dominated private enterprise and government – are not neatly exchanged in the novel as Ranald Macdonald comes to maturity. The Ralph Connor novels consistently demonstrate a strong, residual attachment to the idea that family, and intimate relations with women more generally, are the best incubators of citizenship. Nation does not supplant home but rather acts in dialectical relation with it. A novel like *The Man from Glengarry* was thus particularly well suited to the task of conveying a doubled message: labouring men had to become citizens of the nation, but they needed their mothers and families in order to realize this end. In his advocacy of the physical challenge of the wilderness (instead of the playing field) for the enervated university students who would become his labourer-teachers, Fitzpatrick was obviously alluding to the figure of the muscular Christian, whose battles for "strong, clean, God-conquered" manhood populated the pages of Gordon's fiction. However, Fitzpatrick commonly evoked the need for a "battle" not just for manhood, but also for the merciful, forgiving, and self-sacrificing qualities of women such as Connor's character Mrs. Murray. While admiring the "Herculean thighs and massive limbs of our stalwart toiling sons," Fitzpatrick wished also for the development of "the shapely head and calm divinity of brow"; in other words, the vigorous masculinity that gave the Christian his muscularity in this period was crucial to Fitzpatrick's vision, but these qualities were to be tempered with gentleness and grace.[95] It was not simply that Fitzpatrick was promoting feminized qualities of citizenship, however; he was simultaneously advocating the idea that women possess a special capacity to nurture the individual as a moral citizen. As we have already seen, like his maternal feminist contemporaries, who strongly promoted the affective dimensions of citizenship, Fitzpatrick apprehended the power of the family unit, and of the mother, in particular, to mould moral citizens. In the context of frontier labour camps, where such mothers and families were conspicuously absent, proxies were necessary. If the labourer-teacher was to be a "hero" to the workers around him – the epitome of vigorous skill and strength in labour – Fitzpatrick also imagined him in ideal terms, as a model character of gentleness and steadfastness, a man who "lives not for himself, but for others."[96] These latter qualities are much more commonly associated with the feminized self-abnegation that seems to have little to do with muscular Christianity. Although most recent studies of the history of Frontier College emphasize the "overwhelmingly masculine" construction of citizenship in the first frontier camps, feminized characteristics and influences were in fact crucial to Fitzpatrick's project of cultivating "home-like influences" in the camps.[97] Fitzpatrick believed that such influences could be a powerful antidote to the problem of "jumping" – a practice that demonstrated clear disregard for contract law, that threatened the success of industry and the worker's own individual advancement, and that further imperilled the male worker's identity as breadwinner and head of family.

In adopting this line of thinking regarding women's special role, Fitzpatrick was also stepping into a current of thought that swept up many reform-minded Presbyterians in the early twentieth century – the ideas of Henry Drummond, an evangelist and professor of natural science whose attempts to reconcile evolutionary biology with Christian theology were particularly influential in Canada. Drummond's contention that the Darwinian "Struggle for Life" gave way to a "Struggle for the Life of Others," in which the "Mother Principle" was the guiding force, presented maternal self-abnegation and care as the fount of spiritual development. As a student in Glasgow in the late 1880s, Charles Gordon was captivated by these ideas, and they subsequently appeared in various forms in his popular novels.[98] In *The Man from Glengarry*, for example, it is not the physically and morally powerful minister, Alexander Murray, who leads the protagonist to manhood, but rather the gentle and merciful Mrs. Murray, who has "the power of one who sees with open eyes the unseen, and who loves to the forgetting of self those for whom the Infinite love poured itself out in death."[99] In *Black Rock*, it is Mrs. Mavor alone who has the power to elicit the true gentleness of the miners of the Selkirk Mountains; in *The Sky Pilot*, it is the young minister's combination of masculine expertise on the playing field and feminized characteristics – extraordinarily beautiful violet eyes, eager admiration of others, naive charm, susceptibility to emotion – that make him ultimately so necessary to the rough-edged men and women of the Alberta foothills.

With the exception of a few foremen's wives, cooks, and some remarkable women who served as teachers for the association, women were scarce in frontier camps. Fitzpatrick condemned the absence of women in camp life as one of its "greatest evils": "Only through the presence of women and children can the single man in camp as well as the husband, be taught the proper way of life. No amount of preaching or teaching will take their place."[100] Camp workers had their own strategies for coping with the absence of women: "buck" or "stag" dances were common entertainments in Northern Ontario's lumber camps before the First World War, for example.[101] The homosocial environment of the camps clearly concerned Fitzpatrick, who, by the early 1920s, was advocating family housing for the married man whose "wife and children help him to live the normal life."[102] This worrying absence of women could be addressed in part through labourer-teachers and carefully selected fiction, but Fitzpatrick also emphasized the necessity of the homelike reading tent or cabin, and he often employed the well-tended cabin and its reading matter as a kind of metaphor for the female presence that was lamentably absent in the camps. An instructor in a Parry Sound lumber camp during the 1904–5 season followed the injunction, noting that he was "using every moment at my disposal to make a cosy nest of our little school."[103] Instructors frequently reported improvements such as stoves, lace curtains, photographs and maps on the walls, and good lighting; these improvements, in addition to carefully selected reading material and posted rules discouraging loud talking, swearing, the spitting of tobacco on the floor, and ill treatment of the books and magazines, were, like the Connor novels, meant to temper masculine vigour with "homelike and restraining influences" (see figure 1.2).[104]

The comfortable and home-like reading room and the seemingly female influence it could provide, both in its strong evocation of a "woman's touch" and in the surrogate form of novels such as *The Man from Glengarry*, was also a place where labourer-teachers encouraged workers to write letters home – to maintain or re-establish bonds with their families and to engage in the heterosociability that was notably absent from camp life.[105] Letter-writing materials were always in abundance. In the association's eighth season, labourer-teacher T. Richards reported that his efforts had borne fruit: the worker who played the violin for their Sunday song service had written to Richards, urging him to "keep on with those Sunday night sing-songs, they will do good to some poor soul; they brought me back to the days of my childhood, when everything was gay, and when I used to go to church with my darling old mother. Keep on with them, Tom, you will do good. I have written to my mother, the first for a long time. I was ashamed to write; but I braced up courage at last and wrote a few lines."[106] Just as the early-twentieth-century reform discourse that influenced Fitzpatrick did not always acknowledge the capitalist relations determining its anxiety about home and the family, so this privileging of the wife/mother/family fails to name the actual dependence of the frontier camp economy on the unpaid labour of women. The affective dimensions of citizenship – the centrality to liberal citizenship of the apparently private family and its intimate attachments – are occluded, but so too are the ways in which the unremunerated labour of women contributed to the maintenance of

Figure 1.2 The home-like reading room in an undated photo from the Canadian Reading Camp Association's early period.

this economy. As women's historians like Bettina Bradbury have shown, the shift to industrial capitalism in early-twentieth-century Canada required the unpaid labour of women to perform, on a daily basis, the domestic duties that reproduced the new wage labour. In the context of the Northern Ontario work camp, which demanded the seasonal sundering of the family, this reproductive labour was very difficult to see, but Fitzpatrick's attempts to shape the leisure time of male camp workers unwittingly depended upon it. Moreover, it was not simply housekeeping that was at stake here; absent from the camps was also the affective labour of an idealized femininity that could restrain and temper what middle-class reformers tended to imagine as volatile working-class male conduct. If working-class (and often racialized) women often found themselves at some distance from early-twentieth-century conceptions of idealized femininity, the female characters in Ralph Connor's oeuvre offer idealized proxies for these more troubling subjectivities.[107]

It is now a commonplace to assert that the Social Gospel movement – its leaders, its organizations, and its print culture – was out of touch with and had little influence on the working class.[108] Nevertheless, there is some evidence from both workers and employers that

Fitzpatrick's view of fiction's power in urging men to choose habits of steadiness was accurate. For instance, Charles Gordon's correspondence with enamoured readers includes a 1907 letter from one Frederick S. Hartman, a shantyman from a southeastern Saskatchewan rail construction camp who was powerfully transformed by the Connor novels: "I want to express my deep gratitude to you for converting me and leading me to the light. The new life imparted to me thereby is constantly manifesting itself to me for I find life worth living now and everything seems sort of to harmonize with me. For example – foreigners – Galicians and the like, that to a great extent fill up all the laboring camps, for whom I have always had a strong contempt, I can now see that they too have hearts and are my brothers just the same as my English neighbor." Hartman's letter claims that he and two other shantymen were now reading the Bible and praying every day, and that he has "no doubt that before many days there will be more here added to those that have formed the straight and narrow road."[109]

Moreover, testimony from employers strongly suggests that the pleasant social space of the reading room and the actual act of reading had the effect that Fitzpatrick desired. Employers who wrote to Fitzpatrick in support of his initial efforts were particularly interested in the potential of the reading camps to curb what was often characterized as the "habit" of "jumping." The association's first and second annual reports include many letters to this effect. Prominent lumberman John Charlton's note contends that a "supply of literature of this kind at lumber camps would tend to create a home feeling among a class of men whose services are most desirable." A letter from Felix Bigelow, the foreman at a Nairn Centre camp, claims that such a possibility had been realized in his camp: "[T]he reading camp is a success. In spite of the fact that eighty percent of our men are French Canadians, and fifty percent cannot read English or French, I am surprised to find that a building 20 x 30 feet is filled every evening, and all day Sundays. There is less swearing, gambling, 'jumping' and running to the saloons." Another Nairn Centre foreman, Thomas Shaw, concurred: "Our men appreciate their privilege, are steadier and more reconciled to their lot. The change I am strongly inclined to attribute to this homelike influence." Instructor J.F. Macdonald offered further testimony of the "steadying influence of the reading rooms," and a letter from agent R. Jackson attributes the diminishment of "jumping" and "visits to the saloons," as well as the improved "moral tone" of camp life, to the effects of the reading room.[110]

However, testimonies regarding instructional work were much less sanguine. A considerable number of instructors' reports have been preserved for the 1904-5 season, and of the thirteen labourer-teachers who commented explicitly on their experiences, six of them lamented the difficulty of convincing even a "fair percentage of [the camp men] to take any active interest in the school side of our work."[111] Camp workers evidently preferred the non-structured, self-guided consumption of reading materials that the reading rooms offered, and were less willing to participate in actively shaped lessons. Like their counterparts in nineteenth-century mechanics' institutes, camp men wanted to read but did not particularly want to be told *how* to read or to what end. After 1905, Fitzpatrick apparently accepted the fact that literate, English-speaking workers would not seek out instruction, and he urged his labourer-teachers to focus their teaching efforts on non-English speaking immigrants. However, he long insisted that "while actual attendance on classes may lag," the influence of the labourer-teacher was felt in his "leadership" by example.[112]

W.H. DRUMMOND, POPULAR VERSE, AND IMPERIALIST LIBERALISM

Fiction thus played a central role in the cultural project undertaken by the Canadian Reading Camp Association between 1899 and about 1905. Poetry, a heteronomous form that had long enjoyed a particular symbolic capital that the penny dreadful and the sensational novel had leached from fiction, was also distributed in the first camps. Instructors' evidence suggests that verse of the popular variety, in particular, was frequently read aloud. As I have shown, the one poet whom Fitzpatrick consistently requested before 1905 – in his letters to the Ontario Department of Education and in his annual reports – was W.H. Drummond, the Irish Québécois doctor whose collections *The Habitant* (1897) and *Johnnie Courteau and Other Poems* (1901) were continental bestsellers.[113] Although poetry always constituted a small proportion of the Ontario Travelling Libraries (less than 2 percent of the total number of titles catalogued in 1901, for example), Drummond's books made their way into the libraries after 1902, and, by 1905, fourteen copies of his poems had been added. In 1905, *Johnnie Courteau* was the only poetry title catalogued.[114] Humorous, nostalgic, and sentimental, Drummond's poems are written in a dialect that attempts to evoke the English of Quebec's *habitant* farmers as it sounded to "English-speaking auditors not conversant with the French tongue."[115] Like Charles Gordon, Drummond actively supported the work of the Reading Camp Association: Drummond's 1900 letter, printed in the association's first annual report, wishes Fitzpatrick "all the success your laudable project deserves." Also like Gordon, he donated examples of his work to the first camps – half a dozen copies of his new collection *Johnnie Courteau* in 1902 and another twenty-five copies of this collection, as well as twenty-five copies of *The Habitant*, in 1904.[116]

A complicated imperialism that both uses and diminishes francophone Canada is at the heart of Drummond's verse, and this fact may help explain why Fitzpatrick, who was so deeply shaped by the thinking of George Monro Grant, was drawn to it. Grace Pollock argues that a century-long debate regarding the veracity of Drummond's dialect has ignored the imperialist politics of the poetry. This is a politics that Pollock reads as, on the one hand, idealizing the vigour of the *voyageur* and *habitant* as a tonic for the ailing empire, and, on the other, ensuring the "subordination" of French to British Canadians through the invocation of hierarchies of gender and class.[117] Given the ongoing conflict between French and English Canada at the turn of the century, this poetry quite disingenuously uses the "pauvre illettré," as poet Louis Fréchette calls him in his 1897 introduction to Drummond's *The Habitant*, as a "type national à part" who vouches for the peace that exists between French and English Canadians and the civility of British rule. For example, in poems such as "The Habitant's Jubilee Ode," "Canayens" join in "Wit' res' of de worl' for shout 'Hooraw'" for "Queen Victoriaw." The Conquest "finish it all, an' de English King is axin' us stayin' dere/W'ere we have sam' right as de 'noder peep comin' from Angleterre."[118]

Like his Queen's mentor, Fitzpatrick understood the Social Gospel movement in the context of imperialism; in other words, like Grant, he believed that the "unity of Empire was necessary to maintain a political power making for righteousness on earth." Moreover, as Carl Berger explains, the imperialist ideologies of intellectuals such as Grant were absolutely synonymous with liberty and progress: "In addition to exalting the loyalist tradition, imperialists contended that the history of the Dominion was essentially the story of material progress and the steady advance of liberty and self-government. For them, all Canadian history was ceaselessly moving toward one irrefragable conclusion – the acquisition of full national rights and freedom within an imperial federation." For imperialists like Grant, the propensities to liberty and self-government were often figured as racial inheritances of the Anglo-Saxons, but this thinking was ambiguous: was liberty a racial inheritance or an aptitude that could be acquired? Fitzpatrick, who quoted Grant's call for a "common Imperial citizenship" in his 1919 *Handbook for New Canadians*, evidently shared his mentor's convictions – and, as we shall see, some of his uncertainties.[119] Both liberalism and imperialism drove Fitzpatrick's conviction that Canada's full and equal participation in, and possibly leadership of, an imperial federation would be the culmination of historical progress towards liberty.[120]

As we have seen, a crucial task of the Canadian Reading Camp Association was the recruitment and training of young, urban-dwelling men as labourer-teachers. The labourer-teacher scheme depended on a key reciprocity: what camp workers lacked – gentleness and grace – urban students possessed; what urban students lacked – brawn and vigour – camp workers possessed. Drawing on Canadian imperialists' privileging of the stalwart and vigorous characteristics of the national type, Fitzpatrick recognized the potential threat that urban students posed to the nation's development. He touted the benefits of rigorous physical exercise and manual training for this population, and he sneered at the "waste" of "physical exuberance" in Canada's cities, contending that the issue of the "rich soil and congenial atmosphere" of the city was not simply a "stunted" masculinity but also a nation incapable of properly realizing its potential for growth. Such men needed contact with physical labour in order to "take their places beside the pathfinders of our civilization." In other words, Canada could not assume its primary place in the history of empire, as Canadian imperialists hoped it would, if its middle-class, educated, anglophone sons could not "blaze a trail, excavate a stump scientifically ... portage a canoe or cut a fire guard," as its French Canadian sons in the lumber camps could.[121] Many of Drummond's poems, such as "M'Sieu Smit," subtitled "The Adventures of an Englishman in the Canadian Woods," similarly note the weakness of the British Canadian type and suggest that it might borrow something from the hale and hearty *habitant*. Imperialists frequently used a racial logic to imagine that a mighty "national type" could result from Canada's fusion of the robust, agrarian French Canadian and the willful, self-governing Anglo-Saxon; indeed, some suggested that shared Norman blood would facilitate the fusion. Similarly, Drummond's "The Curé of

Calumette" celebrates the mixing that produced the admirable eponymous character, whose "fader is full-blooded Irish, an' hees moder is pure Canayenne."[122] Without employing racial terminology, Fitzpatrick emphasized the possibilities of such a union in his promotion of the labourer-teacher scheme – the "benefits to both teacher and taught" that would redound to the welfare of the nation as a result of the intermingling of the camp labourer and the urban student.[123] English Canada's male youth needed the brawn and manual skill of French Canada; in turn, French Canada needed the civilization and government of English Canada.

Despite the apparent egalitarianism of this exchange, Drummond's verse implies the unalterable inferiority of French Canadians, suggesting, as Pollock contends, "in the last instance the existence of an essential obstacle – perhaps inherent 'rudeness' – barring French Canadians from ever sounding as sophisticated or educated as English-speaking Canadians."[124] Yet Fitzpatrick insisted that camp workers, including French Canadians and, later, immigrants from northern, eastern, and southern Europe, *could* improve themselves through education. His seventh annual report, for example, argues that camp workers were not "unworthy," "good for nothing else but to be and fill the place of dumb driven cattle." The trouble was "that when men occupy the slave's position, the slave's spirit develops naturally."[125] As we shall see, the association's goal of "improving" non-British immigrant workers was highly circumscribed by a desire for assimilation; however, Fitzpatrick's view of French Canadians was somewhat different. In the first reading camps established before 1905, Fitzpatrick sought French-language materials, surveying Ontario priests in 1901 for appropriate literature for francophone Roman Catholics. He clearly hoped to turn Drummond's permanent "illettré" into an individual who could read in both French and English.[126] This unique treatment of French Canadians is not particularly surprising when one considers the British Canadian imperialist point of view, which prized the "distinctive charm" of French Canadians but worried little about their cultural specificity and occasionally vocal objections to imperialism. According to Berger, imperialists were convinced that the "rapid growth of the English-speaking section of the population, including the 'foreigners' who would be assimilated to the prevailing ideals, would in the end exert a total dominance over the Canadian nationality." Drummond's poems, and Fréchette's commentary on them, enact this process by favouring the figure of the old-timer who recalls a past now long gone and by characterizing the habitant as lost in "souvenirs lointains et mélancoliques."[127]

Berger notes the appeal of rural Quebec to many conservative imperialists, who prized its apparent "backwardness" – its "conservative principles, traditional values, [and] hostility to capitalism." Yet this was a contradictory attraction, full of the paradoxes of early-twentieth-century anti-modernism: these conservative imperialists also "sang the eulogies of progress and welcomed material growth," simultaneously prizing "backward" pastoralism *and* the hearty Norman blood that would engender material and political progress. Conservatives and Liberals alike embraced the profit that industrial and resource development in Canada's North and West signified, but the social progress many claimed it also represented was not easily reconciled with the changes to family life that economic development brought. For instance, the workers served by the Canadian Reading Camp Association were adrift from the moorings of the liberal self – far from their families and, in many cases, without land of their own. French Canadian workers were perhaps particularly at risk of failing to develop as modern, rational citizens; in the imperialist narrative of national history, it was the "mental sluggishness" and "torpid repose" of the Old Regime that the British Canadian love of self-government and material progress had long attempted to discipline.[128]

Popular fiction was used in the first reading camps as a kind of proxy for the absent home and family and as an antidote to the illiberal practice of "jumping"; Drummond's poetry was surely employed to the same purpose. Indeed, Drummond's work is full of stories of courtship and contented marriage, home and hearth. Many of Drummond's personas reject modernity *tout court* and laud the simple joys of rural existence. The speaker of "De Habitant," for example, boasts that the city does not tempt him:

> But I tole you – dat's true – I don't go on de city
> If you geev de fine house an' beaucoup d'argent –
> I rader be stay me, an' spen' de las' day me
> On farm by de rapide dat's call Cheval Blanc.

If there are also verses that laud the strength and daring of the roaming *voyageur* and the *coureur des bois*, Drummond shows a decided preference for the *habitant* and his settled ways. The title poem of Drummond's 1901 collection *Johnnie Courteau* offers a representative example: the eponymous speaker, once "lak de ole coureurs de bois" in his wildness and brute strength, is reformed by his wife, the "nice leetle" Philomene Beaurepaire:

> Den somet'ing come over Johnnie
> W'en he marry on Philomene
> For he stay on de farm de w'ole year roun'
> He chope de wood an' he plough de groun'
> An' he's quieter feller was never seen,
>   Johnnie Courteau![129]

This Drummondian theme of French Canadian "man, and the primary sanctities of the home" clearly appealed to Anglo-Canadian audiences, as a 1907 review in the *Montreal Standard* suggests.[130] Fitzpatrick's preference for this poetry – and, for that matter, for the fiction of Ralph Connor – offers evidence of his own anti-modernist paradox – a paradox that subtended the double emergence of Canada's liberal state and its industrial economy: while the building of the industrial nation required ways of living and being that decentred the traditional household and that privileged the individual, it nevertheless relied on the family, the home, and its reproductive labour.

Literary critics have long insisted that Drummond's poems were popular among English Canadians but rejected by francophones.[131] Indeed, the reception of Drummond's oeuvre in the French-language press was lukewarm at best: it was respectful, detached, and wary. For instance, "Madame Dandurand," the well-known journalist and writer Josephine (Marchand) Dandurand, wrote critical reviews of Drummond's work in her columns in *La Presse* and *La Patrie*. Like Louis Fréchette, Dandurand was a Liberal and a fluent English speaker who wished for "une meilleure harmonie entre les deux groupes linguistiques du Canada." However, Dandurand's uneasiness about the implications of Drummond's popularity offers a marked contrast to Fréchette's enthusiasm.[132] In a 1901 review of *The Habitant*, she castigates Drummond for nurturing a false impression of the people of Quebec, who did not, she insisted, all speak the "idîome bâtard" of Drummond's habitant. In her 1907 memorial for Drummond, she dishes out praise for "ce bon géant à l'âme tendre et compréhensive," but vigorously defends her fellow French speakers, whose "respect instinctif pour notre belle langue fait qu'on ne la voit, pas sans une révolte involontaire, travestie et transigeante." Though thoroughly respectful, Dandurand rejects Drummond's thesis, demonstrated in the poems of *Johnnie Courteau*, that the French language is dying out: "Nous ésperons – pour nous, comme pour le plus grand honneur de l'Angleterre – qu'avec l'amélioration du système d'éducation, notre belle langue va prendre un nouvel essor."[133]

There is ample evidence that French Canadian workers in the frontier camps visited by Frontier College – the "illettrés" at the heart of Drummond's oeuvre – did not simply passively receive Drummond's poems. J.F. Macdonald's testimony offers a good illustration of this point. Macdonald, who went on to become an English professor at Queen's University and the University of Toronto and to write a study of Drummond's work, worked as an instructor for the association just after the turn of the century. He reported to Fitzpatrick in 1902 that camp workers appreciated anything "strongly humorous or pathetic," "particularly poetry," such as the verse in Drummond's *The Habitant*, "old ballads of war or love, much of Burns' poetry," and single poems like Longfellow's "The Wreck of the Hesperus" and Southey's "The Well of St. Keyne," especially when read aloud. In his 1925 study of Drummond, Macdonald describes his experience as a reading camp instructor in three lumber camps near Nairn Centre, Ontario, between 1901 and 1902. According to Macdonald, most of the men in these camps were French Canadian and the rest were Ontario "farm boys." Macdonald recounts the reaction of one group of camp men to a box of books sent from Toronto:

> So far as I remember, the fifty odd volumes were mostly "good" books of the type that no ordinary mortal ever reads for pleasure, but there were two treasures among them, a copy of Drummond's "Habitant," and Butcher and Lang's translation of the "Odyssey." The men who came into the reading shack of an evening would listen to either of these as long as I would read. And they thoroughly enjoyed "The Habitant." After we got acquainted they would correct my pronunciation of French phrases when my Ontario French offended their ears, and sometimes one of them, who was a good raconteur, would launch into a tale suggested by the last poem read. It was obvious they felt that the language was true to life, and believed that the poems were those of a kindly friend who understood and loved them.[134]

If instruction in literacy and numeracy skills was unattractive to many camp workers, the dialogism of the kind of performance that

Macdonald describes above obviously appealed. When the text being read was a popular poem, full of cultural references the workers immediately understood, they could, and evidently did, participate in its construction and its meaning. Macdonald's argument throughout his study of Drummond refutes the idea that the poet's work was offensive to French Canadians, but here he perhaps unwittingly demonstrates not just their appreciation but also their *engagement* of it – their desire to respond to it, to correct Macdonald's French, to extend Drummond's ventriloquized tales with stories of their own. Fitzpatrick privileged the role of the instructor as guide, but as this anecdote suggests, camp workers seem to have responded with vigour to learning that invited them to share their knowledge and experience.

It is not coincidental that the three authors who have received close attention in this chapter are Canadian. In his repeated requests to the Ontario Department of Education and in his annual reports for authors such as Ralph Connor, Ernest Thompson Seton, William Kirby, Louis Fréchette, Gilbert Parker, and W.H. Drummond, Fitzpatrick demonstrated a marked interest in the Canadian writing of his day. This preoccupation reflects neither the literature that was commonly taught in primary and secondary schools at the time nor the state of the early-twentieth-century Canadian publishing industry. Rather, Fitzpatrick's predilection for Canadian authors might be best understood in relation to two key contexts. First, Fitzpatrick was advocating for the value of Canadian-authored fiction at a time when, as Carole Gerson demonstrates, the once-maligned novel was gaining promoters in Canada precisely because it could help nurture a unique national identity. Choosing Canadian authors also perhaps protected Fitzpatrick to some extent from the anxiety of the association's sponsors regarding the moral influence of "shilling shockers" (to use Richard Harcourt's phrase) – the "cheap Coney Island realism" (to use Sara Jeannette Duncan's phrase) that was so often associated in this period with the American popular press.[135] Second, Fitzpatrick's fondness for Canadian authors and their work can be explained by his imperialist nationalism. Many of the authors he preferred also emphasized imperialist themes and figured Canada at the helm of a new age of empire. Although many of the Ralph Connor novels do not directly allude to the empire, the potential relevance for other white settler colonies of their moral messages and allegories of Canada's growing strength is clear. Connor's fan mail amply demonstrates that his writing could function as an important element in the imperialist promotion of Canada as the lead actor in the spectacle of empire. The Social Gospel-inspired missionaries who populate novels such as Connor's *The Sky Pilot* resonated with readers throughout the British Empire. For example, a New Zealander, Robert Buttle, wrote in 1907 to thank Gordon for binding the empire together by noble example: "Living as many of us do on the outskirts of civilization your characters and scenes appeal to us as realities and your thoughts come home to us as inspirations from God stimulating us to lead nobler, and better, and more unselfish lives."[136] In selecting such books, Fitzpatrick seems to have been urging the largely British and French Canadian men in the earliest reading camps to prepare themselves to participate in Canada's glorious century.

The first efforts of the Canadian Reading Camp Association were very beneficial to employers, who clearly desired a less mobile, more steadfast and loyal workforce. Like most reformers influenced by the Social Gospel, Fitzpatrick was hoping to render capitalism more benevolent. Part of his message was directed at employers and, to a lesser extent in this period, the state: these bore the responsibility of ensuring a minimum standard of decency in frontier camps. Barely emergent in the association's first half-decade – in its promotion of the bildungsroman, for example – was the notion of a political citizenship anchored in the national state. It is clear that Fitzpatrick apprehended the role the state might play in supporting cultural, educational, and citizenship programs for working adults, but it was not until after 1905 that he began insisting on the state's responsibility to educate working adults. A stronger message was directed at workers themselves. The relations of production that characterized capitalist resource extraction in Northern Ontario during the early twentieth century demanded that workers be mobile, single, and willing to accept regular periods of unemployment. These relations shaped Fitzpatrick's reading project, which understood the individual as, ideally, the product of a private family environment, and which sought to restore damaged familial bonds through books. This emphasis makes visible the crucial yet occluded role of the family and of women's reproductive labour in a liberal order apparently predicated on the nurturing of the individual male as rational citizen. As this chapter suggests, most camp workers were largely indifferent to the improving forms of culture the Reading Camp Association proffered.

The project of the Reading Camp Association began to alter significantly after about 1905, in the context of the massive turn-of-the-century wave of immigration that crested at the end of the century's first decade. Because such an unprecedented proportion of these immigrants were non-British and, often, non–English speaking, Fitzpatrick's labourer-teachers increasingly encountered work gangs that could not immediately access the association's message through the popular fiction and poetry of authors like Ernest Thompson Seton, Ralph Connor and W.H. Drummond. The shift in pedagogy that occurred in the period prior to and during the First World War was prompted by more than the association's practical challenges in the reading room and classroom, many of which it addressed by developing an English-as-a-second-language program; in a context of increasingly fractious class and ethnic relations, "citizenship" came to function as a keyword for the association's cultural education, offering a tie to bind unruly workers to a benevolent state that the Reading Camp Association was urging into existence.

2

Print for "The Immigrant" and the Limits of Liberal Citizenship, 1906–1919

The period between 1906 and 1919 was one of geographic and bureaucratic expansion but also administrative concentration for the Canadian Reading Camp Association: approximately 40 percent of its work was conducted outside Ontario during these years, but after 1909, it was run from a Toronto office that granted Fitzpatrick and later superintendents proximity to Ontario's business and government leaders. Not surprisingly, given the character of economic development and immigration in this period, the association's expansion had a westward tendency, with new camps cropping up in Manitoba, Saskatchewan, Alberta, and British Columbia; the addition of a western secretary in 1906–07; and the creation of provincial secretaries for each of the western provinces after 1911.[1] In his 1928 study, former labourer-teacher Edmund Bradwin estimates that during the period 1903 to 1914, there were on average two hundred thousand men in any given year who followed "in some form or other the life of the camps"; however, Radforth contends that this number represents the number of men to be found annually in Ontario lumber camps alone in this period.[2] Despite its growth in these years, the association reached only a small proportion of these men: there were approximately eight labourer-teachers and twenty-five reading camps, rooms, and railcars operating in the 1905–06 season. By 1919, as the association was recovering from the diminishment of its operations by the First World War, there were fifty-seven labourer-teachers in as many camps in every province but Prince Edward Island.[3]

Social and economic transformation in this period altered the association's work. In the rail construction camps of the western provinces, the workforce was more transient, obliged to work longer hours, and therefore more difficult to teach, and in all the frontier camps, there were increasing numbers of non–English-speaking workers as a result of the immigration wave stimulated by Minister of the Interior Clifford Sifton's policies – numbers that continued to swell for almost a decade after his departure from office.[4] This latter change had the greatest impact in the West. Yet even in Northern Ontario, camps were altered by the new levels of non-British immigration: in 1909, the region's "gold rush" began to attract thousands of new male labourers, around half of whom were born outside Canada, mostly in continental Europe.[5] According to Donald Avery, this period's economic growth, anchored as it was in railway construction, mining, lumbering, and secondary manufacturing, owed much to "immigrant manpower." The unsafe working conditions, geographic isolation, unstable wages, and poor living conditions typical of the frontier repelled native-born and skilled immigrant workers, with the result that unskilled Slavic and Italian immigrant workers found ready employment there prior to the First World War.[6]

Settler anxiety about "undesirable" immigrants from eastern and southern Europe; wartime fears of German, Austro-Hungarian, Turkish, and Bulgarian "enemy aliens"; and, by 1918, anti-Bolshevik rhetoric that cast eastern European "foreigners" as responsible for all labour radicalism in Canada created a host of new challenges and priorities for the Canadian Reading Camp Association in this period. Labour unrest punctuated these years, particularly around 1912–13 and again between 1917 and 1919, infamously culminating in the Winnipeg General Strike of May and June 1919.[7] Between 1915 and 1920, union membership in Canada grew by more than 40 percent. This increase in membership was accompanied by a diversification of the union landscape in Canada as ethnic-based socialist groups, such as the union locals of the Finnish Social Democratic Party, and industrial unions, such as the International Workers of the World (IWW) and (slightly later) the One Big Union (OBU), were established or expanded. The IWW and OBU experienced particular success in the West among unskilled, immigrant, and seasonal workers – those who had been excluded or sidelined by large and craft-oriented labour organizations such as the central Canadian Trades and Labor Congress (TLC).[8] In the context of state and popular discourses that equated non-British immigrants with the "enemy alien" threat and, particularly in the wake of the Bolshevik Revolution of 1917, labour agitation and radicalism, the Canadian Reading Camp Association found its new *raison d'être*: it turned culture to the purpose of English-language instruction and citizenship education, forms of leisure activity that could potentially combat radical literatures and discontent.

As the association grew and it extended its geographic reach, Fitzpatrick began to diversify the pool of financial contributors, sending fundraisers to Britain and to the West in 1910, for instance. Protestant churches and extra-denominational organizations remained important sources of support. Representatives of railway companies and other industries, such as James Playfair, who owned lumber and shipping businesses in Midland, Ontario, continued to hold privileged positions on the organization's board. Contributions from employers like these remained important sources of income for the association in this period. As the annual reports indicate, the largest donations received in these years (apart from government grants) came mostly from industry leaders like Playfair. Publishers, most of them based in Toronto, continued to support the work of the association during this period: Copp, Clark Co. donated slates and scribblers; many Canadian magazines, including *The Canadian Magazine*, *Canadian Century*, *Busy Man's*, and *The Westminster* provided free copies of their publications for the camps (in addition to featuring articles on Fitzpatrick's efforts); the Toronto *Globe*, with Fitzpatrick's prompting, frequently printed positive articles and editorials about the association's work; and newspapers like the *Montreal Standard*, a popular illustrated weekly, sent complimentary copies to frontier camps, although the war seems to have diminished this practice considerably.[9] After about 1905, Fitzpatrick also regularly asked labourer-teachers to take up voluntary collections in the camps so that workers who had benefited from the association could acknowledge their thanks. In a 1911 letter to instructor T.C. Colwell, Fitzpatrick admits that this collection-taking was also intended to appease men of business who had made large donations but who felt that labourers making "good wages" should contribute to their own welfare.[10]

For all these fundraising efforts, Fitzpatrick was increasingly committed to the idea that responsibility for his work lay with the government. He thus persisted in calling on provincial (and, occasionally, federal) ministers to "extend their systems to meet the needs of our frontier toilers." By 1917, he had succeeded in this insofar as eight provincial governments were now offering financial assistance to the association; but in Fitzpatrick's estimation, "temporary" grants were merely allowing governments to shirk obligations that were rightfully theirs.[11] Of course, as the total contributions made by the various provincial governments grew in this period (from just over one thousand dollars to just under four thousand dollars), so did their influence on the association's work. The increasing priority granted to English-as-a-foreign-language teaching in these years, for instance, was not just a simple case of supplying a demand. As Fitzpatrick wrote to instructor W.J. Agabob in 1913, labourer-teachers needed to pay special attention to the teaching of English to foreigners because it "appeals to the general public and to the Provincial Governments more than any other part of our work."[12] Canadianization was a growing concern for all levels of government in this period: only a small minority of recent non-British immigrants to Canada had assumed citizenship, and it was often assumed that naturalization was an important counterweight to political radicalization.[13] Particularly at the end of the period explored in this chapter, which was marked by rising labour unrest that culminated in the Winnipeg General Strike, citizenship became a crucial term for business elites, as well as an area of increased public investment, particularly at the provincial level. Canadianization thus emerged in the 1910s as the domain in which the Canadian Reading Camp Association could cultivate a particular expertise, an expertise that appeared to be of increasing use and importance to all levels of government, even if the federal government remained reluctant to intervene in educational initiatives linked to citizenship. As the challenge of Canadianization gained new priority, Frontier College devoted itself to the teaching of Canada's dominant language and, perhaps just as importantly, to the cultivation of a pedagogy of liberal citizenship for non-British immigrants.[14] This reoriented pedagogical strategy culminated in Frontier College's *Handbook for New Canadians*, an English-language primer and citizenship guide published in 1919, a few months after the conclusion of the Winnipeg General Strike. In his attempts to bring this handbook to the attention of emergent state bureaucracies, particularly those associated with immigration, Fitzpatrick was staking a claim for Frontier College in the emergent public field of expertise on immigrants and citizenship, while also coaxing a recalcitrant federal government to assume a more formal role in citizenship education.

It is thus hardly surprising that the Canadian Reading Camp Association underwent significant changes between 1906 and the end of the 1910s. In 1919, the association was incorporated as "Frontier College" – the name by which it is still known – and its role as an educator was more firmly attached to its identity.[15] For Fitzpatrick, literacy may initially have been a project of social Christianity, but by the end of the tumultuous 1910s, the association had aimed its mission exclusively at encouraging secular citizenship. But even while secular citizenship assumed an increasingly important role, the association continued to emphasize the problem of illiberalism in the camps. In his study *The Bunkhouse Man*, former labourer-teacher Edmund Bradwin characterizes the frontier work camp of the 1910s as a site of utter lawlessness: "There may be no law east of the Suez, but there is still less on the far-out construction. Rights fade at the last frontier town; they disappear entirely when the end of the steel is passed. Along the grade the head-contractor is supreme ... Only those so favoured may trespass on the company's domain. For, not unlike the Tartar chieftan, the large contractor on the Canadian hinterland bestrides his realm; he is as the Templar, plumed and mounted, in the land of the paynims."[16] Employing a long-standing racialized metaphor that associates tyranny and a lack of rights with the Muslim East, Bradwin insists that a lack of governance had bred decidedly illiberal tendencies within Canada. The racialized nature of Bradwin's comments, however, especially when compared with Fitzpatrick's earliest statements regarding the illiberal tendencies in the camps, indicates that the discourse of "race" was increasingly finding a place in the work of the Canadian Reading Camp Association in these years of growing immigration and the accompanying politicization of identity.

The Reading Camp Association experienced a period of uncertainty between 1906 and 1919 as organizers, teachers, and learners expressed often conflicting views of "literacy," the kinds of print that might be desirable, and the settings in which print might be used or enjoyed by non-British immigrant workers. During the development of the new pedagogy, the popular fiction and poetry of the earliest camps gave way to various new print forms. This chapter considers the use of newspapers and magazines, including the burgeoning immigrant periodical press; Canadian school readers; American materials for the teaching of English to "foreigners"; and, at the end of the period discussed in this chapter, an instructors' and learners' guide to Canadianization, the *Handbook for New Canadians*. Given that it was the first organization to develop a program for adult English-language and citizenship education in Canada, the association lacked models. The diversity of print media employed in the camps in this period indicates the difficulty that organizers and teachers experienced in developing a reading and language-instruction program that might somehow encourage the ideals of liberal citizenship. Non-British immigrant workers posed new challenges to the association. Could these men acquire the proper impulses to liberty and self-government that were essential, in the association's view, to the future of the settler nation? What varieties of print and literary culture could enable this acquisition? As the association developed its pedagogy for liberal citizenship, it adapted its focus on the camp worker's absent home and family to the perceived needs of the non-British immigrant. New literary forms assumed a crucial place in this new pedagogy, but for diverse purposes: oaths and anthems function as typically "public" forms, addressing the individual male would-be citizen, whereas more "private" literary forms such as poems point to the ongoing importance of citizenship's affective dimensions in this period.

ALTERNATIVES TO PRINT

Although the association's emphasis on print continued until well into the twentieth century, rivals to it arose almost immediately that posed interesting challenges – and offered new opportunities – for camp instructors. Like Richard Hoggart's 1957 study *The Uses of Literacy*, Bryan Palmer's research on Canadian workers' history suggests that in the mid-1920s, an increasingly available and influential commercialized mass culture – notably, spectator sports and forms of mass media – portended the fragmentation of working-class community. Yet the centrifugal quality of the frontier camp – the transience it nourished and the cultural and linguistic diversity of the workers it attracted – rendered it a much different kind of site than the urban, working-class neighbourhood (often organized along ethnic lines) for thinking through the impact of mass culture in the early twentieth century. Moreover, as Nancy Christie and Michael Gauvreau point out, the "importance of rural life" until well into the 1930s meant that modern mass culture experienced a "prolonged infancy" in certain parts of Canada.[17] This last point seems particularly relevant to frontier camps, where the impact of mass media such as film was obviously limited. Even so, major rivals to print arrived in the camps soon after the turn of the century – lantern shows, film, and, most notably before 1919, the phonograph – and these proved to be attractive tools for an association that wished to combat "jumping," drinking, gambling, and, later in the 1910s, political organizing.

As the Canadian Reading Camp Association largely abandoned the language of "social Christianity" for the language of liberal citizenship, the hymns it used gradually gave way to popular song, although the latter often appealed to a morality based on home and family that was implicit in many well-known hymns. The "sing-song" – that is, group singing – was a core part of reading room entertainment throughout the period examined in this book. Yet that practice was far from stable; before 1905, there were few phonographs in camps, and what music there was generally came from a donated piano or organ, or simply from voices using sheet music or song books. Hymns dominated these early "sing-songs": the "informal song service" was a Sunday staple in many of the early camps, and Fitzpatrick sent hymn books for this purpose out to those labourer-teachers who requested them.[18] In 1905, instructor John Gray affirmed Fitzpatrick's opinion that labourer-teachers with the ability to "sing and play" were desirable.[19] This practice of group singing is similarly important to the restraining influence Mrs. Mavor exercises on the miners of a western camp in Ralph Connor's novel *Black Rock* and to the late nineteenth-century religious revival depicted in *The Man from Glengarry*. Psalm-singing led by an elder figured in the traditional Presbyterian service of praise, and *The Man from Glengarry* comments on the "innovations" that were altering this music. Conservative church leaders, such as "Straight Rory," condemn these experiments as "new-fangled ranting;" yet in chapters such as "The Wake" and in the depiction of Mrs. Murray's Sunday evening Bible class, the narrator is clearly in sympathy with the community enthusiasm and simple conviction that motivates new forms of collective singing. This Glengarry revivalism, and, more generally, the evangelical Free Church tradition that Fitzpatrick inherited from Pictou Academy and Queen's College, clearly served as a model for the first "sing-songs" conducted by the Canadian Reading Camp Association. However, notwithstanding the term "revivalism," this was nevertheless a sedate and "respectable" kind of singing compared to the earlier, working-class revivalism of organizations such as the Salvation Army, which relied on the culture of popular song, as well as on the spectacle of the parade and the open-air meeting.[20]

The success of the "sing-song" motivated Fitzpatrick to seek other forms of music that would be suitable for the camps. Thus, by about 1910 and until the advent of war forced a new kind of economy, the association commonly purchased phonographs for use in the reading rooms. Commercially available before the end of the nineteenth century, the phonograph and the records it played became cheaper and, hence, more widely available, in the first decade of the twentieth century.[21]

Instructors commonly reported that these machines were tremendously popular among Canadian-born and immigrant workers alike, and many noted that, even where organized classes did not draw men or where card-playing was a formidable distraction, the playing of the phonograph brought great crowds into the tent or reading room.[22] In some cases, workers, in marked contrast to their engagement with print, took up collections in order to buy a phonograph or records for the machine supplied by the association. A record was relatively inexpensive and could be purchased and used collectively; also, it required little time or particular expertise to enjoy; and as instructor J.L Lord noted in 1910, the "privilege" of choosing their own music was probably a novelty for campmen who had so little autonomy over their work or leisure.[23] When labourer-teachers chose music, they generally cited the preferences of the men in the camps, who asked for religious music with a "good swing," such as "Glory Song," and for songs of "love, home, and friendship" of the type that Richard Hoggart identifies with the working-class tradition of "club-singing" that was common in Britain in the early twentieth century: sentimental songs about mothers, family, and childhood, such as the Reverend Robert Lowry's "Where Is My Wandering Boy Tonight?" and Henry Burr's "M-O-T-H-E-R," as well as the music-hall melodrama of Harry Lauder.[24] Like their British counterparts, workers in frontier camps sang along and, in some cases, performed their own concerts.[25] Although songs such as "Where Is My Wandering Boy Tonight?" appealed to a morality common to many hymns – it was published in dozens of gospel hymnals in the early part of the twentieth century – its use of a mother's voice to lament a son's erring and to express her unconditional love for him veers strongly towards the secular and thus a popular morality that required neither pastor nor church. Especially after the advent of the phonograph, the reading room, for at least one evening a week, appeared to be less church than working man's club: if workers were choosing the association's message of home and hearth via the popular song, instructors did not quibble with the medium.

FICTION'S DECLINE

Fiction played an important role in the Canadian Reading Camp Association's earliest reading tents, cabins, and boxcars, but its primacy was short-lived. As noted in the first chapter, the Ontario government inaugurated a system of travelling libraries in 1901, acting on the urgings of Fitzpatrick, who earnestly wished to see library and educational services extended to adult workers in remote areas of the province. But this arrangement, whereby Fitzpatrick requested certain genres, authors, and titles for particular work camps and, for the most part, saw his demands met, did not last long. From the beginning, misplaced and missing books were a problem, and by 1907, the problem had grown to fairly considerable proportions: the Deputy Minister of Education, A.H.S. Colquhoun, wrote to Fitzpatrick to inform him that, of the twenty-four travelling libraries sent to New Ontario between 1901 and 1906, only two had been accounted for (one had been sold without the permission of the Department of Education, and the other had been destroyed with the department's permission in the wake of a smallpox outbreak).[26] Of course, the large number of missing books does not necessarily imply that those books were read; it is also very likely a symptom of the frequent seasonal turnover in the camps and the lack of clarity regarding who was responsible for the libraries. However, instructors' correspondence suggests that the libraries continued to appeal to many workers well into the first decade of the twentieth century. For instance, labourer-teacher E.D. Nott indicated in July 1907 that he had received his library in June and that it had "been in constant circulation since," so much so that he proposed exchanging his books with a nearby camp. Similarly, W.J. Morrison, who was stationed during the summer of 1908 in a Northern Ontario logging camp with mostly English-speaking and Swedish workers, reported his great "surprise" about the interest the men took in the camp's Ontario Travelling Library of about seventy books, which was exhausted in the space of three months.[27]

In 1907, the Inspector of Public Libraries, T.W.H. Leavitt, increased funding for travelling libraries and instituted a new type of library – the "open shelf" library – for use in reading camps and rural study groups. The "open shelf" had movable shelves; a lockable, hinged cover that could serve as a table; pedagogical materials such as copybooks, pencils, and paper; and registers for the purpose of recording book loans and returns.[28] Despite the new libraries' emphasis on the fact that the books belonged to a self-contained system that was under government surveillance, book losses in the reading camps continued. In the summer of 1908, Fitzpatrick agreed to assume personal responsibility for all of the books loaned through the Ontario Travelling Library system, but this was a temporary solution only. By December 1908, the Inspector of Public Libraries, frustrated by the continued losses and the Reading Camp Association's unsettled account, called in all outstanding travelling libraries from

Fitzpatrick's camps.[29] Fitzpatrick later admitted that even the revamped travelling library was not really suitable for camp use: what was needed were inexpensive, paper-bound volumes of popular fiction that could remain in particular camps season after season. He repeated this message in his correspondence with other provinces, such as British Columbia, which began tailoring its long-standing travelling library service to Fitzpatrick's needs in 1912.[30] In 1911, the new Inspector for Public Libraries in Ontario, Walter Nursey, offered two solutions: he donated three cases from the travelling libraries (about three hundred books) to the camps, and he created a dozen cases with "school outfit and reading matter complete in one box" for the 1912 season. Since both of these solutions recycled used reading matter, the books would remain the property of Fitzpatrick's association.[31] Nursey's "outfits" included three compartments: one for reading matter, "chiefly fiction as per your request"; one for school supplies (including spellers and readers); and a third for the association's use. By the end of 1914, the Ontario Department of Education had distributed twelve such boxes to work camps. The last six of these "outfits" contained fifteen titles each (a few had sixteen) and reflected Fitzpatrick's long-standing preference for popular, contemporary authors of romance and adventure, such as Gilbert Parker, Stewart E. White, Conan Doyle, Jack London, Ralph Connor, W.A. Fraser, and Mary C. Crowley.[32]

The fiction that continued to arrive in the reading camps in this period increasingly came accompanied by pedagogical materials – primers, slates, scribblers, pencils – a fact that reflects the association's growing rejection of the passive consumption of print in favour of active pedagogy. Moreover, Fitzpatrick's letters to the Ontario Inspector of Public Libraries in 1919 indicate that by the end of the First World War, even these government-supplied "outfits" "scarcely" met his purpose now that the camps contained so few English-speaking men.[33] Between 1906 and the end of the First World War, the Canadian Reading Camp Association was clearly obliged to shift its emphasis to varieties of print accessible to the growing number of non–English-speaking immigrants in the nation's work camps.

PERIODICALS AND NEWSPAPERS: "READ A GOOD PAPER EVERY DAY"

Canadian periodicals and newspapers experienced explosive growth around the turn of the century. Following Benedict Arnold's contention that mass print culture enabled the imagining of the modern nation, Merrill Distad asserts that the success of the domestic periodical press during a crucial period of Canadian nation-building "played a major role in the creation of distinctive Canadian cultures and a growing national identity." Certainly, that it expanded is undeniable. There were 101 daily newspapers in all of Canada in 1891; by 1913, there were 138. The combined circulation of Canadian weeklies and dailies grew from under three hundred thousand in 1872 to more than one million by the end of the nineteenth century. Similarly, domestically produced general interest magazines with full-colour covers and illustrations, such as *Saturday Night* (originally *Toronto Saturday Night*) (1887–2005); religious magazines, such as *Methodist Christian Guardian* (1829–1925); and agricultural magazines, such as *Grain Growers' Guide (*1908–28) and *Nor'West Farmer* (1882–1936), all enjoyed a significant increase in their readerships around the turn of the century. Boosting this growth was a favourable postal rate for domestic periodicals, as well as the recent development of a national railway network, both of which abetted the federal government's desire to nurture "national consciousness" via print.[34] Newspapers and periodicals also played a significant role in the organization of modern time. If these forms of media functioned as handmaidens to and generators of the precise, scheduled time that was so crucial to the development of industrial capitalism in early-nineteenth-century Britain, one can readily see how their periodicity served the needs of frontier camp employers, who worried about workers' isolation from the routines of urban life.[35]

From its earliest years, the Canadian Reading Camp Association benefited greatly from this healthy domestic periodical press and from advantageous postal rates for domestic newspapers and periodicals.[36] But if the consumption of such print did indeed encourage a "growing national identity," it surely also had great potential for political and cultural division. Before 1919, this seems not to have been a source of great anxiety for Fitzpatrick; nonetheless, it is likely that his increasingly marked preference for guided engagements with print emerged at least in part from concerns over the autonomous reading of periodicals that the culture of the reading room initially encouraged.

Richard Hoggart observes that the quick gratification of a sensational story magazine held more appeal for English workers in the early twentieth century than for twentieth-century middle-class readers, whose lives were shaped by a narrative of progression.[37] This observation holds relevance for early-twentieth-century Canadian frontier camps, as well. The short, often serialized story was a particular favourite among workers in camps. As several instructors noted, workers "have hardly time to read a long story," and fiction that could be consumed in serialized instalments obviated this problem.[38] In rail construction camps, where camp mobility and extremely long hours of labour militated against the slow enjoyment of a novel, short stories in periodicals offered the pleasures of popular fiction with a less significant investment of time.[39] There is evidence that workers in the camps enjoyed short and serialized fiction from popular British and American illustrated magazines, such as *Cosmopolitan, Blue Book, American Magazine, The Graphic, Black and White, Saturday Evening Post, Everybody's Magazine*, and *Popular Mechanics*.[40] Illustrated papers of this sort were also popular with immigrants who could not read English, who would nonetheless "often form in groups to look at the illustrations and study out the accompanying descriptive matter."[41] Less often, instructors suggested that the men sought stories in Canadian periodicals: in the summer of 1912, for instance, instructor J.R. Mutchmore claimed his men were looking for the latest Ralph Connor story in *Westminster Magazine*. W.R. McWilliams, a regional organizer in western Canada during the 1914 season, observed that "nothing is more appreciated than the *Saturday Post* by the men who read continued stories." His report goes on to doubt "whether a quarter of the magazines sent out to camp are ever read by anyone and I find that those who do read as a rule are men who like something better than *Top-Notch Adventure* [an American pulp magazine of adventure fiction] and a score of others of a similar nature."[42] Whether or not McWilliams's contention is accurate, American pulp magazines such as *Argosy* and *Popular Magazine* found themselves omitted from Fitzpatrick's subscription lists in favour of what he described to donors in the Imperial Order Daughters of the Empire in 1916 as "the kind of literature ... we ourselves like best."[43] Inevitably, the magazines sent to camps were Canadian periodicals like *Canada Monthly, Canadian Century*, and *Maclean's*, or more middlebrow, illustrated story magazines from Britain and the United States.

If magazines served as an important source of fiction in this period, it remains true that the association's emphasis on fiction weakened after 1905. The newspaper, however, partly because it could be used as a tool for educating immigrant workers, continued to hold a central, if changing, place in the culture of the frontier reading room. From the beginning, Canadian daily and weekly papers had served as a means of connecting remotely situated camps to cities such as Toronto, Montreal, and Winnipeg (as instructor R.C. Dearle put it, to the "outside world") and to the routines of urban life that were absent from frontier camps.[44] Besides keeping workers connected to a daily and weekly periodicity that was important to the interests of industry, newspapers – like the maps supplied to frontier camps by the federal Department of the Interior throughout this period – communicate a sense of time and space that was important to the workings of empire in peripheral locations.[45]

As we saw in the previous chapter, newspapers were from the beginning of the association's work a popular form of print among camp workers. Unsurprisingly, when war broke out in Europe in 1914, instructors communicated very clearly to Fitzpatrick that camp men were wild for newspapers. Donald L. McDougall, for example, wrote in the summer of 1914 that the reading room "is the Mecca for seekers after war news lately," and R.L. Dorrance reported in the same season that due to the war "attendance in reading room is especially larger and it is the scene of some very exciting debates."[46] Instructors often wrote to ask Fitzpatrick for more local papers (e.g., fewer Toronto papers if the camp was in southern Alberta or on Quebec's north shore), and, occasionally, they communicated the men's displeasure regarding the political character of the papers arriving at the camp. For instance, in 1911, A.D. McConnell complained from his Bala, Ontario, lumber camp that the "majority of the men, and the foreman" were Conservatives who took offence at the quantity of "Liberal" papers on offer in the reading room. Similarly, F.G. Poole wrote in the same season to say that his Cochrane, Ontario, camp received the *Toronto News*, which "tells the Conservative side of politics very well," but since "the fellows are anxious to get the other side of the question," he hoped to soon receive a paper such as the *Daily Globe*.[47]

But the most frequent request that Fitzpatrick received regarding newspapers between 1906 and 1919 was for non-English papers. According to Paul Hjartarson, most of the immigrant communities that arrived in large numbers in the first decade of the twentieth century – Galicians, Italians, European Jews, Russians, Germans, Swedes, and Norwegians – "placed a high priority on setting up schools and presses." Although many of these immigrants, such as the Ukrainians of early-twentieth-century Winnipeg, had access to newspapers in their own language from the United States, setting up a local press that could produce, at a minimum, a weekly four-page paper was a crucial act of community-building. Indeed, Winnipeg, the centre of Ukrainian Canadian print culture in the first half of the twentieth century, boasted five weekly Ukrainian-language papers by 1911.[48] Some government officials involved in the nascent Canadianization efforts of the period, such as Saskatchewan's J.T.M. Anderson, feared that this emergent foreign-language press would harm "national unity and solidarity": "Newspapers are printed in German or Ruthenian or Hungarian or Icelandic, because thousands of their readers cannot read English. Merchants advertise their wares and politicians reach thousands of their supporters through pamphlets printed in a dozen languages. Of course, these conditions are temporarily unavoidable, and nothing else could be expected owing to the heavy tide of immigration during the past decade. But the future of Canada depends on the betterment of these conditions. There must be one medium of communication from coast to coast, and that the English language."[49] Published in 1918 in the context of widespread fears regarding both "enemy alien" and Bolshevik print culture, Anderson's assessment reflects how the state typically viewed the foreign-language press in the late war years. In the early twentieth century, however, these concerns had not congealed to the same extent. Though Fitzpatrick's primary mission was, by the late 1910s, firmly attached to English-language acquisition, which he came to view as soil preparation for the plant of citizenship, he did not initially share Anderson's anxiety regarding the foreign-language press. Perhaps he ascertained, as Hjartarson notes, that the immigrant press could be "double-edged": on the one hand, it was a powerful manifestation of a community's ability to preserve its own language and culture in the new nation; on the other, it "promoted acculturation" through the frequent inclusion of English-language text (often advertisements) and coverage of local and national news.[50] Of course, some foreign-language newspapers espoused a view of self, nation, and government that was amenable to Fitzpatrick's emergent conception of liberal citizenship; others did not.

Particularly towards the end of the first decade of the twentieth century, labourer-teachers, who had no training in the teaching of English as a second language, asked for newspapers, translation dictionaries, or resources in languages other than English. In some cases, instructors sought out materials themselves, sometimes looking to the United States, where immigrant communities established in the nineteenth century had print resources in their own languages. For instance, H.P. Waters reported in 1908 to Fitzpatrick that, hoping to increase his success with his Bulgarian students, he had written to the Bulgarian organ in the United States (the *Macedonia*) to ask about learning materials.[51] Fitzpatrick was very supportive of such efforts; indeed, his own office consistently found appropriate foreign-language newspapers for camps that had requested them, and even for those that had not. In 1909, Fitzpatrick wrote to Charles Combe, who was stationed in Manitoba, that he would attempt to send papers in each of the languages spoken by the men in Combe's camp because this type of print could be a powerful tool in the association's work. Yet he included a note of caution: "You know this work is not only religious. It is primarily educational. We are very anxious that all the workmen improve their spare time taking up elementary studies, as for example, the three R's. We are especially anxious that foreigners be taught the English language. Get them to take more interest in the country and instead of sending their money home, to remain where they become good citizens."[52] In Fitzpatrick's estimation, at least in 1909, foreign-language papers did not harm the labourer-teacher's ability to anchor the immigrant worker to Canadian citizenship.

Crucially, however, Fitzpatrick tended to favour newspapers that were published by immigrant communities in Canada (and that consequently covered Canadian news) and that espoused liberal values. Thus, although Fitzpatrick did not initially hesitate to provide immigrant workers with print in their own languages, his provision was not without political intention. He consistently selected foreign-language papers that spoke for the liberal voice of a given community, and in an era of increasing labour unrest, he avoided all papers that expressed socialist points of view. He set the tone with the French Canadian papers he selected – the liberal papers *La Presse* and *La Patrie*. In 1916, instructor Fred Bell observed from his The Pas, Manitoba, camp that the Austrians in his camp "are very intelligent and I think most of them can read in their own language." Consequently, he recommended that Fitzpatrick send *Kanadyiskyi Farmer* and *Ukrainskyi holos*, both of them Winnipeg-based, Ukrainian-language papers.[53] These papers, which Fitzpatrick subsequently sent, were respectively aligned with the federal Liberal Party and Winnipeg's Ukrainian nationalist community, and both offered alternatives to the socialist Winnipeg papers *Chervonyi prapor* and *Robochyi narod*. Prior to 1917–18, Ukrainian socialists were small in number and influence in Winnipeg; nonetheless, Fitzpatrick had good reason to fear their influence in frontier camps: according to Orest Martynowych, the only educated Ukrainians to visit frontier camps with any consistency before the 1920s were the socialists, who represented organizations such as the Social Democratic Party of Canada (SDPC) and who were successful after 1912 in establishing party branches in Northern Ontario locations such as Timmins, Cobalt, and South Porcupine.[54]

For camps with Italian workers, Fitzpatrick took out a subscription to *L'Araldo del Canada*, an Italian-language paper published in Montreal after 1905. Instructor Norman Davies reported that the Italian workers in his La Tuque, Quebec, camp appreciated the paper enormously.[55] The Italian immigrant community in prewar Canada was neither particularly politicized nor prone to collective action, but its high density of unskilled male sojourners and its consequent lack of political and sentimental attachment to Canada likely made it a concern for Fitzpatrick, who wanted to stifle the practices of remittance and seasonal migration. In choosing *L'Araldo* instead of its counterpart *Corriere del Canada*, which was owned by Canadian Pacific labour agent Anthony Cordasco, Fitzpatrick may have been attempting to avoid the conflict that had culminated in a 1904 Royal Commission tasked with investigating the unscrupulous practices of Italian *padroni* (or labour agents), among whom Cordasco was a chief figure. In the government's view, such practices led to mass unemployment, public dependency, and potential labour unrest in cities like Montreal.[56]

However, Fitzpatrick's language and citizenship manual *Handbook for New Canadians*, published in 1919, clearly indicates that, in the wake of the First World War and the perceived threat of Bolshevism in the camps, his view of foreign-language periodicals had shifted. By the spring of 1918, the government was under considerable pressure to act on seditious foreign-language newspapers, which were widely blamed for the large number of labour strikes in 1917 and which were also being linked to "enemy alien" activity. A September 1918 Order in Council banned "enemy"-language publications containing "objectionable matter" (matter harmful to the war effort or of a socialist or anarchist tendency). A second Order in Council from the same year further banned thirteen socialist and anarchist political organizations, many of which operated in "enemy" languages, as well as any organization advocating political change through "force, violence, or physical injury to person or property." The former Order in Council, PC 2381, was gradually loosened between 1918 and 1919 to allow certain "enemy language" publications to appear under certain conditions (provided they offered parallel English translations, for example).[57] However, in the wake of the 1919 Winnipeg General Strike, amendments to the Criminal Code – later known as Section 98 – were introduced that aimed much more directly at the foreign-language press and its association with radicalism. Those amendments suppressed the production, possession, distribution, and importation of literature "in which is taught, advocated, advised or defended, or who shall in any manner teach, advocate, or advise or defend the use, without authority of law, of force, violence, terrorism, or physical injury to person or property, or threats of such injury, as a means of accomplishing any governmental, industrial or economic change, or otherwise."[58] Evidently eager to assess the state of the foreign-language press in Canada, in 1919 Fitzpatrick surveyed the major English Canadian dailies, as well as foreign-language papers such as *Svenska Canada Tidningen*, a weekly Swedish newspaper published Winnipeg, in order to discern how many foreign-language papers were circulating in Canada and the political character of the various immigrant communities that read them.[59] While still advocating newspaper reading as a means of keeping "in touch with the world," Fitzpatrick used his 1919 handbook to admonish camp workers to both "read a good paper every day" and "aim to read a paper written in the English language."[60] Although there is no extant correspondence for 1917 or 1918, by 1919, instructors were no longer requesting – and seem to no longer have been receiving – newspapers in languages other than English or French. The wartime association of the foreign-language press with both "enemy" activity and labour agitation had surely led to this modified position.

THE "CHILD'S PRIMER"

As the proportion of non-British immigrants in frontier camps increased and as fears about the political loyalties of such workers intensified in the decade leading up to the end of the First World War, Fitzpatrick's emphasis on classes for immigrant men and instructor accountability strengthened considerably. By 1914, he was insisting that labourer-teachers hold classes five nights per week, a demand that some instructors, citing the men's (and, in some cases, their own) long working hours, rejected as impossible.[61] Even before the requirement, many instructors – particularly those in rail construction camps where teaching cars were scarce and working hours were long, and where worker mobility inhibited the formation of relationships – insisted that conditions for teaching immigrants were not favourable.[62] Many others declared modest success with somewhat regular language classes of two to five men, but most of those who made such claims also observed that a departure of a gang of men brought a halt to classes, which were only re-established after great effort on the instructor's part.[63] By 1919, Fitzpatrick also required from each labourer-teacher weekly, one-page registers that recorded number of hours taught per night, attendance at each class, the ethnicities of the men in attendance, and the subjects studied. Significantly, success in forming regular classes increased after the implementation of these registers, which intimates that the register was likely completed as a matter of duty even when classes were not held consistently.[64]

As the association focused increasingly on active pedagogy in the camps, it required resources for teaching. Given the large number of immigrant workers in the camps who neither spoke nor read English, and given that the workers were adults in an era when adult education consisted of nascent, largely philanthropic initiatives such as the YMCA, these resources were hard to come by. One alternative that Fitzpatrick turned to was the primary school reader. Since the latter half of the nineteenth century, agency publishers in Toronto had experienced great success in publishing readers for Ontario elementary schools and, ultimately, for schools in other provinces. The Ontario Readers series became ubiquitous after that province's Superintendent of Education authorized its use in 1884; variously published by Thomas Nelson, Gage, the Canada Publishing Company, Copp, Clark, and the T. Eaton Company, these readers dominated the Canadian schoolbook market throughout the first three decades of the twentieth century.[65] In 1911, Fitzpatrick sought out donations of "Primers and First and Second Readers" from the Ontario Inspector of Public Libraries, and throughout the early 1910s the Toronto Board of Education sent him grammars, spellers, hygienes, geographies, histories, and readers from the Ontario Readers series. Additionally, some of the Toronto publishers donated other readers to Fitzpatrick's cause; for example, the Macmillan Company shipped its New Globe Readers to various camps during the 1907 season.[66]

Labourer-teachers eagerly adopted primary and high school readers for use in the camps. One advantage from their perspective was that the readers allowed them to group men according to ability in a subject; many reports to Fitzpatrick indicate that instructors used the readers to create small classes (usually of two or three men) and to suggest the possibility (very rarely achieved) of progress through the various levels. The regularized, authorized quality that the readers lent to the association's work seems to have appealed greatly to instructors, who were often flummoxed by their remote locations, their lack of teaching experience, the dearth of pedagogical resources at hand, and the apparent impossibility of establishing a camp "school."

Due to the fact that so many of the camp workers in this period were either English speakers with little formal education or immigrants who spoke little English, instructors relied heavily on the first reader, or primer, in their lessons.[67] The first reader in the Ontario Readers series, which after 1909 was published exclusively by the T. Eaton Company, must have initiated some rather comical scenes in reading tents and boxcars across the country: one might only imagine how these textbooks, stocked with poetry and short prose for children as well as illustrations of bonneted maidens, must have been received by the tired immigrant worker who spoke little or no English.[68] These primers were designed not just for children but specifically for *British Canadian* children. For instance, the 1909 edition of the first reader concludes with a series of short prose pieces describing faraway people, places, and customs "not like yours": the low-slung, "mud or stone" house of Ahmet the Syrian boy; the "yellow skin" of the Japanese girl Matsu, whose "eyes are not straight across as our are"; and the black skin, "woolly heads," and "white teeth" of the boys in "banana land."[69] In accordance with prevailing contemporary ideas about primary education as a force for cultural assimilation, the primer interpellates the schoolchild, whom the narrator addresses directly, as participating in a culturally cohesive community that will only ever need to encounter difference theoretically. In order to answer the call of the narrator's "you," therefore, the immigrant child would have been required to imagine herself as different from Ahmet, Matsu, and the boy in "banana land." Surely many immigrant children from northern, central, and eastern Europe, especially those who had experienced homesteading in Canada, considered it strange to encounter a low-slung "mud or stone" house as an oddity, and surely this strangeness was felt by some adult camp workers as well. As Fitzpatrick's 1916 letter to lumberman J.L. Lovering observes, the problem with the elementary readers was also one of level: the "foreigner," he worried, "does not enthuse over child's primers."[70] Dissatisfied with the "child's primer" as a tool for teaching adult men, Fitzpatrick and association employees like Edmund Bradwin worked to locate and develop resources for teaching English as a second language to adult learners.

FROM LANGUAGE DRILLS TO LITERATURE FOR CITIZENSHIP

According to John Sutherland, as non-British and non-French immigration levels rose in the second decade of the twentieth century and as the English/French schooling question receded in importance in relation to new demographic realities, "many English Canadians moved from a reasonably relaxed position on Canadianization to an aggressive policy of assimilation."[71] That shift was also certainly embedded in the context of the First World War, a period during which the state used its unprecedented powers to limit the circulation of print in "enemy" languages and in other languages (namely, Finnish and Russian) associated with socialist activities. This shift towards Canadianization was evident in the Canadian Reading Camp Association's annual reports, which began to pay explicit attention to the "foreigner" in 1906–7. Thus, in his 1907 essay "The Reading Camp and the Foreign Navvy," Edmund Bradwin notes that "foreigners" were abundant in the nation's railway camps and contends that the reading camp instructor was "by no means an inconsiderable force" in the state's duty to "assimilate" into "our national life" the "Italians, Swedes, and Slavs" who laboured in them.[72] In 1912, just as the immigration wave was cresting, the Canadian Reading Camp Association's annual report turned its whole attention to "the immigrant," a strong indication of the extent to which Canadianization had assumed a central role in the association's culture in the period leading up to the First World War.[73] Rendered more or less invisible by the association's shift in attention to Canadianization were French Canadian workers; although, as we saw in chapter 1, these workers had been a significant object of the association's attention during its first half-decade, they receded almost completely from view during the 1910s as the project of citizenship came to be wholly identified with the settler nation's exogenous population.

Not coincidentally, the 1912 annual report was published during a time of intense strike activity, which included the IWW-led strike of Grand Trunk Pacific and CNR railway construction workers in the summer of 1912. As we have seen, such labour radicalism was frequently linked in this period to non-British immigrant workers, despite the fact that most union leaders in Canada, even IWW leaders, were British-born. Yet non-British immigrant workers, organized into separate language locals, constituted the majority of prewar socialist political organizations such as the SDPC. They were also important sources of potential radicalization for the IWW and other union organizers in this period, even if most railway navvies, to take one group as an example, were from peasant backgrounds and did not have a tradition of unionization. During strikes in the Fraser River Canyon in 1912, for instance, the IWW engaged Italian organizers and distributed strike literature in Italian to the region's many Italian navvies.[74] Not surprisingly, then, the Canadian Reading Camp Association's attention to Canadianization efforts soon turned to the development of counter-literacy tools that could be used in the camps to combat this radical print and to create citizen-readers.

Canadianization did not constitute a cohesive settler program or set of goals: while some trumpeted the value of the nation's staunchly British character, others, including imperialists, were interested in the new possibilities that Canadian nationality might bring to the British type. Winnipeg reformer J.S. Woodsworth, for instance, emphasized the potential of the "higher type" to be forged from the best qualities of British and European nationalities. Woodsworth's convictions in this period led him to argue that immigrants might retain unique aspects of their cultures, but that they must also detach themselves from insular and collective lifeways – including socialist politics – that prevented them, in his view, from integrating themselves into Canadian society. In 1917, Woodsworth wrote that his People's Forum "breaks down the artificial barriers that so seriously divide our communities. It takes people out of their own little circles. It broadens their interests and makes them sympathetic toward those who hold different views from their own. It helps to create a common interest, to develop a community spirit and thus to prepare the way for a more disinterested and efficient citizenship." Unsurprisingly, there is evidence that there was a considerable interchange of ideas between Woodsworth, a well-known Social Gospeller and Methodist minister, and the Canadian Reading Camp Association. He and Fitzpatrick corresponded on several occasions, and they were certainly aware of one another's undertakings.[75] Like Woodsworth, whose 1909 study *Strangers Within Our Gates; or, Coming Canadians* ranks immigrant groups according to what Ian McKay calls "the capacity of its units to become the self-sufficient individuals of liberal social theory," many labourer-teachers employed a racial hierarchy to class the men in their camps. Those at the top of the pile – for the instructors as for Woodsworth – were the Scandinavians, who, as one labourer-teacher noted, possessed a "magnificent physique," "industrious, honest, honorable" character, and an "ambitious and progressive" nature that rendered them "the best material for citizens."[76]

"Assimilation," as the association's eighth annual report indicates, was a primary goal of camp education; however, the association cultivated a view of Canadianization similar to Woodsworth's insofar as it idealized the "higher type" that could be produced from the mixing of the preferred traits of British and European peoples. Indeed, that same report includes an anonymous poem, "The Strangers Within Our Gates," that anticipates both the title of Woodsworth's 1909 study and his "higher type" ideal. The poem demonstrates that the association imagined Canadianization as just this kind of mutual exchange between brawny "strangers," who would help "us our wilds to conquer," and British Canadians, who possess a valuable triumvirate of liberty, freedom, and law.[77] Such tropes of mixing draw on the association's earlier representation of the reciprocal exchange that was crucial to the relationship between the labourer-teacher and the worker.

The "higher type" ideal also had general currency in Canada in this period. In his 1915 novel *The Prairie Wife*, for example, Arthur Stringer explores the benefits that might redound to Prairie farmers with the intermixing of the British, a "distinguished race rather running to seed," and Scandinavians, such as Olga Sarristo, the Canadian-born Finn who embodies a "revitalizing, revivifying, reanimalizing, redeeming type." Olga must learn to read and write in English (and her aristocratic British husband will teach her), but her "primitive and natural" spirit is central to the farmer's success on the harsh prairie.[78] Similarly, Ralph Connor's 1909 novel *The Foreigner* opens with an author's preface that declaims: "Out of breeds diverse in traditions, in ideals, in speech, and in manner of life, Saxon and

Slav, Teuton, Celt and Gaul, one people is being made. The blood strains of great races will mingle in the blood of a race greater than the greatest of them all." However, the rhetoric of mutual exchange in a poem such as "Strangers Within Our Gates" or in the other examples above conceals the labour that Canadianization performs: in privileging the British tradition of liberty as that which will overcome ethnic clannishness, the discourse of Canadianization confirms the "natural" positioning of British liberalism, and hence of settler British Canadians, at the centre of the new nation. Moreover, that some groups had few or no preferred traits and no apparent capacity to enjoy liberty reveals that the ideology of mixing that tinctured the association's ideology of Canadianization was structured by rigid limits.

As non-British immigration to Canada and the settler uneasiness that attended it swelled in the second decade of the twentieth century, the assimilation of non–English-speaking children into English Canadian society via instruction in English became the focus of educational policy-makers, particularly in the West, where forms of bilingual schooling were common. Appropriate methods of English-language instruction for immigrant children in Canada were thus much debated as a matter of policy, but the curricular resources and teacher training for such initiatives were very modestly and unevenly developed prior to the Second World War.[79] Largely because many education officials felt that adults could not be weaned from "the habits and customs of their native lands," the population of adult immigrants that Fitzpatrick's association aimed to serve was not at the centre of the debate regarding the education of immigrants.[80] Not surprisingly, therefore, many of the labourer-teachers employed by the Canadian Reading Camp Association in this period felt that the task of teaching adults English as a second language required more training and more resources. W.E. Griffin's 1911 correspondence with Fitzpatrick demonstrates his strong support for the education and "Canadianization" of immigrants but argues strongly for a "definite teaching programme" and for instructors trained in particular methods for teaching immigrants. Others made do with alternative teaching materials: J.L. Lord, who wrote in 1910 to request first readers for his Alberta CPR construction camp, reassured Fitzpatrick that the lack of teaching materials was not insurmountable, "for now I use the Bible for my textbook." Many instructors' letters indicate that the most elementary methods were employed in language classes. Norman Davies, for example, happily reported that he was holding classes five nights a week with nine men of varying nationalities (German, Italian, French, and Russian), but admitted that his method of teaching single words at a time using the blackboard and various gestures was very basic. Reginald Gilbert was similarly pleased to have an average nightly attendance of five men at his Nairn Centre, Ontario, nickel-mining camp, but noted the challenge of teaching a class of Italian, British, and French Canadian students who were working at very different levels.[81] Struggling to find ways to make his association's work with immigrants relevant and effective, Fitzpatrick placed the Canadian Reading Camp Association at the centre of what was a barely emergent Canadian effort to create print resources for the teaching of English as a second language. Yet because the association's efforts targeted adult immigrants rather than children (who have assumed a much larger place in the history of education), its role in the early development of pedagogical materials for English-language acquisition and Canadianization has been largely forgotten.[82]

Although Fitzpatrick did not actively recruit labourer-teachers with second-language skills or non-British backgrounds, when the opportunity arose to engage such men as labourer-teachers, he was generally willing to hire them and place them in camps where their language skills would be of use as long as they had been thoroughly Canadianized. For instance, in 1909, J.F. Sadleir wrote to Fitzpatrick suggesting that a "Galician" worker in his camp might be employed as a labourer-teacher at a site where his native language would be useful. Sadleir assured Fitzpatrick that the man in question, Orest Orner, had attended classes for Galician students at Manitoba College for a year. Fitzpatrick accepted Sadleir's suggestion, adding that he would place Orner in a camp with a large number of Galician workers. In cases where the would-be instructor was clearly lacking this formal training in English, Fitzpatrick was less enthusiastic.[83] Like Saskatchewan's Director of Education Among New Canadians, J.T.M. Anderson, Fitzpatrick was amenable to the prospect of the "properly qualified" "teacher of foreign parentage" who might "reasonably be expected to have gained a knowledge and appreciation of our citizenship." However, like all the provincial education authorities at the end of the second decade of the twentieth century, Anderson advocated the "direct" or "natural" method of English-language instruction: no language but English was to be used in the classroom.[84] The bilingualism that had been tolerated in the public schools of the Canadian West, for example, was under increasing pressure by the end of the First World War.

Throughout the first decade of the twentieth century, the association attempted to modify and adapt its methods and goals to the changing needs of the camps, but as the association grew and concentrated administratively in Toronto, Fitzpatrick's role became less tied to the daily operations of the camps. He was thus obliged to rely on letters from far-flung labourer-teachers to assess these needs. One of Fitzpatrick's earliest efforts to understand the requirements of and challenges faced by labourer-teachers engaged in teaching non-English-speaking men was his 1909 campaign to survey "foreign" learners. That season he sent a notebook to all instructors, asking them to record their conversations with "foreigners" so that he might learn more about the "characteristic learner of each nationality."[85] Assessments such as this – through which the association compiled data regarding camp workers and their needs – became increasingly important to the association's work in the teens.

As early as 1907, the same year that the association's annual report trained its eye on the link between the "Reading Camp and the Foreign Navvy," the Canadian Reading Camp Association was developing its own materials for use in the camps. In their correspondence with instructors during the 1913 season, Fitzpatrick and the association's secretary, Frances McMechan, referred repeatedly to a pamphlet on second-language instruction prepared by Edmund Bradwin – a labourer-teacher turned camp-school inspector who became a director of the association in 1914. Bradwin's authorship of this no longer extant pamphlet confirms the anecdotal evidence that suggests he may have been a primary, though unacknowledged, author of the association's 1919 publication, *Handbook for New Canadians*.[86] The *Handbook* likely drew from a large pool of instructor feedback, as Fitzpatrick's voluminous correspondence with labourer-teachers throughout the war years indicates. In 1916, for example, he sent a sample lesson plan to J. Burke at his Cape Breton mining camp. Burke modified the plan, noted that it contained too much material for a beginner class in English, and sent it back to Fitzpatrick, along with a list of mining terms and definitions that Fitzpatrick had apparently requested.[87]

In 1911, Fitzpatrick ordered the first pedagogical materials for foreign-language instruction in the camps. Like his contemporaries J.T.M. Anderson and J.S. Woodsworth, he relied on materials from the United States, where civic education efforts, fuelled by the early-twentieth-century progressive education movement, had an earlier start: he purchased and distributed to the camps nine sets of Peter Roberts's *English for Coming Americans* series, a publication of the

New York City YMCA. In 1912, the series was adapted for Canadian learners, and there is some evidence that pamphlets in the *English for Coming Canadians* series were used in camps.[88] (The National Council of the Canadian YMCA also published, in 1919, George Reaman's *English for New Canadians*; this was not used in Frontier College camps because, as we will see, its publication coincided with the association's own *Handbook for New Canadians*. Moreover, as Fitzpatrick frequently complained, the work of the YMCA was focused on urban immigrant populations, and *English for New Canadians* privileges the vocabulary of urban experience – "sidewalk," "trolley pole," "register" – over a lexicon more suitable to rural work.) The *Coming Americans* series was published in leaflet form in three groups – series A, the "Domestic Series"; series B, the "Industrial Series"; and series C, the "Commercial Series." Peter Roberts was a proponent of the "direct method" as "the only way to learn"; however, it was his focus on the adult learner – on the working-class immigrant adult learner, in particular – that made his series so relevant to Fitzpatrick. Roberts castigates the conventional approach to second-language acquisition in institutions of higher learning for its literary and academic study of texts and for its consequent inability to teach men to speak comfortably or "express their simplest wants." He advocates instead an approach that emphasizes "common usage," the oral "language of daily life," and, later, basic reading (and to a lesser extent, writing) so that learners might in "their industrial and trade relations be better able to look after their interests." Roberts identifies the lessons in the series as designed to produce "a better employee" and to open a "channel of communication" through which "American ideas and ideals" would reach the "soul" of the immigrant.[89] Undoubtedly, the simple oral-language drills in *English for Coming Americans* also served as a means of teaching "American" habits, hygiene, and culture; for example, the "Domestic Series" comprise drills that verbally enact the proper procedure for washing one's face or using one's utensils.

In the teens, Fitzpatrick also worked to connect the association's efforts to the various levels of state bureaucracy that were emerging to deal with the nation's immigrants. In the spring of 1919, for instance, he consulted Canada's emerging cadre of experts on immigrant education. His letters of inquiry to provincial departments of education in the West generated responses that confirmed that children in urban areas constituted the nuclei of provincial efforts. Fitzpatrick's letter to Saskatchewan led him to the newly appointed Director of Education Among New Canadians, J.T.M. Anderson, who pointed out that his recently published book, *The Education of the New Canadian* (1918), would serve as a valuable resource for Fitzpatrick's research. Anderson added that the recent proscription of teaching in any language but English had added a new component to his work, which he was complementing with a campaign to "man our schools with properly qualified Canadian teachers," the erection of suitable teachers' accommodation in rural, "non-English" districts, and efforts to encourage night schools.[90] There is some indication that a rivalry developed in this period between Anderson, whose work was commissioned and directed by a provincial government, and Fitzpatrick, who had long sought government approval and sponsorship for his work among labourers. Edmund Bradwin lamented the latter's relative marginality to the postwar reconstruction effort, asserting in a 1919 letter that he would like to go to Winnipeg to "fight" for Fitzpatrick's place at the National Conference on Character Education in Relation to Canadian Citizenship, where Anderson, "who was only a country school teacher on the prairie in 1910," was speaking.[91]

Produced through data collection in the camps, correspondence with instructors, and wide consultation with bureaucrats who were tackling the challenges of non-British immigration, the association's *Handbook for New Canadians* was published in 1919. The reorientation of Toronto's Methodist Book and Publishing House under the leadership of Samuel W. Fallis led, among other changes, to the creation of "The Ryerson Press" imprint in July 1919, and the *Handbook* was published under that new imprint in the early winter of 1919.[92] This was a self-financed venture for Fitzpatrick. Although such arrangements were standard company procedure in that era, the first printing of three thousand copies at a cost to Frontier College of just over three thousand dollars drove the association into financial difficulty for years to come.[93] At 327 pages, with each book measuring 13 by 19 centimetres, this was an ambitious publishing project. Faced with this financial burden, Fitzpatrick sought various forms of support as the *Handbook* manuscript was in development. His efforts to secure funding reveal that Fitzpatrick clearly believed that the *Handbook*, an instrument of Canadianization, would find its place in the new state provisions for the education of immigrants. However, as in the association's earliest days, he also appealed to employers with the promise of improved workers.

For instance, Fitzpatrick's 1916 circular to prominent businessmen laments the lack of suitable materials at hand for teaching immigrants English and describes the project as a "test book" meant to "fit the foreign labourer for a place in Canadian life." The book that Fitzpatrick envisioned would contain two hundred work-related words, "suggestions relating to everyday life," information about the government of Canada, and facts about each province, as well as "important Canadian events" in "story form." Fitzpatrick imagined the *Handbook* as a kind of portable citizenship tool for the mobile camp worker: "The ordinary text-books on other subjects are too numerous and cumbersome, as well as too technical. He will be able to carry this book in his pack-sack and with comparatively little assistance acquire a reading knowledge of the language and also a knowledge sufficient to make him a good citizen of Canada." The circular requests that employers purchase in advance (and at the wholesale price) fifty books in order to cover the cost of the publication of the first thousand copies. As both this correspondence and the book's subsequent acknowledgments demonstrate, only four employers, three of whom were already serving on the board of the association, took up these advance subscriptions: H.L. Lovering, president of the association and of the Canadian Copper Company; the Honourable George Gordon, board member of the association, lumber merchant, and Conservative member of the Senate; Sir Joseph Flavelle, meatpacking baron and president of the Imperial Munitions Board during the First World War; and James Playfair, lumber merchant and third vice-president of the association.[94]

Though he made his appeal to employers, Fitzpatrick believed that financing for his association and its publications should flow from the government. Particularly in the second decade of the century, as the association moulded its program in the direction of Canadianization, Fitzpatrick viewed his undertakings as a specifically federal responsibility, one that fell within the purview of the federal government's immigration portfolio. The *Handbook for the New Canadians* states that the Dominion government was obligated to "provide the proper machinery" for the education of immigrants "up to the standards of Canadian citizenship."[95] In 1917, the federal government granted immigration its own department (it had previously been the responsibility of the Departments of Agriculture and the Interior), thus acknowledging the national importance of the portfolio. Fitzpatrick clearly apprehended that his association's interests dovetailed with those of the federal government and seized the opportunity to call on the latter to assume financial and administrative responsibility for citizenship education. Yet even at the end of the period examined in this chapter, federal Superintendent of Immigration and Colonization J.A. Calder did not concur, claiming that the pedagogical work of the association fell under provincial jurisdiction.[96] Left with little hope of securing funds from the federal government, Fitzpatrick sought its authenticating endorsement. In the fall of 1919, when the manuscript was undergoing the last stages of the editing process, he wrote to Calder seeking the "official approval" of the Department of Immigration for his book. The Department could recommend the book "as an aid and incentive to fuller and better citizenship," Fitzpatrick suggested, because it was "intended to give the adult foreigner who wishes to take out citizenship, a knowledge of Canada in brief form under one cover."[97] In writing to Calder, Fitzpatrick was pursuing a new approach to government responsibility for camp workers: the moral diseases of camp men could threaten the nation, but the failure to Canadianize immigrants portended a whole array of new dangers to the nation, especially in the immediate wake of the First World War and the Winnipeg General Strike, a time when fears regarding "enemy aliens" and Bolshevism motivated much federal action. The *Handbook*'s emphasis on basic English-language acquisition responds directly to both the "enemy" language debates that had raged in the late 1910s and had led to the suppression of the foreign-language press and the 1914 Naturalization Act, which added a language requirement (French or English).

The amendments in the spring of 1919 to the 1910 Immigration Act added, among other things, a literacy requirement that obliged prospective immigrants over fifteen years of age who were "physically capable of reading" to be literate in English, French, or "some other language or dialect." This clause did not meet with wholehearted approval in the House of Commons. Senator George McHugh, for example, felt that "literacy is not always a good test of citizenship," and Liberal MP Samuel William Jacobs noted that the state would not "keep out Bolshevists by such a provision" because the Bolshevists "and people of that ilk are able to read and write." Such debates reveal a fear that Amy J. Wan associates with the contemporary Americanization movement in the United States – the concern of government officials that some immigrants were "too literate."[98] Fears of socialist activity and labour unrest also motivated employers, such as James Playfair, whose 1919 contribution was accompanied by the hope that Frontier College could "preach some sense to these Unionists in place of having them go out on strike every few days."[99] Fitzpatrick's modification of the association's historical commitment to literacy in the direction of English-language training *as an element of* citizenship education is perhaps best understood as his canny assessment of where state imperatives were moving, despite the state's reluctance to support his initiative financially.

Like the books on which it draws, such as Peter Roberts's *English for Coming Americans/Canadians* series, the first half of Fitzpatrick's *Handbook for New Canadians* is an English language primer. Despite the fact that knowledge of French provided a route to naturalization, the *Handbook*'s privileged language is English; it renders French more or less invisible as a possible route to citizenship. In the initial lessons, "stock" words are paired with illustrations and then employed in simple sentences that run along the bottom of each page; the more advanced lessons consist of prose sketches that begin with brief texts on simple topics ("To Light a Fire") and progress to page-long texts on more abstract topics ("The Police"). This first half follows the example of the Peter Roberts series and the advice of J.T.M. Anderson quite closely: it emphasizes "functional" spoken English rather than the teaching of grammar; vocabulary is frequently though not exclusively drawn from workers' experiences ("shovel and pick," "hand tools," "gun," "axe and saw"); it advocates the "direct" method (although it includes a vocabulary for more advanced learners that translates common English words into six languages); and it tends to favour the use of whole sentences over the learning of individual words.[100]

Yet the *Handbook* is much more than a language primer: it promotes a settler identity that aggressively links the acquisition of English to Canadian citizenship, implying that the former skill will have relevance only in the context of the latter identity. Operating from the premise that all immigrants to Canada must become naturalized, the *Handbook* insists that the immigrant must do more than simply reside in the nation.[101] Unlike the YMCA's competing titles – Peter Roberts's series and George Reaman's *English for New Canadians* (1919) – the more abstract lessons in the primer and in the second half of the *Handbook*, which comprises booklets dealing with geography, government, naturalization, and "History and Progress," devote extended attention to the individual's place in the capitalist economy, in the progress of national history, and in the geography and government of Canada and the empire. The *Handbook* thus enacts, through its addressee, an English literacy for liberal citizenship that is specific to Canada's emergent settler nation-state.

The admixture of Canadian distinctiveness and the lingering context of empire in the *Handbook* should not be surprising. As Tom Mitchell points out, the development of the *Handbook* during the First World War coincided with a period during which imperialism as the "dominant current of thought" in English Canadian discussions of citizenship education slowly gave way to "a more nationalist approach." Ken Osborne, in his analysis of the four periods of citizenship education in Canadian elementary schools, notes that from the 1920s and until at least the 1950s, a "self-consciously Canadian spirit" entered citizenship education.[102] The "History and Progress" section of the *Handbook* offers a particularly good example of how English Canadian settler nationalism was beginning to emerge from imperialist rhetoric in 1919. The *Handbook* repeats the old imperialist narrative of the Conquest as the triumph of British justice, but it reaches beyond this to figure the nation's independence. Before enumerating the "toleration" and "freedom" granted to French Canadians through the 1774 Quebec Act and the 1840 Act of Union, the *Handbook* points out, for instance, that "Canada had been governed too much from the courts of the Kings of France. With the passing into the hands of the British, Canada awoke to new life." Yet the *Handbook* also pays careful attention to the political and economic progress unique to Canada as a new, independent, modern nation, citing its transcontinental railway as the nation's "greatest contribution to world progress."[103] The "History and Progress" section is thus typical of the historiographical tendency in the early twentieth century towards Whiggish accounts of the past, which figured history as having a "discernable direction and flow." According to Allan Greer, this historiographical propensity produced accounts that figured "Canada as moving towards a goal in the nineteenth century; whether this end point was the construction of a transcontinental, commercial, and political union, the development of parliamentary government, or the preservation and resurrection of French Canada, it was certainly a Good Thing."[104]

Of course, citizenship was not a legal term in early-twentieth-century Canada. Canada's first naturalization legislation, which created naturalized British subjects, was passed in 1868; these same naturalized British subjects could be legally recognized as "Canadians" after 1914, but it was not until 1946 that Canada passed its first independent citizenship legislation, which was adopted as law in early 1947 as the Citizenship Act.[105] If the term "Canadian citizen" was used in the 1910 Immigration Act to designate a specific category of British subject – the individual who was born, was naturalized, or was resident for three years or more in Canada – it was not employed regularly in the federal Speeches from the Throne until the postwar period.[106] Despite its lack of legal reference, the term "Canadian citizen" was one Fitzpatrick used increasingly after 1905 to denote a political identity. As the early twentieth century unfolded and the nation's non-British immigrant population expanded, Fitzpatrick eschewed his previous focus on the citizen as an individual moral character in favour of a larger abstraction – the national citizen. Requiring a social cement and force for assimilation that the immigrant family could not provide, Fitzpatrick turned to the abstraction of national citizenship and to the work of rendering the state and its processes visible to would-be citizens. Despite its reference to a public, political abstraction (the nation), however, this conception of citizenship, like moral citizenship, was intimately tied to private conduct or character. The crucial difference lies in the pedagogical approach embodied in materials such as the *Handbook*, which abstract the individual learner as a potential member of the nation while subjecting him to an increasingly planned method of instruction. This national citizen was the object of new areas of governance: until the end of the first decade of the twentieth century, naturalization was a straightforward process requiring not much more than three years of continuous residence; the Naturalization Act of 1914 not only tightened requirements but also enhanced powers of executive discretion.[107] An important function of the *Handbook for New Canadians* was to attach the non-British immigrant population to this new form of state authority, to make it a commonsensical part of belonging to the nation. This work formed a crucial aspect of the efforts of Frontier College in the 1910s: if the federal government was not in this period willing to assume responsibility for the education of immigrant adults, Frontier College determined that it would render the state and its social capacities visible to non-British immigrants.

Many of those involved in the 1910s with emergent state efforts to deal with the non-British immigrant population, such as school officials grappling with the ever-growing number of immigrant children, were similarly eager to invest citizenship with new political significance. In his 1918 study of the "new Canadian," J.T.M. Anderson decries the lack of "proper training for intelligent citizenship" provided to new immigrants by provincial and federal governments: "Surely the right to become a living link in the great earth-girdling imperial chain of the greatest Empire on earth is too lightly regarded in the apparent anxiety to 'increase production' and develop 'material resources.'" For Anderson, the education of immigrant children was key, and it was not simply the teaching of the English language that mattered but the "Canadianization" of children through the medium of the British Canadian schoolteacher. Such teachers could impart the crucial quality of "self-government" – "intelligence, self-control, and capacity for co-operation." Quoting American economist John R. Commons, Anderson claims that without self-government, "the ballot only makes way for the 'boss,' the corruptionist, and oligarchy under the control of democracy." In Anderson's view, "Canadianization" included not only training in the English language but also the shaping of character and conduct – for example, education in physical hygiene, manners (e.g., eating with a knife and fork), and moral values (e.g., love of truth, avoidance of obscenity, "respect for womanhood").[108] Importantly, Anderson viewed the state-funded school, rather than the family, as the appropriate site for this education. Like Anderson and others in the fields of public health, housing, and education, Fitzpatrick believed that governments were not assuming adequate responsibility for the training of citizens.

LITERATURE AND LESSONS IN LIBERAL CITIZENSHIP

The citizen identity proffered in *The Handbook for New Canadians* is liberal at many levels. First, it retains the British Canadian progressive ideal of "improvement," idealizing individual progress in the form of home and land ownership and warning against clannishness of all kinds – religious, political, or otherwise. Second, while insisting on the primacy of individual responsibility with regard to morality, thrift, sobriety, and hard work, it presents citizenship as an identity to be experienced in relation to a moderately interventionist state that can promote national well-being, economic progress, and harmony between capital and labour. Poems, anthems, songs, oaths, and short narratives – all brief, easily memorized forms that lend themselves to oral recitation – function as key resources in realizing this pedagogy of liberal citizenship. In keeping with the association's long-standing emphasis on the value of literature as a form of moral education, the *Handbook for New Canadians* elaborates the identity of the "good citizen" in the context of a poem:

> The good citizen
> > Loves God.
> > Loves the Empire.
> > Loves Canada.
> > Loves his own family.
> > Protects women and children.
> > Works hard.
> > Does his work well.
> > Helps his neighbor.
> > Is truthful.
> > Is just.
> > Is honest.
> > Is brave.
> > Keeps his promise.
> > His body is clean.
> > Is every inch a Man.[109]

This manly citizen's "just" and "honest" character recalls the "strong, clean, God-conquered" manhood of the association's early-twentieth-century work. Moreover, just as in the earlier period, citizenship in the context of this poem entails many obligations of individual character that are expressed through membership in vertically arranged political communities, whose hierarchical arrangements are mimicked in the poem's lineation. The list solders together "public" and "political" affiliations ("Loves the Empire") and "private," individual behaviours ("His body is clean") and ethical choices ("is just" and "loves God"), demonstrating the necessity of self-governance to the larger categories of "Canada" and "Empire." However, this citizen is no longer simply an individual engaging in a reading act, but rather an abstraction intimately bound up with the text itself – the unnamed "good citizen" who is the object of the *Handbook*'s general address. Unlike the reader of fiction and poetry we encountered in the first chapter, the reader of the *Handbook* is not left much room to interpret, to imagine, or to choose particular characters with whom to identify. If the literary style is different, however, it nonetheless remains a highly literary style. The citizen-reader is offered an abstracted version of himself, and this abstraction offers a ready-made life plot, generally in the form of third- or first-person narratives that present "typical" immigrant experiences.

As part of its efforts to typify the would-be citizen, the *Handbook* employs conventions that would come to characterize government documentary films in the postwar period, forms of realism that, according to Zoë Druick, incorporated realism's "radical potential" – evident in the socialist and social realist documentaries of the 1930s, for example – by "apply[ing] the form to the liberal nation-building project." Radical and liberal documentary alike borrowed from emergent social scientific methods such as statistical probability in order to represent a population through a "typical" figure or representative sample. The resulting representation was useful to state planning because, among other things, it strove to connect a large and diverse population to the new bureaucracies of the postwar state.[110] The strategy of typicality is more common in the informational sections of the *Handbook*, such as the section dealing with naturalization. For example, "Michael Simkovitch" is presented for the learner as a "typical" immigrant, a "good, steady man" who has studied English, worked hard, and changed his name to "John Barley":

> John Barley, his wife, and all children under twenty-one years of age, are now British subjects and citizens of Canada. They share in every way the rights and privileges of Canadians, and are subject to the obligations and duties of a natural-born British subject. They will honour the land of their choice. As true Canadians they will obey the laws and make their lives useful in the land, for it has given them a start in the freedom of a new life. They can share in an Empire founded on principles of liberty to all alike. Peace, contentment, and prosperity will come to John Barley and his family.[111]

Invoking typicality in order to shape *all* individual choices – *all* immigrants are potentially John Barley, transformed via naturalization into Canadians and British subjects – this passage demonstrates the rhetorical power of the apparently objective and omnipotent narrator. Though unidentified, this third-person narrator seems to be the source of the power that is ensuring the immigrant's success and controlling his future. All is predictable once the immigrant is joined to the state via naturalization.

The literary strategy of typicality is especially apparent in the *Handbook*'s attention to naturalization, which constitutes an entire section of the book. It presents naturalization as a means of enjoying "the rights of any subject of George V throughout his worldwide dominions" and certain "protections." The *Handbook* makes only modest claims for the "rights" accorded to naturalized Canadians, perhaps because one of its key examples of a protection accorded by the state – protection from deportation – disappeared as a result of the 1919 amendments to the Naturalization Act, which rendered any naturalized Canadian subject to deportation if he or she was found guilty of the sedition or anti-government activity proscribed by Section 41 of the Immigration Act.[112] Much more robust than its focus on rights is the construction of naturalization as a state-defined identity extended to the immigrant under certain conditions. Naturalization is a "procedure" governed by rules that the immigrant must respect, including residence and language requirements and the expectation that the applicant be a "good man."[113] The *Handbook* not only lays out for the immigrant learner the new state requirements for naturalization that are enshrined in the 1914 Naturalization Act but also reproduces the forms required for application, offers advice about how to fill them out properly, and walks the potential applicant through the complex application process, which, after 1914, included approval of the court decision by the Secretary of State, who retained "absolute discretion" over the decision.[114] Importantly, the male applicant for naturalization is typified in the *Handbook* as a head of household, who is reminded, for example, that in applying he does so not only for himself but also for his wife and children under twenty-one years of age; these too shall become citizens by virtue of his application, but it is the character and conduct of the individual male that matters here. He is the public, political subject.

More intimate and open-ended forms of literary address are also found throughout the *Handbook*, but these too are presented as elements of a formal, instructor-guided pedagogy that leaves little room for independent inquiry. The most obvious site of this form of address is found at the end of the *Handbook*'s reader, which offers a selection of memory gems: an excerpt from George Monro Grant's 1873 book *Ocean to Ocean*; poems (Lord Tennyson's "Sweet and Low," Leigh Hunt's "Abou Ben Adhem," Alexander Muir's "The

Maple Leaf," John McCrae's "In Flanders Fields," and William Wordsworth's "The Solitary Reaper"); and anthems ("God Save Our Gracious King" and "O Canada!"). Just as Fitzpatrick promoted English Canadian authors in the earliest camp libraries, so the *Handbook* peppers its selection of canonical British writers with Canadian authors, such as the imperialist George Monro Grant and the celebrated war poet John McCrae, whose "In Flanders Fields" became a kind of anthem for Canada's postwar spirit of independent national identity. Nevertheless, in an era when imperialist sentiment was giving way to nationalist pride, British poets claimed a crucial place in citizenship's emergent literary canon.

It is not surprising that Wordsworth, a Romantic poet known particularly for his privileging of the "rustic" language of common people as a truer vehicle than artificial poetic diction for the expression of human experience, features among the British poets deemed important to a pedagogy of citizenship for labourers. "The Solitary Reaper" (1805) presents the camp labourer with an image of himself, but defamiliarized as a peasant woman. The lyric stages an encounter between a "Highland lass" and a Wordsworthian persona who is enchanted by a young girl "reaping and singing by herself" yet puzzled by the song, which lies outside the speaker's (English) sense of poetic or even cultural tradition. As Ian Lancashire observes, the girl's song, "like a found poem, springs directly from nature, without literary context. Her 'music' runs like water ('overflowing' the valley) and surpasses the beauty of the celebrated English song-birds, the nightingale and the cuckoo":

> Behold her, single in the field,
> Yon solitary Highland lass!
> Reaping and singing by herself;
> Stop here, or gently pass!
> Alone she cuts and binds the grain,
> And sings a melancholy strain;
> O listen! for the vale profound
> Is overflowing with the sound.
>
> No nightingale did ever chaunt
> More welcome notes to weary bands
> Among Arabian sands:
> A voice so thrilling ne'er was heard

> In springtime from the cuckoo-bird,
> Breaking the silence of the seas
> Among the farthest Hebrides.
>
> Will no one tell me what she sings?
> Perhaps the plaintive numbers flow
> For old, unhappy, far-off things,
> And battles long ago:
> Or is it some more humble lay,
> Familiar matter of today?
> Some natural sorrow, loss or pain
> That has been, and may be again?
>
> Whate'er the theme, the maiden sang
> As if her song could have no ending;
> I saw her singing at her work,
> And o'er the sickle bending;
> I listened, motionless and still,
> And, as I mounted up the hill,
> The music in my heart I bore,
> Long after it was heard no more.[115]

While immigrant workers are clearly being asked to identify with the lyric's labouring figure, the poem addresses labourer-teachers as well. These latter are implicitly urged to open themselves to the unfamiliar but powerfully stirring "music" of their immigrant students. As we have seen and as subsequent chapters will further explore, this coaxing of workers and instructors alike to understand labourers and their experiences through idealized conceptions of work – whether from Social Gospel fiction or from Romantic poetry – is a constant of the early twentieth-century Frontier College project. What most bears noticing here, however, is the fact that the poem – selected by Fitzpatrick and Bradwin from among many other Romantic poems of labour – renders the peasant figure as a woman. Although the strategy of typification I describe above appeals to standard liberal conceptions of the would-be citizen as male, as public representative of the apparently private household, this choice of poem speaks to the ways that liberal citizenship nonetheless requires women, "private" emotion, and intimate relations.

Unsurprisingly, then, bookending the "public" anthems of the literary section are lyrics and memory gems that thematize home as a respite and women as a source of primal comfort: the roaming speaker of Wordsworth's lyric finds solace in the "natural sorrow" of the singing of a "Highland lass"; Tennyson's well-known lullaby conflates home, family, and the "mother's breast; and the speaker of J. Howard Payne's memory gem "Home Sweet Home" decries the "splendor of the world that "dazzles in vain," pining instead for "my lowly thatched cottage again." [116] These enclose anthems – such as Robert Stanley Weir's English lyrics to "O Canada!" (which celebrates the nation as a "land of hope for all who toil / The land of liberty"), "The Maple Leaf," "God Save Our Gracious King," and "O Canada!" – as well as oaths, such as the lesson on the "good citizen" I discuss above, all of which are clearly meant to function as techniques that draw, by turns, on emotional and legal arguments in order to bind the abstracted individual to the state.[117] It is crucial to notice this interplay of lyric and anthem, the apparently private and the apparently public. While indicating the affective dimensions of liberal citizenship that I discuss in chapter 1, this interplay simultaneously demonstrates an uneasiness about the non-British immigrant family. No longer imagined as the ultimate domain of moral authority, the immigrant family was both crucial to the reproduction of capital and a site of dubious self-regulation. In the wake of the immigration wave of the early 1910s, reformers' rhetoric increasingly noted the particular interventions that the state might permit itself with regard to the immigrant family.

Menzies, Adamoski, and Chunn point to the alteration in the early twentieth century of the role of the mother, and their comments are particularly applicable to non-British immigrant and working-class mothers: increasingly "deemed incapable" of fulfilling their roles as moulders of "good citizens" via "traditional child-rearing methods," mothers were understood to require "education for 'scientific' mothering by experts and professionals," even though this "'scientific' mothering" drew deeply on the knowledge of the "private" sphere.[118] If J.S. Woodsworth's 1909 study of the "strangers" at the "gates" of the nation figures "Canadianization" – the instilling of "family spirit" and self-governance – as a kind of mothering of children with "uncertain tempers," the *Handbook for New Canadians* makes it clear that the "mothering" is both at the heart of public interest and an area where the state might permit itself some authority. The lesson "Good Food," for instance, assumes the imperative mood in order to address the would-be citizen and appropriates the gendered domain of diet and nutrition, instructing the worker to "buy only good food," such as "new-laid eggs" and "good, clean milk." "The Low Cost of Health" reminds workers of the many health-giving benefits that might "be had for nothing. For instance, it "costs no more to read good books than trashy literature."[119]

The home and its relationships are important to the *Handbook* in other respects as well. As we have seen, the association's early efforts at building the citizenship of camp workers targeted the practice of "jumping" camp; after 1912 or so this message was redirected at non-British immigrant workers, men whose inclination or ability to settle on the land was in question. For Fitzpatrick, the relation between rural settlement and moral character was paramount. In this he was almost certainly inspired by other early-twentieth-century Protestant reformers, such as his friend Charles Gordon (Ralph Connor), whose 1909 novel *The Foreigner: A Tale of Saskatchewan* sets out to prove the danger of clannish urban immigrant (especially Galician) enclaves and to promote immigrant settlement in rural areas as the salubrious antidote. Accordingly, the association's twelfth annual report, *The Immigrant*, warns that if governments and charitable organizations failed to educate the immigrant worker "we shall see him go back to his native land and take our money with him, or worse, drift into the saloons, shacks, hovels, and already overcrowded tenement houses of our towns and cities."[120] Immigrants could be citizens – ideally, homesteaders securely settled on the land, but also men who worked in seasonal camps in order to finance a homestead – or they could be sojourners and shiftless urban drifters. The report's warning derived from the unique conditions of immigration in this period: while the government officially recruited "agriculturalists," homesteading required capital for improvements, which meant that most recent immigrants worked either seasonally (part-time) in frontier camps to supplement their incomes or abandoned homesteading altogether for the new industrial wage labour of the nation's growing cities. Others, particularly those who fell into non-preferred categories and who came to Canada under any of the various bulk labour importation schemes arranged between the federal government and the railways in the early twentieth century, adopted patterns of sojourning.

Sojourning was a fact of life for many turn-of-the-century immigrants, such as the thousands of Italians, mostly men, who found seasonal employment in Canada's railway, lumber, and mining camps but returned to Italy when conditions permitted.[121] Indeed, according to Donald Avery, federal immigration policy had adapted to this reality by the mid-1910s, seeking to supply labourers where there was demand rather than to recruit for farming only: "The best immigrants would be those willing to roam the country to take up whatever work was available – railroad construction in the Canadian Shield in the summer, harvesting in Saskatchewan in the fall, coal mining in Alberta in the winter, and lumbering in British Columbia in the spring."

The *Handbook*'s pedagogy turns its head from these conditions, instead emphasizing the importance of homeownership and settlement to bona fide citizenship and suggesting that failure in this regard is moral rather than structural.[122] Using first-person narratives and literary strategies of typification, lessons in the primer emphasize the acquisition of private property and homeownership, as well as the virtues of farm life in the western provinces. In one of many such narratives, an unidentified worker exclaims, "I like farm work much better than work in a factory. The open air for me!"[123] This lesson models the benefits of settling on a homestead in an exclamation that avoids the perils of the imperative. Other lessons in the reader, such as "A Visit to an Alberta Farm," "Taking Up Land in Northern Ontario," "The Workman's Family," "Taking Up Land In the West," and J. Howard Payne's memory gem "Home Sweet Home," represent rural homeownership as a reward for hard work. Of course, such lessons simultaneously reject the clannish urban enclaves that are presented as threats in Connor's novel, promoting instead the individual homesteader and his private property. Thrift as the road to private property is a theme common to much of Fitzpatrick's writing in this period, and the *Handbook for New Canadians* pursues it enthusiastically. In "The Paymaster's Visit," a typical immigrant worker models thrift, noting that he will "send some money home to my mother" from the extra he earned working overtime. Such a strategy will allow him to plan for a better future: "I have a good chance now of getting a little ahead." In a lesson titled "The Bank," students are implored to "save a little each week" because even small savings will grow and "some day you will wish to buy a home or go into business in a shop of your own"[124] (see figure 2.1).

THE BANK.

Stock-words.
money
earnings
bank
account
interest
clerk
book
receipt
savings
deposit
habit
home
shop
business
save
start
keep
buy

Try to save some money out of your earnings. You can start a small savings account in the bank.

The bank will pay you interest for the use of your money. When you start an account, the clerk at the bank will give you a small bankbook, which will show you how much money you have in the bank. Keep this little book. It is your receipt for your deposit.

Your savings may not be large, but save a little each week. It is a good habit to begin. Small savings will lead to larger amounts. Some day you will wish to buy a home or go into business in a shop of your own. Begin to save now.

SUGGESTIONS.
  Secure necessary banking forms and have the class learn to recognize and use them. Show:—
    How to deposit money.
    How to withdraw money.
    What a check is, how to endorse a check; and what makes a check good.
  8—H.

Figure 2.1 "The Bank"

CITIZENSHIP'S CONTEST

Given its publication in the fall of 1919, on the heels of the now infamous Winnipeg General Strike and the wave of strikes that accompanied it, it is not surprising that another of the dominant themes in the *Handbook* is the looming threat of Bolshevism. According to Ian Radforth, the culture of work camps had shifted by the end of the First World War: in lumber camps, for instance, prewar workers' homosociality, which was organized around dances and storytelling, was supplanted by political discussions and organizing.[125] In one of Fitzpatrick's 1919 letters to the federal Superintendent of Immigration, he emphasizes the association's active attempts to quell this emergent political radicalism, appealing to popular Anglo-Canadian sentiments regarding the link between the foreign-born and strike activity: "Bolshevik ideas are not only latent throughout Canada, but are openly expressed. In no place is this more apparent than in the camps, where large groups of unskilled workers of foreign extraction usually congregate. The Frontier College Instructors offset much loose talk by their conduct and influence with the men. The work of the College is essentially patriotic."[126] The 1919 annual report, *The Instructor and the Red*, makes similar comments, as does R.C. Dearle's 1919 article for *Canada Lumberman*, which draws on the author's experience as the association's Eastern Inspector to claim that "late events" had amply demonstrated the folly of not requiring immigrants to learn either English or the "privileges and obligations" of citizenship.[127] The 1919 *Handbook* presents itself as a tool that might be employed to combat the "menace" of "unassimilated groups": "We have a right to demand that every man who comes to Canada become a citizen of this country. Unlearned masses of non-English speaking races are fertile soil for future trouble. This has frequently been apparent during the years of recent struggle in Europe."[128] In honing its discourse of Canadianization to resemble a kind of anti-red citizenship and its pedagogy to function as a counter-literacy that could combat the Bolshevik ideas of foreign-born agitators, Frontier College was speaking an idiom that possessed a timely appeal for both business and government.

The workers' revolt that came to a head in Winnipeg during the late spring of 1919 had been preceded by a significant nationwide wave of strikes and, more generally, by a period of intense class conflict. As we have seen, the Dominion government in the context of widespread fears about "enemy aliens" passed Orders in Council in September of 1918 that invoked the War Measures Act to declare illegal more than a dozen socialist organizations, including the IWW and the SPDC, as well as their print publications. While such measures were generally presented in terms of national wartime security, the targeting of Russians and Finns in organizations such as the IWW and the SDPC indicates that the fear of socialism was as great as concerns over "enemy aliens."[129] All of this provided an important rationale for Frontier College activities and for its promotion of a counter-literacy. As instructors' letters from 1919 and that year's annual report, *The Instructor and the Red*, indicate, the presence of socialists in the frontier camps underscored the need for the association to provide a new print pedagogy. In *The Instructor*, Fitzpatrick asserts that "paid agents" of the "I.W.W. and other radicals" were bringing "insidious talk" to the camps, as well as "all sorts of 'red' literature such as 'The Clarion,' 'Federationist,' etc." He further claims to "have been in camps where the only literature one could find was the fiery pamphlets and papers of 'red' propagandists." The only "true remedy" was the "right type of instructor with the aid of books, magazines, papers, games and music."[130] Although "The Clarion," or rather the *Western Clarion*, was the organ of the Socialist Party of Canada from 1905 to 1920 and was thus an admittedly radical paper, the *Federationist* was the organ of the AFL, the body that had absorbed most Canadian craft unions affiliated with the moderate TLC by the end of the First World War. Such craft unions were a far cry from the revolutionary industrial unionism of organizations like the IWW; indeed, the IWW had been founded in response to the AFL's 1905 decision to exclude industrial workers. Fitzpatrick was perhaps unaware of the *Federationist*'s genealogy. In any case, his charge suggests strongly that the *Handbook*'s support for unionization in the workplace had very strict limits. The "remedy" to "fiery" propaganda that *The Instructor and the Red* advocates was as least partly realized with the publication of the *Handbook for New Canadians*: meant to be distributed in the camps as a portable reader and to form the central piece of every instructor's "kit," the book was a key component of the counter-literacy that Fitzpatrick imagined could nurture liberal citizenship.

The immediate postwar period, with its intense class conflict, was a crucial moment in the history of Canadian citizenship. As Tom Mitchell observes, the "constrained juridical citizenship" produced by amendments to the Criminal Code and the Immigration Act in the wake of the Winnipeg General Strike employed coercion and could not be relied on to produce a stable postwar order. Recognition of the limits of explicit coercion led Canada's business elites to launch an "offensive on the cultural and ideological terrain of citizenship and nationhood" that yoked the concept of shared national citizenship to the plough that would turn over labour radicalism and collective claims for expanded citizenship. The *Handbook for New Canadians*, published at the very end of 1919, coincided almost perfectly with this "offensive," which culminated in the National Conference on Character Education in Relation to Canadian Citizenship, held in Winnipeg in October of 1919.[131] While neither the *Handbook* nor the 1919 annual report is entirely sympathetic to the unbending vision of Anglo-conformity and the rejection of "social" and "industrial" citizenship that Mitchell identifies with conference, these texts are nonetheless implicated in the legacy of the Winnipeg conference insofar as progressives stopped short of calling for social and economic transformation and thus "provided a prescription for citizenship that consolidated class inequalities." Like his friend and supporter Charles Gordon, who spoke at the 1919 Winnipeg conference, Fitzpatrick understood the term "citizenship" in the context of his moderate Social Gospel ideals, his belief in a "liberal capitalism with a humane face," and his rejection of class politics.[132] Gordon's 1921 novel *To Him That Hath* elaborates this postwar vision of the "citizen" as a non-partisan individual who works in the interest of community instead of class. Drawing on Gordon's experience as chair of the Manitoba Council of Industry, a body appointed by the Manitoba government in the wake of the Winnipeg General Strike to mediate industrial disputes, the novel advocates mediation over arbitration, and identity derived from citizenship over class identity.[133]

The *Handbook* promotes this sort of liberal capitalism in narratives that emphasize the new forms of state intervention that emerged in response to the strength of prewar industrial unionism and that are strongly identified with the liberalism of Mackenzie King. For example, the federal Department of Labor, established in 1900, and the Industrial Disputes and Investigation Act of 1907 granted to a business-friendly "board of conciliation" the power to vet all industrial disputes in advance of a strike or lockout. The act was unpopular with organized labour, particularly after it was extended to the war industries in the spring of 1916.[134] Employing a narrative voice that strives for objectivity through the use of the third person while occluding its specific location – is this the typical immigrant voice, the voice of the labourer-teacher, the voice of the government, or some other voice? – the *Handbook*'s narratives observe the fair and just mediation of the state in "industrial disputes," including those related to workers' demands for "fair wages." Unionization is not an evil, but rather a "well organized" feature of the Canadian labour economy, regulated by just departments of labour and federal labour bureaus.[135] The collective imagined in these narratives thus rejects the insurgent class-based identities of the period and roots itself in a concept of the responsible citizen. Urging the worker to trust the state, the *Handbook* anticipates what Franca Iacovetta identifies as a key element of the strategy promoted by Canadian social workers in the wake of the Second World War – the effort to overcome what they, in the context of the Cold War, perceived as some immigrants' "misplaced or unhealthy suspicion or distrust of Canadian authorities."[136]

THE LIMITS OF LIBERALISM

Fitzpatrick thus curated and modified his discourse of the liberal citizen in the context of the wave of early-twentieth-century immigration and the mounting class conflict of the prewar and immediate postwar periods. His citizen was someone who could *potentially* fulfill certain personal, ethical obligations of character while also meaningfully participating in the collectivized political life of nation and empire. To realize the citizenship ideal extended by the *Handbook*'s invitation, the abstracted citizen-reader had to recognize the authority of the invitation and hence affirm a structure in which non-settler claims to citizenship were matter of British Canadian settler prerogative.

Furthermore, this potentiality was not universally extended. As I point out in the first chapter, it is possible to speak in meaningful ways about workers' own lack of identification with the mission of the Canadian Reading Camp Association. I will return to this line of argument in subsequent chapters, but here, I am concerned primarily not with the illiberal response of the workers apostrophized by the association but rather with the association's attempts to retain liberalism's rhetoric of universality while constructing definite limits around the figure of the liberal citizen. As Eva Mackey has pointed out, settler nation-building is a "dual process" that entails both the "management of populations and the creation of national identity."

This "dual process" is "a complex and contradictory process of inclusion and exclusion, of positive and negative representations of Canada's internal and external others." The *Handbook* was one of the earliest tools developed in the service of such management. While the capacity to read, understand, and perform the imperatives of the *Handbook* theoretically offered access to national citizenship, this offer constituted what Joseph Slaughter calls the "egalitarian fiction" of the Habermasian public sphere, which "entailed certain systemic exclusions – epitomized in the eighteenth-century revolutionary fixation of white, male, property-owning citizens as the universal class." Such exclusions, Slaughter points out, "are often reproduced, reenacted, and reinforced" in the modern literary forms that have come to be identified with the emergence of the public sphere and the modern nation.[137] Much of the literary labour of the *Handbook* is devoted to the task of narrating a citizen "type." This type is meant to be a universal abstraction – John Barley and the "good citizen" are not meant to be individuals – yet the *Handbook*'s use of other representational strategies, most notably its racialized hierarchy, makes it clear that such abstractions are not meant to extend to non-white would-be citizens.

Noting the rise of nefariously hierarchical constructions of "race" in the late nineteenth century, Daniel Coleman suggests that early-twentieth-century British Canadian "white civility" depended on "paradoxically progressive and conservative, radical and reactionary" impulses. While extending the possibility of "improvement" to all "races," classes, and creeds via the particular capacity of British Canadians to "accommodate and civilize," the discourse of "white civility" also depends on the "constant rediscovery" of inferior others. This contradiction, claims Coleman, forms the "central paradox of liberal modernity," which offers a "limited or constrained universality."[138] Historians adapting McKay's liberal order framework have also been quick to point out the contradictions on which early-twentieth-century "civility" pivoted, as have postcolonial scholars.[139] As Mackey insists, the emphasis on "civility" in this paradox, which was linked to conceptions of British liberty and equality that were defined against American laissez-faire capitalism, persists tenaciously in contemporary formulations of multicultural "tolerance." Such a narrative of national history proffers itself as evidence of Canada's famed "Red Tory" tradition – the alleged tendency of Canadian politics to support collective well-being and, hence, economic principles such as public ownership. The "Tory touch" thesis is abundantly visible in the historiography of adult education in Canada. Gordon Selman, for example, claims that a "communitarian tradition" explains the long-standing national devotion to citizenship education. In Selman's view, Canada, unlike the United States, has a tradition of "communitarianism" that likely explains "why Canadians have focused so much of their attention and creative energies on what has been termed 'the imaginative training for citizenship.'" However, such accounts of the nation's adult and citizenship education traditions obscure the terms under which "white civility" extended belonging to non-British others in early-twentieth-century Canada. As Janine Brodie notes, "the celebration of the Canadian project as an ongoing project in the recognition and accommodation of diversity" is a story only "the dominant group can tell."[140]

While "contradiction" and "paradox" are terms often used to describe the limitations of liberal universality, I prefer to understand the apparent contradictions of Canada's liberal order not under the sign of paradox but rather as constitutive: exclusions come to define the state's conception of itself and the way it rules. As both Janine Brodie and (in a broader context) Lorenzo Veracini point out, Foucault's concept of "biopower" can be useful for thinking through the particularly racialized quality of discourses of citizenship in settler states like Canada. As Brodie notes, with the late-nineteenth-century emergence of biopower and its preoccupation with the production and reproduction of populations, "state racism was engraved onto practices of government," which "sorted subpopulations into biological continuums of good and bad, ascribing hierarchies of superior and inferior." Given social reality through the "legal constructions" of documents such as the 1910 Immigration Act and the definition of "person" in the Indian Act, the biopolitical mechanisms of the settler state have quite clearly elected to let some die in order to make others live. Moreover, according to Veracini, the "settler collective" deploys biopolitical management differently in relation to exogenous (immigrant) and Indigenous Others. Even within the category of the exogenous Other, there are a number of "differently categorized exogenous Others" who are managed differently depending on their relation to what Veracini calls the "settler collective."[141] As Foucault points out in his discussion of biopower and racism in his 1975–76 Collège de France lectures, the new public knowledge of demography addressed not individual bodies and their aleatory characteristics but populations and their knowable features – global birth and death rates, susceptibility to disease, and so on. If population is thus a whole that can be rendered knowable and to some extent predictable, racism fragments this "biological continuum" through the introduction of racial hierarchies.[142] Biopower offers key heuristic tools for understanding the racialized sorting of this period but is less helpful in explaining the conditions of existence for such sorting. In interwar Canada, the ranking of "races" existed in complex relation to the needs of settler-dominated capital, which could not tolerate the labour conflict associated with particular immigrant groups – whether that conflict stemmed from the leftist orientations of those groups themselves or from the conflict with white labourers generated by their presence in the labour market.

Racialized hierarchies form a crucial part of the *Handbook for New Canadians*, which uses a section on "Naturalization" to affirm for the immigrant learner that "races" may be grouped according to "like characteristics" and then ordered according to their desirability as settlers. These lessons indicate how pedagogies of citizenship can function as a means of "making live" by emphasizing attributes such as the Finn's "fine physique" and "passion for education," while disdaining his "radical tendencies," which are "not to be encouraged in a self-governing land." However, the lessons of this section demonstrate the latent instability of these groupings: for example, Finns fall somewhere between "Scandinavians" and "Slavs"; the arrival of Sikhs "raised delicate questions within the Empire, for no class of people have given more valiant service to Britain"; and the "industrious, inoffensive, and well behaved" Chinese sound very much like the "industrious, sober, law-abiding" Norwegians. Resolution is achieved in these lessons only through an appeal to British Canadian unanimity – a biological unity or common "race antipathy" that drives the exclusion or restriction of those who fall into the category of "Orientals."[143] This seemingly neutral gesturing to the collective will of "the people of Canada" is materially motivated: if Chinese labourers provided cheap labour for the Montreal-based syndicate that financed the construction of the Canadian Pacific Railway in the 1880s, their presence in Canada was also a source of ongoing complaint for British Canadian workers, particularly in western Canada.[144] The *Handbook*'s seemingly neutral gesture to "race antipathy" is important: its apparent invocation of common sense is crucial because it functions to undermine the open basis on which naturalization is theoretically proffered to all immigrants. As the *Handbook* notes, five basic things were "required of every 'alien' before he can become a 'citizen'":

1. That he is a good man.
2. That he has resided in Canada or some other part of the British Empire for at least five years within the last eight years.
3. That he has been living in Canada for not less than one year immediately preceding his application for citizenship.
4. That he has adequate knowledge of the English or French language.
5. That he intends to reside in Canada or some part of the British Empire.

If the alien meets these requirements he may become a British subject and enjoy all the rights of a citizen of Canada.[145]

The list makes no mention of racial desirability. The possibility of exclusion, which is presented as resting on the appeal to the collective will of the British Canadian settler population, was actually contingent on the constantly fluctuating needs of capital.

In his 1912 annual report, Fitzpatrick baldly identifies the limits of his liberalism: according to Fitzpatrick, the British Canadian navvy was no longer in existence because "we have dishonoured work with the hands on the frontier." Fitzpatrick's solution was to honour the European navvy because if he stopped coming, Canadians would "be forced to import non-assimilative labour from China, Japan, and India."[146] Fitzpatrick's reference to "non-assimilative" labour suggests that the association never attempted to deploy its pedagogy of citizenship among what are referred to in the *Handbook* as the "Oriental races." However, as reports from several instructors in the 1910s demonstrate, labourer-teachers not only confronted Asian workers in their camps but also occasionally imagined them as potential liberal citizens. In 1911, Fred Waters reported success in his British Columbia lumber camp with "one Chinaman that I have been teaching" who was "very eager to learn to read and write English." Waters proudly concluded: "He says that he wants to become an interpreter."[147] Harold B. Burns's weekly registers indicate that during the summer of 1919 he was teaching reading, writing, spelling, and arithmetic five nights per week to three to six men, including a "little

Chinese lad" who was the son of the rail camp's cook. For at least two weeks, the boy took "a decided interest in the work."[148]

An absolute limit existed, however, in the association's encounter with Indigenous workers. Managed differently by the settler collective, Indigenous Others were subject to particular techniques of population management that rendered them, for instance, non-persons and, later, non-citizens: until 1951, the Indian Act, first made law in 1876, defined a person as "any individual other than an Indian," and Indigenous people were excluded from citizenship until 1956.[149] While many Indigenous men from bands throughout Northern Ontario appear to have sought work in the lumber camps in the first three decades of the twentieth century, such men were "at the bottom of the pile" as far as employers were concerned: for instance, the employer-oriented *Canada Lumberman* warned in 1911 that these men "will work for a time and then take a rest while spending the money they have earned."[150] Industry representatives thus associated Indigenous men with the very qualities the Reading Camp Association hoped to discourage in native-born and immigrant workers – lack of steady commitment, peripatetic wandering, and unreliability. Lacking utility as wage labour, Indigenous people were from this point of view disposable. Edmund Bradwin's report on frontier labour conditions in the 1910s, *The Bunkhouse Man*, rehearses a similar view:

> Strange as it may appear, men of this primal race seem exotic to camps. The bunkhouse itself in the Canadian hinterland signifies an intrusion upon his former domain. Camp activities of whatever kind mean ultimately a narrowing of privileges and customs that for so long have marked his mode of life. The Indian himself draws apart from the continued labour in the camps. The ordered complexity with which considerable numbers of men are handled effectively, the big machines that in their ponderous efforts awaken to new life the solitudes that he so long has called his own, may awe, or even attract for a time, but his stay in a bunkhouse is usually temporary. The Indian more than any other campman is rooted in his own ways, and the methods of the past.[151]

Bradwin's statement offers an apt example of what Lorenzo Veracini identifies as one of the many varieties of "transfer" that settler collectives enact as a means of "cleansing the settler body politic of its (indigenous and exogenous) alterities." In particular, Bradwin's move performs a transfer by means of what Veracini calls "repressive authenticity": modernity's opposite, Bradwin's "primal race" does not yield to the "ordered complexity" of the camp and soon retreats to the "methods of the past."[152] Moreover, Bradwin figures them in absolute opposition to what Ian McKay calls the "*primum inter pares* in the trinity of liberal values ... the precondition of a liberal's identity" – property.[153] The "Indian" lives in a past that is giving way, against his will, to modernity, and he will be left behind. Given this trope of the dying Indian and the immigrant-focused pedagogy of this period, it is not surprising that Indigenous people were utterly absent from the association's promotional literature and appear in the *Handbook* only as a phenomenon of the past. In the Whiggish lesson on "Indians" in the "History and Progress" section, for example, the reader is told that the "native races of Canada *were called* Indians. They *lived* in the regions from the Gulf of St. Lawrence to the Great Lakes."[154] Generally presented as obstacles to liberal modernity, individual Indigenous men such as Joseph Brant are celebrated only when they are represented as serving the cause of the British. Instances of instructors encountering Indigenous workers are rare in the correspondence, but one example serves to demonstrate how semantic erasure performed in the *Handbook* was doubled in the association's practical work: W.M. Diamond's 1916 letter from a Lake Winnipeg fishing camp notes that of the seventy-five men in his camp, at least sixty were "either Indians or half-breeds," and that unlike the immigrant men found in lumber and rail camps, these men spoke English, could "more or less" read and write, and were "satisfied with what they know and don't care to learn more." Although many instructors in the 1910s continued elementary studies with (frequently reluctant) Canadian-born workers, Diamond's letter suggests that a special lack of ambition among Indigenous workers rendered them particularly unsuitable for the kind of improvement the association was aiming to cultivate.[155]

Between 1906 and 1919, the Canadian Reading Camp Association was dramatically transformed. Responding to emergent debates regarding citizenship, themselves determined by the racial and labour conflict of the 1910s and 1920s, the association recast its pedagogical materials and methods while attempting to articulate to government how its work in the field of Canadianization could serve emergent state needs. The association's new name – it was legally incorporated as Frontier College in 1919 – thus indicated more than superficial change. Formerly stewards of the "passive" reading room model and moral-character mentors, labourer-teachers were now expected to be "active" instructors, to manage classrooms, to report on their progress, and to mould non-British immigrant workers into English-speaking citizen-readers who were in right relation with the state. While the instructor's individual influence was deemed crucial in the association's first half-decade, by 1919 this casual but unpredictable relation was subordinated to a more thorough pedagogy, one that addressed each worker in the same way. Thus a pedagogy for liberal political citizenship was born, most tangibly with the 1919 publication of the *Handbook for New Canadians*. This pedagogy came to serve a crucial function in the association's mission during the interwar years. As this pedagogy moved from theory to practice, from the pages of the *Handbook* into the camps, the assumptions it represented met their most formidable test.

3

Using the Pedagogy of Liberal Citizenship, 1920–1929

Given the political and economic uncertainty of the period that immediately followed the First World War, it is perhaps not surprising that Edmund Bradwin, a western inspector who would become principal of Frontier College in the early 1930s, wrote to Alfred Fitzpatrick in 1919 and expressed his doubts about the organization and its mission. Bradwin's letter frankly articulates his concern: "Men Don't Want to Improve. Give them 4 hours a day and not 15% of them would study."[1] Cutting down the most frequently cited reason for the organization's failure to teach significant numbers of men – the problem of overtime or long working hours – Bradwin's letter simultaneously questions one of Fitzpatrick's most basic assumptions – that men, given the opportunity, would want to improve themselves. As Frontier College worked to formalize its educational program in the 1920s, this central assumption, which left the ideologically charged and deeply liberal concept of "improvement" unquestioned, met significant challenges.

The period immediately following the First World War presented Frontier College with a number of difficulties. The labour agitation of 1919 and 1920 and the subsequent nationwide recession, rising prices, falling wages, and growing unemployment during the early 1920s made it exceedingly difficult to place labourer-teachers in camps. Labour camps across the country decreased their workforces during the postwar depression (1920–22); for instance, in British Columbia's logging sector, the province's most important industry, 80 percent of camps were closed at the end of 1920.[2] Indeed, only about thirty-four Frontier College teachers were in the field during 1921. By 1923, this number had grown to forty-nine. The economic turmoil of the early part of the decade had given way to rapid industrial growth and renewed immigration by the late 1920s, but Frontier College did not experience similar expansion. In 1929, the association placed fifty-seven instructors, the same number it had succeeded in sending out in 1919. The number of men the association claimed to have been able to enrol in classes each season also remained more or less constant during the 1920s. Moreover, the total contributions received by the association (from all sources) grew throughout the 1920s but had curved back down to 1920 levels by the 1930s.[3] This levelling off reflected the fact that the 1920s were years of organizational struggle for Frontier College.

The Canadianization program grew to assume a central place in the Frontier College structure during the 1920s. A publicity campaign that appeared in the pages of the *Toronto Daily Star* in the fall of 1920 made the priorities of Frontier College clear to Canadians: "YOU are now asked for a subscription, and you may feel absolutely assured that every dollar you give will be spent wisely and well in transforming the rough, uneducated and untrained foreign labourer into and intelligent and useful citizen of the Dominion" (see figure 3.1).[4] As Tom Mitchell notes, Canada's business elite sought to curb the postwar mobilization of dissent – and displace calls for the reform of economic and political systems – through appeals to "citizenship and nationhood as the ideological core of Canada's liberal capitalist order." Frontier College became one player in what Mitchell terms the "cultural and ideological terrain of citizenship." However, this was a deeply contested terrain: the conspicuous absence of labour movement and agrarian radicals from the 1919 Winnipeg Conference on Character Education in Relation to Canadian Citizenship, which gathered fifteen hundred delegates from business, education, and journalism, is evidence not of their lack of concern with the issue of citizenship, but rather of their conviction that the purpose of the conference was actually to resist those who were agitating for expanded social rights of citizenship.[5]

The demographic reality of the camps in this period offered rich opportunities for Canadianization. The gradual easing of immigration restrictions throughout the 1920s led to an increase in the number of immigrants from Britain, the United States, and Europe from an average of 100,000 persons per year between 1920 and 1923 to an average of 160,000 persons per year between 1927 and 1929. If the ethnicity of immigrants entering Canada was still very much controlled in this period by what Ninette Kelley and Michael Trebilcock call the "tiered" character of the nation's immigration policy, special agreements were arranged to provide labour for those sectors of the economy, such as lumbering, railway construction, and mining, that did not tend to attract British-born immigrant workers. For example, the 1925 Railway Agreement gave the CPR and the CNR great powers to recruit farm workers and agriculturalists from the non-preferred countries of southern and eastern Europe, and it was responsible for bringing more than 185,000 central Europeans (especially German-speaking Russians, Ukrainians, Poles, and Hungarians) to Canada between 1925 and 1929. More generally, the loosening of immigration after 1926 permitted employers to seek permits for immigrants from non-preferred European countries in order to fill specific labour needs. Unsurprisingly, therefore, the proportion of European immigrants to Canada rose from 27 percent of total immigration in 1914 to approximately 46 percent by 1929.[6] The ethnic composition of the frontier camps in which Frontier College worked altered significantly across the 1920s, as well: in 1922, 52 percent of the men in Frontier College camps fell into the categories "English-" and "French-speaking" (Canadian, British, or American); by 1929, these same men constituted only 31 percent of the same population. Within this larger category, it is also worth noting the recorded decline during the 1920s in the number of French-speaking workers, a decline that, as the previous chapter discusses, accompanied the association's increasing unwillingness to view French as a language that could nurture citizenship. "Slav Races" (a large category that included "Jugo-Slavs," "Czecho-Slovakians," Hungarians, Ukrainians, and Poles) were a dominant and growing group throughout this period (always above 30 percent of the population), while Scandinavians (Swedes, Danes, Norwegians, and Finns) increased in number from 3 percent of the Frontier College camp population in 1922 to 21 percent in 1929 (see figure 3.2).

This chapter builds on the preceding one by demonstrating how the association's nascent pedagogy for liberal citizenship was refined in the wake of the publication of its first teaching manual, the *Handbook for New Canadians* (1919). Here I turn to the dissemination and use of this manual. Using contemporary reviews from the liberal media as well as workers' periodicals, instructors' correspondence and weekly registers, students' letters, and samples of students' work, I examine how the new methods developed in the *Handbook* were used in camp classrooms. This chapter analyzes how these methods

Figure 3.1 "Making Good Canadian Citizens Out of Our Foreign Workmen"

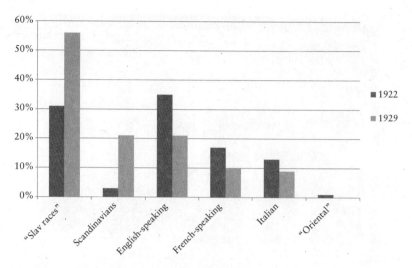

Figure 3.2 Ethnic composition of Frontier College camps, 1922 and 1929

were embedded in the association's growing bureaucracy, which, I contend, was central to Frontier College's efforts during the 1920s and 30s to make the case for federal responsibility in the area of citizenship education. This chapter thus begins to unfold one of the key themes of the second half of this book – how Frontier College's methods for Canadianizing non-British immigrants influenced emergent state efforts in this period. By the mid-1920s it was clear that provincial jurisdiction over education would prevent Ottawa from implementing a national citizenship education program; however, Fitzpatrick continued throughout this decade to correspond regularly with cabinet ministers and other government officials, always attempting to present the association's work as supportive of new or expanding federal responsibilities, such as immigration and surveillance. At the same time, the college ramped up its approach to provincial governments and to industry. As this shift occurred, the college's criticism of industry's failure to provide adequate working conditions softened, and its emphasis on the ameliorative force of education as a tool for engendering liberal citizenship among the new immigrant population increased. Indeed, the 1920s was a key decade in terms of defining both the association's relation to the state and its conception of political citizenship: although it secured a victory from the federal government in the form of a charter that gave it degree-granting powers throughout the Dominion, the provinces (Ontario, in particular) greeted this victory with resentment and pushed back hard. Frontier College was not to be a publicly funded university for working people. If "citizenship education" for the exogenous population of the settler nation was an acceptable form of improvement that placed responsibility on the immigrant to attach himself appropriately to the state, publicly funded degrees by extension that threatened the class structure of the nation were not.

LIBERAL CITIZENSHIP AND THE STATE

The 1920s were tumultuous years for Frontier College: this was the decade during which the organization's character and its relation to the state were solidified, largely as a result of Fitzpatrick's plan to secure a Dominion charter that would allow Frontier College to implement the nation's first extramural degree program. According to George L. Cook and Marjorie Robinson, this plan was not universally accepted by those associated with Frontier College. In Fitzpatrick's view, such a charter would secure the organization's survival and obviate the need for public grants; however, others within the organization, particularly Edmund Bradwin, worried that the charter would come at the expense of government grants and thus of Frontier College's ability to conduct its work in frontier camps. The dissension was perhaps fed by the fact that Fitzpatrick's plan was far more radical than anything the association had attempted to that point: unlike camp-based classes that led to no formal certification, his plan strove to alleviate a fundamental source of social and economic inequality by ensuring common access to university degrees. Fitzpatrick's vision challenged the elitism of Canada's universities by attempting to expand the formal educational opportunities available to workers in remote areas. Moreover, unlike contemporary campus-based programs for adult workers, such as Ontario's WEA (founded in 1918 by then-president of the University of Toronto, Sir Robert Falconer), Fitzpatrick's program was to run off-campus, in the mines and forests where the unskilled worked. One of its goals was thus to narrow the urban/rural divide that was so important to the structure of early-twentieth-century Canada.[7]

In his 1923 book *The University in Overalls*, Fitzpatrick describes his ambition – the "decentralization" of educational systems in Canada, the bringing of higher education to the "masses," the reconciling of the "strife and discord with which modern society is tormented," and the dismantling of hierarchical distinctions between manual and mental labour – not as new but rather as the natural development of the work that Frontier College had been undertaking since the turn of the century. *The University in Overalls* articulates an ambitious plan that encompasses not simply an extramural degree program but also government-assisted homesteading programs that would encourage family settlement in the North rather than the itinerant labour of single men. If the ideas of this book are occasionally radical – Fitzpatrick's desire to undo capitalism's distinction between manual and mental labour recalls Karl Marx's objection in *The German Ideology* to the division between productive and non-productive labour – Fitzpatrick is nonetheless careful to insist that his homesteading plan was not "communistic or utopian" but rather based on the inviolable principles of "individual ownership and personal property." For Marx, we recall, it is precisely such a system of private property that subtends the "contradiction between town and country" that characterizes the division between mental and manual work.[8]

In any case, Fitzpatrick's vision for Frontier College was not to be. Facing immense pressure from Ontario universities that were anxious about standards and eager to protect provincial jurisdiction over education, the Ontario government forced Frontier College to retreat from the federal charter by withholding its grant between 1929 and 1932. Isolated by a board that had come to agree with Bradwin, Fitzpatrick resigned as principal in 1931 and Frontier College continued its work under Bradwin's leadership as a non-governmental organization that sought to ameliorate but not eradicate structural inequalities for working men.[9] Moreover, the demise of Fitzpatrick's vision signals an important step in the association's move away from assessing and acting on structural inequalities and its intensification of its emphasis on culture, literacy, and citizenship education as compensation for capitalism and as tools for managing the non-British immigrant population. It was this latter approach that allowed the organization to survive throughout the interwar years, a difficult period during which Frontier College worked hard to justify its *raison d'être* for would-be donors in government and industry.

Fitzpatrick was keenly aware from the inception of the Frontier College project that state support was not only desirable but also necessary. As its emphasis shifted from moral to political citizenship, from home to state, and from British- and native-born Canadians to non-British immigrants, Frontier College was embedding itself in nascent conceptions of the state's responsibility for social welfare. As Tina Loo, Carolyn Strange, and others have demonstrated, the roots of modern Canadian social welfare legislation sprouted in the 1910s and early 1920s, when compulsory schooling, minimum-wage acts, and mothers' allowance legislation were implemented in most parts of the country and when Ontario passed the nation's first piece of social insurance, the Ontario Workmen's Compensation Act (1914).[10] Throughout the 1920s, Fitzpatrick was clearly trying to shape these new forms of state intervention through appeals to both federal and provincial levels of government.

If citizenship education for adults, which Fitzpatrick believed would bond immigrant workers to the state, was not yet a priority for the federal government at the end of the First World War, other contemporary forms of state intervention offered examples of how the state might use its power to shape practices of citizenship. For example, in the early 1920s the federal government commenced its first experiments in compulsory citizenship education in the context of residential schools for Status Indian children.[11] Moreover, although Ottawa did not actively intervene in the question of citizenship education for adult immigrants during the 1920s, its new administrative capacities with regard to immigration, particularly as embodied in the 1917 creation of a Department of Immigration and Colonization, were suggestive of greater powers. The federal government certainly did in this period employ *negative* powers with regard to citizenship, powers that, for example, prevented certain groups and individuals from accessing citizenship in Canada. During the 1910s and 1920s, the federal government experienced considerable pressure from employers, such as British Columbia's Mountain Lumber Manufacturers' Association and the Manitoba Gypsum Company, to act on the problem of labour agitation, which employers consistently linked to immigration. The proliferation during the late 1910s and 1920s of new mechanisms for selecting and regulating immigration, such as the 1919 amendment of Section 41 of the Immigration Act, which targeted immigrants involved in subversive groups and activities for deportation, demonstrate how the federal government responded. As Barbara Roberts argues, the "anti-radical hostility" of the postwar period "became conveniently and inextricably mingled with anti-alien feeling." The Section 41 amendment, which produced new kinds of state control over immigration while aiming to curb radicalism, illustrates Roberts's point well.[12] In the period prior to the Second World War, therefore, the repression of potential citizenship was of greater concern to the federal government than the *active production* or *encouragement* of citizenship, at least among the adult population.

Nonetheless, the work that Frontier College was undertaking with regard to citizenship education held definite interest for the federal government, and for the newly created Department of Immigration and Colonization, in particular. According to Lorna R. McLean, the "alignment of state and College objectives" in the period after 1919 "facilitated the College's transition into a modern organization." In other words, both saw the value of Canadianizing immigrants and promoting education for citizenship. The federal government was not willing in this period to develop an active pedagogy of Canadianization, but Frontier College was, and Fitzpatrick worked ceaselessly to ensure that Ottawa's expanding bureaucratic functions in the field of Canadianization took note of the efforts of his organization. In 1923, for instance, Fitzpatrick received a request from F.C.C. Lynch, the Superintendent of the Natural Resources Intelligence Service, who wrote to ask for "printed matter relating to your work among foreign immigrants" because the Department of the Interior was "making researches into questions on which this seems to have a bearing."[13] In the fall of 1921, Fred James in the Department of Immigration and Colonization contacted Fitzpatrick, noting that he had heard of the latter's "active and constructive" contributions to the work from Fitzpatrick's old Queen's friend and commissioner of the newly created Royal Canadian Mounted Police (RCMP), Charles Frederick Hamilton. James sent three copies of the department's new handbook *A Manual of Citizenship* to Fitzpatrick for his "criticisms and suggestions"; he also requested a copy of the *Handbook for New Canadians*. Upon receiving the Frontier College *Handbook*, James responded to Fitzpatrick, noting that it will "be useful, I am sure, when we come to the preparation of a new edition of the 'Manual of Citizenship.'" Fitzpatrick's response contains no specific criticisms of the department's own *Manual of Citizenship*, save that its type was too tiny. He compliments the *Manual* for containing "much valuable information in a small space" and concludes by inquiring if the department had interest in purchasing copies of the *Handbook* for use in its "canadianization of foreigners." Robert J.C. Stead, the Director of Publicity for the department and James's superior (and also an author of popular Prairie romances), responded several days later, lamenting the meagre budget of the department and noting the impossibility of making the purchase that Fitzpatrick recommended.[14]

While there are no extant copies in Canadian libraries of the 1921 *A Manual of Citizenship*, extant copies of the 1923 and 1925 editions differ considerably from the *Handbook for New Canadians*. The *Manual* is a tiny, pocket-sized softcover booklet that is dwarfed by the hardcover *Handbook*. Unlike the *Handbook*, which addresses itself to the instructor and the immigrant alike, the *Manual* speaks to the immigrant directly about matters of immediate practical importance: for instance, the "hints for the voyage" section includes advice regarding what to pack and wear on the steamer and the train; where to stay upon arrival in Canada; and money and exchange. More abstract discussions on education, naturalization and voting, and government are reminiscent of the *Handbook*, but these are extremely brief. It is clear from the differences between the texts that the federal government during the 1920s was offering not a citizenship guide of the sort it now authors and publishes – guides that have much more in common with the *Handbook for New Canadians* than with the government's first *Manual of Citizenship* – but rather a brief introduction to Canada for the newcomer. The more ambitious project of Canadianization was not yet imagined to be within Ottawa's purview.[15]

Although the federal government had many compelling reasons to care about citizenship education in the 1920s, its ability to act on this issue was limited by a number of factors. The nature of these limitations is best illustrated in the period's federal debates regarding the possibility of a national education bureau. As Lorna McLean observes, two Conservative motions in 1919 – one in the House of Commons and the second in Senate – critiqued the lack of national unity with regard to education. According to McLean, Conservative and Unionist supporters of these motions drew on arguments of "patriotism, citizenship, and national service" to call for a greater federal role in orchestrating education, noting the well-established role of the National Bureau of Education in the United States, which had recently assumed responsibility for the Americanization of foreigners.[16] Supporters of Frontier College, such as McGill professor and popular humourist Stephen Leacock, took to the pages of Canadian newspapers in this same year in order to observe that the association had for twenty years been "quietly and efficiently" carrying on work that Americans had only recently begun to call Americanization. While

Leacock's argument is somewhat disingenuous – it suggests that the Frontier College's efforts to Canadianize the non-British immigrant formed its founding *raison d'être*, when in fact such efforts did not begin in earnest until well into the first decade of the twentieth century – it demonstrates how supporters of the college were attempting to capitalize on federal debates in order to figure Frontier College as the natural purveyor of federally funded citizenship education.[17]

A third Conservative attempt to gain support for a national education bureau came in early 1920. During this period of proliferating immigration restrictions, federal MPs wrestled with the question of the state's duty to Canadianize the millions of non-British immigrants who had arrived in the previous decade. Conservative MP Michael Steele (South Perth) moved "that, in the opinion of this House, it is essential for the future national welfare of Canada that appropriate measures be taken by the Government to fit and prepare all immigrants of alien origin for assuming the duties and responsibilities of Canadian citizenship." Noting the importance of the 1919 amendments to the Immigration Act, Steele nonetheless observed the need to consider the "assimilation of those already here" and the urgent problem of the "illiterate, non-English foreigner" who "provides a fertile field for anarchy, Bolshevism, and the many other 'isms' and manias that are cursing the world to-day." In Steele's view, the federal government, with its powers over immigration and naturalization, had a responsibility to coordinate and oversee the Canadianizing work that voluntary groups such as Frontier College were undertaking across the country. Steele's motion received much support and was passed on 29 March 1920, but when Conservative MP J.W. Edwards attempted to resurrect his 1919 motion, which called for the creation of a national bureau of education, he was restrained by the acting Prime Minister Sir George Foster, who clearly apprehended the intransigence of Quebec MPs determined to guard their province's control over education.[18] Concerns over jurisdiction would indeed prove to be the roiling waters on which Steele's – and Fitzpatrick's – visions foundered.

As McLean observes, jurisdictional disputes over the education and assimilation of immigrants curtailed federal initiatives and resulted in federal funding for private institutions, such as the urban-oriented YMCA and urban settlement houses.[19] Even so, the federal government remained reluctant throughout the 1920s to grant funding to Frontier College, usually citing its lack of jurisdiction over education. Yet the association did experience one significant success with the federal government in this period in relation to the question of jurisdiction: the passage of the Frontier College Act of 1922, which granted the association the unique ability to operate under the authority of an Act of the Dominion Parliament as an extramural degree-granting institution. Despite the exclusivity of provincial jurisdiction over education, the granting of charters to educational institutions was not an exclusive provincial power in this period, and the federal government was willing in 1922 to test this distinction.[20] However, it was not willing to test that distinction further by committing funds to the organization's operations.

Despite the insistence with which departments in the federal government rejected Frontier College's repeated requests for funding throughout the 1920s, Fitzpatrick did not cease to make demands each year. Perhaps spurred by the signs of support he had received from Liberal Prime Minister Mackenzie King prior to his election in the early winter of 1921, Fitzpatrick made an impassioned plea to the Ministers of Labor, Immigration, and Finance in the spring of 1923, asking each for a grant of five thousand dollars and noting the long history of the association's work and its unique labourer-teacher concept:

> He is not only a guide, philosopher and friend, he not only helps to dignify and ennoble labor, but to combat the pernicious doctrine of agitators. Investigation reveals the fact that there is a widespread movement on the part of not a few foreigners in general, and of Ukrainians in particular, to seek to perpetuate their several nationalities and to criticize and harm our Canadian institutions. The best agent to combat this tendency and to teach, commend, and make enforcement of Federal and Provincial laws practicable, is a well qualified college man as a manual worker amongst our foreign population. He is a leader, not only in work and education, not only in teaching the foreigner to speak one of our national languages – English or French – but in teaching our folk and other songs and in popularising the best in Canadian citizenship and in Canadian and Canadien literature.

After more than twenty years of experience, Fitzpatrick was "more convinced than ever that the instructor as a manual laborer with his fellow laborers is the best cure for Bolshevism and anarchy." The federal government could therefore "do nothing more in the interest of the state than to make it possible to place an instructor as manual laborer in every large work gang."[21] In the same year, Fitzpatrick made a similar claim for Frontier College in his book *The University in Overalls*, in which he asserts that "the right kind of education will go far to reconcile the elements of strife and discord with which modern society is tormented."[22] Linking the state's duty to Canadianize immigrants through the instrumentalization of Canadian culture and the English language to the threat of Bolshevism, which had assumed new importance for all levels of government in the wake of the Russian Revolution, the 1919 Winnipeg General Strike, and the growth of radical unions like the IWW and the OBU, Fitzpatrick fed the employer-fuelled rhetoric of the period, which linked "red" agitation to eastern European immigration. While Fitzpatrick occasionally received signs of encouragement – for example, the Deputy Minister of Labor indicated to Fitzpatrick in early March of 1923 that the Minister of Labor was "inclined to view favourably the idea of a grant" – that grant did not materialize during the 1920s.[23]

Despite this lack of success, Fitzpatrick worked tirelessly throughout the 1920s to keep the work of Frontier College in the federal government's view. For instance, he sent complimentary copies of the *Handbook for New Canadians* and of *The University in Overalls* to numerous federal departments. Moreover, when opportunities arose to give Frontier College some exposure at government-sponsored or -facilitated events, Fitzpatrick seized them. In 1921, for example, the Department of Labor organized a Canadian contingent for a conference on employment in Buffalo, New York, and invited Edmund Bradwin to give a paper on "Unskilled Labor." Although Bradwin initially declined the offer, Fitzpatrick wrote to the department in August of 1921 to say that he would urge Bradwin to reconsider. Bradwin did just that, which suggests the force of Fitzpatrick's belief that cooperation with federal requests was essential to the longevity of Frontier College.[24] Fitzpatrick also exploited every personal connection he possessed in order to make inroads into Ottawa. For instance, the Deputy Speaker of the Commons and a longtime member of the Frontier College board, the Honorable George Gordon, "provided the political entrées at Ottawa" that led to the passing of the federal charter in 1922.[25]

More spectacular, however, is Fitzpatrick's connection to his "old college friend" Charles Frederick Hamilton, the cable censor during the First World War and, after 1919, the Security Board Commissioner for the newly created RCMP. By 1922, Hamilton was the RCMP's Chief Liaison and Intelligence Officer. His job was to compile weekly reports on "Revolutionary Organizations and Agitators."[26] Exploiting his personal connection to Hamilton, Fitzpatrick sought funding from the RCMP in 1923, but Hamilton turned him down, claiming that such funding might "compromise your workers by arousing against them the prejudices of the men most in need of their ministrations."[27] As I discuss in the next section, this incipient relationship between Frontier College and the RCMP is crucial to understanding how the former Reading Camp Association responded to expanding state surveillance of workers – immigrant workers in particular.

Provincial governments, which had a freedom to invest in and oversee education that the federal government lacked, made Canadianization efforts a priority during the early 1920s, when concerns over security and social unrest were heightened. Due to jurisdictional conflicts, the citizenship education that emerged in Canada in the 1920s was far from nationally uniform, as McLean notes: "National, regional, and local organizations and associations, informal and formal, evolved alongside provincial governments to produce institutional variations and 'identities' in the experience of citizenship and education."[28] Yet in every province but Quebec, Canadianization was more or less consonant with a settler identity rooted in Britishness and Protestantism. As I observe in the previous chapter, non-British immigrant children were subjected to an indirect kind of regulation through public schooling throughout the first decades of the twentieth century. In the period following the First World War, state-controlled compulsory education for the purpose of promoting specifically pro-British, Protestant values had triumphed in every province but Quebec. As Loo and Strange suggest, "to preserve democracy and British values against the threat of 'foreign' ideologies, particularly communism, all children had to learn how to be 'proper' Canadians."[29] Anglophone educationalists' support of Canadianization during the 1920s drew on the earlier work of J.T.M. Anderson but was fuelled by the particular contexts of the Winnipeg General Strike and, more generally, postwar labour unrest, as well as by controversies surrounding the public education of dissenting groups such as the Doukhobors. In a 1925 government-commissioned report on public schooling in British Columbia, for instance, J.H. Putman and G.M. Weir invoke Canadianization as a natural goal: "The development of a united and intelligent Canadian citizenship activated by the highest British ideals of justice, tolerance, and fair play should be accepted without question as a fundamental aim of the provincial school system."[30] Rose Bruno-Jofré finds a similar rhetoric of citizenship in Manitoba's *Western School Journal*, which during the 1920s (in the wake of the province's hosting of the 1919 National Conference on Character Education in Relation to Canadian Citizenship) devoted much attention to the necessary relation between individual character – "service, work habits, Christian values, obedience to the law, defence of national institutions" – and "good" citizenship. "Service" in this context referred specifically to voluntarism rather than active political participation. As Bruno-Jofré demonstrates, this thinking about citizenship also permeated the province's elementary- and secondary-level curriculum in the 1920s, which equated the nourishment of good "character" (faith, reverence, obedience, truthfulness, justice, courage, self-reliance, judgment, intellectual and moral power, steadfastness) with Canadianization.[31] As we will see, Fitzpatrick cannily perceived the similarities between the Frontier College project and contemporary provincial efforts to deal with immigrant children. The argument for Canadianization – the cultivation of those character traits necessary to the abstraction of the liberal citizen – as a bulwark against "foreign" and "red" ideologies earned a particularly prominent place in Fitzpatrick's interwar repertoire.

Unfortunately for Frontier College, however, provincial educational authorities continued through the 1920s to privilege the formation of immigrant children over the education and training of their parents and grandparents. In a 1921 plea to provincial leaders and education ministers, Fitzpatrick notes the unique nature of the association's work among adult immigrants on the frontier and characterizes the value of the labourer-teacher: "He is a pivot for sane and ordered opinion; he is an example of the better type of Canadianism; he disseminates a wholesome atmosphere as a teacher and leader." Such benefit was to be had at the cost of five hundred dollars per season per instructor. A tailored version of this letter for the Premier of Ontario points out that seventy instructors, seven travelling inspectors, six movie machines, and accommodations (tents, buildings at more permanent camps) would cost the association fifty thousand dollars for a season. Fitzpatrick committed the association to raising half this amount and asked Ontario for fifteen thousand, while noting that he had requested three thousand each from British Columbia and

Manitoba and one thousand from Alberta, Quebec, Saskatchewan, and Nova Scotia. The Dominion-wide economic recession of 1920–22 rendered the provinces unable to meet Fitzpatrick's plea, and they gave their habitual grants of $4,500 (Ontario), $500 (Manitoba and British Columbia), $250 (Saskatchewan), and $100 (Alberta). Quebec declined to renew a grant it had cancelled in the 1910s; Nova Scotia cancelled its grant.[32]

The gradual economic recovery after 1922 redounded to the association's benefit (its provincial grants totalled just over six thousand dollars in 1920 and fifteen thousand dollars in 1923), but Fitzpatrick's pursuit in these same years of a Dominion Charter to grant degrees alienated the association's greatest benefactor, the province of Ontario.[33] The association managed to cope with great variances in its annual funding, always asking for more money than it received, and it was also successful in managing Ontario's ire for most of the 1920s. But in 1929, a new challenge arose: Fitzpatrick's annual round of letters to the provinces drew the direct disdain of the Premier of Ontario, G.H. Ferguson, who noted that the habitual grant would not be forthcoming because the association had permanently altered the character of its work by seeking a Charter that would allow it to grant degrees:

> This seems to me to be entirely beyond the original conception of this work ... I think you will agree that it is undesirable that we should have a lot of universities springing up all over the Province, particularly when we have had no voice in the powers conferred by their charter. The Department has asked the Frontier College to give its assurance that it will not undertake the conferring of University Degrees. Having taken that position, which I think is a sound one, I am sure you will see the payment of any further grants would simply mean that we were waiving any objection that we had to this feature of the work and approving of the powers that have been granted.

In a 1929 letter addressed directly to Fitzpatrick, Ferguson is clear: "I am at a loss to understand the purpose of attempting to invade the provincial jurisdiction without in any way advising the Province."[34] As a result of the conflict that the charter engendered, Ontario withheld its grant for three years, an action that ultimately caused Fitzpatrick to retreat from his plan to create an extramural degree program. Interestingly, the Ontario government was in this same period giving an annual grant to the Toronto-based WEA for its educational program – a program that similarly touted the benefits of liberal arts education as a means of training workers in "intelligent and effective citizenship." However, if the WEA in this period opened greater opportunities for worker-led education than Frontier College, it did not attempt, as Frontier College did, to challenge the very basis of the post-secondary system.[35]

COUNTING AND THE NEW BUREAUCRACY

One of the important indices of the transformation of Frontier College during the 1920s into a modern organization is its increasing use, across the decade, of methods of counting. These methods emerged from the formal classroom practice that Fitzpatrick began to encourage in the 1910s, but they are also evidence of the association's attempt to render its results in a form that would be visible to emergent state bureaucracies. The annual report for 1920 contains no graphs or charts that demonstrate the association's impact, opting instead, as had been the case since the association's inception, for representative examples. By contrast, the reports compiled for the CNR and CPR in 1924 tabulate instructors' activities in the camps, showing how many workers were engaged in the various kinds of activities offered. They also offer a full list of the names, country of origin, age, and location of workers "enrolled" in Frontier College study programs, complemented by a bar graph that represents the country of origin data. Such techniques of measurement persisted in the decade's remaining annual reports, rendering them longer documents that produced data that Fitzpatrick then employed in his pleas to industry and government.[36]

The organization's developing ability to measure its work in frontier camps was abetted, at least in part, by changes made to the format of the instructors' registers during the 1920s. Possibly inspired by the thorough 1919 seasonal report of instructor John F. Davidson, Fitzpatrick created a prototype for a seasonal register in 1919. By 1921, Frontier College had adopted this model, and it remained more or less standard throughout the decade. The prototype reveals the extent to which the introduction of the *Handbook* was accompanied by a thoroughly new method for tasking instructors with the work of evaluation, measurement, and reporting. The instructor was henceforth very clearly a teacher in a classroom who was responsible for monitoring "student" results. While the new register does not differ greatly from the report format introduced in 1919 – it asks for a weekly, rather than daily, account of time spent teaching, nature of instruction, number of students present, use made of reading matter, and remarks – it also includes a list of "suggestions" for the instructor; a seasonal "summary" (that charts the nationality and progress of each individual student); a personal report ("a review of your work for the season"); a page for the foreman's comments; and blank pages for the pasting of camp photographs. By 1923, the register also included a blank page inviting "a brief note of appreciation from men who have attended your classes."[37]

The association's inclination to produce statistics during the 1920s was of course partly due to the practical difficulty of administering an organization that, while not growing at a rapid rate, was increasingly dispersed across the country. As it attempted to enmesh itself in state functions, Frontier College was also responding to the emergent character of state bureaucracy. In the wake of the first federal study of official statistics, which commenced its work in 1912, Ottawa appointed a Dominion Statistician, R.H. Coats. Coats took up his position in 1915; in 1918, the Dominion Bureau of Statistics was created. Although the Dominion had (by virtue of the British North America Act) possessed the responsibility for the national census since Confederation, the creation of the Dominion Bureau of Statistics at the close of the First World War ushered in an entirely modern system of tracking and enumerating the nation's commercial and social life. According to David A. Worton, the early postwar years were ones of remarkable personnel expansion and "high achievement" for the bureau. Chief among its activities between 1918 and 1923 were the reorganization of the federal census; the establishment of a national scheme of vital statistics; the joint coordination (with the provinces) of agricultural statistics; the unification of statistics for resource and manufacturing industries; the remodelling of statistics for foreign trade and transport; and the establishment of a branch to deal with internal trade. Moreover, the bureau made great strides in its reorganization and coordination of social statistics (dealing with crime, for example), as well as "substantial" beginnings in the treatment of public finance and education.[38]

Because it involved provincial jurisdiction, education posed particular challenges for the new Dominion Bureau of Statistics. By the early 1920s, however, the bureau had established its own Education Statistics Branch, which coordinated areas of responsibility with the provinces, designating to itself the collection of statistics regarding private schools and postsecondary institutions. In 1922, the branch began to publish an *Annual Report of Education Statistics in Canada*.[39] This work led the officials in the Education Statistics Branch to Frontier College. In the spring of 1924, the Chief of Education Statistics, S.A. Cudmore, sent Fitzpatrick his bureau's latest report on education (which includes a brief description of the work of Frontier College) and requested a description of activities and statistics for the year 1923. Beginning in this period, the Dominion Bureau of Statistics began to ask Frontier College for regular bulletins on both education and employment.[40] Frontier College became the object of statistical study, and it, in turn, began to produce data that it could use to make its work relevant to state bureaucracies.

LIBERAL CITIZENSHIP, RADICAL DISSENT, AND THE BUREAUCRACY OF SURVEILLANCE

If, in 1919, Canadian workers participated in no fewer than 427 strikes, the economic recession of the early 1920s slowly drained the energy from this workers' revolt. When prosperity returned, it brought with it the increased concentration of industry (and the birth of resource giants such as Alcan), anti-union violence, strikebreaking, wage reductions, industrial paternalism, and declining union membership across the country, except in Alberta and Cape Breton.[41] As Gordon Hak notes, in the wake of the labour unrest that characterized the late 1910s in the British Columbia logging industry (as elsewhere), logging operators drew on and developed the "corporate employee-management techniques that swept across North America" in this period, such as industrial councils. Moreover, according to Hak, operators in this period also paid more attention to how workers passed their leisure time in the camps. Reading rooms, sports activities, educational classes, religious exercises, and moving pictures, all supervised by a representative of the Young Men's Christian Association, became fixtures in many logging camps. As the *Pacific Coast Lumberman* – an employers' publication – put it in 1919, such recreation was helping the workers "to become better workmen and better men," while bringing them and "their employers into closer relations, breeding harmony and mutual trust, creating loyalty and confidence so that the company can boast of 'the best men in the bush,' and the men in turn will boast of 'their company' as the best there is."[42] If Frontier College had long been contributing to and shaping such employer-friendly efforts to curb radicalism in the camps, it is also important to note that camp leisure seems to have assumed a new urgency after the labour revolt of the late 1910s.

Even in the context of workers' declining militancy in the early 1920s, migratory workers in lumber and other frontier resource camps, always at a political and physical distance from the central Canadian TLC, were courted by the organizations that developed in the wake of the IWW – the OBU (after 1919) and the Communist Party of Canada (CPC) (founded in 1921 and known as the Workers Party of Canada until 1924). Both the OBU (in the early 1920s) and the CPC (before 1925, when "ethnic" members were pushed out as a result of a policy shift) had particular success organizing among non-British immigrant workers who came from the ranks of organizations such as the Ukrainian Labor Farm Temple Association and the Finnish Organization of Canada.[43] In the lumber camps of northwestern Ontario, for example, where working conditions remained poor, five hundred new members (mostly Finns) signed OBU cards in November of 1919, and that number had almost doubled by the middle of the following month.[44] The newly established CPC similarly comprised a significant and growing number of Finnish and Ukrainian members throughout the 1920s. For example, in 1923, Finns and Ukrainians constituted 2,028 and 880 members respectively out of a total of 4,808 CPC members; by the end of the decade, they dominated the CPC.[45] Ethnic groups such as Finnish Canadians did not escape liberal censure for their political affiliations: in both the *Handbook for New Canadians* and Edmund Bradwin's 1928 study *The Bunkhouse Man*, the category of the "Scandinavian" immigrant is arranged so that Finns are discussed last, beneath, it is implied, their racially superior kin from Sweden, Norway, Denmark, and Iceland. The tendentiously racialized hierarchies employed in both of these texts offer a good example of how the apparently "scientific" ordering of humanity was shaped by the political ideologies and labour conflicts of the late 1910s and 1920s.[46]

In this increasingly complex terrain of union and organizational affiliations, Frontier College did not remain neutral. By 1919, the association had placed itself very squarely on the side of the government and of craft unionism, represented by the TLC. This is significant because, under the moderate leadership of Tom Moore, the TLC rejected at its 1918 conference a proposal to reorganize along industrial lines. One direct consequence of this decision was the creation of the OBU at the Western Labour Conference held in Calgary in early 1919.[47] In 1920, Moore became Fitzpatrick's adviser on labour matters; in 1922, he joined the board of Frontier College.[48] This relation came about through Fitzpatrick's efforts to understand the character of the OBU, which labourer-teachers were identifying in their letters by the early 1920s. Howard Chantler, working at a lumber camp in Rock Bay, British Columbia, during the 1920 season, for example, reported to Fitzpatrick that he had met the OBU upon his arrival at camp:

> After putting up my "Frontier College" sign, the men painted one of their own and placed it above mine.
>   OBU
>   Frontier College
> is the sign above the door. OBU stands for One Big Union, to which I now belong, after paying my dues for this month.

Fitzpatrick, evidently though rather surprisingly unaware of the key role played by the OBU in the Winnipeg General Strike, sought Moore's advice. In his response to Fitzpatrick, Moore warned that the OBU was "revolutionary." Fitzpatrick subsequently advised teachers to avoid the organization.[49] In some cases, instructors wrote to Fitzpatrick to report that OBU representatives made life very difficult for instructors who refused to join.[50]

In *The Bunkhouse Man*, Bradwin confirms Fitzpatrick's aversion to the OBU, contending that the "indifference" of the traditional unions to migratory and seasonal camp workers had created a void in which radical organizations such as the OBU thrived. With the "guidance and intelligent sympathy" of organized labour, with fair conditions of employment, and with the "tempering influence" of education, these men would become "a bulwark rather than an enemy of ordered government." For Bradwin, it was not merely the "welfare of the campman" or the making of the individual citizen that was at stake, but rather the "saving of Canada from being stunted in its growth" – its progressive evolution as a modern, liberal nation-state.[51] Not surprisingly, such arguments garnered *The Bunkhouse Man* critical reviews in the leftist press. For example, proletarian poet and millworker Joseph Kalar's 1929 review of Bradwin's book in the Communist-affiliated American magazine *New Masses* is at once admiring – "Professor Bradwin is no pink-cheeked professorial maiden entering timidly the bunkhouse in search of material ... He is a bunkhouse man" – and annoyed – "His repeated reiteration that his intention is not to paint a black picture of contractors and managers of railway systems (largely responsible for the conditions that prevailed during the time of his survey) is irritating." For Kalar, it is clear that organizations such as the IWW had "materially improved conditions" in camps across North America in the prewar period. The sliding in the 1920s of these gains could only be halted by the IWW and the OBU, not by the weak "ointments" of education and reform that Bradwin proffered.[52]

As in the 1910s, the perceived presence of radical agitation in frontier camps offered Frontier College an opportunity. While the railways had long supplied material support in the form of free transportation to the association's principal and its employees, the CPR and the CNR began making regular annual contributions to Frontier College after 1921 as a kind of insurance against strike action in their camps. In return, the association published reports for the railways that enumerated the particular benefits that Frontier College brought to railway construction camps. Zavitz contends that the donations that came to Frontier College in this period from private enterprises such as railways were not given to support Canadianization or citizenship education but rather in the interest of enabling labourer-teachers in their efforts to "talk down" "Bolshevists" and other union organizers; however, given the way the association linked these activities in the period following the First World War, the distinction seems unhelpful.[53] For instance, while the association's annual reports continue to attend to the apparent problem of Bolshevism through the 1920s, they frequently link political radicalism to the issues of immigration and citizenship. The 1921 report, for example, notes the threefold aim of the association: "to educate the worker and give him a fighting chance"; "to educate and citizenize the immigrant"; and "to meet the 'Red' agitator on his own ground." The report then ties this to a grander mission: "Without the clean-living, broadly trained instructors, extremists have a free hand to carry on their work of endeavouring to undermine the foundations of society."[54] Similarly, a Frontier College newspaper advertisement from 1920 suggests that the work of "making good Canadian citizens out of our foreign workmen" is primarily a task that entails familiarizing the worker with "our manners, our customs, our laws, the organization of our society and our national ambitions."⁵⁵ In this context, Frontier College's nurturing of counter-literacy – a pedagogy and print culture that could combat the print and rhetorical power of leftist organizers – retained importance throughout the 1920s.

Many labourer-teachers took the responsibility for countering radicalism seriously, particularly during the early 1920s when the labour agitation of the late 1910s was still a recent memory. Numerous instructors offered evening lectures on topics explicitly designed to soften leftist tendencies among immigrant workers, in particular. N. McKague, for instance, battled the leftist views of his fellow extra-gang workers with lectures that attempted to "prove our democracy by showing how many capitalists of today were once labourers," to "explain and prove the success of" Canadian citizenship, or "to show men that the opportunity to succeed is in the man himself rather than in a better government." Others instructors' registers record lectures with titles such as "socialistic, bolshevistik views explained."⁵⁶ The inside cover of McKague's instructor's report for 1921 visually enacts this approach and interprets it for Fitzpatrick with the caption: "[T]amping with Pochunck a socialist. He used to discuss (quietly) many economic questions with me during day's work. He had a fine vision but was unpractical" (see figure 3.3). Still others, such as J.W. DeNoon in his Northern Ontario CNR extra gang, allowed for more open discussions of topics such as "bolshevism pros and cons." However, DeNoon's report assures Fitzpatrick that he held apart from the influence of such talk: "The agitators all aired their grievances but did not persuade me 'far from it.'"⁵⁷

Some of the reports that offer the most interesting accounts of the radical ideas instructors encountered during the 1920s come from the Atlantic provinces, where the proportion of non-British immigrants in work camps was very low. Although "anti-red" rhetoric in the 1920s was frequently tinctured with anxiety about non-British immigrants, labour radicalism among the Canadian- and British-born populations remained strong throughout the decade in areas such as Cape Breton.⁵⁸ One of Frontier College's experienced instructors in this period, Harry Mutchmor, recorded his adventures at Birch Grove, a Cape Breton coal mining camp, during the summer of 1923. Mutchmor noted that of the two hundred men in his camp, approximately 98 percent were Canadian- or British-born. The

Figure 3.3 Register of N. McKague, 1921

situation that Mutchmor confronted must have been delicate: after the British Empire Steel Corporation assumed control of Cape Breton's coal mines in 1920, the company attempted to introduce a dramatic wage reduction that led to a month-long strike during the summer of 1922. The conflict did not end there but rather simmered through the mid-1920s. Indeed, Mutchmor's classes were suspended in July of 1923 because of a strike at the mine. His position as instructor in this context was difficult, particularly because the Cape Breton district of the United Mine Workers of America, led by J.B. McLachlan, was radically socialist. Mutchmor attempted to offset "radical tendencies" in his camp, but he also reported to Fitzpatrick that he was attending union meetings. In the personal report included in his register, Mutchmor claims that the classroom was not an ideal site for influencing the Canadian- and British-born workers at the Birch Grove camp: "I found I could do a great deal of instructing by sitting and lounging with the men along the fences and around the labour union hall ... the strike opened out a great field for work and I tried to make the best of such an opportunity. I had to be progressive but not radical."[59] Teaching through example rather than formal classroom practice was hardly unique to Mutchmor, even during the 1920s, when Frontier College was vigorously formalizing its educational practice.

Indeed, for all the instructors who met leftist ideas with counter-arguments, there were many who simply towed the old Reading Camp Association line of leading by example. A.S. Kennedy's 1923 report from his Cochrane, Ontario, camp insists that this quiet method worked best: "Above all the men appreciated anyone with an education, mixing with them and doing their work or playing their games. The quiet influence of a sincere instructor in my opinion does much to prevent the inroads of Bolshevist ideas into the heads of men who toil long and hard. The foreigner in the vast majority of cases will admit the wonderful chances he has in Canada."[60] Although the classroom remained the association's privileged site of instruction throughout the decade, instructors were being warned by the mid-1920s to avoid using it as a political soapbox. Beginning in the 1924 season, the reverse side of the title page in each instructor's register bears the following notice: "While you stand for staunch Canadianism, and British Institutions, do not get into arguments, avoid expressing pet opinions, teach rather by example and daily wear and tear. You will be measured by your worth, not your theory. Quietly and unassumingly you are a moulder of Canadianism. What can you give now as a leader in an obscure place? It is a worth while effort." D. Fraser McDonald, an instructor at a Hornepayne, Ontario, CNR camp during the 1924 season, took this message to heart, noting the importance of the instructor's practical example in combatting radical tendencies:

> Discussions pointing out the advantages of the British institutions and the government of Canada were very frequent for it was discovered that the majority of the foreign born and, indeed, many of the Canadian and British born are consistent advocates of Communism or some other phase in the development of Socialism. They attribute the cause of all the various complex social disorders, the mixtures of human prejudices, to one dreadful monster, the Capitalist; destroy him and all these difficulties would be solved. Briefly, their ideas were

all destructive. The task of endeavouring to implant constructive conceptions into their minds was one which required the greatest diplomacy. This was perhaps better accomplished by example than by word of mouth; the sagacity and ability of the instructor is sometimes thus tested very greatly.[61]

Despite the association's apparent sympathy with employers' fears of "red" activity in the camps, labourer-teachers sometimes expressed solidarity with the workers among whom they spent long hours. H. Mutchmor, for example, was keen to name the root causes of the disease he called socialism. Working in 1924 at one of the camps established for the construction of the Welland Canal (in southern Ontario), Mutchmor documented horrendous living conditions – decrepit farmhouses with stagnant standing water in their basements, dirty outdoor privies, and a lack of electricity for lighting and hot water despite the plentiful availability of electricity in the area. "It is not to be wondered," Mutchmor wrote, "that they found relief in getting drunk on 'moonshine' and making a rough-house of it periodically. Nor is it any wonder that Bolshevism and all the other 'isms' find this a favourite soil in which to germinate."[62]

However, most Frontier College instructors in this period did not name the social and structural causes that made life so difficult in the work camps. Much more commonly, instructors' registers identify an antidote to socialism rather than its cause. Indeed, many labourer-teachers pursued the message that Frontier College promoted to potential donors in the period – that the educational work of the association was the best precaution against leftist organizing. R.L. Cockfield's 1927 report from Castle-Trethewey Mines in Bestel, Ontario, for example, observes the power of the Frontier College English class:

> The foreign-born new arrivals at this camp constitute 90% of the workers. They are heartily disliked or disdainfully ignored by the Canadians and so herd to themselves thus forming a phalanx which is pretty difficult to pierce. However, they are here, many of them self-confessed Bolsheviks: before we can Canadianize these men, they must be given even an elementary knowledge of our tongue. Their confidence must be won to show all Canadians are not "Junkers." It has been my aim to win their confidence and give them aspirations toward healthy citizenship.[63]

From his CNR camp in Foleyet, Ontario, instructor George Lasher concurred: "The Bolshevik propogandists are very busy in the north country and receive a ready hearing. Probably not without cause." "All the men want," according to Lasher, "is a knowledge that others think just a little concerning their comfort and welfare and they will be the most loyal of any class."[64] Vic Kaethler, a recent immigrant to Canada and a worker at a Port Arthur, Ontario, CNR camp in 1928, agreed: "I have been in Canada since 1925. I have been working on several lines: on the farm, bush, railroad, etc. Wherever I worked the best chance to learn English I have had has been right here in the Frontier College extra gang no. 6. There should be a Frontier College in every extra gang, wherever foreign people are working, since education is everything. It keeps off the influence of the tribal idea, the communism. I am thankful to the gentlemen who founded Frontier College."[65] In Kaethler's view, and certainly in the view of Frontier College, the learning of English was crucial to the task of combatting the "tribal idea, the communism." The English language and the pedagogy for liberal citizenship laid out in the *Handbook* could nurture individual citizens who conceived of themselves not as members of a radical collective or class but as individuals in a nation.

The previous chapter discusses Fitzpatrick's growing disinclination in the late war years to circulate foreign-language periodicals to the camps. I situate Fitzpatrick's hesitancy in the context of the state repression of the foreign-language press (variously associated with "enemy alien" communities and leftist agitation) in the late 1910s. In Fitzpatrick's 1920 study *The University in Overalls*, it is clear that the foreign-language press continued to be a problematic site for the association, linked as it was to the perceived tendency of some immigrant groups to "cling tenaciously" to print in their native languages. However, Fitzpatrick also points to the potential that such print cultures possessed: "They may be made to serve as channels for disseminating information which the foreign-born need in order to adjust themselves to Canadian life." Fitzpatrick's survey of foreign-language publications had led him to understand their tremendous influence on non-British immigrant communities: "there were published in Canada in 1915, forty-one non- English or non-French newspapers and periodicals, the circulation covering a constituency of nearly 800,000." In Fitzpatrick's view, regulation of this important print culture was necessary; outright repression was not.[66]

However, the association's approach to periodicals during the 1920s seems to have tightened considerably. While there was some latitude regarding foreign-language periodicals well into the 1910s, state repression of this print appears to have prodded Frontier College to retreat to a more conservative policy. For instance, a carefully prepared 1928 report enumerates the names of leading Canadian periodicals and notes their respective circulation figures and "constituencies" (i.e., political leanings). Notably absent are foreign-language periodicals and even popular magazines. The list includes all the major Canadian newspapers of the period, along with two magazines – *Maclean's* and the *Ottawa Congress Journal* – described as speaking "for organized labour – carefully prepared and reliable." Whether or not this is a list of approved publications is not entirely clear, but it seems to serve that purpose. A handwritten list in the same folder reveals that instructors also received *Saturday Night*, the *Canadian Mining Journal*, and *Collier's* – the American periodical known for its serialized fiction and its socially progressive investigative journalism.[67] This prudent list is evidently not exhaustive, however. Guided by the association's recommendations, donors continued to send in a wide range of popular magazines in English. In 1929, for example, the association suggested to donor Josephine T. Goodrich that she send an "ordinary magazines with stories of western life, etc ... There is nothing to beat the *Geographic* and the Illustrated British weeklies. These, when supplemented with the ordinary story magazine and good wholesome books of fiction provide the best reading for men in camps."[68]

The task of creating and circulating a counter-literacy that could combat socialist and communist ideas became increasingly important to Frontier College during the late 1910s; it remained so throughout the 1920s, and it was in this spirit that the *Handbook* was often used. The *Handbook* contains many useful tools for countering leftist arguments, but its approach depends not on direct refutation but rather on emphasizing the common benefits of democratic capitalism. William Ririe, who spent the summer of 1921 working on CPR extra gangs from Alberta to Saskatchewan, reported to Fitzpatrick that the communists in his camp did not quibble with its claims: "The handbook was popular, even the most extreme Bolshevist told me that the subject matter was good and contains no lies." Richard Cockfield's 1929 report from a Castle-Trethewey Mines camp in

Bestel, Ontario, commends the efforts of the association to reach immigrant workers "through our own printed matter, instead of leaving them to the tender mercies (?) of such publications as the 'Vapaus' to gain their knowledge (?) of Canada."[69] *Vapaus* (1917–1974), the Finnish-language organ of the Finnish Organization of Canada, was published in Sudbury, Ontario, about one hundred kilometres south of Bestel. In 1929, the year that Cockfield made his report, *Vapaus* was shut down when its editor, Arno Vaara, was convicted on charges of sedition and libel for making negative comments about King George. Vaara's trial, which garnered national attention, prompted a round of attacks against Finnish socialists at the Lakehead. For instance, the Fort William *Daily Times-Journal*, taking Cockfield's argument one step further, interpreted Vaara's trial as evidence that "Canada is piling up trouble by bringing in people who read foreign newspapers, defy her institutions and create a revolutionary hotbed. It is time to call a halt to bringing in more of them, and it is time to step heavily on those now here."[70] While literacy was never a politically neutral term for Fitzpatrick or for those working for the association, its yoking to an ideal of liberal citizenship and its increasing emphasis on English as the language of literacy after 1919 make it clear that "literacy" was performing deeply ideological work in this period.

An emergent state bureaucracy was important for Frontier College during the 1920s. This was particularly true in relation to new state capacities for the surveillance of radical political activity. As Greg Kealey makes clear, the Union government of Robert Borden (1917–1920) lent its ear to both wartime bureaucrats and Ottawa outsiders such as Sir Joseph Flavelle and Charles Frederick Hamilton, a practice that brought into the "burgeoning bureaucracy a set of business and media linkages previously missing" that helped the federal government pioneer "a number of repressive innovations, including, most infamously, the RCMP and its security and intelligence apparatus.[71] Beginning in the 1920s, Frontier College shaped a role for itself in this emergent bureaucracy of state surveillance. As we have seen, Fitzpatrick's continued attempts to achieve proximity to (and money from) the federal government led him to exploit his personal connection to Charles Frederick (Col. C.F.) Hamilton, a Queen's alumnus who became the RCMP's first intelligence officer in 1922. The RCMP assumed control of national security (from the Dominion Police and the North-West Mounted Police) in February of 1920. Its birth can be credited to the challenges posed by the labour unrest of 1919, but as Greg Kealey points out, federal security forces were investigating links between unionized labour and socialist politics as early as 1918.[72]

Although Hamilton was not willing to commit the RCMP to funding Frontier College, he nevertheless worked in the association's interest in Ottawa during the 1920s. He recommended it to the Department of Immigration and Colonization and also promised Fitzpatrick that, if Frontier College supplied the names and locations of labourer-teachers, he would ensure that Officers Commanding in these districts would be advised to cast a "friendly eye" upon the association and its endeavours.[73] Fitzpatrick evidently took this 1923 letter as a cue; if the RCMP could look out for instructors in the camps, perhaps the RCMP could also imagine the role that instructors might play in surveillance activities. In a 1924 request for funds from the RCMP, Fitzpatrick altered his plea to Hamilton in a very suggestive fashion: "These men are performing a real national service. Their efforts are made unostentatiously and often at a personal sacrifice for the civic well-being of the new-comer and the labourer harassed often by radical talk. In their own field, as intelligence outposts, they tend to supplement the efforts of your own splendid organization."[74] During the 1920s, the RCMP scrutinized the activities of the IWW, the OBU, and the communist-controlled trade unions in locations such as the coalfields of Nova Scotia and Alberta and the lumber camps of Northern Ontario, where large numbers of Ukrainian and Finnish immigrant workers were to be found. The 11 November 1920 report of the Officer Commanding western Ontario offers an example of the RCMP surveillance of frontier work camps during the 1920s:

> There have been small strikes among the employees in five camps along the Algoma Central Railway, during the past month, and a strike of 250 men in Neimi's camp at Ruel is threatened. The men are asking for higher wages and an 8-hour day. The trouble can be laid at the door of the O.B.U. So far there have been no disturbances, and the managers of the camps affected, hope to replace the dissatisfied men. They do not intend to submit to their demands ... The main trouble along the Algoma Central is among the Finns employed in the camps. They are mostly O.B.U. members and a radical bunch. A patrol from Sault Ste. Marie detachment is now in progress along this line.

As Donald Avery observes, in the wake of 1919, the federal government adopted various security measures with the "immigrant population in mind"; immigrant agitators and their organizations were watched closely, and a liaison between the RCMP and the Department of Immigration and Colonization monitored naturalization.[75] As Fitzpatrick seems to have apprehended, this surveillance work represented an opportunity for Frontier College to make itself useful to a state bureaucracy to which it hoped to be relevant.

USING THE *HANDBOOK FOR NEW CANADIANS*

By 1920, each labourer-teacher who set out to work in a frontier camp was equipped by the head office in Toronto with a kit that included a number of copies of the newly published *Handbook for New Canadians*, which was meant to serve both as a kind of textbook for students and as a lesson-planning guide for instructors. As Fitzpatrick's personal correspondence from the early 1920s reveals, the association's arrangement with Ryerson Press did not include promotion or wholesale distribution, and this allowed the association to retain all the profits from copies it sold.[76] In February of 1920, Fitzpatrick wrote to the press to inquire if the price of two dollars per copy was too high, noting that "we are thinking of pushing the sale a little in spring and summer among foreigners."[77] The association did push, but this meant compromising on price. As the instructors' registers for the 1920s indicate, labourer-teachers generally had enough copies for about a tenth of the workers in their camps, and they were asked by the association to attempt to sell these copies for a price of $1.00–$1.25 each to interested students (with a commission of twenty-five cents per copy to the instructor). Sales were not brisk; for instance, in 1923, when instructors were required to enter the commission they earned on *Handbook* sales in their registers, they reported selling an average of 1.5 copies per camp.[78] However, it was quite common for an instructor to note in his report that one or two of his copies had gone missing, had been stolen, or had been given as gifts.

Initial sales outside the camps do not appear to have been significant either. As I note above, the federal Department of Immigration and Colonization did not purchase the title for distribution among new immigrants, as Fitzpatrick had hoped, probably because it had already begun publishing its pocket-sized *Manual for Citizenship*. By the spring of 1921, Fitzpatrick was still working to convince provincial governments, particularly those in the West, to purchase bulk quantities of the *Handbook*. In a 1921 letter to the Saskatchewan premier, W.M. Martin, Fitzpatrick suggests that the association had sold most of the initial print run of three thousand copies and was now hoping to print a "second edition" that could be sold for "a trifle over cost" (eighty-five cents per copy) to provincial and federal governments. He had little success: Martin observed that his government had purchased a "few" copies of another publication of this "kind" – *The Education of the New Canadian*, by J.T.M. Anderson, Saskatchewan's new Director of Education Among New Canadians – and could not possibly use more such books. Fitzpatrick, already clearly feeling some rivalry from Anderson in the small, nascent field of citizenship education, was likely very disappointed with what he interpreted as a provincial solution for a Dominion-wide challenge.[79]

This 1921 correspondence with the government of Saskatchewan slightly overestimates the *Handbook* sales that had actually been achieved by the spring of 1921. It seems that the first lot of copies to be bound (1,045 copies) had been sold by the end of 1920. In October of 1920, Fitzpatrick wrote to Ryerson Press to indicate that "we have almost exhausted our supply" of handbooks, noting also that the cloth-bound covers on the first copies "do not seem to be well finished off at the corners" and wondering if there were perhaps any "bolsheviks in the Ryerson Press putting gravel in the wheels?" His comments suggest that Fitzpatrick imagined the *Handbook* not only as a tool to stem the tide of radical political activity in the camps but also as a text that radical organizations deemed a threat. At this point, Fitzpatrick had another thousand copies bound, but by March of 1921, the press still had 543 bound copies of the book on hand and 955 copies in sheets ready to be bound.[80] A January 1920 advertisement in the *Globe* notes that "several hundred copies" of the book had already been sold. In February of 1920, Fitzpatrick sold eight copies to T. Eaton's Co.; Ryerson Press sold another thirty-five by March of 1920; and in that same year, the International Nickel Company in Copper Cliff, Ontario purchased 150 copies.[81] However, the association's annual report for 1920 lists $2,250.00 worth of handbooks under assets, and by 1923, the number was $615.72 or approximately 615 copies (value was estimated at cost, which was $1.01 per copy for the first three thousand copies). By 1923, therefore, most of the 2,045 bound copies had been sold, given away, lost, or stolen.[82] By 1925, the association required more handbooks for its instructors' kits and made inquiries at the Ryerson Press regarding the feasibility of reprinting. The publisher responded with an estimate (an additional two thousand copies for $1,950), but Fitzpatrick did not proceed, probably because the cost was prohibitive.[83]

By the end of the decade, Frontier College had exhausted its own ability to nurture a print pedagogy for citizenship and was once again looking for pedagogical materials to use in the camps. In 1928 Fitzpatrick also asked for and received from Robert J.C. Stead, director of publicity for the federal Department of Immigration and Colonization, one hundred copies of the *Descriptive Atlas of Canada* for use in the camps. A few months later, Fitzpatrick inquired after civics books, as well. In reply Stead noted that his department had no such books, but he enclosed a copy of a "Canada West booklet" that contained "short sections on franchise, citizenship, etc."[84] During the 1927 season, most instructors had only one *Handbook* in their kit; some, such as Charles Owens in Pangan Falls, Quebec, had none and wrote to ask Fitzpatrick about the possibility of a second edition.[85] However, the publication in 1928 of an abbreviated version of the *Handbook*, *A Primer for Adults: Elementary English for Foreign-Born Workers in Camps*, seems to have solved most of the problems with teaching-material shortages during the 1928 and 1929 seasons: in 1928, for example, most instructors were equipped with a kit of a dozen primers. This primer went through at least six printings between 1928 and 1935.[86] A seventy-two page softcover booklet measuring thirteen by nineteen centimetres, the *Primer* was much cheaper to produce and much easier to transport to camps than the 327-page hardcover *Handbook*. Its abbreviated form also seems to respond to the fact that, as we will see, most instructors did not use the latter half of the *Handbook* for classroom instruction; they favoured instead the first 40 percent of the book, which includes primer material more suitable for basic lessons in English. The *Primer* dispenses with the long description of pedagogical method that prefaces the *Handbook* and also omits many of the lessons in "stockwords," the poems by Tennyson, Hunt, and Wordsworth, as well as the sections on government, naturalization, and "History and Progress." The *Primer* retains the poem describing "the good citizen"; the most nationalist of the anthems and poems ("God Save the King," "O Canada!," "The Maple Leaf," and "In Flanders Fields"); the section on geography; and a timeline of "Thirty Important Dates in Canadian History." This last repeats the Whiggish tendencies of the original

"History and Progress" section of the handbook, condensing the settler nation's history into a now-resolved conflict between the French and the British, making no mention of Indigenous presence on the continent (except for a brief reference to the "cruel Indian wars" of the eighteenth century).

The media coverage that Frontier College enjoyed during the 1920s gives a strong indication of how the *Handbook*'s use dominated the association's pedagogy in this period. Largely due to Fitzpatrick's efforts to correspond with and ingratiate himself to editors of Canadian newspapers as a means of promoting Frontier College and its publications, the association often received favourable attention during the 1920s in the pages of the nation's weekly and daily papers, as well as in trade publications such as *Canada Lumberman and Woodworker* and the *Canadian Mining Journal*. For instance, Nancy Durham's "Circle of Young Canada" in *The Globe* devoted special attention to the association's work during the late summer and fall of 1920. In her "Beside the Campfire" series of book reviews, Durham holds up the *Handbook for New Canadians* as an invaluable instrument of Canadianization: "One of the greatest tasks confronting Canada to-day is making these men loyal friends of the Dominion and supporters of all that is British." The circle followed this review with an invitation calling on young circle members to read labourer-teacher Wallace Moore's accompanying article, "The Frontier College Instructor," and to "remember all you can about this great national undertaking of Canadianizing foreign immigrants."[87] A promotional pamphlet circulated by Frontier College during the 1920s features excerpts from editorials in newspapers from across Canada and the United States, many of which laud the association's work in combatting radicalism. An editorial from the Toronto *Mail and Empire* casts Frontier College as "antidote for radicalism and social unrest generally," and another from the St. John *Telegraph-Journal* notes that the association's efforts in teaching "Canadian ideals and Canadian citizenship" offer immigrant camp workers "Canadianism" as an alternative to "Communism."[88]

The pedagogy that developed alongside the *Handbook* and the *Primer* entailed a new kind of instructor accountability as well as emphasis on students' progress. These changes led to new ways of organizing space. By the early 1920s, the "passive" reading room model with its individuated readers was in free fall; the association was directing all of its energies towards the "active," collective, monitored space of the classroom. As we have seen, one of the methods Frontier College used for measuring student progress after the First World War was the instructor's register. The seasonal register prototype developed by Fitzpatrick in 1920 includes a list of instructions for the Frontier College labourer-teacher. The teacher was henceforth expected to perform, above all, regular teaching work. The list urges the teacher to enter a "memo" each night, to follow the teaching instructions given in the *Handbook*, to "give actual class instruction each day," and to recall that the "Frontier College of your particular camp is YOU, not the car or the tent."[89] This list appeared in the register throughout the decade, and by the mid-1920s it was complemented by a two-page set of "general instructions." Spanning the first two pages of the book, the advice is friendly but detailed, noting that, while the "instructor is not held to hard and fast rules" and will need to assess the specific needs of the camp in question, he or she should "stick to the method, plans, lessons, and themes of the *Handbook*." While the instructions acknowledge the importance of the "clean and attractive" tent or rail car, the emphasis is on classroom work: "The Frontier College expects of each instructor some definite effort in giving instruction each evening after the men have quit work. Keep this in mind. You will find material enough for such general instruction in the *Handbook*, to cover a year's work." Moreover, these "general instructions" are rendered obligatory with the reminder that payment for the season's work is contingent on the submission of the completed register at the conclusion of the work.[90]

The association's encouragement of the planned classroom is reinforced in the *Handbook*, which includes a long description of "method" in its introduction. Instructors are advised not only to establish formal classes but also to maintain "class spirit" by holding class elections, for example. While this suggestion does not appear to have been taken up by many of the instructors working for Frontier College during the 1920s, it features prominently in a promotional article that labourer-teacher Wallace Moore wrote for the *The Globe* in the fall of 1920. Wallace claims that on his second night in his Medicine Hat, Alberta, rail construction camp he held class elections for President and Vice-Presidents, the latter whose duty it was to "be truant officer and interpreter if need arose."[91] The class "government" promoted by the college was certainly linked to the association's desire to familiarize foreign-born students with democratic governance. The *Handbook* further encourages the instructor to assess and divide students according to ability in English – one class for those "beginners who are practically illiterates," another for those capable of writing and speaking some English, and a third for more advanced students. For the two more advanced classes, a sample lesson for an evening class of about one hour is included in the *Handbook*: departing from drills and dictation derived from a chosen lesson in the *Handbook*, the class should conclude with roughly ten minutes "of social intercourse and relaxation ... devoted to some topic of interest in civics or citizenship." The *Handbook* encourages a method of language instruction that emphasizes oral practice and functionality over the teaching of grammar. This remedial work is presented as a stepping stone to instruction in citizenship, which is the goal that follows from all language instruction: "As the working-fund of words is gradually acquired, the instructor, by firing questions back and forward, can convey practical suggestions and advice to his class on home life, cleanliness of habits, foods, and work; and in time he may proceed to more abstract ideas on the duties of citizenship and the place of the new-comer in the country's life."[92]

For all the formality of instruction the *Handbook* urges, labourer-teachers' registers from the 1920s reveal that the pedagogical methods set out in the *Handbook* were frequently impracticable in the context of the frontier camps. Very few instructors managed to form regular classes of distinct grades; of those who did, most formed groups based on distinctions between the non-British foreign-born, on the one hand, and British-, American-, and Canadian-born, on the other. Many labourer-teachers emphasized the very rudimentary nature of the second-language teaching they were undertaking. For instance, in a 1920 letter to Fitzpatrick, instructor W.W. Mustard wrote: "I find your handbook of great value for the few more advanced pupils which we have but the great number we have so far are just learning the language and of course work with them is quite elementary." As in other Niagara Falls hydroelectric camps in this period, the majority of the men in Mustard's camp were Italian.[93] From his railway construction camp in the James Bay region, M.S. McLean reported in 1927 that he used the "introductory picture lessons" in the *Handbook* but after he received the *Pictured Words for New Canadians* pamphlet, he depended on this almost exclusively. Published in 1927 by the Council for Social Service of the Church of England in Canada, *Pictured Words for New Canadians* is an eight-page booklet that presents simple English nouns in grid-fashion, each noun corresponding to a hand-drawn illustration. Like the language primer in the *Handbook*, its selection of quotidian nouns is at once banal and ideological. The words and images arrange the world for the immigrant according to an English Canadian settler logic: for example, an image of a white "man" appears before "woman," which precedes "boy," "girl," and "baby." Towards the end of season, some of McLean's pupils had moved on to Public School Primers, but he notes that one could do little more in one season than "getting the new Canadian started to work at our language and giving him the desire to learn more."[94] C. Bailey was one of the Frontier College instructors placed during the 1920s in a homesteading community. From Cochrane, Ontario, he complained that the *Handbook* was of no use with the Finnish adults and children he was attempting to teach. He asked instead for Finnish-language literature and a Finnish-language newspaper. Benjamin Spock, who later became the famous pediatrician and author of *Baby and Child Care* (1946), spent the summer of 1926 among "Galicians and Poles" in a CPR extra gang in Manitoba. Repeating a claim made frequently in the instructors' registers during the 1920s, Spock observes that his predominantly Galician gang was "friendly and polite and gentle" but clannish and thus in no need of English while working as a team. Spock concludes that it was a "waste of effort to teach this race, at least while they are all in a gang."[95] Indeed, while most instructors' registers from the 1920s report using the *Handbook* or the *Primer* in some way, the vast majority make it clear that classroom work was confined to the most basic of the lessons contained in the first thirty-five pages of the *Handbook*. The more abstract and complex sections devoted to "Geography," "Government," and "History and Progress," and the section of the reader that contains poetry, were apparently very rarely employed. There is the occasional report of an instructor using these sections as background material for a "general talk," but this, too, was rare.

Very occasionally, instructors reported that they were welcomed by workers who desired formal education and the opportunity for self-improvement. From his CPR extra gang in Chapleau, Ontario, H. Bruce Collier reported to Fitzpatrick that he overheard a Lithuanian student in his class chastising a Russian worker who said he had no need for study: "I work all day, come home – read a little at night. Good for me! Your work a little all day, come home – no can read, no can write, nothing but go to bed. All the same, cow, pig!" George Readman went one step further, claiming that the poor attendance in his classes was due to fact that "men were fired who had become so interested in the school that they refused to go out to work overtime." Readman remedied this problem by confining his classes to Sundays.[96]

Beginning in the 1920s, the new emphasis on monitoring the progress of labourer-teachers was accompanied by novel methods for capturing student responses to Frontier College initiatives. Pages in the register soliciting "a brief note of appreciation from men who have attended your classes" were useful for promotional purposes and were unfailingly featured in annual reports or quoted in letters to potential donors during this decade. Fitzpatrick also managed to funnel workers' comments to friendly media, such as *The Globe*, which had long supported the work of Frontier College. In 1925, for instance, *The Globe* reprinted workers' testimonials from the 1924 registers of A.D. Hardie and J.R. Jones as evidence of the "growing Canadianism" of immigrant students in Frontier College camps. In 1929, *The Globe* did this again, this time observing the "child-like frankness" of the foreign-born and the "rosier future" enabled through the work of the association.[97] As the registers from the 1920s make clear, of particular interest to the association was evidence that non-British immigrants were attending classes: "Have the foreign-born write in their own hand. Kindly add information after signature, indicating age and nationality of the adult pupil – also the probable length of time he has been in Canada."[98] In many cases, these comments are of limited use: written in an English clearly dictated by the instructor himself or by an example shared within a group of students with limited English, they tend to be formulaic. For instance, J.M. Robb included in his register a sample of student work by Albert Hundt, who had copied Alexander Muir's patriotic, imperialist poem "The Maple Leaf Forever" from the *Handbook for New Canadians*. Exhorting God to "save our King" and bless "the Maple Leaf forever," Muir's poem was memorized and sung by schoolchildren across Canada in the early twentieth century.[99] Other examples similarly occlude the personality and individuality of the student. In the packet of ten student letters addressed to Fitzpatrick that Richard Carter Gross included in his 1929 register, four of them have identical wording: "Dear Sir, I have been taking the reading and writing English for the past two months and would like to thank you and say that I appreciate it very much." Nonetheless, it is clear that these workers, Ukrainian and Czechoslovakian immigrants in their late thirties, felt moved to express thanks.[100]

The messages from students that appear in instructors' registers from the 1920s are not exclusively formulaic. Most often, however, the unique expressions of students follow a particular theme: the student is deeply grateful for the help he received from his labourer-teacher. "Poor Man," a poem written by Ukrainian immigrant Joseph Simenowitch for instructor John F. Davidson, offers an especially compelling example:

> Oh! I am poor a man,
> I don't know how
> To write to ten.
> > Only you are man,
> > Who can show me
> > How to write to ten.
> Oh! If I don my school,
> I be never man a poor.
> It is first my writing
> Soon will be day of lighting

The relationship here is clearly horizontal. In settings where many labourer-teachers struggled with what instructor E.L. Richards called Canadian and English-speaking men who "know just enough to think they know everything," the non-English speaking immigrant who professed his ignorance openly validated the Frontier College project to its core. According to Davidson, Simenowitch was a "remarkable fellow" with "interesting questions" who "learnt and learnt once and for all whatever you told him." Moreover, and exceptionally, he "had the grace of knowing that he did not know," a characteristic that clearly distinguished him from the English-speaking workers Richards observed. Extending the theme, A. Risterse, a twenty-seven-year-old Dutch immigrant, reported to Fitzpatrick that his instructor R. Holmes "has taught me almost everything to know about the English language and I am only sixteen months in Canada now. With men of his type the road is made easier for the foreigner in this country, and we are given confidence." A note from a thirty-year-old Ukrainian worker, Mike Danchuk, offers not only gratitude but also a narrative of progress – Frontier College was lifting him out of unskilled labour: "He [labourer-teacher D. Fraser McDonald] helped me more in three months than I learned myself in eleven years. This summer I learned to write well and got to be foreman."[101]

Other, rarer messages make visible deep bonds of trust, friendship, and even intimacy that were developed between the worker and the labourer-teacher. One stunning example of such forms of affective attachment is "Summer Evening," the poem that thirty-eight-year-old Mike Kmita, a Ukrainian immigrant, composed for instructor E.M. Reid in 1926:

> It was summer evening
> And pleasant was day.
> When we were working
> At railway to gether wan day.
> You know how it was here.
> Because you saw that all.
> It is golden summer
>   For us and every wan.[102]

Reid's register indicates that he and Kmita likely knew each other quite well: Reid describes Kmita as an "ambitious" student who attended evening classes regularly (fourteen classes in June of 1926 and another seventeen in August). "Summer Evening," however, speaks less of Kmita's indebtedness to Reid and more to their common experience of work and to Reid's knowledge of the things that were important to Kmita's experience of the world. Letters sent to instructors from former students were also from time to time included in registers, and these tell of the affection that was sometimes shared between labourer-teachers and labourers. F. Holko sent a Christmas greeting to instructor William Gottsegen that both models his English and demonstrates his real attachment to Gottsegen:

> All joy to you I send with this greeting.
> I'd be so happy if I could
> Spend a Christmas Day with you.

Worker Francis Madec wrote to instructor H.S. Gross in 1929 to inform him that he was working on the harvest in Manitoba and to share the news that he had met a woman on the train from Portage to Winnipeg: "I am going to get marry for the next month."[103] Other instructors included ephemeral materials from classes, some of which, such as the sketch in Earle W. Carr's register, reveal the artistic skill that could be found in the camps while suggesting a worker's homesickness for a wife, sister, daughter, or mother (see figure 3.4).

As the previous chapter observes, the pedagogy for liberal citizenship set out in the *Handbook* had strict limits. The production of liberal citizens for the settler nation required the production of non-citizens. At the bottom of the racialized hierarchy set out in the "Naturalization" section of the *Handbook*, learners found "Orientals":

Japanese
Chinese
Hindoos[104]

As figure 3.1 indicates, less than 5 percent of workers in camps served by Frontier College in the early 1920s were classified by instructors as "Oriental." By the end of the decade that percentage had fallen closer to zero, perhaps due to the Chinese Immigration Act of 1923, which replaced the long-standing head tax on Chinese immigration to Canada with an instrument of outright exclusion.[105] Nevertheless, some of the workers who found themselves in Frontier College classrooms did fall into this racialized container of undesirability. In the *Handbook*, they read of themselves: "Gambling seems to be a besetting vice of Chinese, probably due to their social isolation. But on the whole the Chinese are industrious, inoffensive, and well behaved. Their industry would make them a splendid asset, but race antipathy has decreed that Canada shall never have a large influx from China. The head tax is large and serves also as a check on immigration."[106]

C.B. Horton, who worked during the summer of 1921 with a CPR extra gang in Lethbridge, Alberta, had an evening class of nine populated entirely by the very Chinese immigrant workers the *Handbook* placed beyond the pale of the project of liberal citizenship. As I note in chapter 2, the *Handbook*'s invocation of "race antipathy" seems at once to be detached from the association's own view and a kind of commonsense defence of the settler society's need to establish limits. However, as Horton's register makes clear, for some settler Canadian labourer-teachers, the prospect of working with Chinese students was more appealing than the intimidating task of corralling "white foreigners," many of whom already had some proficiency in English, into classes. Horton reported to Fitzpatrick that the men in his first work crew – Russians, Poles, Ukrainians, and a few

Figure 3.4 Student sketch in register of Earle W. Carr, 1926

Scandinavians – could all speak English and many could read and write it: "I was the greenest of the lot and all I could do was to hold my own for a start. When I had been there a few days the gang had sized me up and I had neither the courage nor craft enough to start a class." Horton's comments point to a discomfort that many reports from the 1920s register; frontier work for which the labourer-teacher was often physically unsuited and confrontational class politics frequently challenged labourer-teachers' identity and self-assurance. In the case of Horton's camp, the common employer practice of switching crews when disagreements over pay arose led to the arrival later in the summer of 1921 of forty-six Chinese labourers: "As the Chinese were new on the gang and I was not, I at once saw their interpreter and told him what I wanted to do. In a couple of days the class was organized and going strong." The resulting class of nine included the interpreter, Yip Soon, who participated despite the fact that he could already write and read English. The other eight students, all in their twenties and unable to speak or read in English, garnered praise in Horton's seasonal assessment of student progress: one student was a "good student purchased handbook"; another was "very intelligent and interested." An unusually high number of students attending class – six of the nine – purchased the *Handbook*, a fact that suggests the particular commitment of these learners. At the conclusion of his personal report for the season, Horton added: "I do not think I am good enough to tackle a white gang even yet, although I am a nearly perfect mixer, and have no natural antipathy to either white or Oriental foreigners." Here, it is clear that the instructor's ability to imagine himself as a liberal, tolerant, and useful figure in the camp depended, in fact, on those whom the *Handbook* actively produced as non-citizens.[107]

Despite the sanguinity with which Fitzpatrick promoted citizenship education to governments and employers, there is little evidence that the pedagogy for liberal citizenship implemented after 1919 enabled the association to reach a greater number of workers. Ironically, I am able to determine this by examining the data that Frontier College began to produce with great vigour after 1919 – data that was meant to convince governments and employers that the *Handbook* had ushered in an era of educational transformation. The number of men Frontier College claimed to have been able to enrol in classes each season remained more or less constant (at around 1,500 men) between 1923 and 1929.[108] To put this figure in perspective, it is helpful to see that in 1923, for instance, 1,440 workers enrolled in classes, but there were roughly eighteen thousand workers in Frontier College camps that season. Thus, only 8 percent of workers reached by the college enrolled in classes.[109] The 1924 reports generated for the railways demonstrate similar numbers: of the 5,400 men in railway construction camps visited by Frontier College in that year, only six hundred or 11 percent of men could be classed as "adult pupils." Such "pupils," unlike "consistent readers" (19 percent), "part-time readers" (28 percent), and "occasional listeners" (43 percent), actually enrolled in classes.[110]

Moreover, as the instructors' registers clearly show, a proportion of "enrolled" students were not regular attendees of classes (an "enrolled" student may well have attended only one or two classes during the season). For instance, in his register for a Hornepayne,

Ontario, CNR camp, Earle W. Carr reported thirty-two students enrolled in July of 1926; nine of these attended two or fewer classes.[111] A close examination of instructors' registers for 1921 offers further evidence of the fact that the number of regular students in classes tended to be quite low as a proportion of the men in the camps served by Frontier College (see table 3.1). The twenty-four instructors' registers for 1921 in the Frontier College archival fonds show that, with an average camp population of 184, labourer-teachers were not generally able to attract more than ten men to each class offered: while individual instructors experienced varying degrees of success, no instructor was able to bring in more than, on average, 36 percent of the workers in his camp; nine of the twenty-four instructors considered here reported averages of 10 percent or less. If one considers only the ten camps where more than 50 percent of the population was constituted by non-British immigrants, the average number of pupils in each class is slightly higher, 10.9, but this is still only 6.2 percent of the workers in those ten camps. Moreover, given that the records were kept as part of an employment contract (I have already noted that instructors' payment was contingent on the keeping of regular classes), instructors' registers are likely prone to some exaggeration of numbers.[112]

As countless labourer-teachers noted in their registers, the new pedagogy for liberal citizenship, which had at its core the planned classroom and a formal method of instruction, did not appeal to the majority of camp workers. C.W. Hardie's 1929 report from his Fort William, Ontario, camp, suggests that even with a large pool of potential students (Hardie's camp employed 900 men, half of whom were non-British immigrants), the challenges facing the Frontier College instructor were formidable: "The main difficulty in attaining success lies in overcoming the inertia of the men. They are not as a general rule of the intellectual type and are usually interested only in learning enough English to get along. It is very hard for them after a hard day's work to set in and try to absorb a few grains of knowledge when they would much sooner be lying in their bunk reading their newspaper from home."[113] Although echoed by many other labourer-teachers, Hardie's comments are particularly revealing because they add the observation that workers pursued recreational reading on their own time; it was *what* and *how* they were reading that the pedagogy for liberal citizenship attempted to regularize.

Table 3.1
Instructors' results, 1921

Instructor	Work	Location	# Men in camp*	# Nights of instruction	Average # students/night	Average # of students/night as % of # men in camp**
Axford	CNR extra gang	Hornepayne, ON	100 (30/70)	30	7.1	7
Baker	CNR extra gang	Capreol, ON	50 (5/45)	69	3.9	8
Bicknell	CPR extra gang	Smith's Falls, ON	130 (8/122)	61	8.9	7
Bowles	Cdn. Dredging Co.	Port Robinson, ON	26 (20/6)	0	0	n/a
Courtice	H.E.P.C.	Cameron Falls, ON	400 (n/a)	65	23.8	6
Denton	H.E.P.C., Montrose Camp	Niagara Falls, ON	n/a	10	1	n/a
Front	Railroad	Aldershot, ON	50–70 (12.5–17.5/37.5–52.5)	6	10.2	17
Gauthier	CPR extra gang	Louisville, QC	80 (80/0)	54	17.7	22
Green	H.E.P.C.	Cameron Falls, ON	n/a	35	3.9	n/a
Hill	CPR extra gang	Broadview, SK	15 (8/7)	44	5.4	36
Horton	CPR extra gang	Lethbridge, AB	45 (5/40)	10	7.7	17
Imbleau	H.E.P.C., Forebay Camp	Queenston, ON	n/a	25	5.3	n/a
Luxton	CNR extra gang	Lucky Lake, SK	50–90 (5–9/45–81)	49	10.2	15
McKague	CNR extra gang	Orient Bay, ON	90 (7/83)	88	6.7	7
McKenzie	CNR extra gang	Firdale, MB	n/a	23	3.3	n/a
McLean (G.C.)	CPR extra gang	Smith's Falls, ON	130 (8/122)	60	15.4	12

McLean (W.C.)	Connor Bros.	Black's Harbour, NS	100 (99/1)	0	n/a
MacDonald	H.E.P.C., Forebay Camp	Queenston, ON	700 (n/a)	3.4	0.5
Maxwell	Dominion Coal Co.	Birch Grove, NS	250 (225/25)	3.5	1.4
Mutchmor	CNR extra gang	Sangudo, AB	35–75 (14–30/21–45)	10.4	19
Patton	H.E.P.C., Whirlpool Camp	Niagara Falls, ON	600–1600 (60–160/540–1440)	3.2	0.3
Ririe	CPR extra gang	Gleichen, AB	30 (15/15)	4.6	15
Scroggie	BC Timber and Trading Co.	Rock Bay, BC	60 (42/18)	1.6	2.7
Staples	H.E.P.C., Whirlpool Camp	Niagara Falls, ON	n/a	7.4	n/a
Averages			184***	39.7	

Source: Data compiled from the twenty-four (Axford-Staples) instructors' registers found in MG 28, I 124, vol. 119, "Registers, 1921," FC-LAC. The annual report lists more instructors for the season (thirty-four), so the remaining registers are either missing or were not submitted by the individual instructors.

* Total number of men in camp (number of Canadian- and British-born/"foreign-born"). These are the categories employed in the instructors' registers.

** When the # men in camp is a range, the mean is used.

*** I calculated 3,491 total (using the mean for ranges) divided by nineteen camps (the number of camps with data).

THE "PLEASURES AND DIVERSIONS" OF READING AND LITERATURE FOR CITIZENSHIP

Frontier College shifted quite dramatically away from its initial identity as a "reading camp" association during the 1910s and 1920s. However, as in the first two decades of the century, the number of workers reached during the 1920s through the reading room function of the college, while impossible to estimate, was certainly greater than the number reached through classroom instruction, as table 3.1 amply demonstrates. The 1923 annual report notes that for the eighteen thousand workers in forty-six different Frontier College camps, the organization sent out five hundred books of fiction (one book for every thirty-six men), twenty-six phonographs and "several hundred records," fifty-one "leading Canadian dailies" in both French and English, and seven thousand magazines.[114]

Despite the association's shift away from the library and reading room models, it relied on the Ontario Travelling Libraries even into the 1920s, particularly in camps where there were large numbers of English-speaking workers. The problem of lost books continued to plague the association, a fact that in some cases seems to testify to their popularity. A government account of books missing from libraries sent to the Whirlpool and Forebay, Ontario, camps in 1921, for instance, lists one hundred eighteen titles. In response to the problem, Fitzpatrick wrote to W.O. Carson, the Superintendent of Travelling Libraries, to apologize for what seemed to him to be a case of fugitive but not ill-intentioned reading. The library at the Forebay camp at the Chippewa canal had been "much used" and was "very popular." When the summer instructor left for the season, he stored the books, and before the winter instructor arrived "the boxes were broken into and the books were carried off to the bunkhouses and read there." When the new instructor arrived, he collected most but not all of the fugitive titles: "There is no doubt that good use was made of the books firstly under an instructor and secondly when they were supposed to be out of the men's reach. Public money was not wasted even if they are not returned. The only trouble is that men did not return them when read."[115]

The list of missing titles reflects what had become by the early 1920s, partly due to Fitzpatrick's urging, the relatively mixed character of the Ontario Travelling Libraries: nineteenth-century romances and adventure tales such as Sir Walter Scott's *Ivanhoe* (1820) and Robert

Louis Stevenson's *Treasure Island* (1883) mingled with Edward Rice Burrough's tremendously popular novel *Tarzan of the Apes* (1912) and Robert Service's bestselling poems *Songs of a Sourdough* (1907) (two copies of which went missing). Service's book comprises sentimental and darkly humorous poems of the Klondike Gold Rush, the best-known of which today are "The Cremation of Sam McGee" and "The Shooting of Dan McGrew." Service's use of rhyming couplets, colourful characters, and workers' voices contributed to their early-twentieth-century popularity as oral texts that were shared aloud. His poems tend to romanticize the frontier while warning of its moral dangers and, in the style of Ralph Connor, idealizing the worker's absent home. In "The Shooting of Dan McGrew," for instance, the speaker contrasts the mysterious saloon-frequenting woman "known as Lou" to the figure of the wife, who is identified with home and hearth:

> Were you ever out in the Great Alone, when the moon was awful clear,
> And the icy mountains hemmed you in with a silence you most could *hear*;
> With only the howl of a timber wolf, and you camped there in the cold,
> A half-dead thing in a stark, dead world, clean mad for the muck called gold;
> While high overhead, green, yellow and red, the North Lights swept in bars –
> Then you've a haunch what the music meant ... hunger and night and the stars.
>
> And hunger not of the belly kind, that's banished with bacon and beans;
> But the gnawing hunger of lonely men for a home and all that it means;
> For a fireside far from the cares that are, four walls and a roof above;
> But oh! so cramful of cosy joy, and crowned with a woman's love;
> A woman dearer than all the world, and true as Heaven is true –
> (God! how ghastly she looks through her rouge, – the lady that's known as Lou).[116]

Depending as they do on the metaphorical evacuations performed via their figuration of the frontier as the "Great Alone," Service's depictions of the northwest enact what Lorenzo Veracini calls "perception transfer" – the disavowal of Indigenous presence – while emphasizing the authenticity of the speaker's claim to his "four walls."[117] Service's poems thus communicate the settler values central to Frontier College's larger Canadianization project, while figuring the white labourer as a source of potentially valuable moral sense for the nation.

That materials such as Service's collection were only a minor element of the Frontier College pedagogical toolkit by the 1920s demonstrates the association's diminished commitment to the idea that citizenship could be cultivated through individual encounters with idealized representations of home in fiction and poetry; however, as the considerable quantity of poetry in the *Handbook* suggests, this does not mean that the association abandoned the idea that imaginative literature could function as a valuable resource for *guided* citizenship education. As I note above, Fitzpatrick's requests in the early 1920s to the federal government for funding offered fluency in English or French, knowledge of "folk and other songs," and acquaintance with "Canadian citizenship" and "Canadian and Canadien literature" as means of dispelling the "pernicious doctrine of agitators." A spring 1923 editorial in *The Globe* renders Fitzpatrick's plea to government in these words: "The instructor is a leader in the adult study groups formed at the close of the work day. This gives him opportunity to popularize both in song and story the best in Canadian literature. Selected passages of Shakespeare are dramatized, as well as renderings given of the quaint folk songs, both French and English, of the earlier life of the Provinces. All of which serves to strengthen a common Canadian sentiment." While many scholars have shown how Canadian cultural forms, and English Canadian literature in particular, became important to the purpose of liberal democracy in the context of the Cold War, almost no attention has been paid to the pre- and inter-war instrumentalization of Canadian cultures in the war against socialism.[118]

At the same time, the continued recreational use of fiction and poetry in ways that exceeded the association's oversight suggests the importance of the leisure cultures that workers themselves developed in camps with the aid of Frontier College materials. Labourer-teachers sometimes commented on the reading tastes of the workers in their camps, and, as had been the case since the inception of the association, they reported that those who could read in English preferred popular narratives of adventure and sport such as the novels of Zane Grey, the poems of Robert Service, or the tales in the American pulp magazines *Western Story Magazine* (1919–49) and *Top-Notch Magazine* (1910–37).[119] In *The Bunkhouse Man*, Edmund Bradwin confirms, in rather lofty rhetoric, the appeal of popular narratives of adventure in the camps: "Illiterate men who crowd the shanty and the bunkhouse are heartened not by annals of Arthur's court, with chivalry in profusion, or of recorded warriors in epic strife at Troy, but from the versatile doings of one with many human excellences, who shapes his deeds to the commoner sounds of the woods and the camps."[120] Bradwin's analysis of camp life also suggests that there was an existing leisure culture in the camps that such popular narratives could complement rather than supplant: "In surroundings such as these, tales abound of that mystical superman, Paul Bunyan, that forest Zeus, arbiter in all things, great and small, that comprise the days and work of the campman. What with the numerous episodes fittingly recounted of his titan accomplishments, surpassing as they do all others in the experience of man – his mighty feats, however, embellished always with a humanness befitting life and the lowly ways of camps, he has long remained the patron revered of all good bushmen."[121] Other instructors confirmed these middlebrow tastes. Anson Stokes claimed that his library of fifty books was "looked over by a surprising number" of the British-born workers at his Fort William, Ontario, camp. According to Stokes, "some of the most read" titles included histories for schoolchildren such as *Richard III*, *In the Days of Alfred the Great*, and *The Life of General Brock*, as well as the bestselling 1880 novel *Ben-Hur: A Tale of the Christ*.[122]

The 1923 report of James Stewart Daly, whose CNR extra gang in British Columbia was (unusually) populated almost entirely by British- and Canadian-born workers, offers a rare view of the continued value of the reading room function in this period. According to the camp roadmaster, W.O. Eagleson, "the men have stayed longer on this gang than on other gangs where we have no reading car." The labourers who added notes to Daly's report, such as William Acton, commend the reading car as a "fine change after a hard day's work." Another labourer (whose name is not clear) reiterates this point: "It was a great relief for me at night to get away from the bunk car and to go up to the 'Wisdom Box,' which was always bright, and pleasant and well-supplied with magazines." "Diversion more than instruction seemed to be what the men required," Daly's report notes, adding that in this regard the gramophone served a purpose as important as novels, magazines, and newspapers. The reading car gave the men a chance to "get away from the smelly stuffy bunk-cars," while offering them "some of the pleasures and diversions which every body of men should have."[123] British- and Canadian-born workers, it seems, were owed "pleasures and diversions"; non-British immigrant workers were not. Non-British immigrant workers were an increasingly managed population during the 1920s, and their encounter with printed materials was not to be left to the field of "leisure" but rather to be guided, monitored, evaluated, and linked up to nascent conceptions of the national citizen.

4

"Red" Literacy and Counter-Literacy in Relief Camps for the Unemployed, 1930–1936

This chapter turns to the economically and socially turbulent period of the 1930s. After the onset of the Depression, the work of Frontier College was brought into increasing proximity with the state imperatives forged by the crisis of hegemony that followed the economic fallout. The new context for Frontier College efforts was the relief camps for single unemployed men operated throughout the first half of the decade by the Department of National Defence (DND). The conditions that prompted relief camps and that were to be found in them put the association's pedagogy for liberal citizenship under stress for two reasons: because they belied the promise of individual progress and democratic participation that had long formed the core of the association's work, and because the unemployed movement appropriated the nascent idiom of citizenship to seek the state's acknowledgment of its grievances. In this context, the new Frontier College principal (after 1931), Edmund Bradwin, placed a renewed focus on the literary text as a means to turn citizenship towards moral culture and individual reflection and away from its status as a political identity attached to particular entitlements. In camps where individual freedom was restricted, the abstracted type attached by narrative force to the state that one finds in the *Handbook* lost its appeal. In its place, literary culture came to assume its highest prophylactic function for the association: appealing to the Arnoldian idealism that had shaped his mentor, Alfred Fitzpatrick, Bradwin showed little of his predecessor's tolerance for more popular literary forms, opting instead to emphasize the transcendence, introspection, liberty, and sentimental community afforded by poetry. Such uses of the literary were particularly important in the context of the relief camps, which witnessed hundreds of strikes during their brief existence from 1932 to 1936. These strikes and the unemployed movement more generally were dependent on a communications system that attempted to put men in isolated camps in dialogue with one another. This chapter explores the dissemination of this radical print in the relief camps and the ways this print appropriated an idiom of citizenship in order to make its claims, while also drawing on the Frontier College's annual reports, its promotional materials, and instructors' correspondence and registers to analyze the association's attempts to counter leftist organizing through the moral culture of literature.

MAINTAINING "LAW, ORDER, PROPERTY, AND SECURITY": CAMPS FOR THE UNEMPLOYED

The nadir of the Great Depression that spread across the industrialized world after the fall of 1929 was reached in Canada in 1932; by 1933, approximately 32 percent of all wage earners (and this does not include salaried workers) in Canada were without work. Roughly fifteen million Canadians – about 15 percent of the population – were dependent on some form of relief by 1933.[1] Canada, a nation reliant on the export of raw and semi-processed goods, particularly wheat, confronted the challenges of new foreign trade barriers, falling commodity prices, and, in the case of wheat, crop failure. The crises in the nation's primary industries – mining, forestry, and agriculture – were first and foremost felt by the workers these sectors employed, workers who tended to be unskilled, immigrant, and mobile. These same workers also tended to constitute the majority of those employed by sectors directly dependent on the primary industries, such as construction (especially railway and road construction and maintenance). As Lorne Brown notes, during more prosperous years these largely immigrant workers "did much of the most undesirable work at lower than average wages and during the Depression they were the first to be sacrificed."[2] In referring to the "sacrifice" of these workers, Brown is observing not simply that unskilled seasonal workers bore the brunt of job losses and wage reductions, but also that they were most directly affected by inadequate provisions for relief. Single male workers were also particularly vulnerable during the Depression because employers and municipal relief programs, where they existed, tended to favour married workers who were supporting families. The federal Conservative government's 1930

Relief Act granted twenty million dollars to relief programs, which were to be administered by municipal and provincial governments, but the act also effectively placed the responsibility for the unemployment crisis on local and provincial authorities. As out-of-work seasonal labourers flocked to urban centres such as Saskatoon, Winnipeg, and Vancouver in the early 1930s, cash-strapped municipalities responded by cutting off relief to non-residents (generally defined as those resident less than one year in a given municipality), a response that had the effect of denying relief to transient, single men, many of whom were recent immigrants.[3]

The way that various levels of government and diverse publics perceived such men in this period is key both to understanding how the crisis of joblessness was represented and to comprehending how the state came to address the crisis.[4] Throughout the late nineteenth and early twentieth centuries, the Canadian state viewed joblessness through the lens of the British neoclassical tradition, which cast unemployment as a problem of individual choice and therefore as subject to the test of "less eligibility." Since one could always choose to work for less money, relief, as fashioned in Britain's 1834 Poor Law, for instance, needed to be less attractive than the lowest-paid work. In Canada, such thinking retained particular relevance well into the twentieth century because the rural frontier remained, at least in theory, a site where work at a lower wage could always be found. Many viewed urban relief programs as contributing to rural depopulation and as instruments that discouraged the settlement of immigrants in rural areas.[5] This thinking was yoked to newer concerns at the onset of the Depression, particularly the fear that jobless, single, transient men, especially those who were immigrants, were communist agitators who needed the firm hand of the state to coerce them into steady employment. In the summer of 1931, federal Minister of Labour Gideon Robertson acknowledged in a letter to Prime Minister R.B. Bennett that "a large portion" of the transient jobless "are of alien origin and communistic sympathies." A 1931 telegram from the mayor of Winnipeg to Robertson echoes this charge, requesting that the RCMP provide officers "to deal with Bolshevistic leaders agitators and their followers" and advocating the "deportation of all undesirables and particularly communistic leaders not only those who are their public speakers but those behind the scenes who are the real dangerous group." Similar sentiments flooded the media in urban centres, such as Vancouver, where the presence of the unemployed was particularly visible.[6]

The various provisions for relief that trickled down from Ottawa during the first two years of the 1930s were meagre at best, largely because the federal government did not wish to assume responsibility for unemployment, a responsibility that it claimed was in any case *ultra vires*. A new federal Relief Act in 1931 attempted to address the problem of transient men in cities through the provision of funds for provincial road-building programs that could be used to funnel the unemployed out of urban centres and into rural camps. Shortly after this, British Columbia, with some help from Ottawa, began to experiment with a relief-camp scheme. The 1932 Relief Act turned to other solutions: the provision of direct relief over relief work, as well as a back-to-the-land program for jobless families.[7] As the Depression persisted, however, the Bennett government finally turned to the remedy the provinces and municipalities had long been recommending – a system of federally administered relief camps for the physically fit, unmarried, transient unemployed.[8] The federal government's eventual adoption of this scheme can be attributed to the forceful suggestions of General Andrew McNaughton, the Chief of Staff of the DND. McNaughton toured the western provinces in the summer of 1932 to assess conditions and subsequently reported that "a movement in Canada of the unemployed was organizing itself, comparing treatment in different centres, demanding conferences with public bodies, putting forward demands for services and standards, and generally becoming a grave menace to law, order, property, and security in the Dominion." The nation's population of mostly young, single, transient unemployed posed not only a political threat but also more abstract threats to masculinity and, by extension, nationhood. McNaughton, a soldier, was alarmed that the single unemployed "in their ragged platoons were the prospective members of Canada's armed forces should the country become involved in war."[9]

McNaughton recommended that "transients be drafted into concentration camps at strategically located centres to serve the different provinces, and in areas where constructive work can be undertaken."[10] In October of 1932 a program of relief camps for able-bodied, single, unemployed men under the authority of the DND commenced: during the first winter, camps employed approximately two thousand men in eastern Canada, at the Halifax and Quebec Citadels and at various sites for TransCanada Airways. The program subsequently expanded, and by the summer of 1936, when the program ceased operation, there had been military and road-building projects in every province but Prince Edward Island, and 167,171 men had passed through 144 different camps, the majority of which were located in the four western provinces.¹¹ Although the federal government insisted that the single unemployed were not legally obliged to enter the DND camps, other means of compulsion – the denial of provincial or municipal relief, the RCMP's enforcement of laws regarding rail riding – were used to corral men into camps.¹² In all of the camps, men were provided with food, lodging, medical care, necessary clothing when they had none of their own, and an issue of tobacco. They were essentially wards of the state, required to work eight hours per day, five and a half days per week, at the rate of twenty cents per day in accordance with a policy of "subsistence with a modicum of work." This meagre remuneration became, according to Lorne Brown, "one of the chief grievances of camp inmates and one of the major criticisms leveled at the camp system by the opposition political parties, the press, and the public."¹³ The payment men received was not intended to function as a wage; not surprisingly, therefore, men in the camps tended to work at a very low level of productivity, a fact aggravated by frustration at policy that favoured manual over machine labour as a means of maximizing the number of days of relief that could be provided on a single project.¹⁴

Political unrest in camps was constant: in four years, there were no fewer than 359 strikes, riots, and demonstrations. The conflict was greatest in British Columbia, due to the prevalence of political organizers in western camps. Between December 1934 and March 1935, the Vancouver-based Relief Camp Workers' Union (RCWU), which was affiliated with the CPC, tried to organize all camps to strike simultaneously for a "living wage." This campaign failed in Ontario, but the result in British Columbia was the 1935 On-to-Ottawa Trek.¹⁵ Between 27 June 1933 and 31 March 1934, there were fifty-seven "significant" relief camp "disturbances" (such as work stoppages), and at least twenty-one camp workers received prison sentences for their involvement in these actions. Moreover, between the opening of the camps and the end of 1935, more than three thousand men (including the entire population of the Long Branch, Ontario, camp) were expelled from the relief camps as punishment for their involvement in camp unrest.¹⁶ Agitation was greatest on the west coast, but numerous grievances fuelled strikes at camps across the country during the first half of the 1930s. At Lac Seul in northwestern Ontario, thirteen disputes were recorded, eight of which involved grievances over the quality of the food supplied.[17] The DND dealt decisively with political agitation in the camps: at Lac Seul, men accused of "talking in a communistic way to others" in a shared bunkhouse were discharged; others were arrested by the Ontario Provincial Police and escorted from the camp.[18] According to Brown, it was neither the poor wages nor camp conditions that were the fundamental sources of unrest but rather "the sense of indignation felt by the men at the denial of their rights and the waste of their lives." However, Brown's study examines the particular case of the Dundurn camp in Saskatchewan, which was a permanent militia camp with facilities for dining, sleeping, and recreation that were much better than in many other DND camps.[19] The list of grievances issued by the workers of the 1935 relief camp strike that coalesced into a cross-country protest known as the On-to-Ottawa Trek illustrates that protest was indeed fuelled by diverse complaints, including objections to the paltry wage. Among other demands, trekkers asked for a minimum of fifty cents per hour (for unskilled work), protection for camp workers under the Workmen's Compensation Act, the federal provision of a system of non-contributory unemployment insurance, the end of DND control over the camps, and the use of democratically elected committees in each camp.[20] DND control of the camps was clearly a major source of complaint: although camp administrators did not wear military uniforms and a strict code of military discipline was not enforced in the camps, certain civil rights were curbed. The right to make appeals for redress was limited by Section 353 of the Policy and Instructions for the Administration of Unemployment Relief Camps for Single Homeless and Unemployed Men, which proscribed appeals "bearing the signature of more than one complainant" or authored by "organized committees."[21]

"RED" LITERACY AND THE EMERGENT SOCIAL CITIZEN

In his memoir of the 1930s, Ronald Liversedge claims that relief camps did not engender a "'lost generation' philosophy" among the unemployed; on the contrary, he asserts that the camps were "places to rest and recuperate between active forays, but above all they were schools. In those bunkhouses, there were more reading Marx, Lenin, and Stalin, than there were reading girlie magazines."[22] Whether or not this is accurate is debatable, but it is certainly clear that the DND camps were sites of active contest, especially in British Columbia. In the camps, the uses of print culture became extraordinarily politicized.

A large proportion of the unrest in the DND-administered relief camps can be attributed to communist activity. Unlike its craft union counterparts, the CPC during the early 1930s tackled the crisis of joblessness directly, largely though its Workers' Unity League (WUL). The party entered the labour movement in 1930 with the creation of the WUL, which never rivalled the craft union movement in size but which nevertheless led the majority of the strikes that occurred between 1930 and 1934. The WUL endured for six years, a period during which it assumed central importance to the organizational structure of the CPC, which was declared illegal in 1931.[23] Following Comintern directives to unite employed and unemployed workers, the CPC attached its newly created National Unemployed Workers' Association (NUWA) to the WUL in 1930. In 1931, the WUL mounted a national campaign pertaining to the issues affecting the growing unemployed population, which included a mass petition that called for a range of state reforms, including, most notably, a call for the state provision of non-contributory unemployment insurance. This bill garnered 94,000 signatures during the first four months of 1931 and was subsequently delivered by WUL delegates to Prime Minister R.B. Bennett. In February of that same year, some fifty thousand people participated in the Comintern's International Day of Struggle against joblessness. However, the WUL probably never organized more than forty thousand workers, of whom about two-thirds were jobless and only a small fraction of whom (5 to 6 percent) were CPC members. Primarily supported by Finnish- and Ukrainian-born workers, the CPC, through the WUL and NUWA, actively recruited Asian workers who were spurned by bodies such as the Vancouver Trades and Labour Council. The affiliation of jobless organizations may also have helped the CPC attract more elusive Anglo-Canadian members in this period: these grew as a proportion of membership (from about 5 percent to about 25 percent) between 1929 and 1934.[24]

Underground as a result of state proscriptions after 1931, the CPC took the NUWA out of the WUL in March 1932 and created a formally independent body, the National Council of Unemployed Councils (NCUC). John Manley observes that this new body "set cadres the task of convincing the unemployed that one did not have to be a 'red or a Marxist' to join the new organization's permanent 'block' and 'neighbourhood' councils, and freed them to work within reformist organizations in appropriate circumstances." However, if west coast organizers, who already had a thriving movement, did not initially welcome this shift, there were 114 block councils in the Vancouver area with an active membership of over two thousand by the beginning of 1933. The shift enabled the CPC to make some gains in cities where it had experienced little success and to organize mass nationwide events, such as the 1933 National Hunger March to Ottawa.²⁵ Wary of the international rise of fascism, the underground CPC adopted a united front strategy in 1933, which obligated it to conciliate and collaborate with enemies of fascism from across the liberal-left political spectrum and deepened its connections to non-communist organizations. John Manley notes that this approach developed more rapidly in the unemployed movement than in any other area. In August of 1934, for instance, delegates to the British Columbia–based and CPC-affiliated RCWU meeting recommended that "the struggle against the relief camp system be integrated with the struggle against fascism."²⁶ A 1935 shift in CPC strategy, however, meant that the party had more or less abandoned the unemployed movement by mid-decade. In this context it was crucial that the RCWU's efforts to bring pressure to bear on the provincial and federal governments – efforts that resulted in the single most significant national protest movement of the Depression years, the 1935 On-to-Ottawa-Trek – garnered support across a wide political spectrum that included social democratic bodies such as the Co-operative Commonwealth Federation.²⁷

Through a national network of Unemployed Councils; a colourful culture of protest that included strikes, rallies, and marches; and a radical network of print, which included the *Relief Camp Worker* (1934–36), various regional iterations of a paper called the *Unemployed Worker* and *The Agitator*, an RCWU paper illicitly distributed in the DND camp at Dundurn, Saskatchewan during the winter of 1935-1936, CPC affiliates were significant forces in the unemployed movement of the early 1930s.²⁸ The largest of these groups of unemployed workers was the Vancouver-based RCWU. The RCWU moved under the CPC umbrella in the summer of 1933, when it also developed a charter and a constitution. The *Relief Camp Worker* and other organizational tools, particularly petitions circulated by hand, aided the RCWU in its efforts to communicate with unemployed workers in the camps of British Columbia and beyond in order to garner support for tactics such as work stoppages. In the spring of 1935, at a conference in

Kamloops, the RCWU adopted a formal set of demands regarding relief camps and called for a spring strike that would culminate in Vancouver early the following month. In this new context, the *Relief Camp Worker* assumed a new importance to the RCWU's communications strategy. The paper carried the news of the conference and the RCWU's seven key demands to relief camp inmates across the province, accompanied by a call for all union members to participate in the imminent strike.[29] The appeal ushered forth the events that would culminate in the trek to Ottawa: bolstered by constant updates, appeals, and exhortations in the pages of the *Relief Camp Worker* and in the daily strike bulletins issued by the publishing section of the Strike Committee, the RCWU was able to call almost two thousand unemployed workers to Vancouver in the days following the camp walkout on 4 April 1935. What followed was the beginning of the end of the relief camp system: in the wake of fruitless negotiations with Premier Thomas "Duff" Patullo, 831 trekkers departed Vancouver on CPR freight trains, bound for Ottawa and seeking an audience with R.B. Bennett. Bennett, however, had no intention of greeting such a contingent in Ottawa and even less desire to see it pass through radicalized Winnipeg. He ordered the RCMP to halt the trekkers in Regina. A small delegation that included strike lead Arthur "Slim" Evans continued on to Ottawa to make the demands of the trekkers heard, but Bennett was intransigent. The ensuing Regina Riot left one member of the Regina Police dead and many trekkers and police wounded.[30]

A centrifugal movement with a limited communications apparatus, the RCWU relied heavily on the *Relief Camp Worker* to interpret the movement and to rally isolated workers whose mobility was uniquely limited by the relief camp system. According to Victor Howard, the *Relief Camp Worker* was particularly important to the RCWU organizational efforts that preceded and accompanied the events of 1935: the bulletin "found its way into every camp in the province, either by post or in the knapsacks of couriers. Its pages conveyed articles on camp conditions, on union meetings and programmes, on economics."[31] Two of the five elected members of the RCWU executive were devoted to the work of communications – the Literature Agent and the Press Agent – a fact that attests to the centrality of this work to the organization's efforts.[32] Moreover, as the attention garnered by the bulletins issued by Communist-affiliated groups indicates, bulletins were effective means of spreading information. In late 1933, when the RCWU was barely off the ground, officers in British Columbia camps identified the organization to McNaughton and lamented that its bulletin "in spite of all our efforts appears to reach most of the camps." This fact is particularly striking because, as Lorne Brown notes, the circulation of such radical print faced significant obstacles:

> Anyone caught attempting to organize or distributing RCWU leaflets would be expelled from camp immediately and blacklisted throughout the DND camp system. Such people would also be on blacklists in the cities which meant they would be unable to obtain relief. Many were imprisoned, usually for vagrancy. Nonetheless, the organizing continued and took the form of secret "bush committees" in the camps, which would distribute leaflets, coordinate and generalize individual grievances, and provide leadership in strikes and other actions of this nature. When they were discovered and blacklisted they would try to enter other camps under assumed names. A skillful organizer might last some months before the authorities finally caught up with him.[33]

Federal, provincial, and municipal authorities watched the *Relief Camp Worker* carefully: when one of the editors of the bulletin set up an office on West Hastings Street in Vancouver, police constables appeared regularly to pick up copies; police informants used the paper to gather information; and the bulletin was read aloud in the House of Commons on more than one occasion in order to sound the warning bell about unrest in the relief camps.[34]

This particular surveillance and repression belongs to a wider context that chapter 2 discusses: in the wake of the Winnipeg General Strike of 1919, amendments to the Criminal Code replaced the earlier, temporary provisions (under the War Measures Act) that had rendered socialist organizations and their publications illegal. Added to the Criminal Code in 1927, Section 98, as Andrea Hasenbank puts it, "operates most pointedly on the circulation of ideas within the public sphere: ideological, not physical, association is the true locus of criminality."[35] Not repealed until 1936, Section 98 rendered organizations attempting to bring about "governmental, industrial, or economic change" by "use of force, violence, terrorism, or physical injury to person or property" unlawful, while specifically targeting the production and circulation of radical print. According to subsection 8,

[a]ny person who prints, publishes, edits, issues, circulates, sells, or offers for sale or distribution any book, newspaper, periodical, pamphlet, picture, paper, circular, card, letter, writing, print, publication or document of any kind in which is taught, advocated, advised or defended, or who shall in any manner teach, advocate, or advise or defend the use, without authority of law, of force, violence, terrorism or physical injury to person or property, or threats of such injury, as a means of accomplishing any governmental, industrial or economic change, or otherwise, shall be guilty of an offence and liable to imprisonment for not more than twenty years.[36]

As Dennis G. Molinaro details in his study of Section 98, the CPC's focus on the unemployed movement in the early 1930s prompted the federal government to coordinate an effort to declare the CPC an unlawful organization in violation of Section 98. In the summer of 1931, a police raid involving the RCMP, the Ontario Provincial Police, and Toronto police succeeded in arresting party leader Tim Buck, as well as eight other party members. Due to the emphasis on seditious print in Section 98, the raid focused not simply on arresting party members but also on the seizure of radical print. The Toronto office of the CPC paper the *Worker* was raided, and "books, membership lists, and letters between party members praising the Soviet Union, in addition to Marxist literature from the Soviet Union, were used as evidence."[37] Print was thus at the heart of the political contests of this period, a fact that is crucial to understanding the charged context in which the *Relief Camp Worker* and papers like it circulated.

As in other parts of the industrialized world, the party paper – and print in general – played a key role in the political cultures of Canadian workers during the early twentieth century.[38] In choosing the newspaper form, of course, workers were to a significant extent mimicking a print culture whose values ran counter to their own, a fact that has caused significant debate in print-culture studies regarding leftist periodical culture. Nicholas Thoburn, for instance, declines to include periodicals as radical "anti-books" because to warrant this designation "would require a self-critical and disruptive relation with the organizations and audiences with which media are associated ... that is inimical to the consolidating tendencies of movement media." Unlike the pamphlet, the leftist periodical's "correlation between movement and medium" renders it "just that little bit too obedient, 'tiresome' even – ordered and contained by the requirements of a movement."³⁹ Others have been more sanguine about the movement paper, particularly those who focus on the material particularities of its production and hence of its circulation. Unlike the large weekly and daily papers of the early twentieth century, the movement paper tended to be mimeographed in relatively small quantities (not more than five thousand copies per print run), produced via the somewhat crude technology of a typed stencil attached to a rotating cylinder (or cylinders), into which paper was fed by hand.⁴⁰ Writing at the end of the Second World War, Theodor Adorno applauded such mimeographed papers as forms of "older media," which, "not designed for mass production, take on a new timeliness: that of exemption and improvisation. They alone could outflank the united front of trusts and technology. In a world where books have long lost all likeness to book, the real book can no longer be one. If the invention of the printing press inaugurated the bourgeois era, the time is at hand for its repeal by the mimeograph, the only fitting, the unobtrusive means of dissemination."⁴¹ While Adorno's sentiments are shaped by his loathing of mass culture in any form, his privileging of the mimeographed paper is valuable insofar as it points to that which distinguishes this medium from its mass-produced counterpart: the simple technology involved in this small-scale production meant that political organizations like the RCWU could either own the means of production or easily find small, sympathetic printing companies to do the work for them. Movement papers are also, as Régis Debray argues, shaped by the interpretive imperatives of the movement in ways that both limit their potential audience and attempt to establish extraordinary identification in their readers: "Mainstream newspapers, product of a media conglomerate, are conceived as black boxes: events come in and information goes out. A class or party newspaper plays a different role: transforming a conception of the world into small change, a philosophical system into everyday slogans. Events are centralized by, and under, the idea; individual energies by the leadership. In contrast to the paper-as-mirror, the paper-as-guide fulfils the role assigned by Kant to the schema: intermediary and interpreter between the pure concept and the appearance of things."⁴²

The *Relief Camp Worker* was produced with great resourcefulness: before the RCWU set up an office with a typewriter on West Hastings Street, volunteers, armed with one page worth of material each, would "spread out over the city," looking for a typewriter and scrounging up stencils so that the eight typed pages could be mimeographed by a company on Cordova Street.[43] Produced weekly on thin foolscap, each page of the folio measuring 21.5 by 35.5 centimetres, the paper sold for three cents per copy – one cent more than the daily *Toronto Evening Star* in the same period – but each copy could of course be shared by many readers in a camp.[44] Editor (and RCWU executive member) Ronald Liversedge recalls that late 1934, in particular, was

> a busy time, with much correspondence coming in, wonderful reports from the camps all over the province, testifying to the high degree of organization which had been reached. Smokey Cumber, our president, wrote the editorial for the paper, and I did the rest. We would usually have two pages of camp reports, or excerpts from reports, thus, the boys in camp were kept up to date on what was going on in the other camps, some news of our prison population, trade union news, maybe some international news of special interest to us, financial statements.[45]

Although the RCWU executive seems to have maintained tight control over the mandate and content of the bulletin, material was provided by RCWU organizers, mostly from British Columbia but also from Alberta, and editors constructed feedback loops in the form of "Camp Reports" and a "Question Box," both of which strove to make camp workers present in each issue. The most obvious instance of reader-contributed material was the regular (generally two-page) "Camp Reports" section, which included news about camp conditions, impending strikes or other labour actions, gains made through collective action, appreciation of RCWU literature, and requests for more reading material, such as the one sent in by a Revelstoke camp in 1934, which notes the urgent need for "good literature in camp" because it "plays a prominent part in the education of the workers, bringing them to the point of taking up the issue of the class struggle."[46] The RCWU communications circuit thus attempted to both meet and provoke demand for radical print.

In addition to being more dialogic than the major Canadian dailies of the period, the *Relief Camp Worker* is more diachronic in its attempts to function as what Debray calls a "paper-as-guide": although much of its news was of the moment, it also includes a regular "Workers' Education" column that elucidates a chronological "working-class history" in a series of articles that move from the prehistoric world to the present, always linking changes in the means of production to "different methods" in the "social life" of humankind.[47] These columns render digestible the theoretical literature of Marxism for the camp worker, illustrating dialectical materialism via practical examples in world history.

Although it mimicked the physical appearance of a bourgeois newspaper, it also functioned as a corrective to the more powerful mainstream press. In October of 1934 a column titled "According to the Yellow Press" appeared, calling itself "a review" from the worker's point of view "of anything of note that has appeared in the capitalist press."[48] Later, in the context of the 1935 strike, contributors to the *Relief Camp Worker* refuted the claims of the mainstream press (to which camp workers gathered in Vancouver presumably had increased access), as well as of the "fascist" leaflets distributed at RCWU events and gatherings that suggested, for instance, that "Moscow agents and agitator leaders" were leading the strike without the broad support of workers in the camps.[49] As a further means of countering the mainstream press, the *Relief Camp Worker* actively promotes an alternative communist reading culture, of which it, of course, formed a part. Beginning in the fall of 1934, it began running occasional notices in response to the fact that "many workers have written in asking for literature." The accompanying list of publications (with prices) consists mainly of Canadian, American, and Soviet periodicals – including the CPC's *The Worker* and *The Young Worker* – all of which could be procured from the RCWU office in Vancouver.

As many studies of interwar leftist periodical culture have demonstrated, visual and literary cultures were tremendously important to the rallying work of the movement paper. Like many communist and leftist periodicals from this decade, the *Relief Camp Worker* employs visual culture that drew on the deep well that was the iconography of radical protest during the Depression. Liversedge notes in his memoir of the 1930s that executive member John Matts was largely responsible for the paper's illustrations, which would have been added to the master stencil with a stylus. His "workers were always depicted as upright, honest, clear-eyed, strong-jawed specimens of humanity and his police were always depicted as the Neanderthal type in boy scout hats, clutching a big club in big hairy paws."[50] Many of the cartoons, particularly those published during the strike activity of 1935, portray workers in the plural – massed together, placards held high – rather than the singular proletarian type of much leftist iconography in this period.

While the *Relief Camp Worker* is not as literary as some other CPC organs from this period, such as *Masses*, it did, in the tradition of the workers' paper, regularly include poems, either anonymously authored or submitted by readers. These poems are not hived off or presented in a special "literary" section; instead, poetry was treated like any other form of communication. Cary Nelson contends that the work of interpreting poems in leftist movement papers entails a sense of their "rapid use" and "their capacity to participate in history" rather than "their supposed capacity to transcend it":

> Given poetry's history of identification with transcendentalizing (or at least transhistorical) idealization, there is, of course, a real tension built into its publication in the transitory medium of newsprint. Newspapers themselves sometimes marked poetry's difference by placing it in a special box, but that difference was also complicated by poetry's multiple relations with other items in the paper. When the *Daily Worker* put poems on its features page – along with letters to the editor, notices of events, and recipes – poetry's difference did not prevent it from being seen as an object designed for practical use in everyday life.[51]

Poems in the *Relief Camp Worker* were meant to be read and used. Like the correspondence from the camps and reports of RCWU meetings and rallies, the poems focus not on the privacy of an individual experience or emotion but rather on camp life or on the more general trials of the unemployed. A poem like "In Regina City on Dominion Day" offers a good example of the way that verse was turned to the purpose of shaping workers' understanding of a current event. Published in the immediate wake of the return of the Ottawa trekkers to Vancouver, it interprets the riot for western workers who might understand it as a defeat, turning the confrontation at Regina into a noble and controlled "orderly retreat" of "strikers returning to the camps / Showing the way like shining lamps." In other cases, poems are explicitly and self-consciously treated as an alternative means of narrating current events: the "poetically inclined" worker who reported on a strike in an Oyama, British Columbia, camp in the 14 March 1935 issue opted to recount the struggle in his camp in rhyming quatrains.[52]

Moreover, like the forms of communication they complement, the poems invoke rallying cries that connect the paper's voice to what Nelson identifies as the larger "revolutionary chorus" that connected diverse workers' protest cultures during this period. "Workers in the Slave Camps," submitted to the paper by "F.W.M. in Camp 341," concludes in a typically imperative mood:

> Organise and struggle
> Struggle with all your might,
> Then will come our System
> So, comrades, on with the FIGHT![53]

As Nelson notes, the "revolutionary chorus" of which F.W.M.'s rallying cry forms a part was a highly intertextual site where workers' chants, left poetry, fiction, drama, journalism, manifestos, editorials, political speeches, and visual media all met. Poetry had a distinct role to play in this chorus: although, as I have noted, the *Relief Camp Worker*'s poems were clearly meant to be read and used like any other element in the paper, they also drew on the particular richness of imagery, figure, and rhyme in ways that borrowed from and added to the verbal and visual density of a protest culture of chants, songs, and visual iconography. For example, while most of the poems in the *Relief Camp Worker* are clearly directed at camp workers themselves, one of the most poignant, J.W. Barrett's "The Camp Striker," attempts to make relief camp conditions visible and hearable to a public in the context of the strike that first gathered in Vancouver in April of 1935:

> I've tired of the awe,
>   Of the army law,
> And the life of a galley slave;
>   And I strike in my might,
> For freedom and right,
>   From the chains of a living grave.
>
> Why should they pen
>   Ten thousand men,
> In camps that you cannot see?
>   Why should I wait,
> For my future fate,
>   In this secret soldiery?
>
> You'll never know
>   The world of woe

I've suffered through the years,
  'Till you've heard the tales
Of my souls travails,
That ring in your listening ears.⁵⁴

With its powerful apostrophe of the residents of Vancouver, its interrogative plea, its insistence that the unseen reader will "never know" the speaker's troubles, its summoning of the reader's "listening ears," and its use of common symbols of oppression, "The Camp Striker" leverages a power that was crucial to the strikers' efforts to secure public support and collective mobilization.

Some of the RCWU's seven key demands lent themselves to poetic rendering better than others. The paper's poems are full of alliterative claims for "work and wages," condemnation of the military administration of the camps (which creates a "secret soldiery"), and rhetorically powerful appeals to slavery, which bear a strong residual connection to the enslavement of African Americans and the more general denial of liberal freedoms that slavery represented.⁵⁵ "Work for wages" and the cessation of military control figured among the seven demands articulated at the 1935 Kamloops conference that preceded the Vancouver strike of that same year; however, other demands – the protection of the Compensation Act, the provision of first-aid supplies, the recognition of democratically elected workers' committees, the introduction of non-contributory unemployment insurance, the restoration of workers' right to vote, and the repeal of Section 98 of the Criminal Code and Sections 41 and 42 of the Immigration Act – seem to have offered less fruitful poetic opportunities.⁵⁶ Nonetheless, these other demands made their rounds through the paper in editorials, cartoons (frequently appearing on placards held high), and reports of various kinds.

Together, these demands form "the idea" Debray refers to in his discussion of the movement paper; although they are presented through the diverse verbal and visual forms the paper employs, they meet under a single sign: the citizen. As the *Relief Camp Worker* never failed to notice, camp workers were citizens stripped of the liberal freedoms the state ostensibly guaranteed. John Matts's cartoon for the 16 May 1935 issue presents this argument in the form of a striking worker whose placard states simply and without exclamatory punctuation, "All we want is food and our rights as citizens" (see figure 4.1). One of Liversedge's 1934 editorials puts it this way: "The privileges that we are asking are only the same that other industries are already enjoying. Why are we deprived of these rights? Are we not, as Canadian citizens, entitled to such?"[57] Liversedge's rhetorical strategy is effective: he is asking only for what others already have, and in pursuing what are framed as the basic rights of Canadian citizenship, he casts his demands in the moderate language of liberal rights and freedoms, while combatting a rhetorical tendency during the 1930s to pit "reds" and "radicals" against "citizens."[58] Yet his strategy was not entirely ingenuous: alongside many other leftist organizations in this decade, the RCWU was actually demanding *more* than the state had ever conceded. British Columbia workers had been covered by a Compensation Act since 1902, but there was no comparable federal legislation in the 1930s, and unemployment insurance was not introduced by the federal government until 1940 (and it was not non-contributory).[59] The RCWU was thus pushing not only for "rights" conceived as they are in classic liberal theory (civil and political rights, such as the right to vote), but also for a new kind of right – the right to state provision for social security, or what sociologist T.H. Marshall, in the context of postwar Britain, theorized as the social rights of citizenship.[60] These articulations of citizenship's relation to social rights sit in marked contrast to rights as they are understood in Frontier College's 1919 *Handbook for New Canadians*. In the *Relief Camp Worker*, citizenship is a collective practice defined by social needs that the state has an obligation to meet; in the *Handbook*, citizenship is an identity defined by an individual's duties to the state and by the civil and political rights that shape these duties.

"COMRADESHIP," COUNTER-LITERACY, AND MORAL CULTURE

As we have seen, Alfred Fitzpatrick worked tirelessly thorough the 1910s and 1920s to bring the work of Frontier College to the attention of the Department of Immigration and Colonization, the Department of Labour, the Prime Minister's Office, and the RCMP. A new opportunity to attach its work to the federal government arose in the early 1930s in the form of the DND relief camps. Even prior to the establishment of DND relief camps in 1932, the various relief camp schemes that had operated across the country since 1930 had come to serve as what James Struthers calls the "natural state substitute" for the bush camps that had been so crucial to the primary industries

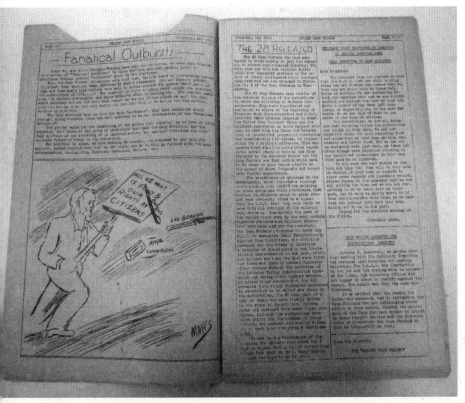

Figure 4.1 "Fanatical Outbursts," *Relief Camp Worker*, 16 May 1935

that were the heart of the Canadian economy.[61] It is not surprising, then, that Frontier College soon found a role for itself in government-run relief camps. Moreover, in taking up the call to offer services in government camps, Frontier College was participating in what John Manley identifies as a broad middle-class effort to "ensure that the CPC did not enjoy unopposed access to the 'native' unemployed." Its work in this period might be compared to the undertakings of the YMCA, the YWCA, Women's Institutes, the Imperial Order of Daughters of the Empire, Junior Leagues, or the Rotarians, all of whom used "sporting activities, training schemes, and make-work projects" to maintain a distance between the jobless and radical organizers of the unemployed.[62] More often than not, governments employed voluntary organizations to spearhead entertainment and leisure efforts in the relief camps; however, state apparatuses were also put to work in new ways that acknowledged the need not simply for remedial education or occupational training but also for what Gordan Selman calls "personal self-development and the cultivation of the liberal arts": in British Columbia, for example, the Department of Education funded classes in folk dancing, commercial art, and singing, as well as academic correspondence work, for relief camp residents.[63]

The Depression years also witnessed more general development and expansion in the field of adult education. In tandem with the period's radical organizing and a flourishing socialist and communist print culture, strong liberal institutions for adult education, many of which employed the instrument of the study group, emerged. During the early 1930s, the Antigonish Movement in eastern Nova Scotia birthed the establishment of credit unions and marketing cooperatives in fishing, agriculture, and housing, all supplemented by study clubs, mass meetings, and rallies. With leadership from Reverend James Tompkins and Reverend Moses Coady of St. Francis Xavier University in Antigonish, the community development and cooperative education principles nourished by this movement functioned as a "middle way" – the "Antigonish Way" – between capitalism and socialism, forces that were aggressively vying for control in the region during the interwar period. A similar "community development" program was developed at McGill University in the late 1930s to serve the anglophone communities of the eastern townships. Many of the first provincial associations of adult educators were also established in the 1930s, including those in Prince Edward Island, Ontario, and Manitoba. These regional developments were complemented by the emergence of what would go on to become a significant national, non-governmental institution in the development of adult education – the Canadian Association for Adult Education (CAAE), founded in 1935. The first director of the CAAE, E.A. ("Ned") Corbett, was formerly the director of the Department of Extension at the University of Alberta and was, like Alfred Fitzpatrick, a former Presbyterian minister influenced by the Social Gospel movement. A nationalist and a fervent promoter of liberal democracy, Corbett actively engaged provincial and federal governments in his visions of participatory citizenship and deeply shaped postwar government programs in the field of citizenship education. Edmund Bradwin attended the founding meeting of the CAAE and served on its board of directors during the 1930s.[64]

At the end of 1931, Ontario's Department of Northern Development began corresponding with Fitzpatrick in order to arrange the placement of Frontier College instructors at relief camps dedicated to the construction of the Trans-Canada Highway. This continued, but by the end of that year, plans for the use of Frontier College instructors in the new DND camps were under way.[65] However, it was not until the spring of 1933 that a formal agreement was reached between the DND and Frontier College. According to the agreement, Frontier College would provide one instructor for "educational and recreational work" to each camp with more than 250 men. The DND would classify these instructors as "clerks," which entitled them to thirty dollars per month, board, and lodging. Any additional Frontier College instructors in a given camp would be classed as "ordinary labourers" and would receive twenty-five cents per day, board, and lodging (generally supplemented by an honorarium from Frontier College). As had long been the case, instructors were to act as labourer-teachers – to toil alongside the men during the day and to teach at night. The DND agreed to pay the cost of transportation for Frontier College staff. Each district was to have a Frontier College-appointed Supervisor of Educational and Recreational Work whose task it would be to direct the work of instructors, to "bring about uniformity," and "generally, to keep up the standard."[66] As Bradwin's correspondence during the 1930s makes clear, this "standard" hinged explicitly on the duty of the labourer-teacher to avoid political discussions. In cases where "decision is unavoidable," Bradwin insisted that instructors "should be found lined up with the officials who carry responsibility at a camp." Frontier College assumed the task of providing books and the DND of furnishing sports equipment (through its "Unemployment Relief Comforts Fund"). Each potential instructor was to complete an application form created by the DND and was required to pass a medical exam prior to employment.[67] By the end of 1933 (seven months after the agreement), Bradwin reported to the DND that he had placed eighty-seven representatives in federal and provincial relief camps during that year. That number declined to fifty-seven during 1934 and 1935 and spiked back up to 165 in 1936, the year that the DND camps were discontinued. Frontier College responded to DND requests for instructors and exercised little control over where they were located. Even though almost one third of the relief camp population was located in British Columbian camps, and even though, as we have seen, strike activity was concentrated in the western camps, Frontier College instructors were directed to Ontario: 76 and 65 percent of its labourer-teachers were sent to Ontario camps in

1933 and 1935, respectively. Bradwin was certainly willing to send men to British Columbia, as his letters to the DND indicate, but General McNaughton seems to have had concerns that Frontier College would "interfere with the educational work being done by the Department of Education in British Columbia."[68]

DND correspondence with Bradwin indicates that the former saw great value in the "wholesome and constructive influence" of labourer-teachers, who worked hard to "re-establish the morale" of the single unemployed.[69] The collaboration between the DND and Frontier College that extended from mid-1933 to mid-1936 demonstrates the extent to which Frontier College, under the new leadership of Edmund Bradwin just as had been the case when Fitzpatrick was principal, desired a formal association with the state. The association's commitment to work in relief camps caused it all manner of administrative and financial difficulties, but it had the advantage of placing Frontier College and its work with adult men in frontier camps in direct view of the federal government.[70]

The role the DND imagined for Frontier College in the relief camps cast the association's task as one that would go beyond the mere physical necessities provided by the state. The task of conserving the "manhood" of the jobless was a priority for countless government officials during the Depression. As we have seen, for example, General McNaughton's motivation for the relief camp scheme was fuelled by a discourse of threatened masculinity. For McNaughton, the challenge of conserving manhood was linked directly to the fact that the unemployed constituted the future ranks of Canada's military. McNaughton's specific concern was undergirded by the more general ways in which the crisis of joblessness challenged what Michael Ekers calls the "normative expectations" that "men should engage in waged work and be individualistic, productive, and physically strong." As Menzies, Adamoski, and Chunn observe, "for men, engagement in paid labour outside the family was key to their claims for civil, political, and social rights and thus to their own status as citizens." Also, unemployment eroded the basis of the distinction common to early-twentieth-century relief between the deserving and the undeserving poor, which "represented the boundary between normative and deviant masculinities."[71] The right to work and to improve one's lot is central to the masculine identity that is at the core of liberalism. The task of Frontier College in the relief camps was thus closely linked not only to its long-standing work of cultivating "healthy and sound

Canadianism," but also to the particular work of preserving the masculinity of the unemployed.

As Edmund Bradwin put it in his 1933 annual report, "unemployment camps confront the people of Canada with a serious situation. Because of the unusual circumstances under which they are working, the men are naturally prone to discontent. Perhaps no other group of unskilled labour requires such careful leadership as the men in the relief camps." In this same report, Bradwin strikes a note that sounded consistently through the Frontier College reports on relief camps: formal educational opportunities were important, but the "lasting factor" of the Frontier College contribution to the DND project was the "personal influence of the instructor himself." Bradwin describes the instructors as "carefully selected," physically fit university students ranging in age from twenty-two to thirty but notes that most important are the "broad human qualities" that make them "companions with their fellow workers and constructive leaders in conserving manhood among the men of the camps." [72] In its selection of the young men who would be tasked with "conserving manhood," Frontier College maintained in this period a preference for the "Canadian and British-born"; however, Bradwin made exceptions for well-educated immigrants or for those who were acceptably "white," such as the Danish-born schoolteacher Alfred Frederickson and the Chinese Canadian grandson of the Canadian missionary known as the "Great Mackay of Formosa."[73]

The "manhood" that Bradwin sought to preserve is presented here as neutral; however, this particular "manhood" had many crucial ideological functions in this period. It served as a "human" and personal alternative to the widely critiqued military administration of the camps, and it privileged individual responsibility over (proscribed) collective action, while simultaneously appropriating the idiom of "comradeship" in order to associate the term with homosocial bonds of friendship and trust that could help the individual overcome trying times. In his July 1935 advice to instructor A.E. Graham, Bradwin spells out the instructor's responsibility to lead by cultivating "contact and influence," "judgement and discretion," while also noting the particular political ends of such behaviour: "In these serious days where there is talk of Trekking and Marching to Ottawa, discussions will arise in a camp. Every representative of Frontier College – no matter what his personal opinion may be – can only take one position, and that is to stand solidly behind constituted authority. If at any time men should be allayed and soothed in their thinking, it is when things are tense. Otherwise fuel is added to the fire and men incited to further action."[74] As many of the documents contained in the annual reports for the 1930s suggest, the defence of "constituted authority" was imagined as working best through the contact and friendship that the labourer-teacher model enabled. By the end of the decade, the college's promotional photographs of workers and instructors bore captions boasting of the "comradeship that comes from association in the day's work."[75]

Of course, a significant challenge that faced this appropriated idiom of comradeship was the fact that Frontier College instructors, despite the labourer-teacher model, had never really experienced camps as workers did. The honoraria that Frontier College granted to instructors over and above the remuneration they received from their camp employers had long distinguished them from their fellow labourers; in the context of the relief camps, where the issue of work for reasonable wages was newly politicized, this difference may have taken on new meaning. As I note above, even those teachers hired by Frontier College to work in the smaller relief camps received honoraria to supplement the camp stipend of approximately six dollars a month. Claims of "comradeship" in this context now seem somewhat questionable.

The goal of "comradeship" represented a considerable shift away from the citizenship education work the association had undertaken in the 1910s and 1920s. The reasons for this are complex. The relief camps visited by Frontier College instructors in the early 1930s housed more British- and Canadian-born men and fewer foreign-born men than the camps the association frequented during the 1920s. For example, in the camps visited in 1933 for which registers exist, the proportion of British- and Canadian-born men was much greater (62.9 per cent) than it had been in the camps visited in the previous decade (31 per cent in 1929) (see figures 3.1 and 4.2). The shift away from citizenship education and the use of the *Handbook* in the context of relief camp work must be understood in this context. However, as many of the instructors' registers from this period indicate, foreign-born men continued to be the most eager students; the muted emphasis on citizenship education might thus have had more diverse causes than simply a smaller proportion of foreign-born men.

Annual reports and instructors' registers from the early 1930s offer ample evidence that labourer-teachers struggled to counter the effects

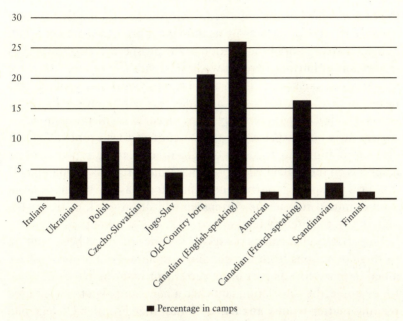

Figure 4.2 Ethnic Composition of Frontier College Camps, 1933. These data are compiled from the forty-one (Barnes to Zimmerman) instructors' registers found in MG 28, I 124, vol. 126, "Registers, 1933," FC-LAC. I used the information given in the bar graph at the end of each register. I did not count the Willard register because he was not stationed in a relief camp.

of "talk from those who have subversive purposes."[76] While the *Handbook* had been put to this end during the 1920s, it was in the context of the relief camps a poor rival for the exhilarating calls to action and immediate political solutions offered by the *Relief Camp Worker*, strike pamphlets, and the like. Lacking in the relief camps were many of the compelling reasons that labourer-teachers had long given for the foreign-born to take up naturalization. The single unemployed who found themselves in relief camps were denied, among other rights, the right that is presented in the *Handbook for New Canadians* as "a privilege and a duty" central to citizenship – the vote: the majority of men in relief camps were effectively disenfranchised because they had not been in the camps long enough to meet the residential qualifications required to vote in federal elections. The Bennett government refused to extend the right of absentee voting to camp inmates, and as the 1935 federal election loomed, this disenfranchisement became one of the central issues around which the RCWU rallied the unemployed.⁷⁷ More generally, the *Handbook*'s liberal narrative of citizenship as individual progress culminating in homeownership bore little relation to the prospects facing the jobless in the camps. Furthermore, as we have seen, the workers who were organizing strike actions in the relief camps vigorously deployed the term "citizen" as a means of articulating their claims to the basic rights and freedoms ostensibly guaranteed by a liberal-democratic society. It is not surprising in such a context that Frontier College chose to diminish its focus on citizenship education in favour of an emphasis on the individual responsibility and fortitude of "manhood." A critical pedagogical instrument in this effort was one that had played a more muted role in the citizenship education work of the 1910s and 1920s: the literary text.

Most DND relief camps possessed libraries that had been built up through donations from surrounding communities. Frontier College aided in this effort as part of its agreement with the DND: in 1934, for example, the association launched a new campaign to solicit used reading matter from Canadians. Noting that Frontier College had distributed fifty-eight thousand books and magazines during 1934, the brochure pleads for "many thousands" more, "particularly illustrated magazines, British weeklies, books of healthy fiction, travel, biography, history, and text books" (see figure 4.3). The 1936 annual report boasts the distribution of eighty-six thousand books and magazines to men in relief camps.⁷⁸ By 1935, the DND had established a box library system in its British Columbia relief camps: during the summer of 1935, each camp in the province had three box libraries, with each box containing "fifty volumes of fiction and ten of educational interest, such as biography, history, travel, drama, etc." The DND concluded that these 180 books were adequate for most camps for three months, at which point the libraries were traded with those of other camps. A 1936 report on the DND relief camps observes that the camps "invariably" possessed libraries of 200 to 350 books.⁷⁹

The demand for reading matter was not simply a Frontier College–generated solution to idleness, although the association received letters from camp superintendents that affirmed the role that reading could play in "keeping the men contented."⁸⁰ With more leisure time on their hands than labourers in conventional work camps possessed, unemployed camp residents avidly sought reading material. As the registers from relief camps demonstrate, there was a great appetite for printed matter, and particularly fiction, in relief camps. A 1935 letter signed by twenty-six men from a Trenton, Ontario, camp expresses appreciation for the "interesting and enjoyable" "works of fiction," but the men clearly hankered for more: "and may we respectfully state that there is not a sufficient number or variety of them to meet our needs. We sincerely solicit your aid in helping us augment and maintain our library and will thankfully receive any volumes that you may send us."[81] Although not perhaps the "healthy fiction" that Frontier College requested in its 1934 campaign, popular genre and pulp fiction, whether in novels or in illustrated magazines such as the American *The Argosy* (1882–1978) and *Detective Story Magazine* (1915-1949), seem to have been especially desired. Instructor Clarence Baker's system of library organization offers a case in point: of the 260 works of fiction in his library, 120 of them were classed as either "Mystery, Horror, and Detective Stories" or "Adventure and Action Stories." Apparently speaking from experience, Baker notes that men must be warned about novels in the library that do not conform to these generic preferences: "It is the business of the Instructor to guard the reader against 'duds,' unsuitable books that will discourage him and keep him from coming for another book. For example, sensational romances by female novelists of the pre-war period should be weeded out and put aside or destroyed." Interestingly, it is not the popular quality of this literature that concerned Baker but rather its assumed femininity. As chapter 1 explores, popular adventure fiction formed part of the earliest libraries of the Canadian Reading Camp Association. By the 1930s, the constant threat of radical print and the growth of the American pulp industry, which peaked in the interwar period and formed part of the tsunami of American periodical publications that flooded the Canadian market in the early twentieth century, combined to create a situation in which Frontier College instructors tolerated reading that would have been dismissed as "sensational" just after the turn of the century. It is harder to say what purpose these serials served for men living in relief camps: the masculine world conjured in pulp genres such as the hard-boiled detective story perhaps offered a reassuring alternative to the emasculation of joblessness.[82]

At the level of the labourer-teacher's selections, and at the level of the principal's office, literary preferences remained distinctly more highbrow. When they mention the active incorporation of imaginative literature into lessons and discussions, instructors' registers from the 1930s offer examples with canonical prestige, such as George Eliot's

Figure 4.3 "Reading Matter for Campmen"

Silas Mariner; John Keats's poem "St. Agnes Eve"; Alfred Lord Tennyson's *The Idylls of the King*; Thomas Carlyle's *On Heroes, Hero Worship, and the Heroic in History*; and the plays of Shakespeare.[83] This embrace of higher-brow literary taste during the 1930s was certainly encouraged by the head office in Toronto. In the early 1930s, Frontier College adopted a new motto, "Vita sine Litteris mors est," meaning "life without letters is dead."[84] The Latin suggests Fitzpatrick's earlier degree-granting ambitions for Frontier College, but in the early 1930s it bore a more direct reference to Bradwin's desire to have labourer-teachers act as "pivots for citizenship, yes, and culture and refinement." Labourer-teachers' final reports often echo such sentiments. Reginald Perry, for example, viewed his task in the Arnoldian terms of bringing "the light of knowledge and truth to men deprived of the ordinary cultural influences of society."[85] While the conception of the literary attached to Frontier College work had from its earliest days been Arnoldian, the tolerance for popular genre fiction and popular sentiment that characterized Fitzpatrick's work in the association's first half-decade contrasts with Bradwin's elitist appeals to the power of literature, which he consistently praised as able to elevate men with its "higher" tone and sentiment. Bradwin's selections were not always highbrow in character, but it is clear that in the relief camp context he was much less interested than Fitzpatrick had been in promoting popular fiction. To men who had time but no freedom, Bradwin offered transcendence, elevation, and introspection.

Bradwin lavished particular attention on poetry as a tool for cultivating the "finer perception" of men. As a response to the particularly challenging conditions that instructors faced in relief camps – conditions that led to a few instructors being accused of promoting "the expression of discontent" – Bradwin sent "helps" to men in the field.[86] These brief notes often included ideas for general talks or for more focused lessons, and many of them pointed to poetry as a key resource. Such "helps" reminded the labourer-teacher not to ignore the simple yet powerful tools that poetry offered: "As you well know, men in camps are not susceptible to the teaching of literature – particularly poetry of sustained thought and study, and yet I question whether young men in a classroom at college have a finer perception of what is real and genuine in the message of any simple poem, rich with a human background, than the rough-handed, big-hearted men who so often congregate in the camps." Despite his many years of experience in the camps and his academic training in industrial history, sociology, and economics, Bradwin, like Fitzpatrick before him, retained a more or less romantic view of camp workers. In Bradwin's case, this is somewhat surprising given the prevalence, by the early 1930s, of both labour unrest and realist literary modes of representing labour. In print forms ranging from the workers' press to Canadian novels such as Douglas Durkin's *The Magpie* (1919) and Martha Ostenso's bestselling *Wild Geese* (1925), Bradwin would have found alternatives to the idealized "big-hearted men" of his "help." Moreover, Bradwin turned in the early 1930s not simply to poetry, but to Romantic poetry – a poetry renowned for its idealized portraits of labourers and common folk. Complementing the deployment of the poetry of William Wordsworth in the *Handbook for New Canadians*, Bradwin's "helps" and letters of advice to labourer-teachers promote the poetry of Henry Wadsworth Longfellow and Alfred Lord Tennyson, as well as the epigrams of the leader of German Romanticism, Johann Wolfgang von Goethe.[87]

In a "help" that seems to date from 1933, Bradwin enclosed a copy of American poet Henry Wadsworth Longfellow's "The Bridge," a poem whose "artistry is so unobtrusive and the sentiment and expression so pensive that a simplicity results, which makes a direct appeal to the heart of any man." In choosing Longfellow, a poet who achieved a degree of popularity in the latter half of the nineteenth century that no American poet has rivalled since, Bradwin was reaffirming popular taste, but he was doing so in a slightly belated fashion: by the 1930s, Longfellow had fallen out of favour with American realists, naturalists, and modernists, who disdained his idealism and sentimentality.[88] "The Bridge," which appeared in *The Belfry of Bruges and Other Poems* in 1846, is written in the style of a popular ballad, a form commonly identified with workers' poetry and not unlike the rhyming tetrameter lines one finds in the *Relief Camp Worker*. Yet if the ballad of the *Relief Camp Worker* was being turned to the effort of rallying workers to strike, Longfellow's ballad turns it to the purposes of exploring empathy for one's fellow man and thematizing the eternal nature of time. In his "help," Bradwin quotes only the final four quatrains of a fifteen-stanza poem:

> And I think how many thousands
> Of care-encumbered men,

Each bearing his burden of sorrow,
Have crossed the bridge since then.

I see the long procession
Still passing to and fro,
The young heart hot and restless,
And the old subdued and slow!

And forever and forever,
As long as the river flows,
As long as the heart has passions,
As long as life has woes;

The moon and its broken reflection
And its shadows shall appear,
As the symbol of love in heaven,
And its wavering image here.

Originally localized as "The Bridge Over the River Charles" (the river that separates Cambridge from Boston, Massachusetts), but by the time of its first book publication in 1846 bearing the more universal title "The Bridge," Longfellow's poem employs a first-person speaker who recalls his youthful burdens of care, while observing that now it is only the "sorrow of others" that gives him grief. Like Goethe's epigrams, which appealed to Bradwin for their reflections on the "contented" life, "The Bridge" fashions true wisdom and sympathy as qualities that emerge from solitude. Of Goethe, Bradwin wrote: "But perhaps one of his finest sayings may be expressed as follows: character is gained in the stream of life, but knowledge must be acquired in solitude." Such "solitude" and reflection, so key to Romantic thought, obviously bore an important role in the context of Depression-era camps, where collective thought and action loomed large.[89] The DND's Policy and Instructions for the Administration of Unemployment Relief Camps for Single Homeless and Unemployed Men presents as "one of the most fundamental and most necessary rules" for the administration of relief camps the forbidding of "anything bearing the appearance of combination to obtain redress of alleged grievances." Bradwin's "helps" place poetry in the service of this aim, encouraging men to imagine themselves in solitude rather than in "combination."[90]

Bradwin was insistent that, in presenting this poem to camp men, the instructor should avoid

> anything you have been told about it by a professor. Read it to the men, in the light of your own experience. Every man in the camp can be thrilled and helped by the quiet message conveyed in this lyric, because it visualizes life, and all men have their own experience of life. There is another thought; how often the small and unpretentious poems outlast the bigger works erected with such literary skill, but which do not live and wear throughout the centuries. Write this little poem on the blackboard; recite it; have some of the men repeat it, singly or in unison, have individuals in the group give you in a few sentences their impression of the poem – as to its meaning and its message. Have some member of the class point out what, to him, is a measure of beauty in the language of the poem, and why.

Bradwin closes the "help" with an acknowledgment of the instructor's knowledge of his "own" men: "You know your men, you know the poem – relate the two, for there is a human message contained in it."[91] We might understand Bradwin's emphasis on the poem as an instrument for the teaching of moral culture – it offers a "human message," a "help" for the troubled soul, a source of "beauty" – in the context of an approach that, as I discuss in chapter 1, was characteristic of the cultural idealism that shaped the teaching of English literature in Canadian universities, such as Bradwin's *alma mater* Queen's University, well into the twentieth century. While Bradwin studied history and economics at Queen's, he inherited from his mentor Fitzpatrick a strong sense of literature as a vehicle for what Henry Hubert calls the "new idealism" of Canada's early-twentieth-century post-secondary literature curriculum. According to Hubert, "a primary object" of this new idealism was to ensure the students' continued faith in traditional cultural values, which in Canada consisted of the belief in the primacy of the intellectual life – as opposed to faith in material reality – along with their commitment to the higher welfare of society, which translated into a firm commitment to the British Crown and to a British political ideology, combined with a denial of self-aggrandizement deriving from material philosophies and pleasures.

In fashioning "The Bridge" as something that can both "thrill" and "help," Bradwin is pointing to its moral function, a function linked to its representation of reflection in the solitude of nature as a source of empathy and commitment to those "thousands / of care-encumbered men" who lie outside the self. This commitment is easily translated into concern for what Hubert calls the "higher welfare of society" – –a concern rooted not in "material philosophies and pleasures" such as dialectical materialism, but in the ideals of empire and, by the 1930s, the ideals of national progress.[92] As many of his "helps" reveal, Bradwin held deep convictions regarding the "higher welfare" of the Depression-plagued nation, and his concerns offer a good example of how liberal ideals grappled with conceptions of collective good during this period. In an undated "help" from the 1936 annual report, Bradwin acknowledges the threat of "extreme thinking" but also notes that resistance to all change is folly: "You should know that the way of all permanent progress lies between these two points of view. A continuance in any other course is a perversion of all true and orderly advance obscuring the goal which in the end would count most for the furtherance of human life, and civilization, and happiness." At the beginning of 1935, before the significant strike action on the west coast that precipitated the termination of the relief camp system, Bradwin commented in similar terms on the unemployment insurance that organizations like the RCWU were demanding. Urging instructors to "talk the matter over with your classes," he advocates "measures and steps that lead toward orderly and progressive advance," while cautioning that "any new plan of social insurance will still retain for the individual the fact of his own responsibility: even in the face of collective action it will be of advantage to show individual thrift."[93] This thinking accommodates "orderly and progressive" collective social change, but only insofar as the essential primacy of individual responsibility, morality, and freedom remains intact. Such a philosophy dovetails perfectly with Longfellow's poem, which figures individual moral reflection as a condition essential to the possibility of the larger social categories the poem invokes – "thousands / of care-encumbered men," but also the American nation, expanding as it was under the Jacksonian manifest destiny of the period of its first publication.

Moreover, Bradwin's emphasis on feeling – the "thrill" that poetry can engender and the "impression" this might produce – over fine-grained analysis of the poem's form speaks to the complexity of the work he wanted it to do in the classroom. The poem might be read "singly," and this surely speaks to its thematization of individual reflection, but it might also be read, Bradwin suggests, "in unison." This is a sentimental poem, written on the late edge of a popular movement in sentimental literature (predominantly fiction) that crossed the Western world between the mid-eighteenth and the mid-nineteenth centuries. In the stanzas Bradwin omits but that workers would have seen in complete versions of the poem, Longfellow writes:

> I stood on the bridge at midnight,
> As the clocks were striking the hour,
> And the moon rose o'er the city,
> Behind the dark church-tower.
>
> I saw her bright reflection
> In the waters under me,
> Like a golden goblet falling
> And sinking into the sea.
>
> And far in the hazy distance
> Of that lovely night in June,
> The blaze of the flaming furnace
> Gleamed redder than the moon.
>
> Among the long, black rafters
> The wavering shadows lay,
> And the current that came from the ocean
> Seemed to lift and bear them away;
>
> As, sweeping and eddying through them,
> Rose the belated tide,
> And, streaming into the moonlight,
> The seaweed floated wide.
>
> And like those waters rushing
> Among the wooden piers,
> A flood of thoughts came o'er me
> That filled my eyes with tears.

Read "in unison," such lines urge collective sympathy with the anguished speaker (who is, in turn, appropriately sympathetic). Such sympathy is crucial to the kind of "sentimental community" that Margaret Cohen, extending Benedict Anderson's concept of the "imagined community" of the modern nation generated in and through mass print forms such as the newspaper and the novel, describes as the "affectively charged association" that literature of sentiment labours to produce among readers. Tears, which feature in "The Bridge" as in all other literary instances of sentimentality, are synecdochal of sentimental community because, according to Cohen, "they are a universal human response and thus signify the universality of this community's potential membership, comprising the same formally equal individuals that are citizens of emerging liberal society." The sympathetic response, Cohen specifies, is "available to anyone regardless of rank, social status, age, gender, or nationality; all that is required is the taste to be moved." At the same time, the popularity of sentimental forms in emergent liberal societies of the eighteenth and nineteenth centuries may be attributed, Cohen asserts, to the fact that communities of sentimentality form "idealized instances of the liberal public sphere" in which individuals may exercise their freedom without impinging on the freedom of their fellow citizens. This freedom is one of "morals and taste" – "aesthetic-moral judgements" that, particularly when liberal democratic freedoms become problematic at the "level of practice," come to serve as alternative and affectively powerful forms of liberty. Moreover, as Lauren Berlant's work on sentimentality's genealogy in American culture indicates, the community of taste that Cohen identifies forms an important origin for what Berlant calls the "intimate public sphere" – an ambivalently political space where citizenship is defined through the expression of sentimentality and complaint.[94] The alternative freedom Cohen identifies is precisely that which Bradwin was inviting unemployed men to enjoy: in the context of the relief camp, where the liberal promise was deeply compromised, the idealized instance of the liberal public sphere made available through sentimental community offered an important opportunity, one that was not limited by class, education, or wealth.

Cohen's theorization of sentimental community as an "idealized instance of the liberal public sphere" offers a rich interpretive tool for analyzing the association's use of the term "comradeship" in this period. The "comradeship" deployed by Frontier College refers not to class-based bonds that form the basis of a collective identification, but rather to the act of being together without compromising the freedom of one's fellow citizens. Bradwin's "helps" also encourage collective activities in order to cultivate the "feel" of group belonging. Although these activities had long formed a part of the Frontier

College repertoire, they assumed new priority in the relief camps, particularly those forms that were conducive to sentimental feeling. Most often, he advised group singing, an activity that one labourer-teacher described as "something to stir the hearts of lonely men," but he also suggested orchestras and other musical activities, as well as sports. Registers offer ample evidence that instructors took this advice to heart. Instructor H.G.E. Rhodes's outdoor Sunday "sing-songs" served the purpose of bringing men of a "dozen different nationalities and as many more religious beliefs" together in order to sing "old songs," such as "The Moon Comes Over the Mountains" and "Abide With Me." According to Rhodes, the men who could not read the song lyrics in English joined in by "following the tune."[95] The sentimental community that is useful for understanding how forms such as the sentimental song circulated in relief camps may also be productively linked to Lauren Berlant's concept of the intimate public. As in an intimate public, the forms of collective feeling-together that Bradwin promoted "sought to displace the filtered story of instability and contradiction from the center of sociality" in order to achieve the "*affect of feeling political together*."[96] In the relief camps, instability and contradiction were symptoms of the structural complexities of the economic fallout – complexities often occluded from view in Bradwin's "helps." Although his "helps" frequently broach "public" and "political" topics, among them the 1933 Economic Conference, "encouraging world developments," and the 1933 federal budget, Bradwin's texts frequently displace the political – the possibility of effecting change in the public sphere through meaningful collective action – with appeals to individual responsibility and morality. He underscores the importance of "the individual's own responsibility," and of individual entrepreneurial effort, which can overcome material disadvantages, and he points to the "great need and worth of private initiative."[97] The intimate public sphere, which produces this "*affect of feeling political together*," "downsizes" citizenship to precisely the kinds of "personal acts and values," that concern Bradwin here.[98]

As we have seen, there were other important affective dimensions to the conceptions of citizenship that attended the early-twentieth-century work of Frontier College. Part of the work that an emergent pedagogy for citizenship undertook was the endorsement (and, by implication, the censure) of particular kinds of intimate emotional relationships. If, in the first half decade of the association's work, the creation of the citizen-reader was thought to depend on cultivating his (absent) wife though the proxies offered by fiction and poetry, by the 1910s and 1920s the kinship relations embodied in non-British immigrant families were understood to require state intervention in the domain of the household. In the context of the relief camps, where the workers were unmarried, the concern was less for absent wives than for the *potential* heterosexual union that joblessness and loss of dignity might jeopardize. H.A. Weir, a school inspector with the Nova Scotia Department of Education, worries in his 1939 study "Unemployed Youth" that long periods of worklessness were particularly disastrous for young men under the age of twenty-five: "There is no need to emphasize the decline of self-respect, the disregard of individual responsibility, and the lowering of the general morale which are the inevitable results of lengthy periods of unemployment … Youthful enthusiasm is soon smothered in an atmosphere of idleness and dole." More concerning, for Weir, were the results of a survey conducted in the late 1930s by the Ontario Young Men's Council of the YMCA, which demonstrate that unemployed youth were forgoing "those personal functions which should be the right of every normal individual, namely, marriage, the rearing of children, and the establishment of a home." Weir links the "individual responsibility" and the taking up of "personal functions" to a healthy citizenship, concluding his study with a warning that the absence of such citizenship could imperil national progress. Bradwin shared Weir's concerns regarding the "untethered" lives of relief camp men, which did little to nourish the "healthy Canadian citizenship" and individual responsibility that family, in Bradwin's view, engendered.[99] The literary forms Bradwin favoured – tilted to the purposes of cultivating individual moral reflection – were clearly linked to these larger concerns regarding citizenship's crucial affective dimensions.

What kind of response did this reoriented pedagogical method encounter in the relief camps? As we have seen, the single most obvious obstacle that stood in the way of Frontier College classroom work though the 1910s and 1920s was the simple one of exhaustion: thirteen-hour days were simply not conducive to evening study. However, in the context of the relief camps, this obstacle evaporated. Most men in relief camps were obliged to work eight hours a day, five and a half days per week, which left a good deal of leisure time. Moreover, the labour itself, though physically demanding, did not proceed at a pace that would have rendered the workers incapable of further activity at the end of the day. As in previous decades, the unguided use of reading matter in relief camps appears to have been considerable. The registers for the 1930s include a place at the bottom of each monthly page to record "Approximate No. of Readers of Books, Magazines, and Newspapers." Not all instructors filled out this section, but in the camps of the twenty-six instructors in 1933 who did record this information alongside their total camp populations, it is clear that reading was a popular activity: there was an average of 101 monthly readers per instructor, and the average size of their camps was 264 men.[100]

By contrast, it does not appear that the study and discussion sessions led by Frontier College in the relief camps held wide appeal. In 1933, the first season during which Frontier College instructors took up positions in DND relief camps, there were a total of 8,010 men in the camps reached by Frontier College for which instructors' registers exist, and these instructors were able to attract, on average, twenty-five students each month – under 1 percent of the enumerated camp population (see table 4.1). To put the figures in comparison, it is helpful to know that in 1923, 8 percent of the workers in camps reached by Frontier College enrolled as students for classes. In 1924, the same figure was 11 percent.[101] The decrease during the 1930s is significant. Tellingly, James E.R. Shaver, the instructor who realized the highest enrolment as a proportion of the men in his camp during 1933 (44.7 percent), did not attract many men to daily classes: in June of 1933, his daily average attendance (for eight classes) was 10.5 (or 15.9 percent of men in the camp), and in July (for twenty-three classes) this number was 8.5 (or 12.9 percent of men in the camp).[102] Finer-grained analysis of daily attendance for all the camps would likely produce similar results; however, many of the registers for this year lack this precise measure.

While many instructors attributed their lack of success to factors that had long posed difficulties for Frontier College – "jumping," the advanced age of the men – others pointed in their registers to the challenge that the Depression posed to the liberal narrative of individual development the association proffered. From his Canoe Lake, Ontario, relief camp, for instance, A.J.H. MacDonald noted that "due to the period of depression it is harder to convince Canadian borne men of the need for extra training when there are more than a few well trained men working in the gangs along with them." Robert McRae's register observes that the same problem was affecting the association's ability to attract foreign-born learners: "It was found that very few men actually wished to study. A foreign-born worker in the camp explained to me that most of his fellow-born country-men had little prospects in Canada and were looking for the earliest opportunity to return to Europe and accordingly were not very ambitious to improve themselves in the English language as they might have been when times were more booming."[103]

It is especially revealing to examine the poorest results in table 4.1. W.A. Trott and H.G.E. Rhodes, who were in the DND camp at Dundurn, Saskatchewan, from July to September 1933 and from November of 1933 to March of 1934, respectively, reported particularly low average monthly attendance – just under 5 and 3 percent, respectively. As Lorne Browne's history of Saskatchewan relief camps indicates, the DND opened the Dundurn camp hastily in the spring of 1933 in response to strike activity in a provincial camp in Saskatoon that had led to thirty arrests and the death of an RCMP officer. Two thirds of the initial six hundred men at Dundurn were transferred from this Saskatoon camp. Largely because of close RCMP surveillance and the particular difficulties of organizing in Dundurn as the only major DND camp in the province, the RCWU's organ for Dundurn, *The Agitator*, does not appear to have been in circulation before 1935, and unrest at the camp did not erupt into strike action until December 1935. Nonetheless, discontent was present prior to 1935: between May and December 1933, 115 inmates were expelled for disciplinary reasons, including the possession of a "socialist book."[104] Despite this apparently unsettled atmosphere, Rhodes's representation of his time in the camp is restrained, mentioning the possibility of unrest in the most muted way. In a 1933 lecture, for instance, he noted that the men of the Dundurn camp were receptive to "occasional little inspirational discussions," such as "the one we had a short time ago on Longfellow's little poem 'The Bridge.'" Rhodes's register also indicates that he broached more political topics but was careful to emphasize his rational and statistically backed presentation of economic issues: "Into the English classes I have worked several discussions on the general basis of economics, the reports of the Dominion Bureau of Statistics have been helpful in this. It is interesting to note that these men, whose difficulties in life are nearly always economic rather than political, can quite easily grasp the significance of this and change their ideas of reform from political to economic." Such a message seems not to have attracted many auditors: an "Economics and Ethics Discussion" organized by Rhodes

Table 4.1
Instructors' results, 1933

Instructor	Location	# of men in camp	Avg. # of men enrolled as students Per month	Avg. # of men enrolled as students per month as % of # of men in camp*
Barnes	Trenton, ON	500–860	34.6	5
Bischoff	Spence's Bridge BC	75	14	18.6
Bradley	Borden, ON	125–160	13.5	9.5
Brunton and Rush	Port Credit, ON	800	39.3	4.9
Buckley	Barfield, ON	35	11	31.4
Cairncross	Wagoming, ON	n/a	15	n/a
Cockburn	Princeton, BC	72	17	23.6
Collins	Lac du Bonnet, MB	100	16	16
Dalton	Rockcliffe, ON	n/a	n/a	n/a
Fraser	Trenton, ON	200	28	14
Glashan	Petawawa, ON	400	33.5	8.4
Hawkins	Pearl, ON	n/a	16.5	n/a
Hartley	Kenora, ON	100	32.75	32.8
Hinchcliffe	Petawawa, ON	n/a	53	n/a
Horton	Nakina, ON	108	15.6	14.4
Hunter	Corbeil, ON	100	17.5	17.5
Jenner	Trenton, ON	500	37	7.4
Lantz	Pagwa, ON	90	28	31.1
Murray	Deux Rivières, ON	n/a	18.3	n/a
MacCallum	Lac du Bonnet, MB	90	9	10
MacDonald	Kenora, ON	120	39	32.5
MacDonald	Kingston, ON	260	27	10.4
McDonald	Hope, BC	100–125	19	16.9
Meek	Camp Borden, ON	65	10.5	16.2
Moorhead	Hope, BC	n/a	n/a	n/a
Newbie	Pagwa, ON	n/a	13.7	n/a
Poole	Nakina, ON	90	21.6	24
Presson	Ottawa, ON	185	23.6	12.8

Rhodes	Dundurn, SK	1100–1500	38	2.9
Scott	Saint John, NB	149	11	7.4
Shaver	Gillies' Depot, ON	66	29.5	44.7
Sisler	Diver, ON	100	28.3	28.3
Strachan	Gillies' Depot, ON	n/a	23.3	n/a
Tregidga	BC	100	20.2	20.2
Trott	Dundurn, SK	200–450	16	4.9
Turner	Valcartier, QC	1000–1500	112	9
Webster	Amesdale, ON	100	15.3	15.3
Welch	Bonfield, ON	100	18.3	18.3
Westcott	Kitchener, BC	80	25	31.3
Zimmerman	Deux Rivières, ON	115	20.6	17.9
Totals		8010**		
Averages		258.4	25.3***	

Source: These data are compiled from the forty-one (Barnes to Zimmerman) instructors' registers found in MG 28, I 124, vol. 126, "Registers, 1933," FC-LAC. I did not count the Willard register because he was not stationed in a relief camp. The 1933 annual report lists more instructors for the season (eight-five), so the remaining registers are either missing or were not submitted by the individual instructors. A report for 1934 claims that 4,859 men enrolled in "definite class work" during 1933; this number must be based on the results of this larger number of instructors, but whether this number accounts for the fact that registers represent monthly enrolment and often repeat names from month to month is unclear. "Reports, 1933," MG 28, I 124, vol. 108; "Reports, 1934," MG 28, I 124, vol. 108, FC-LAC.

* When the # of men in camp is a range, the mean is used.
** I calculated 8,010 total (using the mean for ranges) divided by thirty-two camps (the number of camps with data).
*** Average of the thirty-eight camps for which there are data.

on 9 January 1934, for example, attracted only seven of the camp's 1,100 to 1,500 men. Another class on 22 March 1934 incorporated a "Bureau of Statistics Report" into an English lesson but attracted only a few more listeners.[105]

By contrast, W.A. Trott's register obliquely observes the presence of unrest in the Dundurn camp, focusing on those who rejected radicalism but defining them against their more politicized counterparts. The register notes that "a large number – say 15% to 20% – of the men in the camp are men that have had small businesses, that have been chemists, or have been used to thinking etc in the past and these men are keenly interested in the future of Canada and the interest emphatically does not take the form of threats or revolution or bloodshed." Trott's attempts to host "general discussions" on topics such as "economics," "government," and "behaviour" were, like Rhodes's, not particularly successful, attracting 3 percent of the camp population at best.[106] Bradwin, convinced by 1934 that the smaller, isolated camps provided a better opportunity for Frontier College than the larger, centrally located camps, and well aware of the potential for strike activity in each camp, did not send further labourer-teachers to Dundurn.[107]

THE RIGG COMMISSION AND FEDERAL RESPONSIBILITY FOR LABOURERS' CULTURAL EDUCATION

Although Frontier College struggled to keep itself in the view of all levels of government prior to the 1930s, it entered a new phase of intimacy with the federal government in the context of its work in relief camps. Frontier College was not merely a passive institution attached benignly to the DND camps: it attempted, perhaps not very successfully, to involve itself in the daily lives of men in hundreds of relief camps across the country during the first half of the 1930s. However, its role in the federal relief camp scheme extended beyond classwork, discussions, and recreation: Edmund Bradwin was in fact instrumental in shaping the federal government's response after the mid-1930s to what was a conflict-ridden relief camp system. In the fall of 1935, DND relief camps faced their final challenge: in the wake of the On-to-Ottawa Trek, the Regina Riot, and the election of the Liberal government of Mackenzie King in October, the new Minister of Labour Norman Rogers established a committee to survey relief camp conditions in approximately fifty camps west of Valcartier, Quebec. With an eye to the "eventual transfer of such camps to the jurisdiction of the Department of Labour," the minister charged the committee with examining the "desirability of continuing the Relief Camps on their present basis or in any other form."[108] Along with R.A. Rigg, a senior civil servant in the Department of Labour, and Humphrey Mitchell, former Labour MP from Hamilton East who lost his seat in 1935 but who returned to the federal government as (Liberal) Minister of Labour in 1942, Bradwin was called to serve on this committee.

The Rigg Commission, as it came to be known, submitted its interim report at the end of January 1936. Based on interviews with MPs, DND personnel, and municipal and provincial officials, as well as "innumerable personal interviews" with men in the camps, questionnaires filled out by labourer-teachers, and observation of relief camps in the United States, the commission recommended keeping the camps open for a "temporary period" with the proviso that a work-for-wages system, such as they had observed in American relief camps, be implemented. The report is clear about the particular threat the camp system posed to young men between eighteen and twenty-five who had "not acquired the habit of working or the sense of individual responsibility to society." Under normal conditions, these men "would have given a good account of themselves," but under Depression conditions, they "constitute a real menace to the maintenance of our existing institutions." Moreover, the large relief camps, such as the camp at Dundurn, Saskatchewan, afforded organizations such as the WUL the "most suitable opportunity for the successful propagation of subversive ideas and the stimulation of the spirit of rebelliousness." Given this threat, and although the commission members found the camps to be perfectly adequate in terms of facilities, they advised the Minister of Labour to close the relief camps "as soon as possible in the best interest of the State and for the sound, healthy development of the majority of the men now in the camps."

The terms of reference for the Rigg Commission were quite narrow. With the exception of assessing the "adequacy of existing facilities for re-establishing men now in Relief Camps in industrial and agricultural employment," their work was confined wholly to the analysis of the camps themselves rather than to alternatives to the camps that organizations such as the RCWU were proposing, such as a system of unemployment insurance. The emergent social citizen made visible in the *Relief Camp Worker's* demands for non-contributory unemployment insurance is thus barely discernable in Rigg, Mitchell, and Bradwin's report. Moreover, their assessment of the camp system brazenly ignored most of the RCWU's key demands. Although asked to examine any matter "in relation to the administration of Relief Camps which you deem to be of importance," the report omits mention of the effective disenfranchisement of relief camp residents and the proscription of workers' committees and other collective complaint mechanisms. However, without acknowledging its relationship to the RCWU or the unemployed movement, the Rigg Commission did adopt one of its key demands – work for wages. For the authors of the report, the advantages of a work-for-wages policy were numerous, and first among them was ".the creation of self-respect and the spirit of initiative and individualism among the men of the camps." Furthermore, men with wages in their pockets could pay for their own board, transportation, and clothing, and more work would be accomplished in the camps by more motivated workers. Cabinet responded to the Rigg Report by announcing that federal relief camps would be shut in July 1936. The government pledged to increase the monthly wage in the camps to fifteen dollars a month for the months prior to the closures, and for the period following the closures, it arranged with the two national railways to provide summer work for ten thousand relief camp residents and promised to assist the remaining ten thousand men in camps in finding farm work.[109]

Although appealing to individual initiative and tepid in its conception of social citizenship, the report's work-for-wages proposal endorses an interventionist state and its responsibility for unemployment. Such an endorsement is further evident in another Rigg recommendation – that the Employment Service of Canada "afford adequate provision for the re-establishment of relief camp workers in industrial and agricultural employment as opportunity to do so arises." The Employment Service of Canada was a national network of labour exchanges established in 1918 as a response to the labour shortage of the spring of 1918, but it gained its principal *raison d'être* from the demobilization efforts of the following autumn. Jointly financed and administered by Ottawa and the provinces, the service had an auspicious beginning under the progressive direction of Bryce Stewart, who conceived of unemployment as a structural, industrial problem and not merely as a challenge of reconstruction. However, under the direction of R.A. Rigg, the service had fallen victim to federal indifference and the austerity measures of the King Liberal government in the early 1920s. Noting Bennett's aversion, and later Mackenzie King's, to recognizing unemployment as a structural problem of industrial capitalism that required an expansion of the state, James Struthers cites the decline of the Employment Service as a key aspect of the federal government's inability to deal effectively with the crisis of joblessness that erupted in the early 1930s. The members of the

Rigg Commission were essentially arguing the same thing: a robust federally managed network of labour exchanges could help manage a national labour force. Not until four years later, in 1940, when Mackenzie King was finally moved by the outbreak of war and a future demobilization to admit federal responsibility for the unemployed, did a national employment service and legislation on unemployment insurance emerge.[110]

In the midst of these contests over state responsibility, Frontier College gained a new foothold at the level of the state. As Bradwin explains in a November 1935 letter addressed to labourer-teachers in the field,

> Recently I was called to Ottawa and asked if I would go on this committee to make a report on Relief Camps and offer a solution for the present situation. It has no political significance whatever for I have never been in politics, but an impartial estimate of the camps is to be made with some suggestions for their amelioration and probably elimination ... This little recognition which has come reflects, I think, credit on Frontier College and particularly on its field staff. Surely it indicates that those in authority are not unobservant of an organization that for thirty years has been endeavouring to give its best to men, particularly the migratory and untethered workers in isolated camps![111]

Bradwin's enthusiasm is plain. In his estimation, the work of Frontier College had finally come into the federal government's view. In the report of the Rigg Commission, Bradwin's hand is most evident in the section that deals with recreation in the camps. Interestingly, this section emphasizes not simply the importance of educational work among camp labourers, but also the special quality of the labourer-teacher model, which is contrasted to the extension work of the provincial Departments of Education:

> Campmen, whether from the isolation of their work or from whatever reason, are as a class proud and sensitive; they feel frequently a sense of neglect. They will respond, however, to the companionship and counsel of the teacher who is a labourer with them. Camp education can never be limited solely to teaching. The campman will give heed to the man who works alongside him, sharing the common tasks in all kinds of weather,

rather than to the man with a staff appointment who does not partake in his work and activities.

If provincial departments of education met with "considerable indifference" and "suspicion" in the relief camps, the Frontier College method enabled a form of what might be called alternative scientific and cultural education:

> The older men in the camps are not easily enrolled as students – much of life already lies behind them. Too often, also, the older man at camp is sensitive and not prone to admit any deficiency in his schooling, particularly among youths. Many men, however, of this group, can be interested in general discussions, or informative talks if presented in a practical way – science in some form, events in world history, biography, or the dramatization of a selected passage from literature, will attract and hold interested listeners among the older men.[112]

In presenting the "companionship" work of Frontier College as a positive force not simply in relief camps but in work camps more generally, Bradwin and his co-authors strongly imply the importance of an institution like Frontier College to what they suggest should be a federal strategy for dealing with the Canadian labour force. It was clear to Bradwin by the early 1930s that no federal grants for educational work would be forthcoming. The argument made by Rigg, Mitchell, and Bradwin comes at the funding question from another direction: it frames Frontier College's efforts to provide "companionship and counsel" to workers in the context of a set of labour-related questions for which the federal government, the authors imply, should be responsible.[113]

In the relief camps where Frontier College undertook its work in the interwar period, we thus see how nascent conceptions of an interventionist state (responsible for a national labour force, for example) coincided with an older cultural idealism to suggest new ideas about how the state might use culture in the new areas where state knowledge and bureaucracy were being urged to expand. Yet the contests waged over print, pedagogy, culture, and citizenship that I explore in this chapter also point to the importance of pre–Second World War contexts for understanding the more general emergence of citizenship in Canada. While I invoke T.H. Marshall's postwar work in the discussion of the *Relief Camp Worker*'s agitation for the social rights of citizenship and in the analysis of the Rigg Commission, I am attempting to demonstrate how, *pace* Marshall's evolutionary narrative of citizenship's ever-expanding civil, political, and social rights, the postwar institutionalization of citizenship's social rights in Canada was preceded by a set of interwar contests over the meanings of these social rights. Attending in this chapter to "red" or radical literacy is a way to resist the progressivist narrative of Canadian citizenship, a narrative does not account for the role of struggle in the emergence of citizenship regimes. Veronica Strong-Boag and others have pointed out that the history of a citizenship regime must also account for those who have sought inclusion in its exclusionary structures, contested its terms, or rejected its relevance.[114] Étienne Balibar puts it more bluntly when he insists that social citizenship was not merely a philanthropic concession made by the bourgeois state under the guise of "'repairing' the pathological effects of the Industrial Revolution and unrestrained capitalist exploitation or even a logical consequence of capitalism's need to regulate the market that threatened to destroy the moral/physical integrity of the labour force upon which it depended for the production of surplus value." If these factors "had an impact upon the transformations of the contents of citizenship in the 'developed' capitalist countries where organized class struggles took place," a "third element in competition with the other two was required in order to provoke their combination": "Today we can argue that *this element was 'socialism,'* in the diversity of its different strains, formulations, and organizations."[115]

Conclusion

As the chapters in this book make clear, Frontier College nurtured and developed relationships with departments and agencies of the federal government across the first few decades of the twentieth century, despite the many refusals and obstacles it confronted. While it focused mainly on the government of Ontario in its earliest years, its own westward expansion, prompted by the early-twentieth-century boom in railway construction in the West, urged its principal's growing apprehension that immigration, labour, and citizenship were nationwide challenges requiring federal solutions. Frontier College thus increasingly made itself particularly visible to the bureaucratic bodies that were emerging in Ottawa during the 1910s and 1920s to deal directly – in the case of the Department of Immigration and Colonization – or indirectly – in the case of the RCMP and the DND – with federal challenges linked to immigration and labour. This conclusion turns to the period immediately following the decades analyzed closely in this book to consider how Frontier College's early-twentieth-century efforts in frontier camps were taken up in the context of the federal government's postwar citizenship regime. In the latter half of the conclusion, I turn to the question of social citizenship, interrogating representations that frame it as a lost ideal and reconsidering the moments of contest that have constituted its meanings.

FRONTIER COLLEGE AND NATIONAL CITIZENSHIP, 1935–59

As we have seen, Frontier College struggled throughout the interwar years against federal insistence that citizenship education was not to be a federal responsibility. Although many federal civil servants made this point clear to Fitzpatrick as early as the 1920s, Frontier College persisted, and made some inroads, as its Depression-era work for the DND attests. By the mid-1930s, however, the point was still largely falling on deaf ears. In a 1934 letter to Harry Cassidy, a political scientist at the University of Toronto and a well-known member of the reformist League for Social Reconstruction, Bradwin states his firm belief in the federal nature of his association's work and implies his frustration that this conviction was not shared in Ottawa:

> I need not point out to you that educational classes are not the whole work of the Frontier College – in fact, I would put this phase of the work, in some camps at least, as a lesser part of our activities. Would one say, for instance, that naturalization, the conserving of manhood, and the inculcating of healthy citizenship are not a Dominion work? Certainly all these powers are vested in the Federal Government. These aspects constitute a big proportion of the work in the mind of any instructor who is alive to his possibilities and enthused with the full purpose of Frontier College.[1]

Two years later, however, some marginal movement on this point was realized. In 1936, the federal Department of Labour began to give Frontier College an annual grant – the first annual federal grant the association received. Although this was temporarily suspended during the Second World War, an annual grant of five thousand dollars was reinstated in 1945 and continued well into the postwar period.[2] In this same period, the citizenship education that Frontier College had long identified as a federal responsibility became just that.

As this achievement of federal funding attests, Frontier College was an important player in the postwar development of a federal citizenship regime – a regime that defined key policy directions (and funds) but that largely relied on the provinces and organizations like Frontier College and the CAAE that were at some remove from the government. Moreover, the federal bureaucracies for citizenship that were developed after the Second World War were aware of Frontier College's long-standing efforts to educate workers for citizenship and leveraged this legacy to promote their own activities and policies. Frontier College was not absorbed by the state; instead, it gained new public funding for its efforts, a fact that curiously exacerbated the way that it had always existed as an organization that intersected when it could with shifting state priorities – federal efforts to educate for citizenship during the 1950s – and with state interest in the combined forces of citizenship and literacy after the mid-1960s.

Immediately preceding and during the First World War, and again in the wake of the Second World War, the Canadian state's intervention in the field of adult education expanded considerably. The federal government's 1913 Agricultural Instruction Act, which launched a federal–provincial relationship on vocational and technical education for adult workers that endured until the 1960s, was the first significant federal action. As I note in chapter 4, the CAAE was established in 1935 with E.A. Corbett as its first secretary and Edmund Bradwin as a member of its board of directors; Bradwin remained on the board of the CAAE during the Second World War and into the postwar period. In the early 1940s, the CAAE began working in concert with emergent federal efforts to educate for citizenship and to encourage participatory democracy. It collaborated with the federal government in citizenship education initiatives, such as the National Farm Radio Forum (1941–65) and the Citizens' Forum (1943–65), both of which it sponsored jointly with the Canadian Broadcasting Corporation (CBC). As the social progressivism of the National Farm Radio Forum particularly demonstrates, social democrats within the CAAE were committed to a citizenship based on a reconstructed postwar society that included social planning and public ownership (including an expanded federal role in education and federal funding for the work of the CAAE). These same CAAE progressives also promoted training for active citizenship (which included the expression of ideas and even critiques of government); encouraged an "internationalist" outlook and orientation; and, following a turn of phrase coined by John Grierson, the first Commissioner of the National Film Board (NFB), called for "imaginative training for citizenship," a training, in other words, not simply for literacy, knowledge, or skills, but for what Grierson called "civic appreciation, civic faith and civic duty."[3] Building on a model that Frontier College had developed in the late 1910s with its "general discussion" format, the National Farm Radio and Citizens' Forum functioned with the help of pamphlets designed by the CAAE for leaders of the local discussion groups attached to these initiatives.[4]

Such state involvement in adult education in Canada significantly curbed the radical potential of the early-twentieth-century worker-led initiatives in education that I discuss in the Preface. According to Gerald Friesen, throughout the 1930s, 1940s, and 1950s, unions increasingly abandoned the ideal of "community-wide social change" in favour of "tools courses" as the state's efforts to "use adult education vehicles such as the study club to build a classless, democratic, and cohesive community" ramped up. Despite accusations from "big business" that CBC programs such as Citizens' Forum harboured "pro-CCF, even communist, anti-capitalist sentiment," citizenship education was imagined in state discourse of the late 1940s and 1950s as a democratizing force that would neutralize the insidious class loyalties of another era.[5]

During both world wars, the federal government, with the assistance of voluntary organizations, including Frontier College, undertook the task of educating Canadian soldiers stationed overseas and at home, but it was particularly in the context of the Second World War effort that the federal government's interest in actively promoting citizenship sharpened: in 1941, it established the Advisory Committee on Cooperation in Canadian Citizenship (CCCC), which was meant both to educate new Canadians about government policy and to help the government and non-immigrant Canadians understand the needs of new Canadians. The CCCC accomplished its work partly through the volunteer organizations and provincial departments of education that had come together in 1940 as the Canadian Council of Education for Citizenship. This council assumed new life in the late war years as the state's new Citizenship Division, and in 1945 it was transferred to the Department of the Secretary of State. The adoption of Canada's Citizenship Act in early 1947 granted the federal Citizenship Division, and the federal government more generally, a legal basis for its involvement in citizenship education (a basis that it had previously lacked, as I explore in chapter 3). In 1950, with the creation of the Department of Citizenship and Immigration, the Citizenship Division, renamed the Citizenship Branch, found a new home. As Reva Joshee explains, provincial pressures on this federal vision of citizenship education produced a particular focus on language training, which spoke to the practical needs of the provinces. The mandate of the Citizenship Branch was an outward-looking one: it was meant to "assist governmental and non-governmental agencies engaged or interested in facilitating the adjustment and integration of newcomers."[6]

If the then newly established Department of Immigration was asking Frontier College for copies of its citizenship materials in the early

1920s, by the late 1940s, the relationship was reversed: in 1947, Frontier College regularly requested and received copies of citizenship materials published by the Department of the Secretary of State and the Department of Citizenship and Immigration, such as *How to Become a Canadian Citizen*; *Our Land, Our History, Our Government*; and a series called *Learning the English Language*. While Bradwin's correspondence with these departments demonstrates that they were aware of Frontier College's long-standing efforts to educate workers for citizenship, it is clear that institutional memory, limited by shifting ministers and the mercurial nature of federal departments, was not long enough to create deep knowledge of the *Handbook for New Canadians* and the pedagogical work for citizenship it had been attached to since the late 1910s. Whether because of this lack of memory or because of a desire for the "professional" development of state citizenship education, the *Handbook* and the shorter *Primer for Adults* do not seem to have been used as explicit models by federal citizenship officials in Ottawa in the late 1940s and early 1950s.[7] However, the federal citizenship materials developed after the passage of the Citizenship Act bore, according to Reva Joshee, "a remarkable resemblance" to materials developed in the first part of the century by organizations such as Frontier College: although the former tended to avoid the British-centric qualities of prewar materials, they nonetheless retained the latter's insistence that only those of non-British origin required citizenship training and that (British) Canadian ways were superior.[8]

This resemblance is ironic, given that the emergence of citizenship and citizenship education in postwar federal bureaucracies was strongly linked to the concepts of integration and cultural pluralism. As Joshee notes, the postwar state emphasis on integration must be understood in the context of a colonial-settler state that needed to distinguish itself from both Britain and the United States. Cultural pluralism emerged as the "symbolic cornerstone" of this distinction, and "citizenship and citizenship education were to be used to promote and develop the new identity." In moving the second reading of the Citizenship Bill in 1946, Paul Martin employed language that anticipates what the federal government would later call multiculturalism: "Fortune has placed this country in the position where its people do not all speak the same language and do not all adore God at the same altar. Our task is to mould all these elements into one community without destroying the richness of any of those cultural sources from which many of our people have sprung." Linked to this discourse of pluralism was a policy developed in the Department of Citizenship and Immigration in the early 1950s promoting the "integration" of immigrants, which had the twin goals of encouraging "participation in common citizenship" and "appreciation of diverse cultural contributions." While the distance between this discourse of pluralism and the liberal citizenship elaborated in the 1919 *Handbook for New Canadians* may seem great, it did not seem so to Department of Citizenship and Immigration officials, who cast integration as a Canadian ideal "that had been developing for over fifty years" and as a "natural reflection of the political and cultural pattern of our society."[9]

Not surprisingly, then, federal agencies were keen by the 1950s to attach the legacy of Frontier College – and particularly, its work in citizenship education among non-British immigrants – to a nationally and internationally promoted image of Canadian pluralism. The NFB, a federal film agency founded in 1939, offers another example of the federal government's increasing involvement in the education of adults. As immigration exploded in the decade and a half that followed the end of the Second World War, new government bodies, particularly those housed in the new Department of Citizenship and Immigration – the Citizenship Branch, Indian Affairs, the NFB – assumed responsibility for citizenship education – a responsibility that Frontier College had been urging since the turn of the century. In this period, the NFB's mandate was extended to include citizenship education and the promotion of reconstruction-era state services and policy, including Cold War foreign policy.[10] A potent marker of this shift is the NFB film *Frontier College* (1954), written and directed by Julian Biggs. Produced in the context of dozens of government documentary films that sought in this period to, as Zoë Druick notes, represent "the population in order to help predict and manage it," *Frontier College*, like other contemporary documentary films that represent citizenship education at work in the classroom, "both provides citizenship education and demonstrates the apparatus of such a pedagogy."[11] This is an important observation: drawing on a well-established civil society effort to educate for citizenship, as well as its older technologies – labourer-teachers, blackboards, books, phonographs, and group singing – *Frontier College* simultaneously embodies the new state technologies for citizenship education that would alter the sites the film represents.

As an example of a documentary genre that Druick calls "government realism," *Frontier College* draws on the social scientific epistemologies that shaped Reconstruction-era state planning. Representational strategies such as typification, which, as I discuss in chapter 2, were employed by Frontier College as early as 1919, generalize particular information through the figure of the socially typical citizen. The young labourer-teacher of the film, Robbie, who also provides the voiceover narration, never directly names himself (we hear his name only passively when he is addressed by other characters). Typicality matters to this film in terms of its representation of the "integration" of non-British immigrants, the term favoured by the nation's reception workers and by officials in the Citizenship Branch in the period following the Second World War. According to Franca Iacovetta, such workers argued that "successful integration involved a two-sided and gradual give-and-take process in which old and new Canadians interacted with each other, actively engaging in meaningful cultural exchanges and developing new and enriched understandings and interrelationships." Only then could a "stronger and more harmonious society" emerge. Such a "two-sided approach to integration" required "citizenship training for both newcomers and the general Canadian public." As Iacovetta notes, that officials in the Citizenship Branch did not see the contradiction between their self-described "enlightened," liberal, and social-scientific methods and "their presumption of superiority vis-à-vis the newcomers ... was an irony common to democracies." Such superiority was more than a matter of attitude: anticipating liberal multiculturalism, citizenship officials tended to understand cultural pluralism as "a celebration of individual talents and achievements, and thus of liberal capitalism's opportunities and freedoms, and of cultural forms, such as food, dance, and music, that were considered to be least threatening to the state and its dominant classes." Indeed, recalling a strategy practised by Frontier College since the 1910s, left-liberals and leftists frequently agreed in this period with the liberal view that Soviet influence could best be mitigated through an emphasis on the salubrious effects of democracy; demonstrating these benefits would be the task of citizenship educators. The film *Frontier College* insists that this integration work, although now undertaken among "D.P.'s" by the many postwar experts – psychologists, social workers, reception workers, psychiatrists – who found roles in government bodies established to deal with the integration of immigrants, was not new to Canada.[12]

The film's narrator and principal figure is presented to the audience as a typical Anglo-Canadian university student – a male in his early twenties named Bob Simpson. Drawing on many of what had become, by the early 1950s, standard tropes of Frontier College's self-presentation, Biggs's film stresses the mutually transforming experience of integration: the weak-bodied instructor who must harden up; workers who are imperilled by a cheap leisure culture; the initial failure of the classroom experiment; the camaraderie and friendship that must precede instruction, which will come about organically if all is handled well and if the instructor can demonstrate good character and receptivity to workers' needs (insofar as these are cast apolitically, such as the need for wholesome food); and the depth of the friendships formed, which redound as much to the benefit of the labourer-teacher as to that of the students. Cast as a neutral figure on the ground of a simmering "private little war" between the immigrant Italian and German workers in a northern Ontario CNR rail construction camp, Bob or "Robbie" must devise strategies to counteract the nationalist songs that are used as verbal weapons on the work site. After unselfconsciously winning the workers' loyalty through his honest desire to help "little Herman" write a persuasive response to an ad in a Lonely Hearts column, Robbie begins to organize night classes in his railcar. At one end of the car, he has a "full house" for English-language instruction, and, at the other, he is able to put the Germans and the Italians "side by side for a change."

Robbie is appreciative of the immigrants' esteemed national cultures; however, as the film's cultural gatekeeper, it is he who decides which elements of German and Italian culture are suitable for incorporation into Canadian life. He models this in a scene in which he plays German and Italian classical music, including Beethoven's Fifth Symphony and Gioacchino Rossini's William Tell Overture, on his phonograph. While this scene suggests how European high culture might be sewn into the fabric of Canadian democratic life as a common language that conflicting groups might adopt, Robbie further populates the film's cultural field with his teaching of "I've Been Workin' on the Railroad" to a group of immigrant labourers assembled around him. This American folk song has somewhat apocryphal origins: although it appears to be a work song linked to the great era of railway building, it seems to have its actual roots in a songbook published by Princeton University in 1894.[13] More collegiate than folk, the song brings together the German and Italian workers with their Anglo labourer-teacher in an interethnic chorus bound by collegiate friendship rather than class or ethnic identity.

Significantly, Robbie's attention to cultural forms as tools in the work of citizenship education participates in a more general Cold War discourse that privileged high culture as a means of promoting liberal democracy on the international stage. Robbie not only displaces nationalist anthems with classical music and apolitical work songs but also succeeds in diverting workers from the lures of American mass culture and towards the pleasures of English Renaissance drama. As Robbie's time in the rail construction camp begins, the camera offers glimpses of the recreational activities that fill workers' spare hours, described ironically by Robbie as forms of "self-education": besides indulging in their fondness for beer drinking, workers while away the hours in their bunks with texts such as American self-help guru J. Louis Orton's 1929 *Hypnotism Made Practical* and a copy of the comic book *Tales from the Crypt*. The particular choice of *Tales from the Crypt* is meaningful: the American comic book industry experienced a period of unparalleled expansion in the immediate postwar years, and the particular appeal of its product to young readers rendered it subject to increasing public criticism. A bimonthly horror comic, *Tales* was published twice a month between 1950 and 1955 by the Educational Comics (EC) company, whose president William Gaines found himself the target of public vitriol in the spring of 1954, when the Subcommittee on Juvenile Delinquency of the US Senate Judiciary Committee scheduled hearings on the comic book industry. According to Jean-Paul Gabilliet, EC's profitable ventures after 1950 into racy comic genres such as horror, suspense, and science fiction made Gaines an "industry scapegoat." When prominent comics publishers rallied together to pen a Comics Code that would regulate the industry's moral standards, Gaines was forced to abandon *Tales from the Crypt* and its ilk in favour of new titles that followed the industry standards.[14]

Banking on the currency of the scandal surrounding *Tales from the Crypt*, *Frontier College* alerts its original viewers to the inadequacy of certain texts as vehicles for education in liberal citizenship. Interestingly, in the association's earliest days, founder Alfred Fitzpatrick, we recall, advocated popular narratives of adventure for workers. However, the Cold War context produced the belief among many that democratic principles were threatened not only by communism but also by the much closer danger of American mass culture.[15] *Frontier College* takes up the Cold War challenge most specifically in its representation of high cultural forms as vehicles for integration, sane dialogue, and the mutual respect upon which freedom must be based. For example, one significant mark of Robbie's success in the camp is his ability to turn the men from the sensational pages of *Tales* to oral classroom readings of Shakespeare's *Macbeth*. The film explicitly links *Tales* to what the Massey commissioners decried in their 1952 *Report on National Development in the Arts, Letters, and Sciences* as "the less worthy American publications" that were seeking to "threaten our national values, corrupt our literary taste and endanger the livelihood of our writers."[16] Nevertheless, the film itself stands as evidence of what Druick identifies as the paradoxes inherent in the Massey Report, which, oriented as much to the policies of new international bodies like the United Nations Education, Scientific and Cultural Organization (UNESCO) as to national needs, articulates contradictory arguments that denigrate popular culture and the new mass media while promoting technologies such as film, for instance, as educational tools for democracy.[17] The film's argument thus contradicts its form, as well as the potential that form implicitly announces.

If *Frontier College* makes use of an older tradition and older technologies of citizenship education, its form makes it clear that such work is giving way to a more modern era. It is nevertheless clear that, in a period when government documentary tended to treat citizenship as an opportunity to make the state's administrative capacities visible to the immigrant or as an occasion to perform its Cold War foreign policy for an international audience, Frontier College offered important symbolic opportunities for the state. *Frontier College* was screened all over the country and, to a lesser extent, internationally: by 1960, the NFB calculated that there had been 2,230 domestic screenings and that it had been subject to fifteen international field loans. Camps where Frontier College worked were also important sites of experimentation for the NFB, as a collaborative 1955 study titled "The Use of Films and Filmstrips as Educational Aids for Frontier College Instructors in Isolated Camps of Canada" indicates.[18] The film enabled various state departments to represent their efforts to integrate immigrants as possessing a long history and to support federal messaging on the relationship between liberal democracy and culture. In using film to narrate the story of Frontier College, the NFB was making these stories available for telling in international contexts, as well. Indeed, there is evidence that state uses of Frontier College in international contexts were not confined to the 1954 NFB film: various government offices sought to attach themselves to Frontier College on the international front, representing the organization as one that could be used, in the words of Department of Secretary of State official A.D.P. Heaney, "to promote international understanding between peoples of different cultures," or, in the view of the Department of External Affairs, to represent a vision of Canada at "our missions abroad."[19]

The fact that literacy emerged in the 1960s as the keyword of an international discourse of development promoted by the cultural organizations that subtended American hegemony in this period, such as UNESCO, also arguably redounded to the benefit of Frontier College. In the latter half of the twentieth century, Frontier College became an important presence in such international cultural organizations: as Gordon Selman notes, Canadian adult education is highly regarded in an international field dominated by UNESCO as a result of the organizations, movements, and programs – such as the Antigonish Movement, the National Farm Radio Forum, the NFB, and Frontier College – that defined the field in the decades following the Second World War. More generally, Canadian organizations like the CAAE – on whose board Frontier College representatives held places throughout the postwar years – went on to become, in the 1960s and 1970s, key contributors to UNESCO's global literacy efforts: most notably, former CAAE president James Robbins ("Roby") Kidd was instrumental in promoting the reputation of Canadian adult education initiatives internationally, through his membership in UNESCO's Advisory Committee on International Understanding and Cooperation; his establishment in 1958 of a non-governmental foreign assistance venture called the Overseas Book Centre; and his roles as first chair (in 1959) of the Committee on Adult Education (of the World Confederation of Organizations of the Teaching Profession), as president of the Second UNESCO World Conference on Adult Education (1960), as chair of UNESCO's Committee for the Development of Adult Education during the 1960s and its Experimental World Literacy Programme (1967–73), and as the first chair of the International Council for Adult Education. A more obvious instance of Frontier College's international prominence in this period is the fact that it was honoured, in 1977, with UNESCO's Literacy Prize.[20]

RETHINKING SOCIAL CITIZENSHIP'S DEMISE

During the 1970s and 1980s, the Department of the Secretary of State was particularly committed to the concept of "active citizenship," which Roberta Russell describes as follows: "Program activities designed during those years were designed to foster the development of attitudes, skills, and knowledge needed for an informed and active citizenry. Active citizenship was encouraged through information, voluntarism, and promotion of the day-to-day practice of citizenship values." As Russell observes, "social and economic" participation was central to this vision, a fact that demonstrates how, since at least the mid-1960s, literacy, citizenship, and economic development have come to be articulated together. This co-articulation parallels global developments: according to Joseph Slaughter, postwar cultural organizations such as UNESCO valourized literacy, embodied in the citizen-reader, as "an essential technology for balancing the asymmetrical geopolitical conditions of an emergent international world system and as an engine of the internationalist teleologies of human personality and socioeconomic development" embedded in documents such as UNESCO's 1972 Charter of the Book.[21] In the 1986 Speech from the Throne, this view of literacy as central to social and economic participation was placed on the national agenda, and the following year the National Literacy Secretariat in the Department of the Secretary of State was established. Its mandate was to develop partnerships with provinces, volunteer and community groups, labour, and the private sector; to provide funds for literacy research and for community literacy initiatives; and to generally support the view that literacy is an essential prerequisite for full and active participation in Canadian society."[22]

This long-standing association of citizenship and literacy to economic development has, in the more recent past, narrowed to produce a more limited conception of the work that literacy and citizenship training might do. Public funding for adult literacy programs that do not fit the current model of skills training has been steadily evaporating for more than a decade: since 2006, federal cuts to literacy funding have resulted in the closure of countless literacy organizations across the country, as well as the dismantling of the National Literacy Secretariat, which was never solely focused on literacy as training for the workplace.[23] More generally, influenced by the Organisation for

Economic Co-operation and Development's international literacy surveys, which tend to reduce literacy to economic productivity, state conceptions of literacy have shifted significantly in the past twenty years. For example, the closure of the National Literacy Secretariat led to the creation of the Office of Literacy and Essential Skills within Employment and Social Development Canada, a reorganization that clearly indicates the new functionality that characterizes the state definition of literacy.[24] Although Frontier College seems to have been largely spared the scalpel that has eviscerated literacy programs across the country, the kind of work it is able to do has not remained untouched by the new state priorities. Its famed labourer-teacher program, for instance, has recently been reinvented as the Workplace Literacy and Essential Skills Program, which is promoted as a program that will foster "higher individual and overall productivity, workplace safety, and a more skilled and engaged workforce."[25]

Erica Martin describes the shifting ground under contemporary adult education in Canada in these terms: what was once a "community-based movement, which encouraged societal change," became a "professionalized provider of autonomous skills to individual students." Over the course of its history, Martin contends, Frontier College has struggled with the coexistence of and contradictions between these conceptions of education. Frontier College's dual negotiation of state imperatives and more radical views of literacy and its purposes is evident in the association's centennial materials, which are explicitly critical of state approaches that emphasize "skills training" or education for employment as the only acceptable goals of literacy work. In their essay "Frontier College: A Century of Lifelong Learning Outside the Boxes," for example, Philip Fernandez and Sarah Thompson accentuate the ongoing ways that government austerity, generational poverty, and a precarious labour market entrench social differences that "lifelong learning" – the "knowledge and the ability to learn on an ongoing basis" – might mitigate.[26] One thinks here of earlier Frontier College arguments, such as Alfred Fitzpatrick's radical critique in his 1922 book *The University in Overalls* of the social and economic hierarchies that leave workers excluded from higher education and "educated" men and women unable to perform manual labour. However, a longer historical view of the kind this book offers also obliges us to consider how the early-twentieth-century creation of a literacy for liberal citizenship that was primarily aimed at cultivating obedient and productive workers and that harnessed the sentimentality of the intimate public sphere shares much with current emphases on skills training for employment, individual adaptability, and family as a network of private support in precarious times.

It has now become commonplace to link the late-twentieth-century transformation of adult literacy and education more generally to the ascendance of what is described, following David Harvey and others, as neoliberalism. In citizenship studies, this turn has been variously interpreted as the emergence of a "neoliberal citizenship regime," "denizenship," and "entrepreneurial" citizenship. [27] As Bryan S. Turner has it: "the erosion of social Marshallian citizenship (both as an identity and as a bundle of rights) is slowly converting citizenship into a form of membership that resembles temporary, limited, and unpredictable denizenship. Citizens are more clearly secure than denizens in terms of formal rights to welfare and to voting. However, a range of social developments relating to marketization are transforming social citizenship and the relationship between the citizen, the state and civil society is becoming more tenuous and less predictable." Focusing specifically on the Canadian context, Janine Brodie understands this same shift through the term "entrepreneurial" citizen, a state-promoted conception of citizenship that "attempts to link Canadian identity and unity to the perceived demands of the emerging global economy" while eroding the social rights of citizenship and accentuating individual responsibility and entrepreneurial flexibility. This concept of "entrepreneurial" citizenship has been taken up in many recent critiques of Canada's citizenship guide, *Discover Canada*, which was revised by the Conservative government of Stephen Harper in 2010 to reflect, according to Laura Tonon and Tracey Raney, "the importance of personal responsibility" and "a disciplined, hard-working, self-reliant citizenry."[28]

Despite the power of the argument that frames literacy and citizenship with a narrative representing "neoliberal" and "entrepreneurial" conceptions of the citizen as a decline from the heights of the postwar social citizen, I would like to conclude by pointing briefly to the ways this book contributes to the necessary work of assessing how exactly the term neoliberalism helps us understand the ways that literacy, citizenship, and global capitalism are entwined in the present moment. Social citizenship must not be cast as a lost ideal; rather, it must be analyzed through historical studies of the deep compromises and costs that have given it meaning. Is there then a "social" worth recuperating in social citizenship?

As I point out in the Introduction, one of my intentions in writing this book has been to challenge a dominant evolutionary narrative of social citizenship, one that downplays contests over definitions and meanings of citizenship and the role of non-state actors in these meanings while underestimating both the limitations and costs of the social citizenship rights that emerged in the postwar period. These two points are related: it is helpful to think about how contests over the meanings of the social rights of citizenship in early-twentieth-century Canada came to shape the limits of those same rights as they were institutionalized at the level of the state in the postwar years. As we have seen, early-twentieth-century middle-class reformers such as Alfred Fitzpatrick and Edmund Bradwin were not alone in their desire to expand citizenship in the direction of social rights, particularly as these rights were represented in opportunities for adult education in rural areas. However, as I show in chapter 4, their demands were deepened and transformed during the interwar period by, among others, workers who apprehended the limitations of nascent state conceptions of citizenship. As historians of the reluctantly expanding welfare state have amply demonstrated, the demands of the unemployed movement were to some extent realized – in the 1940 Unemployment Insurance Act, for example – but whatever victories were achieved were won in the context of what Ian McKay, borrowing from Gramsci, casts as a process in which "the left program of new democracy was contained in the middle years of the twentieth century through a seemingly conciliatory, ultimately profoundly disintegrating, process of 'passive revolution' in which, unusually in world terms, Canadian liberalism vanquished its enemies within and without." The Unemployment Insurance Act did not enshrine a non-contributory plan, for example. Moreover, as Janine Brodie points out, if there were numerous postwar state provisions for social security and social welfare in addition to Unemployment Insurance – the 1944 National Housing Act; the 1944 Family Allowances Act (the nation's first universal social program); and the 1951 Old Age Security Act – social security programs such as Unemployment Insurance tended to be "constructed for the male breadwinner," in part because the nation's labour movements themselves promoted the Fordist family wage. At the same time, notes Brodie, social welfare provisions such as the Family Allowance Act were "usually less generous and means-tested" and "reserved for women and others on the fringes of the paid labour force." The most significant pieces of social welfare legislation – the 1965 Canada Pension Plan, the 1966 Medical Care Act, and the 1966 Canada Assistance Plan – were not adopted until the mid-1960s; by the early 1970s, the "social Canadian" ushered forth by such universal welfare provisions found herself the object of austerity measures.[29] It is also crucial to notice, as Indigenous legal scholar James (Sákéj) Youngblood Henderson points out, that analyses of citizenship's social rights neither adequately account for the distinct status of Indigenous peoples in Canada nor oblige "Canadians and their institutions to comply with constitutional supremacy and share sovereignties of treaties."[30]

Critiques of neoliberalism in citizenship studies as in the history of adult education tend to cast the "denizen" as a degradation of a historical ideal embodied in the postwar social citizen. T.H. Marshall, we recall, understood social citizenship as the last of three distinct stages in the development of a liberal-democratic citizenship that evolved beyond civil and political rights to become more inclusive. As Brodie puts it, social citizenship is "represented by Marshall as an apex in the evolution of liberal citizenship rights, and as irrefutable evidence of the legitimacy of liberal government." Yet there is good reason to question the costs of social citizenship or what exactly its rights legitimated. In Sarah Brouillette's view, they underwrote "America's postwar hegemony, when its industrial capacity set the standard for the ratcheting up of global competition that characterizes capitalism in its expansive phase." That is not all: we cannot "in good conscience overlook the environmental and social effects of the growth and expansion of industry and the catastrophes attendant upon American efforts to hold on to its precarious hegemonic status in the decades that followed."[31] The early-twentieth-century contests over citizenship that this book explores – contests that deeply shaped one of the nation's earliest citizenship-education programs as a counter to the literacies of the left, broadly speaking – challenge us to move beyond the liberal common sense that even critiques of neoliberalism, it seems, struggle to cast aside.

If the social of social citizenship requires interrogation, so, more generally, does the conception of the social that has long undergirded liberalism. In the present moment, the ideology of Canadian liberalism has become particularly durable, especially as it is juxtaposed to forms of right-wing populism and white nationalism. As this book attempts to demonstrate, this durability was partly produced through its historical grounding in a notion of the individual who exists within an intimate rather than a collective construction of social relations. Literacy, literature, and citizenship played mutually supporting and interconnecting roles in the early-twentieth-century consolidation of this intimate sociality. We are still living with a version of this liberal conception of the social. As Melinda Cooper points out, neoliberal economists and legal theorists have since the 1970s been seeking to reinstall the private family as "the primary source of economic security and a comprehensive alternative to the welfare state." As we question the legacies of social citizenship, we must surely also think about the forms of the social that are moving to supplant it, particularly because they can seem so benign, relying as they do on commonsense appeals to private family responsibility. Cognizant of Marx's critique of citizenship in "On the Jewish Question," Giovanna Procacci suggests that there is in fact a "social" in social citizenship worth recuperating, a "social dimension" of citizenship that "has been the source of a socialization process of citizenship and rights according to a logic different from liberalism."[32] Whether this "social dimension" of citizenship can be thought beyond its relation to liberalism remains a pressing question.

Notes

PREFACE

1 Williams, *Keywords*, 134–38. See also the Introductions to Graff, *The Literacy Myth* and Graff, *Literacy and Social Development*. For an account of the ways the specialization of the term "literature" to "creative" or "imaginative" works is linked to the growth of industrial capitalism in late-eighteenth- and early-nineteenth-century Britain, when the "liberating 'imagination'" associated with "literature" came to function as a counterweight to wage-labour production and the narrowing of "social relations to functions within a systematic economic and political order," see the section "Literature" in Williams, *Marxism and Literature*, 45–54.
2 Altick, *The English Common Reader*, 85, 141, 189; Eagleton, "The Rise of English." On evangelical and utilitarian conceptions of guided reading for the emerging middle class, see chapters 5 and 6 of Altick's *The English Common Reader*. On the "rise of English," see also Baldick, *The Social Mission*; and Viswanathan, *Masks of Conquest*.
3 Verrette and Lamonde, "Literacy and Print Culture," 453–4, 457; Graff, "Respected and Profitable," 66; Verrette, "Measuring Literacy," 453–4. When noting that Canada achieved nearly "full literacy" in 1921, Verrette is speaking of what is often called "nominal" literacy, or the ability to sign one's name. For debates regarding the use of this ability as an index of literacy, see Curtis, "Beyond Signature Literacy." The Canadian census began to measure literacy in 1861, but the question on literacy was not consistent across decades, the methods used to collect data in rural and urban environments were not always identical, and the data rely on self-reporting. See Verrette, *L'alphabétisation au Québec*, 29, for more information about the questions asked. As Verrette and Lamonde point out, variations in

questions may have actually led to a decline in literacy in, for example, Ontario, where the rate went from 96.7 percent in 1861 to 78.7 percent in 1891. "Literacy and Print Culture," 556n5.

4 Vincent, *Literacy and Popular Culture*, 119–28; Graff, "Respected and Profitable," 68–74, 81–2; Graff, *The Literacy Myth*, 19. For the implications of such questioning on the history of reading, see Price, "Reading," 316.

5 In 1911, the census inquired specifically after literacy rates among the foreign-born. The questions sought information regarding one's ability to read and/or write *in any language*. In the measure of non-British, foreign-born males twenty-one years of age and older, 82.81 percent could read and write; the rate for Canadian-born males of the same age was 89.76 percent. However, greater gaps appear in the rates for foreign-born men of this age who were living outside urban areas: for example, in Cape Breton, Nova Scotia, the foreign-born rate was 49.21 percent; in Chateauguay, Quebec, it was 11.73 percent; and in Mackenzie, Saskatchewan, it was 54.64 percent. Canada, *Fifth Census of Canada*, 497, 507–8, 510; Canada, "Fifth Census of Canada, 1911," 15. Contemporary commentators suggested that the proximity between the percentages for Canadian-born and non-British, foreign-born men was due to the fact that children of recent immigrants reported in the former category. Anderson, *The Education of the New Canadian*, 180.

6 Graff, *The Literacy Myth*, 321.

7 Ryerson is quoted in Graff, "Respected and Profitable Labour," 58. For accounts of these early efforts to educate workers, see Draper and Carere, "Selected Chronology," 44–9; Selman, Cooke, and Dampier, *The Foundations*, 63; and Candy, "From Homo canadiannus," 6–7. On mechanics' institutes in the pre- and post-Confederation periods, see Blanchard, "Anatomy"; Eadie, "The Napanee Mechanics' Institutes"; Fergusson, *Mechanics' Institutes*; Ferry, *Uniting in Measures of Common Good*; Keane, "A Study"; Lewis, "The Goderich Mechanics' Institute"; Ramsay, "Art and Industrial Society"; Robins, "Useful Education"; and Wiseman, "Phoenix in Flight."

8 Selman, Cooke, and Dampier, *The Foundations*, 62–4.

9 This is not to say that workers' publications did not evince interest in education. In Canada's earliest labour periodicals *Ontario Workman* (1872–1874) and *Palladium of Labor* (1883–1886), Harvey J. Graff finds workers' general support for the public education that Egerton Ryerson was promoting in the last half of the nineteenth century. Yet Graff also notes that the conception of public education in the labour press of this

period differs quite substantially from what Ryerson and other middle-class school reformers were advocating: contributors to the labour press did not prioritize the making of better workers; they advocated a combination of work and study rather than the pursuit of study alone; and they understood education and literacy as means (although not the exclusive means) of politicizing and instilling class consciousness in workers. See Graff, "Respected," 62–5. Palmer provides particularly rich evidence of the workings of this associational life in nineteenth-century Hamilton, Ontario, in the second chapter of his book *A Culture in Conflict*. On farmers' associations in the nineteenth century, see Draper and Carere, "Selected Chronology," 46; and MacPherson, *Each for All*.

10 "The Aberdeen Association: The First Three Years," p. 1, file 12, MG 127 1B5, vol. 5, AP-LAC.

11 "What to Do with Old Books and Magazines: Report of the Aberdeen Association 1898," p. 24, file 12, MG 127 1B5, vol. 5, AP-LAC. For a discussion of the low postal rates on domestic periodicals in late- nineteenth-century Canada, see Distad, "Newspapers and Magazines," 294–5.

12 "What to Do with Old Books and Magazines: Report of the Aberdeen Association 1898," p. 12, file 12, MG 127 1B5, vol. 5, AP-LAC.

13 Robinson, *Muckraker*, 165, 169. In the early 1880s, Stead became editor of the *Pall Mall Gazette*, which became known during his tenure for its daring investigative and sensational journalism, including an exposé of child prostitution in London that earned him a jail sentence in 1885. See Dawson, "Stead, William Thomas (1899–1912)."

14 Baylen, "Stead's Penny 'Masterpiece Library,'" 712–15. Whatever the purpose of the series, its popularity attests to the nineteenth-century "transformation of the reading public" from an elite to a mass social group – a transformation that occurred in British North America as well as in Britain. Altick, *The English Common Reader*, 314–15.

15 This is how James Robertson, federal Commissioner of Agriculture, described the mission of the Aberdeen Association. "What to Do with Old Books and Magazines: Report of the Aberdeen Association 1898," p. 30, file 12, MG 127 1B5, vol. 5, AP-LAC.

16 In its constitution, the association declared itself "undemoninational" and announced its intention to "rigidly avoid any semblance of religious or political bias." It committed its members to "send out such literature as shall suit the religion and as far as possible the tastes of the readers." The questions sent out to applicants consistently inquired about nationality and religion. "What to Do with Old Books and Magazines: Report of the Aberdeen Association 1898," p. 4, file 12, MG 127 1B5, vol. 5, AP-LAC.

17 "What to Do with Old Books and Magazines: Report of the Aberdeen Association 1898," p. 11, file 12, MG 127 IB 5, vol. 5, AP-LAC; "The Aberdeen Visitor," p. 4, file 12, MG 127 IB 5, vol. 5, AP-LAC.
18 "What to Do with Old Books and Magazines: Report of the Aberdeen Association 1898," p. 33, file 12, MG 127 IB 5, vol. 5, AP-LAC.
19 As the Aberdeen Association declined, the Victoria League assumed its work in Canada; the Glasgow branch no longer played a key distributive role for Canadian locals, although it continued to supply the growing demand for books in South Africa and the less settled parts of Australia. "Aberdeen Association for the Distribution of Good Literature to Settlers in Canada," file 12, MG 127 IB 5, vol. 5, AP-LAC. Lady Aberdeen's association offered assistance to the Canadian Reading Camp Association from the latter's earliest days, sending "comfort bags" with basic hygiene supplies, books, and magazines to the reading camps between about 1901 and 1908. Fitzpatrick, *Library Extension: Travelling Libraries and Reading Camps*, p. 14, MG 28, I 124, vol. 107, FC-LAC. Fitzpatrick's annual reports acknowledge the support of the Aberdeen Association, particularly the Toronto and Winnipeg branches, until 1908.
20 Friesen, "Adult Education and Union Education," 169–70. For a fuller account of the history of the WEA, see Radforth and Sangster, "'A Link between Labour and Learning'" and Friesen and Taksa, "Workers' Education in Australia and Canada." The British WEA (founded in 1903) is discussed at some length in chapter 8 of Rose, *The Intellectual Life*. For the Antigonish Movement, see Alexander, *The Antigonish Movement*; and Lotz and Welton, "'Knowledge for the People.'" For the Women's Institute Movement, see Crowley, "The Origins of Continuing Education for Women"; Dennison, "'Housekeepers of the Community'"; and Sheehan, "Women's Organizations."
21 MacPherson, *Each for All*, 12, 110–11.
22 For a good overview of the literature on educational initiatives among immigrant workers (and particularly those Eastern European workers who arrived after 1905), see McKay, *Reasoning Otherwise*, 398–407. For urban Jewish communities, see Abella, *A Coat of Many Colours*, 115–16; and Tulchinsky, *Taking Root*, 259. For Ukrainian communities, see Petryshyn, *Peasants in the Promised Land*, 163, 169; Martynowych, *Ukrainians in Canada*, 265, 297, 270–1, 277; and Krawchuk, *The Ukrainian Socialist Movement in Canada*. For Finnish communities in Fort William and Port Arthur, Ontario, see Beaulieu, *Labour at the Lakehead*, 22; and Metsaranta, *Project Bay Street*, 100–48.
23 Mitchell, "'The Manufacture of Souls,'" n.p.; Radforth and Sangster, "'A Link Between Labour and Learning,'" 49–76.

24 Canadian universities (especially what is now Queen's University) were experimenting with extension from the late nineteenth century; however, in the early twentieth century, important new extension programs were set up by the University of Alberta (1912) and St. Francis Xavier University (1920, as part of the Antigonish Movement). Tippett, *Making Culture*, 58–62. Tippett surveys a variety of early-twentieth-century cultural educational initiatives aimed at working-class adults in *Making Culture*, 51–8.
25 Sutherland, *Children in English-Canadian Society*, 206.
26 Draper and Carere, "Selected Chronology," 50; Schuessler and Schuessler, *School on Wheels*, 37. See also McLeod, "A Short History," 26.
27 Murray G. Ross describes Canada's early YMCA leaders as "disposed to what would in their day be termed 'liberal' views, both theological and other. They were impatient with denominational pettiness and strong supporters of interdemoninational activity," as well as promoters of education in unconventional contexts, such as railway yards and lumber camps. Ross, *The Y.M.C.A. in Canada*, 69–71.
28 Mills, *Fool for Christ*, 52–53. Mills is analyzing the content of Woodsworth's 1917 article "Nation-Building."
29 Fitzpatrick, *Library Extension in Ontario: Travelling Libraries and Reading Camps*, 3–4, MG 28, I 124, vol. 107. The year 1899 is often given as the founding date of the association, and Fitzpatrick likely began some initial work in this year, but it seems that the association was formally created in July 1900. Robinson, "The History," 28. Robinson suggests that the association operated three reading camps in 1900–1; the first annual report makes clear that there was a fourth, although this last may not have operated out of a separate cabin. Fitzpatrick, *Library Extension in Ontario: Travelling Libraries and Reading Camps*, 3–4, MG 28, I 124, vol. 107. Fitzpatrick claimed in a 1901 interview that he built three of the camps at his own expense. "Free Reading Camps," 10.
30 Both Robinson and Morrison cite the figure of twenty-four reading rooms in 1903. Robinson, "The History," 18; Morrison, "Black Flies," 35. In his 1902–3 annual report, Fitzpatrick claims there were thirty reading camps in operation during the period (see page 22 of Fitzpatrick, *Home Education Extension: Reading Camps, Camp Schools, Reading Tents, Camp Churches, with Third Annual Report of Canadian Reading Camp Association 1902–03*, 3rd Annual Report, MG 28, I 124, vol. 107, FC-LAC). By 1912–13 (just prior to the period of decline during the First World War), there were seventy-one labourer-teachers and four field supervisors, and between 1904 and 1919, approximately 40 percent of the association's work was conducted in camps outside Ontario (by 1919, there were instructors in every province but Prince Edward Island). Tents were

used in camps until the mid-1920s, when they were discontinued, probably because of growing employer cooperation in the provision of shacks. Robinson, "The History," 19, 40–1, 18.
31 Martin, "Action and Advocacy," 64–7; Robinson, "The History," 38.
32 For a fuller account of the nation's economic "transformation" in this period, see Brown and Cook, *Canada, 1896–1921*.
33 Morrison, "Black Flies," 37–8.
34 *The Immigrant, with Twelfth Annual Report of the Canadian Reading Camp Association, 1912*, n.p., MG 28, I 124, vol. 107, FC-LAC. Immigration increased steadily after the turn of the century, reaching its peak (400,870 individuals) in 1913, the year after Frontier College's annual report declared the organization's commitment to citizenship efforts. For a table detailing annual immigration to Canada between 1852 and 1992, see Avery, *Reluctant Host*, 11.

INTRODUCTION

1 Mackey, *The House of Difference*, 3; "Frontier College," Parks Canada, accessed 6 April 2016, http://www.pc.gc.ca/APPS/CP-NR/release_e.asp?id=1333&andor1=nr. According to its Annual Report for 2017, between April 2016 and March 2017, Frontier College received 8 percent of its total funding from the federal government and 45 percent of its total funding from provincial and territorial governments. Annual reports may be consulted on the Frontier College website: "Annual Reports," Frontier College, accessed 31 May 2018, https://www.frontiercollege.ca/About-Us/Annual-Reports-Financial-Statements.
2 Selman, *Citizenship and the Adult Education Movement*, 3–5. For an analysis of the racist ideologies and exclusionary measures embedded in the 1906 and 1910 Immigration Acts, including the particular targeting of Chinese and other Asian immigrants, see Kelley and Trebilcock, *The Making of the Mosaic*, 135–63.
3 Canada, Citizenship and Immigration Canada, *Discover Canada*, 11–13, 20.
4 Harrol and Simpson, "Introduction," 7.
5 See Habermas, *Structural Transformation of the Public Sphere*.
6 See Bothwell, "Something of Value?"
7 Brodie, "The Social in Social Citizenship," 33. Most of the studies of citizenship in Canada have focused on the years following the Second World War, when the Cold War added a new urgency to the state's project of regulating the identity of the "national citizen." In concert with the work of historians collected in Adamoski, Chunn, and Menzies, eds., *Contesting*

Canadian Citizenship, I add a particular focus on the early-twentieth-century elaboration of the concept of the "citizen." On the making of the meanings of citizenship in the first half of the twentieth century in Canada, and particularly the issue of citizenship education, see the essays collected in Adamoski et al., *Contesting Canadian Citizenship*; and Hébert, *Citizenship Transformation in Canada*; as well as Chen, *Tending the Gardens of Citizenship*; Druick, *Projecting Canada*; Heathorn, *For Home, Country, and Race*; Martynowych, "'Canadianizing the Foreigner'"; McLean, "Education, Identity, and Citizenship" and "'The good citizen'"; Osborne, "Education Is the Best National Insurance"; Prokop, "Canadianization of Immigrant Children"; Selman, *Citizenship and the Adult Education Movement*; Strong-Boag, "Claiming a Place"; and Walter, "Literacy, Imagined Nations, and Imperialism." The scholarship dealing with citizenship education in the later period is obviously vaster. Important studies include the essays collected in Gauvreau and Christie, *Cultures of Citizenship*; and Hébert, *Citizenship Transformation in Canada*, as well as Iacovetta, *Gatekeepers*; Schugurensky, "Adult Citizenship Education"; Selman, *Citizenship and the Adult Education Movement*; and the essays collected in the December 1996 issue of *Canadian and International Education* (especially Joshee, "The Federal Government"; and Osborne, "Education is the Best National Insurance").

8 For the "new" liberalism argument, see Ferguson, *Remaking Liberalism*. For the influence of the Social Gospel movement, see Allen, *The Social Passion*; and Cook, *The Regenerators*. For an alternative view that summarizes the influence of the (broadly defined) left on an emergent welfare state, see McKay, "For a New Kind of History."

9 Mouffe, "Democratic Citizenship," 226–7.

10 Menzies, Adamoski, and Chunn, "Rethinking the Citizen," 17.

11 Jenson, "Fated to Live," 634. According to Jenson, a citizenship regime comprises the "institutional arrangements, rules and understandings that guide and shape state policy; problem definition employed by states and citizens; and the range of claims recognized as legitimate."

12 See Marshall, *Social Policy*. The literature on the influence of Marshall's ideas on the postwar citizenship regime in Canada is vast, but a good discussion may be found in Brodie, "Citizenship and Solidarity." For a discussion of Marshall's influence on citizenship regimes across the West, see Turner, "Contemporary Problems."

13 For an analysis of the fact that social citizenship rights in Britain were not merely creations of the nation-state, see Somers, "Citizenship and

the Place of the Public Sphere." Drawing on the work of Jacques Donzelot, Brodie identifies the "tentative and uneven" character of the social rights of citizenship that emerged in Canada after the Second World War. For more on this point, see the Conclusion, as well as Gorham, "Social Citizenship and Its Fetters." Brodie further asserts that the social rights of citizenship were in the 1960s "woven into the nationalist story of who Canadians were." This conflation of social citizenship rights and Canadian identity persists in the present, asserts Brodie, despite the fact that neoliberal policy has fundamentally altered the meaning of the social. Brodie, "The Social in Social Citizenship," 31–40; Donzelot, "The Promotion of the Social," 397, 399; Brodie, "Citizenship and Solidarity," 382–6. See also Procacci, *Gouverner la misère*, for a discussion of the conflicts between formal equality and positive inequality in social citizenship.

14 McKay, "The Liberal Order Framework," 623, 630, 634.

15 There is a very helpful discussion of liberalism and the early-twentieth-century "race question" in chapter 6 of McKay, *Reasoning Otherwise*. See also Avery, *"Dangerous Foreigners"*; Harney, "Men Without Women"; Lindström, *Defiant Sisters*; Loewen, *Family, Church and Market*; Martynowych, "'Canadianizing the Foreigner'"; McLaren, "Creating 'Slaves of Satan'"; Perry, "Women, Racialized People"; Prokop, "Candianization of Immigrant Children"; Radforth, *Bushworkers and Bosses*; Ramirez, "Brief Encounters"; Sandwell, "The Limits of Liberalism"; Sandwell, "Missing Canadians"; Strong-Boag, "Who Counts?"; and Wilde, "Literacy at the Resource Frontier." Most of the essays collected in Iacovetta, with Draper and Ventresca, *A Nation of Immigrants*, are pertinent to the question of how an emergent liberal order confronted non-British immigrant cultures (especially Chan, "Bachelor Workers"; Forestell, "Bachelors"; and Lindstrom, "I Won't Be a Slave"). Franca Iacovetta's work on postwar immigrants, although it deals with a later period, similarly deals with the often uncomfortable fit between Canadian liberalism and immigrant subjects. See Iacovetta, *Gatekeepers*; and her "Making 'New' Canadians."

16 Gramsci, *Selections from the Prison Notebooks*, 34, 242. The two most important Canadian examples of studies that examine citizenship as a form of liberal governmentality are Chen, *Tending the Gardens of Citizenship*; and Druick, *Projecting Canada*, both of which draw on Michel Foucault's late theorization of governmentality. Theorists such as Giovanna Procacci, Jacques Donzelot, and Nikolas Rose have

subsequently developed this field. The "reflexive historical sociology" of Bruce Curtis, although it is not specifically focused on citizenship, is also important for its contribution to the study of education from a governmentality perspective. See, in particular, his *Building the Educational State* and *Ruling by Schooling Quebec*. For a summative discussion of the debates that McKay's use of Antonio Gramsci has engendered, see Constant and Ducharme, "Introduction," 15–17.

17 On the importance of non-state actors (and particularly organizations inspired by evangelical Protestantism and maternal feminism) to the establishment of the structures that anticipated the welfare state, see Chen, *Tending the Gardens of Citizenship*; Christie, *Engendering the State*; Guest, *The Emergence*; Mitchison, "Early Women's Organizations"; and Valverde, *The Age of Light, Soap, and Water*. For a review of the key literature on moral regulation and the role of non-state actors, see Loo and Strange, *Making Good*. Chen, Valverde, and Loo and Strange all analyze the emergence of citizenship and moral regulation in relation to liberal governmentality.

18 Curtis, "'After Canada,'" 181–2.

19 Christie, *Engendering the State*, 12–13.

20 McKay, "The Liberal Order Framework," 634–5.

21 Gramsci, *Selections from the Prison Notebooks*, 261; Feola, "Fear and Loathing," 54; Johnson, "The Politics of Affective Citizenship," 496; Berlant, *Cruel Optimism*, 224; Berlant, The *Queen of America*, 5; Berlant, *The Female Complaint*.

22 Welton, "Introduction," 2–3. For "insider" histories of Frontier College, see Cook, "Alfred Fitzpatrick" and "Educational Justice for the Campmen"; Cook and Robinson, "The Fight of My Life"; Forest and Morrison, "The Women of Frontier College"; Fernandez and Thompson, "Frontier College"; Krotz, with Martin and Fernandez, *Frontier College Letters*; Morrison, *Alfred Fitzpatrick* and *Camps and Classrooms*; and Wigmore, "Mining the Frontier College Archives." Some unpublished theses have also undertaken preliminary studies. See Kidd, "The Frontier College Labourer-Teacher"; Martin, "Action and Advocacy"; Robinson, "The History of Frontier College"; and Zavitz, "The Frontier College." More recent essays attempt to understand Frontier College's early period in relation to gender politics and the politics of imperialism. See McLean, "'The good citizen'"; Walter, "Adult Literacy Education" and "Literacy, Imagined Nations, and Imperialism"; and Wilde, "Literacy at the Resource Frontier."

23 Selman, *Citizenship and the Adult Education Movement*, 4–5. See also Selman, Cooke and Dampier, *The Foundations*; and Selman, *Adult Education in Canada*.
24 McKay, "The Liberal Order Framework," 641–2.
25 Until 1951, the Indian Act, first made law in 1876, defined a person as "any individual other than an Indian." Henderson, "*Sui Generis*," 435n16. In 1956, the Citizenship Act was amended to grant formal citizenship to status Indians and Inuit. An Act to Amend the Canadian Citizenship Act, 1956 S.C., ch. 6, s. 2. Balibar contrasts "external exclusion" to forms of "internal exclusion" – when an "'external border' is mirrored by an 'internal' border," or when the "condition of foreignness is projected within a political space or national territory to create an inadmissible alterity," or when, on the contrary, "an additional element of interiority and belonging is introduced into an anthropological category, in such a way as the push the foreigner out." *Citizenship*, 68.
26 Veracini, *Settler Colonialism*, 16–17, 26, 33–4; Quayson, "Paracolonialism," 6. Eva Mackey similarly discusses the ways in which settler nation-building entails both the "management of populations" and the "creation of national identity." *House of Difference*, 23.
27 Hébert and Wilkinson, "The Citizenship Debates," 17.
28 Sandwell, "Missing Canadians," 247. Among these "a-liberal" historical subjects who lived "outside" and "alongside" the emerging liberal order, Sandwell counts peasants; those who persisted well into the twentieth century with forms of collective, sometimes religiously defined community; and First Nations peoples (particularly with regard to their practices of hunting, fishing, and trapping). For work that explores the continued importance of rural society throughout the first half of the twentieth century, see Sandwell, "'Read, Listen, Discuss, Act,'" "Missing Canadians," "Notes Toward a History of Rural Canada," and "Rural Reconstruction," as well as Christie and Gauvreau, *A Full-Orbed Christianity*. Although Canada was officially more urban than rural after 1921, Sandwell points out that this fact must be viewed in the context of what was defined as "urban." Until 1951, this definition was not dependent on the population of the community. It was only in 1941 that the majority of Canadians lived in communities with populations larger than one thousand people. Sandwell, "'Read, Listen, Act, Discuss,'" 172–3, 189n9.
29 Gramsci, *Selections from the Prison Notebooks*, 34.
30 McKay, *Reasoning Otherwise*, 378; Radforth, *Bushworkers and Bosses*, 103. As Erica Martin admits in her study of Frontier College, there have

been many estimations of the association's success in various periods and locations, but they are ultimately only estimates. Fitzpatrick's annual reports, meant for promotional purposes, likely inflated the organization's success. See Martin, "Action and Advocacy," 83.

31 Long, *Book Clubs*, 8.
32 Rose, *The Intellectual Life*, 256. The classic studies of working-class reading, influenced by the tradition of British cultural studies, are either (like the Frankfurt School) less than sanguine about the cultural consumption practices of working-class communities (e.g., Richard Hoggart's 1957 book *The Uses of Literacy*), or dedicated to a vision of an "authentic" and autonomous working-class culture (e.g., Thompson's *The Making of the English Working Class*). Bryan Palmer's 1979 book *A Culture in Conflict* was at the forefront of what is now called the "new" labour studies, which draws deeply from the "culturalist" approach to labour and class modelled by E.P. Thompson's 1963 classic *The Making of the English Working Class*. Many studies of working-class leisure cultures and associational life in Canada have followed. Examples that consider education, reading, and cultural initiatives include Friesen, "Adult Education and Union Education"; Friesen and Taksa, "Workers' Education in Australia and Canada"; Marks, *Revivals and Roller Rinks*; and Radforth and Sangster, "A Link Between Labour and Learning." Histories of Canada's non-British immigrant communities offer a wealth of information regarding early-twentieth-century education and reading initiatives, which were generally undertaken in languages other than English or French. See this Introduction, note 15. As Jason Martinek has observed, histories of education, literacy, and reading tend to be oriented to middle-class readers and reading. *Socialism and Print Culture*, 6. Other histories of workers' reading that, like Martinek's, work against the tendency he identifies include Lyons, *Readers and Society*; McHenry, *Forgotten Readers*; Pawley, *Reading on the Middle Border*; Rose, *The Intellectual Life*; and Smith, *Hard-Boiled*. While Rose's has been the most influential of these, his empiricist assumptions about the coherence and stability of oral and written accounts of reading, as well as his tendency to focus on the most skilled, literate, and affluent members of the "working classes," produce an overly optimistic view of the possibilities of the history of reading for labour history. Rose's empiricist tendencies are linked to his opposition of the history of audiences and literary criticism, an opposition that hinges on, in Rose's estimation, the empirical grasp of the former and the ideology of the latter. For a useful critique of such oppositions and their

relation to cultural studies in the United States and Britain, see Janice Radway's revised (1992) introduction to *Reading the Romance*.

33 On the "new" literacy studies, see Street, "What's 'New'" and *Literacy in Theory and Practice*; and Prinsloo, "Literacy and the New Literacy Studies." For qualitative histories of reading, see, for example, Cavallo and Chartier, *A History of Reading in the West*; and Towheed, Crone, and Halsey, eds., *The History of Reading*. See also Darnton, "First Steps." As James English notes, recent sociologically oriented work on reading and readers by Roger Chartier and others has both "helped to dislodge the traditional literary-critical conception of 'the' reader as a generalized text processor" and promoted understanding of "the reception side of literary practice as a complex and changing social space in which the kind of reading we do (silent, secular, academic, unshared, et cetera) is a recent and decidedly nontypical development." As English also notes, such an approach shares much with Gramscian cultural studies. "Everywhere and Nowhere." In joining literary studies to citizenship studies with the aid of sociological and historical methods, I question the way that literary studies treats citizenship – as a series of textual representations that, in Jonathan Kertzer's words, mould the nation "in the minds of citizens." Diana Brydon, one of the few scholars of Canadian literatures who has called for interrogation of the "roles of citizens and institutions within the contexts of literary study," offers a critical prompt, but one that has not been taken up with much vigour. Kertzer, *Worrying the Nation*, 12; Brydon, "Metamorphoses of a Discipline," 2. One other significant exception to my claim regarding the relation of Canadian literary studies to citizenship is Donna Pennee's influential essay "Literary Citizenship," which examines the role of pedagogy in producing critical citizenship. Pennee draws on Len Findlay's conception of "critical citizenship" and Smaro Kamboureli's theorization of "negative pedagogy" (in Findlay's "Always Indigenize!" and Kamboureli's *Scandalous Bodies*). There is a large body of contemporary literary scholarship in Canada that seeks to understand literature's cultivation of alternative (read non-national) forms of citizenship. See, in particular, the publications that have resulted from the work of the TransCanada Institute, most notably the essays collected in Kamboureli and Miki, eds., *Trans.Can.Lit* (especially Cho, "Diasporic Citizenship: Contradictions and Possibilities"); Cho, "Diasporic Citizenship"; and the essays collected in Fleischman, Styvendale, and McCaroll, eds., *Narratives of Citizenship*. Literary scholarship that focuses on earlier (and particularly pre–Second World War) conceptions of citizenship is less robust in quantity, but important studies include Kulba,

"Citizens, Consumers"; Morris, "From 'Stalwart Peasant' to Canadian Citizen"; Sheffer, "'Citizen Sure Thing'"; Smith, "Fiction and the Nation"; and Tough, "'Civilization Had Given Him the Vote.'"

34 Murray, *"Come, bright improvement!,"* 159. Burgeoning international interest in book history and print culture studies has prompted increased attention in Canada to all manner of questions related to the nation's material culture of print. The monumental *History of the Book in Canada* project includes, in all of its three volumes, sections on readers and reading. In the third volume, which deals with the twentieth century, there are a number of short articles that point to the tremendous gaps in historical knowledge regarding readers and reading. See, for example, Verrette, "Measuring Literacy"; Murray and Rotundo, "Surveying the Habit of Reading"; and Knight, "Reaching Out." In Canada as elsewhere, the study of reading is generally marginalized within the field of book history. Indeed, the canonical theoretical model of the field, Robert Darnton's communications circuit, leaves the relationship between the reader and every other stage of the circuit in question. See "What Is the History of Books?" Some recent scholarship on the history of reading in Canada is beginning to close these gaps, yet the cultural consumption and reading practices of workers and immigrants, particularly in the period of great immigration following the turn of the nineteenth century, are activities that beg further exploration. See Karr, *Authors and Audiences*; Edwards, *Paper Talk*; Fuller, "Listening to the Readers"; Fuller and Rehberg Sedo, *Reading Beyond the Book*; Fuller and Rehberg Sedo, "A Reading Spectacle"; and Murray, *"Come, Bright Improvement!"*

35 Williams, *The Sociology of Culture*, 12–13, 139, 140, 141, 33, 186. Williams is deeply influenced by Pierre Bourdieu's interest in how the education system contributes to symbolic production and its "decisive role in the generalized imposition of the legitimate mode of consumption." Bourdieu, "The Field of Cultural Production," 37. See also Bourdieu and Passeron, *Reproduction in Education*; and Bourdieu, *Distinction*. The "reflexive" sociology of literature has been taken up, for example, in Baldick, *The Social Mission*; Eagleton, "The Rise of English"; Graff, *Professing Literature*; Hunter, *Culture and Government*; Murray, *Working in English*; and Viswanathan, *Masks of Conquest*. Viswanathan notes that she focuses on how English rulers imagined Indians rather than on how "Indians actually received ... or resisted the ideological content of British literary education" because she is interested in what English attempts to institute literary education in India and to anticipate Indian response say about the fragility of colonial rule. She also notes that such work is

beyond the "literary, textual analysis" she employs. *Masks of Conquest*, 11–12.
36 Storey, *Cultural Consumption*, 152–3.
37 Darnton, *The Case for Books*, 4, 5. There are countless studies that link the emergence of the Enlightenment to the practice of reading. Important ones include Darnton, *The Great Cat Massacre* and *The Forbidden Bestsellers*; Sher, *The Enlightenment and the Book*; and Warner, *The Letters of the Republic*.
38 Viswanathan, *Masks of Conquest*, vvi–xviii. See also Curtis, *Building the Educational State* and *Ruling by Schooling Quebec*.
39 "Frontier College," 268–9.
40 Draper, "Introduction," 37; Walter, "Literacy, Imagined Nations, and Imperialism," 56.
41 Martin, "Action and Advocacy," 12–13. See the sources cited in this book's Preface, note 22.
42 Derrida, *Mal d'archive*, 2–3.

CHAPTER ONE

1 Recent articles on Frontier College have focused on the connections between books and citizenship in the association's early camp work. See Bruce, "Reading Camps"; McLean, "'The good citizen'"; and Walter, "Literacy, Imagined Nations, and Imperialism." To this scholarship, I add an emphasis on Fitzpatrick's liberalism, his conception of literature, his use of particular authors in the first camps, the association's receptivity to workers' cultural preferences, and workers' responses.
2 Matthews and Kerr, *Historical Atlas of Canada*, 30; Radforth, *Bushworkers and Bosses*, 14, 26–8.
3 Bradwin, *The Bunkhouse Man*, 63–75.
4 *Library Extension in Ontario: Travelling Libraries and Reading Camps*, p. 7, MG 28, I 124, vol. 107, FC-LAC; Radforth, *Bushworkers and Bosses*, 27.
5 Still, Northern Ontario's economic boom after the turn of the century, coupled with the influx of non-British immigrants in the same period, created a population with a much larger concentration of both French Canadian residents (just under 24 percent) and non-British residents (just over 25 percent) than in the rest of the province. See Zaslow, *Opening of the Canadian North*, 192. Even in the first half-decade of the twentieth century, some instructors reported a significant "variety in nationality" (Italian, Scandinavian, Austrian, Ukrainian, Finnish) in the Northern Ontario camps. See *The Education of the Frontier Laborer, with Fifth*

Annual Report of the Canadian Reading Camp Association, p. 32, MG 28, I 124, vol. 107, FC-LAC. See also the letter to Fitzpatrick from John Miller on the inside front and back covers of the fourth annual report: *Camp Education Extension, with Fourth Annual Report of Canadian Reading Camp Association 1903–04*, MG 28, I 124, vol. 107, FC-LAC.

6 Bradwin, *The Bunkhouse Man*, 76–8; Radforth, *Bushworkers and Bosses*, 39.

7 Fitzpatrick, "Social Amelioration in the Lumbering Camps," 15; Fitzpatrick, "The Neglected Citizen in the Camps," 43; *Camp Education by Contact, With Ninth Annual Report of the Reading Camp Association, 1909*, p. 15, MG 28, I 124, vol. 107, FC-LAC.

8 Allen, *The Social Passion*, 17. Ramsay Cook distinguishes between Social Gospellers who heralded the "Kingdom of God on earth" and those who anticipated the "secular city." *The Regenerators*, 229. (Fitzpatrick's faith in this "secular city" is very clearly demonstrated in his 1905 article "The Neglected Citizen in the Camps.") McKay, *Reasoning Otherwise*, 232–33.

9 *Library Extension in Ontario: Reading Camps and Club Houses*, pp. 3–6, MG 28, I 124, vol. 107, FC-LAC. The books in the travelling libraries were difficult to disinfect due to the paste in their bindings. This problem appears to have affected the circulation of McLennan Travelling Libraries to the camps; the first library sent from McGill in January 1901 to a camp in Nairn Centre, Ontario, was returned to Montreal in November of that year for fumigation. Fitzpatrick does not appear to have made further requests for these books, but perhaps the advent of the Ontario Travelling Libraries after 1901 made books from McGill unnecessary. See Registers 1901–1955, RG 40 Libraries, MTL-MLMU.

10 Fitzpatrick, "Life in Lumbering," 49, 51.

11 Valverde, *The Age of Light, Soap, and Water*, 18–19; Fitzpatrick, *The University in Overalls*, 8.

12 *Library Extension in Ontario: Travelling Libraries and Reading Camps*, p. 1, MG 28, I 124, vol. 107, FC-LAC.

13 *Home Education Extension*, p. 8, MG 28, I 124, vol. 107, FC-LAC. This emphasis on education as an inexpensive form of crime prevention runs throughout the history of education in Canada. For example, Egerton Ryerson, Chief Superintendent of Schools in Upper Canada, promoted mechanics' institutes and public libraries for adults as a means of rendering individuals unlikely to "sink down into melancholy, slothfulness or resort to places of sensual and intemperate indulgence for relaxation or pleasure." Qtd. in Candy, "From Homo Canadiannus," 8–9.

14 See the discussion of such worker-led initiatives in the Preface, notes 20, 21, and 22.
15 Christie, *Engendering the State*, 20.
16 Ibid., 21–2.
17 Johnson, "The Politics of Affective Citizenship," 496. On the importance of the couple, the nuclear family, and the special authority of white, middle-class women to forms of settler colonial rule, see, for example, Henderson, *Settler Feminism*; Povinelli, *The Empire of Love*; and Stoler, *Carnal Knowledge*.
18 For a discussion of how this kind of argument is characteristic of classic liberalism, see Holmes, "Liberal Guilt." For an example of how education and the social good were similarly linked by Scots who brought Smith's thinking to Canada, see McCulloch, *The Nature and Uses of a Liberal Education*, 6–8.
19 For a complete list of the board members, see *Home Education Extension: Reading Camps, Camp Schools, Reading Tents, Camp Churches, With Third Annual Report of the Canadian Reading Camp Association, 1902–3*, p. 21, MG 28, I 124, vol. 107, FC-LAC.
20 Fitzpatrick, "Life in Lumbering and Mining Camps," 49, 51; Radforth, *Bushworkers and Bosses*, 104; *Camp Education Extension*, p. 10, MG 28, I 124, vol. 107, FC-LAC.
21 *Library Extension in Ontario: Reading Camps and Club Houses*, p. 18, MG 28, I 124, vol. 107, FC-LAC.
22 Altick, *The English Common Reader*, 9–10; Hubert, *Harmonious Perfection*, 9–15.
23 Wilson, Stamp, and Audet, eds., *Canadian Education*, 39.
24 Fergusson, *Mechanics' Institutes in Nova Scotia*, 11–13.
25 Hubert, *Harmonious Perfection*, 29; Phillips Casteel, "The Dream of Empire," 137.
26 Morrison, *Alfred Fitzpatrick*, 12–13.
27 Gauvreau, *The Evangelical Century*, 24. For a discussion of the Free Church movement – the modernization of old Calvinist orthodoxy in late-nineteenth-century Canadian Presbyterianism, see Crerar, "'Crackling Sounds,'" 123–36; and Gauvreau, *The Evangelical Century*, 19–31.
28 Morrison, *Alfred Fitzpatrick*, 21–2; Hubert, *Harmonious Perfection*, 83. On the influence of Arnoldian idealism on the new discipline of English literary studies in Canadian universities in the last third of the nineteenth century, see also Fee, "Canadian Literature."
29 Phillips Casteel, "The Dream of Empire," 144. Phillips Casteel also makes the excellent point that McCulloch's satirical *Letters of Mephibosheth Stepsure* coolly assesses the fact that the "true value of the study of

rhetoric for the Scots and other members of the British Empire may have rested not so much in assimilating to Englishness as in self-advancement and material gain." "The Dream of Empire," 149.
30 Draper and Carere, "Selected Chronology," 47. Queen's commenced its extension program in 1888; the University of Toronto followed three years later.
31 McKillop, *A Disciplined Intelligence*, 217–18; Cook, *The Regenerators*, 186; Berger, *The Sense of Power*, 32–3. For a discussion of how Grant's idealism is connected to the Free Church movement, see the first chapter of Fraser, *The Social Uplifters*.
32 Fitzpatrick to Tom Moore, 6 April 1922, MG 28, I 124, vol. 27, "General Correspondence," FC-LAC.
33 Morrison, *Alfred Fitzpatrick*, 24.
34 Registers 1901–1955, RG 40 Libraries, Rare Books and Special Collections, MTL-MLMU. In 1899, the family of Hugh McLennan endowed McGill's travelling library service, which operated until the late 1960s, mostly in rural Quebec. On 4 February 1901, Charles Gould, the university librarian at McGill, wrote to Fitzpatrick to inform him that, in accordance with Fitzpatrick's request, he was sending a travelling library to a camp at Nairn Centre. Gould was clearly uncertain about the contents of the library, given that his system of travelling libraries had never before been sent out to logging or mining camps: "We have some doubts as to what would be most useful in this new phase of travelling library work, and I hope you will regard this library in the light of an experiment, and will give me frankly such suggestions as its use may lead you to think practical." Fitzpatrick, *Library Extension in Ontario: Travelling Libraries and Reading Camps*, p. 37, MG 28, I 124, vol. 107, FC-LAC. For the Aberdeen Association, see "What To Do With Old Books and Magazines: Report of the Aberdeen Association, 1898," file 12, MG 127 IB5, vol. 5, AP-LAC. For more information about the Aberdeen Association, see the Preface and Mein, "The Aberdeen Association."
35 Bruce, "Reading Camps," 75–81.
36 *Camp Education Extension*, p. 10, MG 28, I 124, vol. 107, FC-LAC.
37 Fraser, *The Social Uplifters*, 1–7.
38 Viswanathan, *Masks of Conquest*, 19.
39 Altick, *The English Common Reader*, 136–40.
40 Baldick, *The Social Mission*, 65–6.
41 Curtis, "'Littery Merit,'" 285–6. For other analyses of the pervasiveness of a "utilitarian/proscriptive" approach to reading in mid-nineteenth-century Upper Canada, see Murray, "Teachers Must Read"; and Gerson, *A Purer Taste*, 17–35.

42 Altick, *The English Common Reader*, 132.
43 Blanchard, "Anatomy," 395. For a map indicating the historical spread of mechanics' institutes in British North America, see Wadland and Hobbs, "The Printed Word," 136–7.
44 Ontario, Ministry of Education, *Special Report*, 10.
45 Eadie, "The Napanee Mechanics' Institutes," 214–15.
46 Blanchard, "Anatomy," 396–7.
47 Ontario, Ministry of Education, *Special Report*, 43.
48 Lamonde, McNally, and Rotundo, "Public Libraries," 262.
49 Toronto Mechanics' Institute, "Schedule to Annual Report, Schedule B," 30 April 1876, RG 2-146, MS 918, reel 1, PLB-AO.
50 Robins, "Useful Education," 30–1.
51 Montreal Mechanics' Institute, *Catalogue of Books*. For similar examples, see Lyons, "New Readers in the Nineteenth Century," 335; Murray, *"Come, bright improvement!,"* 274n74; and Palmer, *A Culture in Conflict* 51–2. Bryan Palmer notes the tendency in the scholarship of mechanics' institutes to conflate middle-class dominance with workers' acquiescence and counters this with frequent demonstrations of the ways that workers made their cultural preferences known. *A Culture in Conflict*, 49–50.
52 Hardy, *The Public Library*, 62, 63, 58–61. Carole Gerson notes the common appeal in English Canadian literary periodicals of the late Victorian period to the "Golden Age" of Sir Walter Scott's romances and contends that this preference for Scott marked a "neat reversal" in which the common distrust of imaginative writing and the demand that "fiction justify itself by relating didactically to the real world" was turned into a distrust of realistic literature and a demand that "fiction revert to simple entertainment." *A Purer Taste*, 35.
53 Sutherland, *Children in English-Canadian Society*, 183–8.
54 McKillop, *A Disciplined Intelligence*, 205.
55 Fitzpatrick, "Life in Lumbering and Mining Camps," 49.
56 *Home Education Extension*, pp. 23–4, MG 28, I 124, vol. 107, FC-LAC. As this report indicates, Fitzpatrick engaged eight such labourer-teachers in 1902–3, with the balance of his instructional staff provided by missionaries and a medical doctor. According to James Morrison, the concept of the labourer-teacher came from Angus Grey, a reading camp instructor and librarian who proposed the idea in the winter of 1903 as a remedy to the problem of poor attendance in his cabin. *Alfred Fitzpatrick*, 27–8. Fitzpatrick's suggestion that this plan had already been put in place for the winter of 1903 contradicts Morrison's account; nevertheless, Grey's role in

the birth of the labourer-teacher is a central feature of the institutionally authored history of Frontier College, a fact that suggests the organization's consistent privileging of pedagogy and guidance over self-directed reading, as well its commitment to teaching methods forged by field experience. See references to the story of Angus Grey in Fernandez and Thompson, "Frontier College," 12; and Robinson, "The History of Frontier College," 36–37.

57 *Camp Education Extension*, pp. 11–12, MG 28, I 124, vol. 107, FC-LAC; Fitzpatrick, "Social Amelioration," 15; Berger, *The Sense of Power*, 140–41.
58 *Camp Education Extension*, pp. 10, 13, MG 28, I 124, vol. 107, FC-LAC.
59 *Library Extension in Ontario: Travelling Libraries and Reading Camps*, p. 36, MG 28, I 124, vol. 107, FC-LAC.
60 "Travelling Libraries," 8; "Books for Michipicoten," 10.
61 *Library Extension in Ontario: Travelling Libraries and Reading Camps*, p. 17, MG 28, I 124, vol. 107, FC-LAC.
62 "Free Reading Camps," 10.
63 Sutherland, *Children in English-Canadian Society*, 186–7.
64 Fitzpatrick, *The University in Overalls*, 8.
65 For a discussion of Scots Canadian cultural idealists' Arnoldian conceptions of the reading act and suitable reading matter, see Phillips Casteel, "The Dream of Empire," 142–43; and Fraser, *The Social Uplifters*, 1–7.
66 Viswanathan, *Masks of Conquest*, xvi.
67 Fitzpatrick to Richard Harcourt, 2 September 1901; and Fitzpatrick to Harcourt, 14 October 1901, RG 2-29-4-4, MS 913, DELC-AO.
68 Fitzpatrick, *Library Extension in Ontario: Travelling Libraries and Reading Camps*, MG 28, I 124, vol. 107, FC-LAC, 48.
69 "The Ontario Library Association," 271.
70 "Rural School Reading," 7.
71 "Registers of Books 1901–1907: Register of Books Received and Labelled by the Ontario Travelling Library," RG 2-146, MS 918, reel 1, PLB-AO. In the fall of 1901, Harcourt was already modifying individual cases of books; in response to an application from a camp in Cache Bay, for example, he promised to send the "elementary readers" and books in French that they requested. Harcourt to A.J. Young, 26 September 1901, RG 2-29-4-4, MS 913, DELC-AO. However, the Department of Education was slow to understand the meaning of "elementary" reading, sending, for example, the French-language works of Jules Verne, Alphonse Daudel, Alexandre Dumas, Honoré de Balzac, and François René de Chateaubriand to camps

in response to requests like the one cited above. Richard Harcourt to William Tyrrell, 27 September 1901, and Tyrell to Harcourt, September 1901, RG 2-29-4-4, MS 913, DELC-AO.
72 Fitzpatrick to Harcourt, 1 January 1904, and Fitzpatrick to Harcourt, 14 January 1904, RG 2-29-4-13, MS 913, DELC-AO.
73 *Camp Education Extension*, p. 26, MG 28, I 124, vol. 107, FC-LAC; *The Education of the Frontier Laborer*, p. 36, MG 28, I 124, vol. 107, FC-LAC; *Camp Education Extension*, p. 71, MG 28, I 124, vol. 107, FC-LAC.
74 "Registers of Books 1901–1907: Register of Books Received and Labelled by the Ontario Travelling Library," RG 2-146, MS 918, reel 1, PLB-AO.
75 Fitzpatrick, *The University in Overalls*, 10.
76 Gerson, *A Purer Taste*, 132, 142. On this point, see also chapter 1 of Doyle, *Progressive Heritage*.
77 F.W. Watt points out that the three earliest of these labour periodicals published some creative writing, including M.A. Foran's serialized novel *The Other Side*, which appeared in the *Ontario Workman* beginning on 27 June 1872: "A melodramatic tale of factory life, trade unionism, and the eventual triumph of the labour movement over the tyrannical oppression of the capitalist class, it is noteworthy as an early fictional critique of industrial urban society, its class divisions and its economic basis." "Literature of Protest," 464–65. The *Western Clarion* was the organ of the Socialist Party of Canada from 1905 to 1920. T. Phillips Thompson's *Labor Reform Songster* is a pamphlet of simple verse adapted to familiar musical settings of hymn tunes and political anthems; the poems rely on "generalized allusions to capitalist exploitation, militant exhortations to revolutionary action, and repetitive refrains expressing the sufferings and hopes of workers." Doyle, *Progressive Heritage*, 35, 37–8.
78 Willmott, *Unreal Country*, 21. The human concerns of this period's animal stories have been observed many times. In the early twentieth century, naturalists such as John Burroughs and Theodore Roosevelt decried the flagrant anthropomorphism of the animal story as Seton and contemporaries such as Charles G.D. Roberts practised it, and contemporary critics tend to read *Wild Animals* as allegorical. See Taylor, "Seton, Ernest Thompson," 1035. Nevertheless, Seton's tales were likely popular with utilitarian educational reformers precisely because the author insisted (in his "Note to the Reader") on his "realistic" (rather than allegorical or anthropomorphic) representation of animal life.
79 Seton, *Wild Animals I Have Known*, 15.
80 Ibid., 215–16, 232.

81 Johnson, "National Species," 339; Jones, "Wildlifewriting?," 138.
82 Seton, *Wild Animals I Have Known*, 220–1, 247, 237.
83 "Lumber Camp Libraries," 17.
84 Fitzpatrick, *Library Extension: Travelling Libraries and Reading Camps*, p.12, MG 28, I 124, vol. 107, FC-LAC; "Free Reading Camps," 10. For the criticism of anti-Catholic feeling in Ralph Connor novels, see M.C.M, [Untitled], 429. Similarly, a Catholic priest from Haileybury, Ontario, wrote to Fitzpatrick in 1907 to complain that *Raymond the Fox*, a book in one of the Ontario Travelling Libraries, was "calculated to wound the feelings of Catholics." J.R. O'Gorman to Fitzpatrick, 17 July 1907, MG 28, I 124, vol. 3, "Magazines, 1907," FC-LAC.
85 In a 1908 letter, Fitzpatrick thanks Gordon for his "valuable assistance," noting that he had "doubled" his contribution in the preceding year and had "accommodated the Association with a temporary loan." He then asks Gordon to consider endorsing a fundraising letter with his signature because of his "great patience and interest in these men" and because "you have pictured their life better than anyone else, and your name has more weight on this subject, than that of any other." Fitzpatrick to Gordon, 7 March 1908, MG 28, I 124, vol. 3, "Gordon, C.W., 1908," FC-LAC. Fitzpatrick's correspondence with Gordon and Gordon's support of the organization continued for many years. In the annual reports for the 1920s, for example, he is listed as one of the organization's principal "patrons." A 1921 letter from Gordon to Fitzpatrick indicates that Gordon continued to make financial contributions to the association during the 1920s, a fact that is confirmed by the Annual Report for 1921, which records a $25.00 contribution from Gordon. Gordon to Fitzpatrick, 20 June 1921, MG 28, I 124, vol. 25, "Manitoba Government," FC-LAC; and *Treasurer's Report of the Frontier College, 1921*, p. 14, MG 28, I 124, vol. 107, "Annual Report," FC-LAC. In the fall of 1921, Fitzpatrick corresponded with Gordon regarding the *Handbook for New Canadians*; Gordon read the book and provided some lines of praise that Fitzpatrick subsequently used in the promotion of the book. Fitzpatrick to Gordon, 17 October 1921, MG 28, I 124, vol. 25, "General Correspondence," FC-LAC.
86 *Library Extension in Ontario: Reading Camps and Club Houses*, pp. 34, 25, MG 28, I 124, vol. 107, FC-LAC.
87 "Registers of Books 1901–1907: Register of Books Received and Labelled by the Ontario Travelling Library," RG 2-146, MS 918, reel 1, PLB-AO.
88 *Camp Education*, p. 39, MG 28, I 124, vol. 107, FC-LAC.

89 Fitzpatrick to Gordon, 20 December 1901, MSS 56, box 48, folder 1, Department of Archives and Special Collections, CGP-UM. Between 1899 and 1914, Gordon's novels made the top ten on the Canadian Bestseller List of the trade journal *Bookseller and Stationer* fourteen times. That was more than any other author, and his work also sold well internationally. See Karr, "Popular and Best-Selling Fiction," 399.
90 Fitzpatrick, *Library Extension: Travelling Libraries and Reading Camps*, MG 28, I 124, vol. 107, FC-LAC.
91 Connor, *Black Rock*, 34, 36.
92 Connor, *The Man From Glengarry*, 342.
93 Slaughter, *Human Rights, Inc.*, 20–1, 32.
94 Coleman, *White Civility*, 82, 113; see also 120–3.
95 *Home Education Extension*, p. 19, MG 28, I 124, vol. 107, FC-LAC.
96 *Camp Education by Contact*, p. 7, MG 28, I 124, vol. 107, FC-LAC; Fitzpatrick, *The University in Overalls*, 126.
97 Walter, "Literacy, Imagined Nations, and Imperialism," 54; Fitzpatrick, "Social Amelioration," 15. For more on the figure of the muscular Christian and its resistance to feminized Christianity, see Curtis, "The Son of Man and God the Father"; and Tosh, *A Man's Place*. For other analyses of the way that conceptions of masculinity, in particular, shaped Fitzpatrick's project, see McLean, "'The good citizen'"; and Wilde, "Literacy at the Resource Frontier." For further explorations of the ways that Charles Gordon and the Ralph Connor novels negotiate *both* masculinity and femininity, see Coleman, *White Civility*, 139–45; and Marshall, "A Canoe, and a Tent and God's Great Out-of-Doors.'"
98 Mack, "Modernity Without Tears," 142–5. See also Coleman, *White Civility*, 139.
99 Connor, *The Man from Glengarry*, 300.
100 Fitzpatrick, *The University in Overalls*, 14, 16.
101 Radforth, *Bushworkers and Bosses*, 95. On the homosocial culture of Canada's early-twentieth-century frontier camps, see Forestell, "Bachelors, Boarding-Houses, and Blind Pigs"; and chapter 3 of Perry, *On the Edge of Empire*.
102 Fitzpatrick, *The University in Overalls*, 15.
103 *The Education of the Frontier Laborer*, p. 24, MG 28, I 124, vol. 107, FC-LAC. Fitzpatrick's emphasis on the reading room as an "alternative site of male sociability" connects his work to that of the nineteenth-century reformers who sought to mould white, working-class masculinity through temperance campaigns and organizations such as mechanics' institutes, which aimed to "replicate the political and social functions of the

nineteenth-century, middle-class home." Adele Perry points out that such "alternative sites" were deemed particularly necessary on the frontier (her study is focused on colonial British Columbia). *On the Edge of Empire*, 80, 87.

104 *Library Extension in Ontario: Reading Camps and Club Houses*, p. 21, MG 28, I 124, vol. 107, FC-LAC.
105 The term "heterosociability" is from Perry, *On the Edge of Empire*, 88.
106 *Canada's Frontiersmen, With Eighth Annual Report of the Reading Camp Association, 1907–1908*, p. 17, MG 28, I 124, vol. 107, FC-LAC.
107 Bradbury, *Working Families*, 26–27. Adele Perry observes that the masculinity imagined by nineteenth-century reformers on Canada's western frontier was "pessimistic" insofar as it insisted that working-class men, in particular, required careful regulation by family (or by institutions serving as families). Perry's comments are helpful for thinking about the surveillance of working-class masculinity in the context of the early-twentieth-century reform movement, as well. *On the Edge of Empire*, 95. See also essays by Chan, Forestell, and Harney in Iacovetta et al., eds., *A Nation of Immigrants*. On the way that early-twentieth-century reformers in Canada dealt with the "troubling" qualities of working-class, racialized, and Indigenous women, see, for example, Valverde, *The Age of Light, Soap, and Water*; and Devereux, *Growing a Race*.
108 For arguments that demonstrate the failure of Social Gospel initiatives among working-class boys, see Mangan and Walvin, "Introduction," 5; and Springhall, "Building Character," 67–70.
109 Frederick S. Hartman to Gordon, 8 March 1907, MSS 56, box 49, folder 7, CGP-UM. Nancy Christie and Michael Gauvreau posit that Ralph Connor's fan mail proves that his novels were "instrumental in converting numerous middle- and working-class Canadians," but this fan mail includes only a very few letters from readers who are clearly working class. See *A Full-Orbed Christianity*, 36–7; and, for a reading of Connor's fan mail that argues for the broadly middle-class character of his correspondents, see Karr, *Authors and Audiences*, 152–69. The "Galicians" of Hartman's letter were immigrants from Galicia, a province of the Austro-Hungarian Empire that became part of Poland after the First World War and that sent thousands of Polish, Ukrainian, and German immigrants to Canada in the late nineteenth and early twentieth centuries.
110 Fitzpatrick, *Library Extension: Travelling Libraries and Reading Camps*, pp. 20, 33, 34, MG 28, I 124, FC-LAC; *Library Extension in Ontario: Reading Camps and Club Houses*, pp. 29–31, MG 28, I 124, FC-LAC.

111 Fred Miller to Alfred Fitzpatrick, 1905, MG 28, I 124, vol. 1, "Instructors' Correspondence (Broatch-Ross), 1905," FC-LAC. The thirteen letters I am referring to may be found in this volume of correspondence, as well as in the association's fifth annual report, *The Education of the Frontier Laborer*.

112 Fitzpatrick, *The University in Overalls*, 121–22. In May 1905, for example, Fitzpatrick advised an instructor in Humboldt, Saskatchewan, that "the work you have to do is largely a matter of primary education. Your chief duty will be to get those Galicians to read and write. Of course the English speaking boys will take advantage of the books and magazines." See Fitzpatrick to Donald J. Fraser, 20 May 1905, MG 28, I 124, vol. 1, "Instructors' Correspondence (Broatch – Ross), 1905," FC-LAC.

113 The first print run of *The Habitant*, published by G.P. Putnam's Sons in New York, was not large enough to supply even the Canadian market, and was reprinted more than twenty times in a decade. Drummond's second collection, *Johnnie Courteau*, also published by G.P. Putnam's, was reprinted six times in five years for markets in the United States and Canada. Macdonald, *William Henry Drummond*, 11, 13. The reprinting of *The Habitant* obviously continued long after Drummond's death in 1907: McLennan Library at McGill University owns a copy of the collection from the forty-ninth printing.

114 "Registers of Books 1901–1907: Register of Books Received and Labelled by the Ontario Travelling Library," RG 2-146, MS 918, reel 1, PLB-AO.

115 Drummond, *The Habitant*, xi.

116 Fitzpatrick, *Library Extension in Ontario: Travelling Libraries and Reading Camps*, p. 27, MG 28, I 124, vol. 107, FC-LAC; Fitzpatrick, *Library Extension in Ontario: Reading Camps and Club Houses*, p. 40, vol. 107, FC-LAC; Alfred Fitzpatrick to Richard Harcourt, 28 November 1904, RG 2-29-4-13, MS 913, DELC-AO. Drummond's donated books were not catalogued in the Ontario Travelling Library.

117 Pollock, "William Henry Drummond's True 'Canayen.'"

118 Fréchette, Introduction, vi; Drummond, *The Habitant*, 129–30.

119 Berger, *The Sense of Power*, 32, 109, 117. For this extended quotation of Grant's book *Ocean to Ocean*, see Fitzpatrick, *Handbook for New Canadians*, 123. For the history of the concept of "imperial citizenship," see Morton, "Divided Loyalties?"

120 Although Berger identifies this brand of imperialism with Canada's conservative political tradition, his analysis offers striking evidence of the liberalism that has informed this tradition. Analysis of Canada's conservative tradition in relation to the liberal order framework can be found in

Constant and Ducharme, "Introduction," 11–12; and Bannister, "Canada as Counter-Revolution."
121 Fitzpatrick, *The University in Overalls*, 76, 85, 92, 87; Fitzpatrick, *The Diffusion of Education, with Eleventh Annual Report of the Reading Camp Association, 1911*, p. 10, MG 28, I 124, vol. 107, FC-LAC.
122 Berger, *The Sense of Power*, 131–32, 144–45; Drummond, *Johnnie Courteau*, 13.
123 Fitzpatrick, "Social Amelioration," 15.
124 Pollock, "William Henry Drummond's True 'Canayen,'" 125.
125 *Camp Education Extension*, p. 13, MG 28, I 124, FC-LAC.
126 See, for example, Bishop Lorrain of Pembroke to Richard Harcourt, 14 November 1901, RG 2-29-4-5, MS 913, DELC-AO. Although some imperialists called for the suppression of Catholicism, not all did. George Monro Grant was among those who disagreed that national unity would require uniformity of religion and language. Berger, *The Sense of Power*, 136. Fitzpatrick, whose camps were undenominational, clearly concurred.
127 Berger, *The Sense of Power*, 152; Drummond, *The Habitant*, vi.
128 Berger, *The Sense of Power*, 140, 131, 112. Among other texts, Berger cites John McMullen's The *History of Canada from its First Discovery to the Present Time* (1855), J.G. Bourinot's *Canada Under British Rule, 1760–1900* (1901), and William Withrow's *A History of Canada for the Use of Schools* (1876) as examples.
129 Drummond, *The Habitant*, 7; *Johnnie Courteau*, 5.
130 Qtd. in Noonan, "Drummond – The Legend and the Legacy," 186.
131 Gerald Noonan's study of the reception of Drummond's poetry has shaped contemporary critics' views, but Noonan, by his own admission, did not consult the French-language reviews that were not already translated into English. He thus relied in several cases on translations of articles from Québécois newspapers that appeared in the English-language press but that tended to translate positive rather than critical commentary. See Noonan, "Drummond – The Legend and the Legacy."
132 Line Gosselin, "Marchand, Joséphine (Dandurand)," *Dictionnaire biographique du Canada*, vol. 15. Université Laval/University of Toronto, last modified 2005, http://www.biographi.ca/fr/bio/marchand_josephine_15E.html.
133 Madame Dandurand's review of *The Habitant* in the 15 December 1901 issue of *La Patrie* is quoted in Noonan, "Drummond – The Legend and the Legacy," 182. The 1907 memorial is from Dandurand, "William H. Drummond," 4.

134 *Library Extension in Ontario: Reading Camps and Club Houses*, p. 29, MG 28, I 124, FC-LAC; Macdonald, *William Henry Drummond*, 97.
135 Gerson, *A Purer Taste*, 18, 28. The Duncan quotation is also from Gerson, and it first appeared in the former's column in *The Week* 3 (7 October 1886), 723. By the end of the First World War, Canadian literature had achieved only "sporadic representation" in the nation's elementary, secondary, and post-secondary classrooms, despite the fact that a native textbook publishing industry developed in Toronto in the last half of the nineteenth century. Robert, Verdyun, and Friskney, "Canadianization of the Curriculum," 57. Penney Clark observes that the revised *Ontario Readers*, published by the T. Eaton Company and authorized for use in classrooms in Ontario, Nova Scotia, and Prince Edward Island between 1909 and the mid-1930s, contained an overwhelming proportion of British to Canadian authors. "Great Chorus," 691.
136 Robert Buttle to Gordon, 7 July 1907, MSS 56, box 50, folder 1, CGP-UM.

CHAPTER TWO

1 Robinson, "The History of the Frontier College," 40–41. The position of western secretary was first held by Joseph Wearing; he is acknowledged in the seventh annual report. See *Camp Education Extension*, p. 64, MG 28, I 124, vol. 107, FC-LAC. The eleventh annual report lists provincial secretaries for Ontario, British Columbia, Manitoba and Saskatchewan, and Alberta. See *The Diffusion of Education, with Eleventh Annual Report of the Reading Camp Association, 1911*, p. 2, MG 28, I 124, vol. 107, FC-LAC.
2 Bradwin, *The Bunkhouse Man*, 7; Radforth, *Bushworkers and Bosses*, 27.
3 *The Frontier Laborer, with Sixth Annual Report of the Reading Camp Association, 1905–1906*, p. 9, MG 28, I 124, vol. 107; and *The Instructor and the Red. Nineteenth Annual Report*, n.p., MG 28, I 124, vol. 107, FC-LAC. Even in 1919, most of the association's work was undertaken in Ontario camps (thirty-four of the fifty-seven instructors in this year were in Ontario).
4 On the question of the transient workforce in rail construction camps, see Edmund Bradwin's "The Reading Camp and the Foreign Navvy," in *Camp Education Extension*, pp. 22–5, MG 28, I 124, vol. 107, FC-LAC. On Clifford Sifton's immigration policies from 1896 to 1905, see Kelley and Trebilcock, *The Making of the Mosaic*, 113–66.
5 Forestell, "Bachelors, Boarding-Houses, and Blind Pigs," 253–4.
6 Avery, *Reluctant Host*, 60–1, 67. For a detailed description of the working and living conditions on the western industrial frontier in the period preceding the First World War, see chapter 1 of Bercuson, *Fools and Wise Men*.

7 For a discussion of the strike waves of this period and the conditions that prompted them, see Kealey, "1919," 16–21; and chapter 4 of Palmer, *Working-Class Experience*. Clifford Sifton's tenure as Minister of the Interior was followed by two Immigration Acts (1906 and 1910) that, in response to British Canadian fears regarding "undesirable" immigrants, greatly increased federal powers of deportation and exclusion. Kelley and Trebilcock, *The Making of the Mosaic*, 138–40. For a discussion of the legislation that created "enemy aliens" and, ultimately, internment, see Avery, *Reluctant Host*, 71–5; and Kealey, "State Repression," 286, 292–3. See also the table "Strike Activity in Canada, 1912–1921" in Kealey, "State Repression," 283.

8 The IWW was founded in 1905 as a response to the American Federation of Labor's (AFL) decision not to support the organization of industrial workers. Influenced by European syndicalism, the IWW promoted the organization of all workers in one industry into one union and aimed to both destroy capitalism via the general strike and to create a workers' state administered by trade unions. Palmer, *Working-Class Experience*, 187–88; Heron, *The Canadian Labour Movement*, 40–3; Radforth, *Bushworkers and Bosses*, 111–14. Established in 1919, the OBU was an industrial union formed by thousands of unskilled and semi-skilled workers who rejected the moderate politics and exclusionary practices of both the AFL and the TLC. The TLC's perceived failure to oppose conscription during the First World War also contributed to the birth of the OBU. See Bercuson, *Fools and Wise Men*, 68–86; and Kealey, "State Repression," 291–2, 310. As more regionally focused studies suggest, the IWW and the OBU found considerable traction among unskilled immigrant workers (see, for example, chapter 6 of Radforth, *Bushworkers and Bosses*; Part Two of Beaulieu, *Labour at the Lakehead*; and Creese, "Exclusion or Solidarity?").

9 Fitzpatrick to Copp, Clark, Co., 13 May 1910, FC, MG 28 I 124, vol. 6, "Newspapers and Magazines"; Fitzpatrick to R.L. Calder of *The Canadian Century* (Montreal), 20 June 1910, MG 28 I 124, vol. 6, "Newspapers and Magazines," FC-LAC. For a sense of how the war negatively affected the number of newspaper publishers who were willing to send free newspapers to the camps, see the 1919 correspondence in MG 28, I 124, Vol. 21, "Newspapers and Magazines," FC-LAC.

10 Fitzpatrick to T.C. Colwell, 11 July 1911, MG 28, I 124, vol. 6, "Instructors' Correspondence (Appleton-Willis), 1911," FC-LAC.

11 *The Frontier College, with Thirteenth Annual Report of the Reading Camp Association*, 1913, n.p., MG 28, I 124, vol. 107, FC-LAC; and *The Diffusion of Education, with Seventeenth Annual Report of the Reading Camp*

Association, 1917, p. 5, MG 28, I 124, vol. 107, FC-LAC. Fitzpatrick was increasingly insistent in his address of provincial governments in this period. In 1911, for instance, he wrote to the premier of Ontario, the Conservative Sir James Whitney, to ask him for a "personal loan" that would ease the association's financial difficulties while it waited for the government to increase the annual grant. Whitney was outraged, treating the request as "more or less of a joke," and, needless to say, denied the request. Whitney to Fitzpatrick, 2 December 1911, MG 28, I 124, vol. 7, "Ontario Govn't (Premier Whitney)," FC-LAC.

12 Fitzpatrick to W.J. Agabob, 21 May 1913, MG 28, I 124, vol. 10, "Instructors' Correspondence, 1913," FC-LAC. For a table that tabulates the varying contributions of the provincial governments to Frontier College during the period covered in this chapter, see Zavitz, "The Frontier College," Appendix A, "Government Grants to Frontier College from 1901-2-1930."

13 Of the total number of foreign-born assessed in the 1911 census (and who reported a year of arrival), 52.3 percent had arrived between 1905 and June 1911. Of these, more than 56 percent had remained in the country long enough to obtain naturalization but only 22.2 percent had obtained citizenship (via naturalization) at the time of the census. Canada, *Special Report*, 15.

14 For the rather high literacy rates of the foreign-born as recorded in the 1911 census, which measured their ability to read and write in any language, see the Preface, 13.

15 The name "Frontier College" was used long before the incorporation. The 1913 annual report, for example, is titled *The Frontier College*.

16 Bradwin, *The Bunkhouse Man*, 198.

17 Palmer, *Working-Class Experience*, 229–36; Christie and Gauvreau, *A Full-Orbed Christianity*, 47. For Christie and Gauvreau, this fact is evidence of the continued influence until at least the 1930s of the Protestant churches on British Canadian culture.

18 For example, the fifth annual report notes that labourer-teacher Donald J. Fraser received hymn books from Fitzpatrick, which enabled him to have a "good sing with the boys" on Sunday evenings. *The Education of the Frontier Laborer*, p. 28, MG 28, I 124, FC-LAC.

19 Gray to Fitzpatrick, 8 April 1905, MG 28, I 124, vol. 1, "Instructors' Correspondence (Broatch-Ross), 1905," FC-LAC.

20 Connor, *The Man from Glengarry*, 102, 135–49, 183–4. On the revival culture of the Salvation Army in Ontario during the 1880s, see Chapter 6 in Marks, *Revivals and Roller Rinks*. For a discussion of the Free Church movement in Canada, see this book's Chapter 1, n27.

21 "History of Edison Sound Recordings: History of the Cylinder Phonograph," *Library of Congress*, accessed 15 February 2015, https://www.loc.gov/collections/edison-company-motion-pictures-and-sound-recordings/articles-and-essays/history-of-edison-sound-recordings/history-of-the-cylinder-phonograph.

22 For example, R.C. Dearle reported in 1911 that all the men at his northern Ontario lumber camp were "delighted with the gramophone and it is now one of the prime favorites at the camp." In the same year, E.G. Law and James Menzies claimed that, although classes were difficult to organize, their gramophones could bring fifty to one hundred men or more to their tents. During the 1912 season, S.F. Kneeland made repeated requests for a gramophone (which he eventually received), and he claimed it helped him to begin work with those who could not read at all, besides serving as a distraction from poker in the bunkhouse and as a mutual interest for Canadian-born and immigrant men. Dearle to Fitzpatrick, 30 January 1911; Law to Fitzpatrick, 18 June 1911; and Menzies to Fitzpatrick, 28 January 1911, MG 28, I 124, vol. 6, "Instructors' Correspondence (Appleton-Willis), 1911"; and Kneeland to Fitzpatrick, 21 May 1912 and 20 July 1912, MG 28, I 124, vol. 8, "Instructors' Correspondence (Ansley-Wilson), 1912," FC-LAC.

23 Lord to Fitzpatrick, 9 July 1910, MG 28, I 124, vol. 5, "Instructors' Correspondence (Banting-Wearing), 1910," FC-LAC.

24 J.R. Mutchmore to Fitzpatrick, undated letter, MG 28, I 124, vol. 8, "Instructors' Correspondence (Ansley-Wilson), 1912"; Norman Bethune to Fitzpatrick, 12 November 1911, MG 28, I 124, vol. 6, "Instructors' Correspondence (Appleton-Willis), 1911"; and J. Ian Way to Fitzpatrick, 20 June 1916, MG 28, I 124, vol. 17, "Instructors' Correspondence (Aitcheson-Turnbull), 1916," FC-LAC. For Hoggart's discussion of "club-singing," see *The Uses of Literacy*, 109–23.

25 Thomas A. Garratt reported in 1914 that the men in his Markstay, Ontario, lumber camp enjoyed the gramophone very much and had also held a concert, at which "one French Canadian sang several 'Lauder' songs and his 'Scotch' was enough to make one weep with laughter. The songs were not of beautiful rendering, often being out of tune, but the spirit and goodwill were there and so everything went well." Garratt to Fitzpatrick, 15 February 1914, MG 28, I 124, vol. 14, "Instructors' Correspondence (Agabob-Rutherford), 1914," FC-LAC.

26 Colquhoun to Fitzpatrick, 24 April 1907, MG 28, I 124, vol. 3, "Ontario Government (Dept. of Education)," FC-LAC. In January 1905, a Conservative government replaced the Liberal government of Ontario,

and Richard Harcourt's role as Minister of Education was assumed by Robert Pyne (with Colquhoun as his deputy minister).
27 Nott to Joe Wearing, 21 July 1907, MG 28, I 124, vol. 3, "Instructors' Correspondence (Broatch-Phillips), 1907"; Morrison to Fitzpatrick, 5 February 1909, MG 28, I 124, vol. 4, "Instructors' Correspondence (Banting-Wilson), 1909," FC-LAC.
28 Bruce, "Reading Camps," 90–1.
29 Fitzpatrick to Colquhoun, 11 July 1908, MG 28, I 124, vol. 6, "Ontario Government 1/2"; Colquhoun to Fitzpatrick, 1 December 1908, MG 28, I 124, vol. 6, "Ontario Government 2/2," FC-LAC.
30 Fitzpatrick to Robert Pyne, 29 June 1910, MG 28, I 124, vol. 6, "Ontario Government," FC-LAC; Fitzpatrick to Herbert Killam, 15 March 1912, MG 28, I 124, vol. 10, "British Columbia Government," FC-LAC.
31 Nursey to Fitzpatrick, 28 September 1911, MG 28, I 124, vol. 7, "Ontario Government (Inspector of Public Libraries)"; Nursey to Fitzpatrick, 21 December 1911, MG 28, I 124, vol. 7, "Ontario Government (Inspector of Public Libraries)," FC-LAC.
32 Nursey to Fitzpatrick, 3 Octpber 1913, MG 28, I 124, vol. 13, "Ontario Government, Department of Education," FC-LAC.
33 Fitzpatrick to W.C. Carson, 3 June 1919, MG 28, I 124, vol. 21, "Ontario Government," FC-LAC.
34 Distad, "Newspapers and Magazines," 294–5, 299–300.
35 Several media and print culture scholars have noted the association between the modern periodical and newspaper and the secular temporality of modernity. See, for example, Somerville, *The News Revolution in England*. For a view of the nineteenth-century development of industrial time that points to both the temporal symmetry and asymmetry of periodicals, see Turner, "Periodical Time." Modifying Tom Nairn, Benedict Anderson makes the more general point that the "diurnal regularities of the imagining life," embodied in print forms such as the newspaper, aided in converting class inequality into the abstract equality of national citizens. *Imagined Communities*, 35.
36 In some cases, the association and its partners, such as the Aberdeen Association, received free shipping from the Postmaster General and from rail companies such as the Canadian Pacific Railway. See this book's Preface, xv–xxv.
37 Hoggart, *The Uses of Literacy*, xxv–xxvi.
38 E.H. Clarke to Fitzpatrick, 9 August 1908, MG 28, I 124, vol. 3, "Instructors' Correspondence (Brokenshire to Weaver), 1908," FC-LAC.

39 J.R. Mutchmore's 1912 letters from a Northern Ontario camp to Fitzpatrick observe that the camp's "switch" was near his reading tent and that men consequently came into the tent for short periods of time. Short fiction, he suggested, would offer them a practical alternative to novels. Mutchmore to Fitzpatrick, undated letter 1912, MG 28, I 124, vol. 8, "Instructors' Correspondence (Ansley-Wilson), 1912," FC-LAC.

40 Gordon Doolittle, Fred Bell, E.H. Clarke, and F.G. Poole all wrote to Fitzpatrick's Toronto office with magazine titles that the men liked or were asking for: Doolittle to Fitzpatrick, 17 July 1914, MG 28, I 124, vol. 14, "Instructors' Correspondence (Agabob-Rutherford), 1914"; Bell to Pauline Smith, 20 May 1916, MG 28, I 124, vol. 17, "Instructors' Correspondence (Aitcheson-Turnbull), 1916"; Clarke to Fitzpatrick, 6 July 1909, MG 28, I 124, vol. 4, "Instructors' Correspondence (Banting-Wilson), 1909"; and Poole to Miss McMechan, 16 July 1911, MG 28, I 124, vol. 6, "Instructors' Correspondence (Appleton-Willis), 1911," FC-LAC.

41 E.T. Hacking to Fitzpatrick, 16 January 1909, MG 28, I 124, vol. 4, "Instructors' Correspondence (Banting-Wilson), 1909," FC-LAC.

42 Mutchmore to Fitzpatrick, undated letter 1912, MG 28, I 124, vol. 8, "Instructors' Correspondence (Ansley-Wilson), 1912"; McWilliams to Fitzpatrick, 12 July 1914, MG 28, I 124, vol. 14, "Instructors' Correspondence (Agabob-Rutherford), 1914," FC-LAC. *Top-Notch Magazine* (1910–1937) was initially a pulp magazine targeted at teenage boys containing mostly sports-themed stories; by the 1930s, it had become a men's adventure magazine featuring pulp sports fiction, westerns, detective stories, and science fiction. Alexandra Blair, "Top-Notch Magazine," *The Pulp Magazines Project*, accessed 9 June 2017, http://www.pulpmags.org/content/info/western-story-magazine.html.

43 Fitzpatrick to Chapters of the Imperial Order Daughter of Empire, 5 October 1916, MG 28, I 124, vol. 18, "I.O.D.E," FC-LAC.

44 Dearle is only one of countless instructors who claimed that if efforts to conduct classes were meeting with little success, the newspapers of the reading room were always in demand. Dearle to Fitzpatrick, 30 January 1911, MG 28, I 124, vol. 6, "Instructors' Correspondence (Appleton-Willis), 1911," FC-LAC.

45 For evidence of Fitzpatrick's ongoing relationship with the Department of Interior, see MG 28, I 124, vol. 7, "Federal Government"; and vol. 10, "Federal Government," FC-LAC. Drawing on the work of Benedict Anderson, Pierre Walter notes how the association's representation of space and time in publications such as the *Handbook for New Canadians* served its imperialist politics. "Literacy, Imagined Nations, and Imperialism," 47.

46 McDougall to Fitzpatrick, 11 August 1914, and Dorrance to Fitzpatrick, 16 August 1914, MG 28, I 124, vol. 14, "Instructors' Correspondence (Agabob-Rutherford), 1914," FC-LAC.
47 McConnell to Fitzpatrick, 15 December 1911, and Poole to Miss McMechan, 4 August 1911, MG 28, I 124, vol. 6, "Instructors' Correspondence (Appleton-Willis), 1911," FC-LAC.
48 Hjartarson, "Print Culture," 44, 49–50. A table compiled by the federal government that indicates the nationalities of the immigrants who arrived in Canada between July 1900 and December 1907 appears in Woodsworth, *Strangers Within Our Gates*, 22–23. See also Kelley and Trebilcock, *The Making of the Mosaic*, 124–34.
49 Anderson, *The Education of the New Canadian*, 93.
50 Hjartarson, "Print Culture," 44.
51 Waters also contacted a Bulgarian missionary to inquire about obtaining New Testaments in Bulgarian, which Waters thought would be a "capital thing" to have in his camp. See Waters to Fitzpatrick, 31 July 1908, MG 28, I 124, vol. 3, "Instructors' Correspondence (Brokenshire-Weaver), 1908," FC-LAC.
52 Fitzpatrick to Combe, 23 June 1909, MG 28, I 124, vol. 4, "Instructors' Correspondence (Banting-Wilson), 1909," FC-LAC.
53 Bell to Pauline Smith, 20 May 1916, MG 28, I 124, vol. 17, "Instructors' Correspondence (Aitcheson-Turnbull), 1916," FC-LAC. Other instructors thanked Fitzpatrick for "Ruthenian" papers or asked for *Kanadyiskyi Farmer*, such as Wilbur C. Lowry and Fred Baragar. Lowry to Fitzpatrick, 3 July 1912, MG 28, I 124, vol. 8, "Instructors' Correspondence (Ainsley-Wilson), 1912"; and Baragar to Fitzpatrick, 31 May 1914, MG 28, I 124, vol. 14, "Instructors' Correspondence (Agabob-Rutherford), 1914," FC-LAC.
54 Martynowych, *Ukrainians in Canada*, 276–77.
55 Davies to Fitzpatrick, 26 August 1913, MG 28, I 124, vol. 10, "Instructors' Correspondence, 1913," FC-LAC. Until the First World War, Montreal had the largest concentration of Italian immigrants, largely because the greatest employer of Italian labour was the Canadian Pacific Railway, and Montreal was the centre of the company's operations. See Ramirez, "Brief Encounters," 10–15. At the turn of the century, three Italian-language newspapers were established in the city: *Corriere del Canada* (1895), *La Patria Italiana* (1903), and *L'Araldo del Canada* (1905). Jansen, *Italians in Multicultural Canada*, 20.
56 For discussions of the sojourning practices and political tendencies of Italian workers in Canada in the prewar period, see Harney, "Men Without Women"; Ramirez, "Brief Encounters"; and Ramirez, *On the Move*, 94–106.

For further discussion of *Corriere del Canada*, Anthony Cordasco, and the Royal Commission, see Ramirez, *Les premiers Italiens*, 46–53.

57 Avery, *Reluctant Host*, 74–5. The complete text of the Orders in Council can be found in Swyripa and Thompson, eds., *Loyalties in Conflict*, 190–96. "Enemy" languages included German, Bulgarian, Ukrainian, Estonian, Ruthenian, Hungarian, Turkish, Russian, Finnish, Croatian, Syrian, Roumanian, and Livonian. See also Kealey, "State Repression," 293–300; and Kealey, "The Surveillance State," 184–7. Kealey contends that "ethnic chauvinism" was less important than class conflict (and the general fear of socialism) in motivating these Orders in Council, but I tend to agree with Dennis Molinaro that both ethnicity and class were at play. See Molinaro, *An Exceptional Law*, 20. For more on state restriction of the press during the First World War, see the chapters on censorship in Keshen, *Propaganda*; and Bausenhart, "The Ontario German Language Press."

58 An Act to Amend the Criminal Code, 1919 S.C., ch. 46, s. 1. Membership in subversive organizations was also targeted by this amendment to the Criminal Code. See Molinaro, *An Exceptional Law*, 35–43. Molinaro points out the essential continuity between the Orders in Council PC 2381 and PAC 2384 and the 1919 amendments to the Criminal Code (which eventually became Section 98).

59 Nils Brown to Fitzpatrick, 31 January 1919, and Fitzpatrick to R. Atkinson (of the Toronto *Daily Star*), 23 December 1919, MG 28, I 124, vol. 21, "Newspapers and Magazines 1/2, 1919," FC-LAC.

60 Fitzpatrick, *Handbook for New Canadians*, 108.

61 For various accounts of the new requirement to teach five nights per week, as well as objections to the requirement, see MG 28, I 124, vol. 14, "Instructors' Correspondence (Agabob-Rutherford), 1914," FC-LAC.

62 See, for example, J.G. Moore to Miss McMechan, 23 July 1911, MG 28, I 124, vol. 6, "Instructors' Correspondence (Appleton-Willis), 1911"; and C. Brubacher to Fitzpatrick, 24 June 1919, MG 28, I 124, vol. 20, "Instructors' Correspondence (Anderson-Stewart), 1919," FC-LAC.

63 See, for example R.C. Dearle to Fitzpatrick, 30 January 1911, MG 28, I 124, vol. 6, "Instructors' Correspondence (Appleton-Willis), 1911," FC-LAC, or the correspondence of Alfred Holmes from the summer of 1914, MG 28, I 124, vol. 14, "Instructors' Correspondence (Agabob-Rutherford), 1914," FC-LAC.

64 For examples of the new weekly register, see MG 28, I 124, vol. 20, "Instructors' Correspondence (Anderson-Stewart), 1919," FC-LAC.

65 Clark, "The Publishing of School Books," 335–9.

66 Fitzpatrick to Walter Nursey, 30 May 1911, MG 28, I 124, vol. 7, "Ontario Government (Inspector of Public Libraries)"; Fitzpatrick to Mr. Kerr, 29 April 1914, MG 28, I 124, vol. 16, "Ontario Government 4/4"; Macmillan Co. to Fitzpatrick, 8 July 1907, MG 28, I 124, vol. 3, "Magazines 1907," FC-LAC.

67 Labourer-teacher Ossian Lyr, for example, wrote to the association's Toronto office in 1911 asking for more primers to do elementary language teaching at his camp at Missinaibi River, Ontario. Lyr to Fitzpatrick, 11 June 1911, MG 28, I 124, vol. 6, "Instructors' Correspondence (Appleton-Willis), 1911," FC-LAC.

68 Penney Clark describes how the findings of Ontario's 1907 Textbook Commission led to the development of a revised series of *Ontario Readers* authored by Dr. D.J. Goggin, a "respected educator," and a committee of school superintendents and principals. The T. Eaton Co. won the tender for the publication of these readers, and Eaton's *Ontario Readers*, first issued in 1909, remained authorized until the 1930s. "Great Chorus," 686–91.

69 *The Ontario Readers*, 79, 93, 118.

70 Fitzpatrick to H.L. Lovering, 31 August 1916, MG 28, I 124, vol. 17, "Instructors' Correspondence (Aitcheson-Turnbull), 1916," FC-LAC.

71 Sutherland, *Children in English-Canadian Society*, 202.

72 *Camp Education Extension*, pp. 22–3, MG 28, I 124, vol. 107, FC-LAC.

73 In 1912, immigration to Canada from all sources was 375,756. The following year, immigration peaked at 400,870. Avery, *Reluctant Host*, 11. The 1912 annual report is titled "The Immigrant."

74 Bercuson, *Fools and Wise Men*, 37, 41–2.

75 Woodsworth, "Nation-Building," 96; Woodsworth, *Strangers Within Our Gates*, 48. On Woodsworth's work with the All-People's Mission and the People's Forum, see this book's Preface, as well as the first two chapters of Mills, *Fool for Christ*. On the influence of imperialism on Woodsworth's theory of the "higher type," see Sutherland, *Children in English-Canadian Society*, 209, 212. For a discussion of Woodsworth's writing on the "race question" prior to the First World War and his negotiation of a desire for both the preservation of Anglo-Canadian identity and the birth of a new "pan-Canadian" identity, see Mills, *Fool for Christ*, 42–56. For Fitzpatrick's correspondence with Woodsworth, see MG 28, I 124, vol. 10, "General Correspondence, J.S. Woodsworth," FC-LAC. Like Fitzpatrick, though much later (in 1918), Woodsworth ultimately left the church in order to pursue his social reform work.

76 McKay, *Reasoning Otherwise*, 379. The quotation that follows is from a letter from instructor F.C. Moyer to Fitzpatrick that is reprinted in the annual report. *Camp Education Extension*, p. 44, MG 28, I 124, vol. 107, FC-LAC. See also Bradwin, *The Bunkhouse Man*, 100–2.
77 *Canada's Frontiersmen*, pp. 7, 35, MG 28, I 124, vol. 107, FC-LAC.
78 Stringer, *The Prairie Wife*, 203, 248.
79 Of course, this construction of the value of English exceeded the project of British Canadian nation-making: as Gauri Viswanathan observes in *Masks of Conquest*, the teaching of the English language and its literature served a crucial function in propping up the British Empire during the nineteenth century; the language played a similar role in later colonial education in places such as the Philippines. See also Baldick, *The Social Mission*, 70–2; and Willinsky, *Learning to Divide the World*, 189–243. On the casting of English as a language "inherently conducive to liberty" in the colonial Philippines (1905–1932), see Schueller, "Colonial Management." For accounts of Canadianization as an element of educational policy for immigrant children in early-twentieth-century Canada, see Heathorn, *For Home, Country, and Race*; McLeod, "A Short History"; and Sutherland, *Children in English-Canadian Society*, 202–15. For regionally focused studies, see, for example, Bruno-Jofré, "Citizenship and Schooling"; Martynowych, "'Canadianizing the Foreigner'"; and Prokop, "Canadianization of Immigrant Children." For a discussion of the limited curricular resources and teacher training for English-as-second-language instruction prior to the 1950s, see Gidney and Millar, "How to Teach English," 103–7.
80 "To Aid the Immigrant," 6; Anderson, *The Education of the New Canadian*, 9. See also Prokop, "Canadianization of Immigrant Children," 2.
81 Griffin to Fitzpatrick, undated letter 1911, MG 28, I 124, vol. 6, "Instructors' Correspondence (Appleton-Willis), 1911"; Lord to Fitzpatrick, 12 August 1910, MG 28, I 124, vol. 5, "Instructors' Correspondence (Banting-Wearing), 1910"; Davies to Fitzpatrick, 29 July 1913, MG 28, I 124, vol. 10, "Instructors' Correspondence, 1913"; Gilbert to Fitzpatrick, 29 April 1914, MG 28, I 124, vol. 14, "Instructors' Correspondence (Agabob-Rutherford), 1914," FC-LAC.
82 For example, the association's contribution is not mentioned in Mary Ashworth's standard historical account of the development of English-as-second-language instruction in Canada. See *Immigrant Children*. Similarly, Gidney and Millar ("How To Teach English") omit Fitzpatrick from their history of the early-twentieth-century development of pedagogy for

immigrant children in Canada; Ken Osborne does not mention the association in his overview of citizenship education in Canada, "Education Is the Best National Insurance"; and Paula Romanow omits Fitzpatrick from her discussion of the pre-1950 adult education movement (see "'The Picture of Democracy We Are Seeking,'" 111). Recent exceptions include McLean, "'The good citizen'"; and Walter, "Literacy, Imagined Nations, and Imperialism."

83 J.F. Sadleir to Fitzpatrick, 21 April 1909, MG 28, I 124, vol. 4, "Instructors' Correspondence (Banting-Wilson), 1909," FC-LAC. Fitzpatrick seems to have ignored F.M. Carpoff's request to be placed on the association's payroll, probably because it was clothed in lately acquired English: "Here I am studying with six seven pupils with hope to encrease as far as it could be possible." Carpoff to Pauline Smith, 9 August 1916, MG 28, I 124, vol. 17, "Instructors' Correspondence (Aitcheson-Turnbull), 1916," FC-LAC. For a similar example, see the letters of Mike Jeiry to Fitzpatrick: FC, MG 28, I 124, vol. 17, "Instructors' Correspondence (Aitcheson-Turnbull), 1916," LAC.

84 Anderson, *The Education of the New Canadian*, 157. The ethnic identity of elementary school teachers of immigrant children was a contentious issue in this period, particularly in the West, where teachers were often hailed by education officials as crucial models of British Canadian identity. Osborne, "Education Is the Best National Insurance," 38. Anderson details the benefits of the "direct" method in Chapter 8 of *The Education of the New Canadian*, 116–42. For a discussion of the "direct method," its development from European and North American methods (including the "Berlitz method"), and its earliest Canadian proponents, including Anderson and Saskatchewan high school teacher and inspector Norman F. Black, see Gidney and Millar, "How to Teach English." The proscription of any language other than English in Manitoba public schools after the 1916 Thornton Act was followed in Saskatchewan by the 1918 hiring of Anderson and the promotion of the "direct" method. Sutherland, *Children in English-Canadian Society*, 212.

85 Fitzpatrick to W.J. Dodman, 19 June 1909, MG 28, I 124, vol. 4, "Instructors' Correspondence (Banting-Wilson), 1909," FC-LAC.

86 See MG 28, I 124, vol. 10, "Instructors' Correspondence 1913," FC-LAC. In correspondence with the federal Department of Labour in 1949, Bradwin claimed that a version of the *Primer for Adults* was in use as early as 1907. Bradwin to A. MacNamara, 6 May 1949, MG 28, I 124, vol. 90, "Dept. of Labour-1949," FC-LAC. In the document "Resume of Frontier College Work (Retrospect of one-third of a century)," Bradwin is

credited with having prepared "the first system of lessons in English for foreign-born nationals that was issued in this country." This "system," the document implies, eventually became the *Handbook for New Canadians*. See "Annual Reports, 1934–1935," MG 28, I 124, vol. 109, FC-LAC. Fitzpatrick dedicated the *Handbook* to Bradwin, who "has given so many years of his life as an instructor and Canadianizer in bunkhouses and camps of Canada."

87 J. Burke to Fitzpatrick, 14 November 1916, MG 28, I 124, vol. 17, "Instructors' Correspondence (Aitcheson-Turnbull), 1916," FC-LAC.

88 Fitzpatrick ordered by mail one set of lessons in each of the three series (A, B, C) from *English for Coming Americans* for nine instructors (five in Alberta, one in British Columbia, and three in Ontario). Fitzpatrick to Manager, Association Press, 26 June 1911, MG 28, I 124, vol. 7, "Newspapers and Magazines Correspondence, 1911," FC-LAC. Both Anderson and Woodsworth included bibliographies of US sources in their studies of Canada's newly diverse society. See Anderson, *The Education of the New Canadian*, 260–61; and Woodsworth, *Strangers Within Our Gates*, 6–7. On the Americanization movement and its textbooks, see Chapter 2 of Wan, *Producing Good Citizens*. Edey Maggie requested a "half-dozen leaflets" in the *English for Coming Canadians* series in May of 1914. Maggie to Fitzpatrick, 24 May 1914, MG 28, I 124, vol. 14, "Instructors' Correspondence (Agabob-Rutherford), 1914," FC-LAC.

89 Roberts, *English for Coming Americans*, 44, 10, 12–13, 78, 31.

90 Anderson to Fitzpatrick, 31 March 1919, MG 28, I 124, vol. 21, "Saskatchewan Government," FC-LAC. See "Government Correspondence" in this same volume for further letters of inquiry to provincial departments of education and their responses.

91 Bradwin to Fitzpatrick, 7 October 1919, MG 28, I 124, vol. 154, "Correpondence–A. Fitzpatrick," FC-LAC. In 1920, instructor C.D.G. Longmore wrote to Fitzpatrick with a similar message: "You started, and carried on the work Anderson harps on, when he was a little boy in a public school. So please advertise our work more, and get on the platform, here, there and everywhere." Longmore contrasted the "personal contact" behind Fitzpatrick's knowledge with the "reading knowledge" of immigrants possessed by Anderson. Longmore to Fitzpatrick, 5 March 1920, MG 28, I 124, vol. 22, "Instructors' Correspondence, 1920," FC-LAC.

92 For information on the history of the Ryerson Press and its relationship to the Methodist Book and Publishing House, see Janet Friskney, "The Birth of the Ryerson Press Imprint," *Historical Perspectives on Canadian*

Publishing, McMaster University, http://hpcanpub.mcmaster.ca/hpcanpub/case-study/birth-ryerson-press-imprint?page=0%2Co.

93 Fitzpatrick decided on three thousand copies after he received the following estimate from the press. In September of 1919, E.J. Moore informed the principal that the book would run approximately 321 pages and would include nine two-colour maps and two tri-colour engravings. The "price for the 'sheets' or letterpress section, including typesetting, paper, presswork, folding, gathering and sewing, will be now, for 3,000 copies, $2,700.00; for 5,000 copies, $3,325.00; for 10,000 copies, $4,850.00." Cloth-covered boards were not included in this price. Moore to Fitzpatrick, 16 September 1919, MG 28, I 124, vol. 153, "Correspondence-A. Fitzpatrick," FC-LAC. See also General Office to Fitzpatrick, 21 October 1919, MG 28, I 124, vol. 153, "Correspondence-A. Fitzpatrick," FC-LAC. The final invoice for $3,044.30 was received in January of 1920. The Ryerson Press to Fitzpatrick, 31 January 1920, MG 28, I 124, vol. 154, "Correspondence-A. Fitzpatrick," FC-LAC. The subsequent chapter discusses the fact that the publication of the *Handbook* led the association into financial difficulty. Fitzpatrick encountered this self-financing arrangement with an earlier manuscript, as well. In 1911, when Fitzpatrick approached Briggs regarding the publication of his manuscript *Gates of Hell*, Briggs proposed an arrangement by which Fitzpatrick would pay to have the book produced ($465 for one thousand copies plus some other charges for binding, alterations to proofs, and special dyes for the cover design). Briggs assured Fitzpatrick that the company would not take commission if the books were not sold on the retail market. Briggs to Fitzpatrick, 8 September 1911, MG 28, I 124, vol. 7, "Newspapers and Magazines, 1911," FC-LAC.

94 Fitzpatrick to H.L. Lovering, 31 August 1916, MG 28, I 124, vol. 17, "Instructors' Correspondence (Aitcheson-Turnbull), 1916", FC-LAC.

95 Fitzpatrick, *Handbook for New Canadians*, 3.

96 Calder to Fitzpatrick, 31 March 1919, MG 28, I 124, vol. 21, "Federal Government," FC-LAC.

97 Fitzpatrick to Calder, 10 November 1919, MG 28, I 124, vol. 21, "Federal Government," FC-LAC.

98 Wan, *Producing Good Citizens*, 42. On the language requirement in the Naturalization Act, see Kelley and Trebilcock, *The Making of the Mosaic*, 162–63. For the debates regarding the literacy requirement in the 1919 amendments to the Immigration Act, see An Act to Amend the Immigration Act, 1919 S.C., ch. 25, s. 3; *Debates*, 1919, vol. 1, 422; *Debates*, 1919, vol. 2, 1884.

99 See Playfair to Fitzpatrick, 16 June 1919, MG 28, I 124, vol. 21, "General Correspondence," FC-LAC.
100 In its use of the "look and say" rather than the centuries-old syllabic system of literacy instruction, Fitzpatrick's *Handbook* follows not just Anderson and Roberts but a more general trend in late-nineteenth- and early-twentieth-century Anglo-American educational philosophy. Colclough and Vincent, "Reading," 289.
101 The *Handbook*'s introduction proclaims that "we have a right to demand that every man who comes to Canada becomes a citizen of this country," and recommends using the naturalization record of those already in Canada to determine which countries will supply future immigrants to Canada. Fitzpatrick, *Handbook for New Canadians*, 1–2.
102 Mitchell, "'The Manufacture of Souls,'" n.p.; Osborne, "Education Is the Best National Insurance," 44–5.
103 Fitzpatrick, *Handbook for New Canadians*, 243, 278.
104 Greer, "1837–1838: Rebellion Reconsidered," 3.
105 Joshee, "The Federal Government," 108–9. Joshee points out that Canadian citizens legally continued to be British subjects until 1977.
106 An Act Respecting Immigration, 1910 S.C., ch. 27. For a discussion of "state citizenship discourses" in Speeches from the Throne from Confederation to 1946, see Brodie, "White Settlers," 98–107.
107 Kelley and Trebilcock, *The Making of the Mosaic*, 162–3.
108 Anderson, *The Education of the New Canadian*, 8, 38, 89, 146–50.
109 Fitzpatrick, *Handbook for New Canadians*, 56.
110 Druick, *Projecting Canada*, 16. For discussions of more radical uses of the documentary in the interwar period, see Mason, *Writing Unemployment*; and Rifkind, *Comrades and Critics*. On the use of typicality in postwar government documentary film, see Druick, *Projecting Canada*, esp. chapter 5.
111 Fitzpatrick, *Handbook for New Canadians*, 199.
112 Kelley and Trebilcock, *The Making of the Mosaic*, 184–5. On the 1919 amendment to Section 41 of the Immigration Act, see also Avery, "Dangerous Foreigners," 90–92. First introduced in 1910 but amended in 1919, Section 41 authorized the deportation of anyone not a Canadian by birth or naturalization who espoused or was affiliated with an organization that advocated overthrowing the government. British subjects with Canadian domicile (in 1919, five years' residence) could be deported under this law.
113 Fitzpatrick, *Handbook for New Canadians*, 183–99.
114 Kelley and Trebilcock, *The Making of the Mosaic*, 163.

115 This is the poem exactly as it reproduced in the *Handbook*. Fitzpatrick, *Handbook for New Canadians*, 129. Ian Lancashire, "William Wordsworth, 'The Solitary Reaper,' Commentary," *Representative Poetry Online*, University of Toronto Libraries, accessed 28 September 2017, https://rpo.library.utoronto.ca/poems/solitary-reaper#20.

116 The "memory gem" collection enjoyed widespread use in late-nineteenth-century classrooms. Consisting of "brief prose excerpts, abridgements of long poems, and short verse," the memory gem was, as the name suggests, meant to be memorized. Rubin, "They Flash," 262.

117 Fitzpatrick, *Handbook for New Canadians*, 122, 126–7, 129. For a history of the writing, performance, and publishing of "O Canada!," see Gilles Potvin, Helmut Kallman, and Andrew McIntosh, "O Canada!," *The Canadian Encyclopedia*, accessed 11 February 2015, http://www.thecanadianencyclopedia.ca/en/article/o-canada.

118 Menzies, Adamoski, and Chunn, "Rethinking the Citizen," 28.

119 Woodsworth, *Strangers Within Our Gates*, 202–3; Fitzpatrick, *Handbook for New Canadians*, 82, 86.

120 *The Immigrant*, n.p., MG 28, I 124, vol. 107, FC-LAC. As McKay points out, this was not simply a liberal argument; it also powered much of the nativist sentiment in the early-twentieth-century Canadian labour movement and in the nation's early socialist formations. *Reasoning Otherwise*, 384–95.

121 On the "geographical mobility" and "occupational pluralism" of eastern and southern European immigrant men in the early twentieth century, see Avery, *"Dangerous Foreigners,"* 8–9 and Chapter 1. On the sojourning practices of Italian men, see Harney, "Men Without Women"; Ramirez, "Brief Encounters"; and Ramirez, *On the Move*. On immigrant sojourning in this period more generally, see Heron, *The Canadian Labour Movement*, 32–3.

122 On the importance of homeownership to the way that social reformers in the 1910s employed the term citizenship, see Purdy, "Building Homes, Building Citizens," 513–15.

123 Fitzpatrick, *Handbook for New Canadians*, 73.

124 Ibid., *Handbook for New Canadians*, 67, 105.

125 Radforth, *Bushworkers and Bosses*, 95.

126 Fitzpatrick to Calder, 11 February 1919, MG 28, I 124, vol. 21, "Federal Government," FC-LAC.

127 I am quoting from an unpublished typescript found in "R.C. Dearle," MG 28, I 124, vol. 20, "Instructors' Correspondence (Anderson-Stewart), 1919," FC-LAC.

128 Fitzpatrick, *Handbook for New Canadians*, 1–2.
129 For the way in which the 1918 Orders in Council targeted perceived Bolshevism among Russian, Finnish, and Ukrainian workers, in particular, see Beaulieu, *Labour at the Lakehead*, 59.
130 *The Instructor and the Red*, n.p., MG 28, I 124, vol. 107, FC-LAC. For examples of instructors' letters that identify the presence of "Bolsheviks" in the camps, see E.A. Bicknell to Fitzpatrick, 14 July 1919; Lavern Churchill, "Register, 20 August 1919"; Merlin C. Eynon to Fitzpatrick, 12 June 1919 and 23 August 1919, MG 28, I 124, vol. 20, "Instructors' Correspondence (Anderson-Stewart), 1919," FC-LAC.
131 Mitchell, "'The Manufacture of Souls,'" n.p.
132 Mitchell, "'The Manufacture of Souls,'" n.p.
133 The "citizens" of *To Him That Hath* are very clearly those who never subscribe to, or who later abandon, partisan political positions. Workers and employers alike might fail to be citizens, as the characters Simmons and McGinnis demonstrate. The novel's model citizen is Jack Maitland, the son of the lumber mill owner and a manager who is figured as capable of transcending class divisions, even if the novel ultimately reinforces these same divisions through its marriage plots. Unsurprisingly, capitalist relations of production remain undisturbed by the novel's vision of citizenship. Connor, *To Him That Hath*.
134 Heron, *The Canadian Labour Movement*, 47; Bercuson, *Fools and Wise Men*, 60–61.
135 Fitzpatrick, *Handbook for New Canadians*, 75, 84. Charles Gordon served on several Boards of Conciliation and Investigation established by the 1907 Act, and this experience served him in his work as chair of the Manitoba Council of Industry after 1919. "Charles William Gordon (Ralph Connor): An Inventory of His Papers at the University of Manitoba Archives and Special Collections," *University of Manitoba Libraries*, accessed 24 August 2017, http://umanitoba.ca/libraries/units/archives/collections/complete_holdings/ead/html/gordon.shtml.
136 Iacovetta, *Gatekeepers*, 62. On this same point, see Chapters 3 and 5 of Druick, *Projecting Canada*.
137 Mackey, *The House of Difference*, 23, 24; Slaughter, *Human Rights, Inc.*, 157.
138 Coleman, *White Civility*, 132–33, 13. For a fuller discussion of the debates of Canadian imperialists regarding "race" and its ability to determine – or not – an individual's capacity for change, see Berger, *The Sense of Power*, 117. See also this book's discussion of the uses of W.H. Drummond's poetry, chapter 1, 60–1.

139 Darren Ferry notes that the limits of liberalism became more visible in the last decades of the nineteenth century "as the demarcations of nation, gender, and particularly socio-economic gradations between classes, became increasingly intricate and complex." Ferry, *Uniting in Measures of Common Good*, 8. To this consideration of liberalism's limits, Adele Perry adds the question of "race," which operated to relegate "non-Western peoples to various states of reduced humanity, savagery, unfreedom, or containment." Perry, "Women, Racialized People," 275. McKay discusses liberalism's "race" limits in Chapter 6 of *Reasoning Otherwise*. Postcolonial scholar Uday S. Mehta contends that there is a "politically exclusionary impulse" at the heart of seventeenth-century liberalism that had a tremendous influence on liberal practice in the nineteenth century. Mehta's examination of John Locke insists that the universal capacities described in his work conceal "specific cultural and psychological conditions" that function as "preconditions for the actualization of these capacities." Such "taken for granted" conditions are in fact nothing more than the assumed cultural norms of Locke's social context, but they exercised a powerful "exclusionary imprint in the concrete instantiation of liberal practices" in nineteenth-century India, for example. "Liberal Strategies of Exclusion," 61, 70.

140 Mackey, *The House of Difference*, 23–4; Selman, *Citizenship and the Adult Education Movement*, 3–5; Brodie, "White Settlers," 93. For the most influential theorization of the "Tory touch," first formulated in the mid-1960s, see Horowitz, "Conservatism, Liberalism, and Socialism." George Grant (son of George Monro Grant) also articulated an influential formulation in *Lament for a Nation*.

141 Brodie, "White Settlers," 97, 105; Veracini, *Settler Colonialism*, 16–20.

142 Foucault, *"Society Must Be Defended,"* 243–4, 254–5.

143 Fitzpatrick, *Handbook for New Canadians*, 200, 203, 205–6, 220–1.

144 See Chan, *Gold Mountain*; and Creese, "Exclusion or Solidarity?"

145 Fitzpatrick, *Handbook for New Canadians*, 185.

146 *The Immigrant*, n.p., FC, MG 28, I 124, vol. 107, LAC.

147 Waters to Fitzpatrick, 30 July 1911, MG 28, I 124, vol. 20, "Instructors' Correspondence (Appleton-Willis), 1911," FC-LAC.

148 Burns, "Register, 31 August 1919," MG 28, I 124, vol. 6, "Instructors' Correspondence (Anderson-Stewart), 1919," FC-LAC.

149 See this book's Introduction, n25.

150 Qtd. in Radforth, *Bushworkers and Bosses*, 34. Radforth consults reports of the federal Indian Affairs Branch as evidence for his contention that Indigenous men found work in the logging camps of Northern Ontario.
151 Bradwin, *The Bunkhouse Man*, 103.
152 Veracini, *Settler Colonialism*, 33–50.
153 McKay, "The Liberal Order Framework," 627.
154 Fitzpatrick, *Handbook for New Canadians*, 233 (emphasis added).
155 Diamond to Pauline Smith, 9 July 1916, MG 28, I 124, vol. 17, "Instructors' Correspondence (Aitcheson-Turnbull), 1916," FC-LAC. One 1924 register offers a different view of the potential of the Indigenous student: W.B. Mather in Longlac, ON, reported that 10 percent of his students were "Chippeway Indians," one of whom, Tom Odecom, attended twenty classes and made "fair" progress. "W.B. Mather," MG 28, I 124, vol. 120, "Instructors' Registers, 1924," FC-LAC.

CHAPTER THREE

1 Bradwin to Fitzpatrick, 7 October 1919, MG 28, I 124, vol. 154, "Correpondence-A. Fitzpatrick," FC-LAC.
2 Bercuson, *Fools and Wise Men*, 216; Hak, "British Columbia Loggers," 86. According to Bercuson, the economic recession of 1920–21 brought a 15 percent wage decrease across Canadian industry, an unemployment rate that reached 16.48 percent for unionized workers in the spring of 1921, and declining union membership across the country.
3 The figures describing instructor placement are taken from the following annual reports: *Coming of Age, Annual Report 1921; The Frontier College, with Twenty-Second Annual Report; The Frontier College, with Twenty-Third Annual Report*, MG 28, I 124, vol. 107; and *General Report, Frontier College Activities Among Foreign-Born Labourers Throughout Canada, Season 1929*, MG 28, I 124, vol. 109, FC-LAC. For total contributions throughout the 1920s, see this chapter, n33; for enrolment figures, see table 3.1.
4 Other advertisements in the same paper during the same year asked readers to support the "patriotic work" of "Canadianizing" and "citizenizing" foreign workers. "Canadianizing Foreigners," 6; "Financial Help Is Needed," 4.
5 Mitchell, "'The Manufacture of Souls,'" n.p.
6 Kelley and Trebilcock, *The Making of the Mosaic*, 192, 198–202, 213–14.
7 For the WEA, see the this book's Preface, n20.

8 Fitzpatrick, *The University in Overalls*, ix, xi, 70; Marx with Engels, *The German Ideology*, 72.
9 I take the details of this conflict from Cook and Robinson, "'The Fight of My Life.'" The correspondence between Frontier College and the government of Ontario that deals with this conflict may be found in the "Ontario Government" folders in MG 28, I 124, vols. 42, 44, 46, and 47, FC-LAC.
10 Loo and Strange, *Making Good*, 123. On the emergence of social security in the period contemporary with the First World War, see also Guest, *The Emergence of Social Security*, 38–63; and the discussion of "reluctant welfarism" in Moscovitch and Drover, "Social Expenditures," 20–26.
11 Ian McKay argues for the need to understand the federal government's handling of the "Indian Question" not just as a misunderstanding or manifestation of racism, but also as the "fufilment of liberal norms": "It was perhaps in the residential schools that the full utopianism of a vanguard liberalism came to the fore, for within these Christian/liberal manufactories of individuals, pre-eminent laboratories of liberalism, First Nations children were 'forced to be free,' in the very particular liberal sense of 'free,' even at the cost of their own lives." "The Liberal Order Framework," 637.
12 Roberts, *Whence They Came*, 90, 73; Kelley and Trebilcock, *The Making of the Mosaic*, 180. See also this book's chapter 2, n112. Other new restrictions on immigration in this period, such as the 1923 Chinese Immigration Act, were not directly linked to perceived problems of radicalism but were instead produced by nativist sentiment. Strange and Loo, *Making Good*, 117–22. For a more general discussion of the new powers over immigration arrogated by the state through 1919 amendments to the Immigration Act, see Kelley and Trebilcock, *The Making of the Mosaic*, 187.
13 1 May 1923, MG 28 I, 124, Vol. 30, "Canadian Government," FC-LAC.
14 James to Fitzpatrick, 26 October 1921; James to Fitzpatrick, 2 November 1921; Fitzpatrick to James, 9 November 1921, and Stead to Fitzpatrick, 15 November 1921, MG 28, I 124, vol. 25, "Government of Canada," FC-LAC.
15 Canada, Department of Immigration and Colonization, *A Manual of Citizenship*. I am citing the 1923 edition here; the 1925 edition contains only very minor textual differences. Its size and format are the same.
16 McLean, "Education, Identity, and Citizenship," 9–17. The National Bureau of Education in the United States was established within the Department of the Interior in 1867.
17 Leacock, "Frontier College," 9.
18 *Debates*, 1919, vol. 1, 812–13, 815, 818, 832–3. See McLean, "Education, Identity, and Citizenship," 17–23, for a discussion of Steele's and

Edwards's motions and the debate they engendered. The division of legislative power in the British North America Act created more general conflict during the late nineteenth and early twentieth centuries, a period during which the Dominion power over naturalization and aliens might have developed into federal authority over the basic rights of citizenship. According to Robert J. Sharpe, it is not surprising that this did not happen, largely because of the "legitimate claims of provincial power." "Citizenship," 229–30.

19 McLean, "'The Good Citizen,'" 236–7.
20 In 1923, the Deputy Minister of Justice wrote to Fitzpatrick (who had previously requested the minister to inform him if the 1922 Frontier College Act was *ultra vires*) to advise him that "the exclusive provincial power to make laws respecting education does not necessarily exclude a power in the Dominion to incorporate a body for promoting or imparting education." The minister concluded his letter, however, by noting that the 1922 Act was nonetheless "questionable" in terms of its validity. 23 May 1923, MG 28, I 124, vol. 42, "Dominion Government," FC-LAC. For further discussion of the question of jurisdiction in relation to the Frontier College Act, see Cook and Robinson, "'The Fight of My Life.'"
21 Fitzpatrick to Hon. James Murdock, Minister of Labour, 1 March 1923, Fitzpatrick to Hon. Charles Stewart, Minister of Immigration, 13 March 1921, and Fitzpatrick to Hon. R.S. Fielding, Minister of Finance, 1 March 1923, MG 28, I 124, vol. 30, "Dominion Government," FC-LAC. Fitzpatrick established a correspondence with Mackenzie King in the early 1920s, when King was leader of the Opposition. Fitzpatrick sought King's support for Frontier College and clearly hoped that King, if elected in December of 1921, would follow through with a grant. For King's noncommittal though friendly reply, see King to Fitzpatrick, 29 November 1921, MG 28, I 124, vol. 25, "General Correspondence," FC-LAC.
22 Fitzpatrick, *The University in Overalls*, xi.
23 Deputy Minister of Labor to Fitzpatrick, 9 March 1923, MG 28, I 124, vol. 30, "Dominion Government," FC-LAC.
24 Fitzpatrick to Stewart Bryce, Department of Labor, 15 August 1921, and Director of Employment Service of Canada to Bradwin, 13 September 1921, MG 28, I 124, vol. 25, "Government of Canada," FC-LAC.
25 Cook and Robinson, "'The Fight of My Life,'" 96n45.
26 Kealey, "The Early Years," 133. For more on Hamilton's role as cable censor in the First World War, see Kealey, "State Repression," 284, 287. As Keshen notes, Hamilton was also the *Globe*'s South African War correspondent. *Propaganda*, 72. In his 1921 letter to Fitzpatrick, the assistant

to the Director of Publicity for the Department of Immigration and Colonization notes that he has heard about the work of Frontier College from Fitzpatrick's "old college friend" C.F. Hamilton. Fred James to Fitzpatrick, 26 October 1921, MG 28, I 124, vol. 25, "Government of Canada," FC-LAC. For information on Hamilton and his role in the state intelligence developed in the wake of the First World War, see Kealey, "The Early Years," 133.

27 Hamilton to Fitzpatrick, 28 February 1923, MG 28, I 124, vol. 30, "Canadian Government," FC-LAC.

28 McLean, "Education, Identity, and Citizenship," 24. For a discussion of particular provincial developments in citizenship education in the 1920s, see Bruno-Jofré, "Citizenship and Schooling"; and Osborne, "Education is the Best National Insurance."

29 Loo and Strange, *Making Good*, 114. See also Sutherland, *Children in English-Canadian Society*, 202–15. The restrictions on public schooling produced by anglophone and Protestant anxiety about immigrant populations are numerous and complex, but the case of Manitoba is perhaps the best known. I refer in chapter 2 to the proscription after 1916 of any language but English in Manitoba's public schools (see n84). Another interesting and well-known case involves state efforts to coerce the Doukhobor population of Saskatchewan and British Columbia into public schools. See McLaren, "Creating 'Slaves of Satan,'" for a compelling account of the situation in British Columbia, where the Doukhobor population resisted many elements of state control, including public schooling.

30 Putman and Weir, *Survey of the School System*, 38.

31 Bruno-Jofré, "Citizenship and Schooling," 114–19.

32 Fitzpatrick to Robert Grant, 5 February 1921, and Fitzpatrick to A.H.U. Colquhoun, 18 March 1921, MG 28, I 124, vol. 25, "Ontario Government," FC-LAC; Fitzpatrick to Hon. Geo. P. Smith, 28 February 1921, and J.T. Ross to Fitzpatrick, 1 August 1921, MG 28, I 124, vol. 25, "Alberta Government," FC-LAC; Fitzpatrick to Hon. Dr. R.S. Thornton, 28 February 1921 and Jessie Lucas to Dr. R.S. Thornton, 21 April 1921, MG 28, I 124, vol. 25, "Manitoba Government," FC-LAC; Fitzpatrick to G.H. Murray, 15 November 1921, and Deputy Provincial Secretary to Fitzpatrick, 22 November 1921, MG 28, I 124, vol. 25, "Nova Scotia Government," FC-LAC; Fitzpatrick to L.A. Taschereau, 18 February 1921, and Taschereau to Fitzpatrick, 16 June 1921, MG 28, I 124, vol. 25, "Quebec Government," FC-LAC; Fitzpatrick to N.M. Martin, 28 February

1921, and "Treasury Note from Government of the Province of Saskatchewan," MG 28, I 124, vol. 25, "Saskatchewan Government," FC-LAC.
33 For a table that documents the varying contributions of the provincial governments to Frontier College during the period covered in this chapter, see Zavitz, "The Frontier College," Appendix A, "Government Grants to Frontier College from 1901–2 – 1930."
34 G.H. Ferguson to Hon. Dr. H.J. Cody, 28 September 1929, MG 28, I 124, vol. 42, "Ontario Government"; Ferguson to Fitzpatrick, 10 June 1929, MG 28, I 124, vol. 42, "Ontario Government," FC-LAC.
35 Radforth and Sangster, " 'A Link Between Labour and Learning,'" 47.
36 See "Railway Reports, 1925"; *General Report Frontier College Activities Among Labourers Throughout Canada, 1926*, MG 28, I 124, vol. 107, FC-LAC; *General Report Frontier College Activities Among Labourers in Camps Throughout Canada, Season 1927*, and *General Report Frontier College Activities Among Foreign-Born Labourers Throughout Canada, Season 1929*, MG 28, I 124, vol. 109, FC-LAC.
37 "Davidson, John F., 1920," MG 28, I 124, vol. 22, "Instructors' Correspondence," FC-LAC. For the invitation included in 1923, see "Registers, 1923," FC, MG 28, I 124, vol. 120, FC-LAC.
38 Worton, *The Dominion Bureau of Statistics*, 63–81. See Chapter 5 of Worton for a fuller description of these activities during the interwar period. Worton points out that the staff of the Dominion Bureau of Statistics grew from 123 in 1918–19 to 253 in 1923–24. Two-thirds of the new positions were full-time. *The Dominion Bureau of Statistics*, 83.
39 Ibid., 105–6.
40 S.A. Cudmore to Fitzpatrick, 2 April 1924; M.C. MacLean to Edmund Bradwin, 23 April 1924; and S.A. Cudmore to Fitzpatrick, 2 April 1924, MG 28, I 124, vol. 31, "Dominion of Canada," FC-LAC.
41 See the table "Strike Activity in Canada, 1912–1921" in Kealey, "State Repression," 283; Palmer, *Working-Class Experience*, 214–21.
42 Hak, "British Columbia Loggers," 86; "'Y' Work Among Lumbermen," 34; Austin, "The Y.M.C.A. in the Camps of B.C.," 56.
43 Heron, *The Canadian Labour Movement*, 55–63; Avery, "*Dangerous Foreigners*," 116–28; Beaulieu, *Labour at the Lakehead*, 65–150. See Chapter 2, n8 for a description of the IWW and the OBU.
44 Beaulieu, *Labour at the Lakehead*, 75. Beaulieu notes, however, that the OBU was soon supplanted in the Lakehead region by the competing forces

of a resurgent IWW, which had a particular appeal for radical Finnish workers, and the CPC.

45 In both 1925 and 1928, Finns made up 60 percent (up from 42 percent in 1923) of the party's members, and by the end of the decade, Finns and Ukrainians represented approximately 90 percent of the party's membership. Beaulieu, *Labour at the Lakehead*, 100–1, 108, 133, 150. Beaulieu points out that despite this dominance, Finns did not figure prominently in the party leadership, and that by mid-decade they found themselves the objects of the party's desire to dismantle the autonomy of the language federations.

46 See Fitzpatrick, *Handbook for New Canadians*, 201–6; and Bradwin, *The Bunkhouse Man*, 100–3.

47 Berguson, *Fools and Wise Men*, 68–86.

48 For Moore's acceptance of Fitzpatrick's offer to join the board, see Moore to Fitzpatrick, 11 April 1922, MG 28, I 124, vol. 27, "General Correspondence," FC-LAC.

49 Chantler to Fitzpatrick, 9 May 1920, MG 28, I 124, vol. 22, "Instructors' Correspondence," FC-LAC; Zavitz, "The Frontier College," 61.

50 R.N. Howson to Fitzpatrick, 9 March 1920, MG 28, I 124, vol. 22, "Instructors' Correspondence" FC-LAC. D. Fraser McDonald recounted to Fitzpatrick the story of two Russian workers who plotted a camp-wide strike and "strongly urged" McDonald to join them because of his influence with the men. McDonald did not want to use his influence for a strike for "which there was no justification" and chose to go to work the next morning, as did about sixty other men. The twenty strikers were discharged and proceeded to ransack the Frontier College car. "D. Fraser McDonald," MG 28, I 124, vol. 120, "Registers, 1924," FC-LAC.

51 Bradwin, *The Bunkhouse Man*, 224–5, 234, 237.

52 Kalar, "Review of *The Bunkhouse Man*," 16.

53 Zavitz, "The Frontier College," 35, 57. See also Zavitz, "The Frontier College," Appendix H, "Railway Grants to Frontier College, from the first donation to 1930."

54 *Coming of Age*, Annual Report 1921, p. 11, MG 28, I 124, vol. 107, FC-LAC.

55 "Making Good Canadian Citizens Out of Our Foreign Workmen," MG 28, I 124, vol. 143, "Clippings 1920–1929," FC-LAC.

56 "N. McKague," MG 28, I 124, vol. 119, "Instructors' Reports, 1921"; "W. Cecil Johnston," MG 28, I 120, vol. 120, "Registers, 1923," FC-LAC.

57 "J.W. DeNoon," MG 28, I 124, vol. 120, "Registers, 1923," FC-LAC.

58 On this point, see Frank, "Class Conflict." Frank points to the role of a "strongly homogenous" labour force and a tradition of militant trade unionism among mine workers from the Scottish lowlands in the labour conflicts of the Cape Breton coal industry during the early 1920s.
59 "Harry Mutchmor," MG 28, I 124, vol. 120, "Registers, 1923," FC-LAC.
60 "A.S. Kennedy," MG 28, I 124, vol. 120, "Registers, 1923," FC-LAC.
61 "D. Fraser McDonald," MG 28, I 124, vol. 120, "Registers, 1924," FC-LAC.
62 "H. Mutchmor," MG 28, I 124, vol. 120, "Registers, 1924," FC-LAC.
63 "R.L. Cockfield," MG 28, I 124, vol. 122, "Registers, 1926" FC-LAC.
64 "George Lasher," MG 28, I 124, vol. 120, "Registers, 1923," FC-LAC.
65 "Walter Shell," MG 28, I 124, vol. 123, "Registers, 1928," FC-LAC.
66 Fitzpatrick, *The University in Overalls*, 131–2.
67 MG 28, I 124, vol. 40, "Newspapers and Magazines, (1/2), 1928," FC-LAC. For information on *Collier's*, see Brad Bullock, "Newsstand: 1925: *Collier's Weekly*," accessed 8 May 2017, http://uwf.edu/dearle/enewsstand/enewsstand_files/Page736.htm.
68 "Bookkeeper to Miss Josephine T. Goodrich (Windsor ON)," 29 June 1929, MG 28, I 124, vol. 42, "Newspapers and Magazines, 1929," FC-LAC.
69 "W. Ririe," MG 28, I 124, vol. 119, "Registers, 1921"; "Richard Cockfield," MG 28, I 124, vol. 124, "Registers, 1929," FC-LAC.
70 Qtd. in Beaulieu, *Labour at the Lakehead*, 144. Beaulieu points out that Vaara and *Vapaus* were also at the centre of the struggle that emerged between the CPC and the Finnish Organization of Canada in the late 1920s in the wake of Stalin's Bolshevization plan, which aimed to dissolve the particular ethnic interests of organizations affiliated with the CPC. On *Vapaus*, see also Multicultural History Society of Ontario, "Vapaus," *SFU Digitized Newspapers*, Simon Fraser University. http://newspapers.lib.sfu.ca/vapaus2500-collection.
71 Kealey, "State Repression," 284.
72 Kealey, "The Surveillance State," 182–203.
73 Hamilton to Fitzpatrick, 28 February 1923, MG 28, I 124, vol. 30, "Canadian Government," FC-LAC.
74 Fitzpatrick to Hamilton, 7 May 1924, MG 28, I 124, vol. 31, "Government," FC-LAC.
75 Beaulieu, *Labour at the Lakehead*, 76, 79–80; Kealey and Whitaker, *R.C.M.P. Security Bulletins*, 288; Avery, "*Dangerous Foreigners*," 118, 126.

76 Nevertheless, the Retail Department of the press did retain 260 copies, which it sold for a small profit of twenty cents per copy. Retail Department, The Ryerson Press, to Fitzpatrick, 29 September 1921, MG 28, I 124, vol. 25, "Saskatchewan Government"; Manufacturing Department, The Ryerson Press to Fitzpatrick, 17 March 1921, MG 28, I 124, vol. 25, "Saskatchewan Government," FC-LAC. See also The Publication Department to Fitzpatrick, 19 February 1920, and E.J. Moore to Fitzpatrick, 27 February 1920, MG 28, I 124, vol. 154, "Correspondence–A. Fitzpatrick," FC-LAC.
77 Fitzpatrick to E.J. Moore, 20 February 1920, MG 28, I 124, vol. 154, "Correpondence–A. Fitzpatrick," FC-LAC.
78 These data are compiled from the thirty-one (Alexander-Stevenson) instructors' registers found in MG 28, I 124, vol. 120, "Registers, 1923," FC-LAC. The highest number sold in a single camp in 1923 was twelve (W. Mitchell); seventeen of the thirty-one labourer-teachers reported no sales.
79 Fitzpatrick to Martin, 22 March 1921, and Martin to Fitzpatrick, 9 April 1921, MG 28, I 124, vol. 25, "Saskatchewan Government," FC-LAC. On Fitzpatrick's rivalry with Anderson in the emergent field of citizenship education, see chapter 2, 93.
80 Fitzpatrick to W.L. Cope, 13 October 1920, MG 28, I 124, vol. 23, "Newspapers and Magazines," FC-LAC; Cope to Fitzpatrick, 17 March 1921, Cope to Fitzpatrick, 24 December 1920, and Cope to Fitzpatrick, 31 December 1920, MG 28, I 124, vol. 25, "Saskatchewan Government," FC-LAC.
81 Fitzpatrick, "Handbook for New Canadians," 2; Fitzpatrick to The Ryerson Press, 25 February 1920, "Memorandum of Credit and Report of Sales," and Fitzpatrick to E.A. Collins (International Nickel Company), 29 April 1920, MG 28, I 124, vol. 154, "Correspondence–A. Fitzpatrick," FC-LAC.
82 *The University and the Frontier*, 1920, n.p., MG 28, I 124, vol. 107, FC-LAC; *The Frontier College, with Twenty-Third Annual Report*, n.p., MG 28, I 124, vol. 107, FC-LAC.
83 Ryerson Press to Edmund Bradwin, 19 February 1925, MG 28, I 124, vol. 34, "Newspapers and Magazines," FC-LAC.
84 Fitzpatrick to Stead, 1 May 1928, and Stead to Fitzpatrick, 17 July 1928, MG 28, I 124, vol. 40, "Dominion Government," FC-LAC.
85 "Charles Owens," MG 28, I 124, vol. 123, "Registers, 1927," FC-LAC.
86 For possession of the primers, see registers for the 1928 season in "Registers, 1927," MG 28, I 124, vol. 123, FC-LAC. Many of these

registers indicate that the "Handbooks" in the kit are actually "Primers." Although the Amicus listing for *A Primer for Adults* (Frontier College Press) indicates that it was published in 1926, this does not seem to be accurate. For example, it was not until late in 1928 that Fitzpatrick sent text for the "forenote" that was later included in the *Primer* to William Cope, head of the printing department at Ryerson Press. Fitzpatrick to Cope, 15 November 1928, MG 28, I 124, vol. 40, "Newspapers and Magazines (1/2), 1928," FC-LAC. Copies of the *Primer* are very rare: Library and Archives Canada holds two copies, which they describe as the third and fifth "editions" (1930 and 1933, respectively); these are actually reprintings of the 1928 edition. A sixth edition is referenced in the document "Resume of Frontier College Work (Retrospect of one-third of a century)." See "Annual Reports, 1934–1935," MG 28, I 124, vol. 109, FC-LAC.

87 Durham, "Beside the Campfire," 12; Durham, "Rules for Membership," 32; Moore, "The Frontier College Instructor," 32. For examples of Fitzpatrick's increasing practice of corresponding with editors of Canadian newspapers in order to bring the work of Frontier College to their attention during the 1920s, see the folder "Newspapers and Magazines" in MG 28, I 124, vols. 21, 23, 25, 34, 36, 38, and 40, FC-LAC. In 1919 and again in 1920, *Canada Lumberman and Woodworker* sought and obtained from Fitzpatrick promotional articles regarding Frontier College. See G.B. Blaricom to Fitzpatrick, 27 December 1919, and G.B. Blaricom to Fitzpatrick, 22 July 1920, MG 28, I 124, vol. 23, "Newspapers and Magazines," FC-LAC.

88 "Frontier College: Press Excerpts From Recent Editorials," MG 28, I 124, vol. 143, "Clippings, 1920–1929," FC-LAC.

89 "Davidson, John F., 1920," MG 28, I 124, vol. 22, "Instructors' Correspondence," FC-LAC.

90 See, for example, registers for the 1926 season in "Registers, 1926," MG 28, I 124, vol. 122, FC-LAC.

91 Fitzpatrick, *Handbook for New Canadians*, 12; Moore, "The Frontier College Instructor," 32.

92 Fitzpatrick, *Handbook for New Canadians*, 9, 6, 12.

93 Mustard to Fitzpatrick, 10 September 1920, MG 28, I 124, vol. 22, "Instructors' Correspondence, 1920," FC-LAC.

94 "M.S. McLean," MG 28, I 124, vol. 122, "Registers, 1927," FC-LAC; *Pictured Words for New Canadians*, 1. The pamphlet urges more advanced learners to seek out the *Handbook for New Canadians*, George Elmore Reaman's *English for New Canadians*, and Peter Roberts's *English for Coming Canadians*.

95 "C. Bailey," MG 28, I 124, vol. 122, "Registers, 1927"; "B.M. Spock," MG 28, I 124, vol. 122, "Registers, 1926," FC-LAC.
96 "H. Bruce Collier," MG 28, I 124, vol. 123, "Registers, 1928"; "George Readman," MG 28, I 124, vol. 120, "Registers, 1924," FC-LAC.
97 "Touching Tributes," 13; "Toil and Teaching," 20.
98 The page inviting student comments first appeared in the register in 1923. See "Registers, 1923," MG 28, I 124, vol. 120, FC-LAC.
99 "J.M. Robb," MG 28, I 124, vol. 123, "Registers, 1928," FC-LAC. First published in 1867, Muir's poem appears at the end of the Reader section of Fitzpatrick's *Handbook for New Canadians* (where it is titled "The Maple Leaf"). It was one of the most popular anthems in late-nineteenth- and early-twentieth-century Canada. Sugars and Moss, eds., *Canadian Literature in English*, 315–16.
100 "H.S. Gross," MG 28, I 124, vol. 124, "Registers, 1929," FC-LAC.
101 "Davidson, John F., 1920," MG 28, I 124, vol. 22, "Instructors' Correspondence"; "E.L. Richards," MG 128, I 124, vol. 122, "Registers, 1926"; "R. Holmes," MG 128, I 124, vol. 120, "Registers, 1924"; "D. Fraser McDonald," MG 28, I 124, vol. 120, "Registers, 1924," FC-LAC.
102 "E.M. Reid," MG 28, I 124, vol. 122, "Registers, 1926," FC-LAC.
103 "William Gottsegen," MG 28, I 124, vol. 123, "Registers, 1927"; "H.S. Gross," MG 28, I 124, vol. 124, "Registers, 1929," FC-LAC.
104 Fitzpatrick, *Handbook for New Canadians*, 200.
105 Kelley and Trebilcock, *The Making of the Mosaic*, 206–7. Note that this exclusion on Chinese immigration remained in place until 1947, the year the National Citizenship Act was made law. The exclusion mechanism worked as it was intended to: between 1923 and 1947, only fifteen Chinese persons were given permission to emigrate to Canada. Kelley and Trebilcock, *The Making of the Mosaic*, 208.
106 Fitzpatrick, *Handbook for New Canadians*, 221.
107 "C.B. Horton," MG 28, I 124, vol. 119, "Registers, 1921," FC-LAC.
108 For lists of instructors in the field and for claims regarding enrolment in classes, see the following annual reports: *Coming of Age, Annual Report 1921, The Frontier College, with Twenty-Second Annual Report*, and *The Frontier College, with Twenty-Third Annual Report*, MG 28, I 124, vol. 107, FC-LAC; *Annual Report of Frontier College Activities Among Labourers in Camps Throughout Canada, Season 1927*, and *General Report, Frontier College Activities Among Foreign-Born Labourers Throughout Canada, Season 1929*, MG 28, I 124, vol. 109, FC-LAC.
109 *The Frontier College, With Twenty-Third Annual Report, 1923*, p. 45, MG 28, I 124, vol. 107, FC-LAC.

110 *Frontier College Combined Railway Reports 1924*, n.p., MG 28, I 124, vol. 107, FC-LAC.
111 "Earle W. Carr," MG 28, I 124, vol. 122, "Registers, 1926," FC-LAC.
112 Exaggeration as well as errors were very likely quite common. A.J. Hill, a labourer-teacher for an extra gang in Saskatchewan, entered his class for 14 August 1921 twice: in the first instance, he claimed fifteen students were in attendance; in the second, he claimed the number was twelve. "A.J. Hill," MG 28, I 124, vol. 119, "Registers, 1921," FC-LAC.
113 "C.W. Hardie," MG 28, I 124, vol. 124, "Registers, 1929," FC-LAC.
114 *The Frontier College, With Twenty-Third Annual Report, 1923*, p. 45, MG 28, I 124, vol. 107, FC-LAC.
115 "List of Books Missing," 24 April 1921, and Fitzpatrick to W.O. Carson, 19 May 1921, MG 28, I 124, vol. 25, "Ontario Government," FC-LAC.
116 Service, *Songs of a Sourdough*, 52. *Songs of a Sourdough* went through fifteen impressions in its first year of publication alone. The poems were a staple of Canadian school textbooks throughout the early twentieth century. New, "Service, Robert," 1033–34. My mother, who was born in 1944 near Haliburton, Ontario, recalls that her uncle, who worked as a manual labourer in the region and who had no more than elementary school education, could recite Service poems, including "The Cremation of Sam McGee," by heart.
117 Veracini, *Settler Colonialism*, 37. See also Johnston and Lawson, "Settler Colonies," 364–5, for an analysis of this kind of transfer in settler colonial narratives.
118 For Fitzpatrick's plea to federal officials, see Fitzpatrick to Hon. James Murdock, Minister of Labour, 1 March 1923, Fitzpatrick to Hon. Charles Stewart, Minister of Immigration, 13 March 1921, and Fitzpatrick to Hon. R.S. Fielding, Minister of Finance, 1 March 1923, MG 28, I 124, vol. 30, "Dominion Government," FC-LAC. For his 1923 editorial, see Fitzpatrick, "The Frontier College," 4. On the ways in which Canadian cultural forms assumed new importance in the context of the Cold War, see Dowler, "The Cultural Industries"; Litt, *The Muses*; and Druick, *Projecting Canada*, Chapter 5.
119 Requests for Zane Grey novels can be found in "Paul Alexander" and "A. Harmeyer," MG 28, I 124, vol. 124, "Registers, 1929," FC-LAC. Howard Chantler reported in 1920 that he had been working to make the reading room "more presentable" by cleaning it and "covering the walls with pictures, etc. from magazines, and parts of Robert Service's poems, which the men seem to enjoy reading." "Howard Chantler," MG 28, I 124, vol. 22, "Instructors' Correspondence, 1920," FC-LAC. Comments regarding

Western Story Magazine, *Western* (likely *Western Story*), and *Top-Notch Magazine* can be found in "B.J. Thomson," MG 28, I 124, vol. 122, "Registers, 1925"; and "H.L. Sharpe," MG 28, I 124, vol. 123, "Registers, 1927," FC-LAC. Described as the "first all-western pulp," *Western Story Magazine* arrived on newsstands in July 1919. Priced at ten cents, the inaugural issue boasted that its readers would be treated to "Big Clean Stories of Outdoor Life." Alexandra Yancey, "Western Story Magazine," *The Pulp Magazines Project*, accessed 9 June 2017, http://www.pulpmags.org/content/info/western-story-magazine.html. For *Top-Notch Magazine*, see chapter 2, n42. C.R. Wright noted that he generally liked the selections of books and magazines sent by Frontier College but complained that "detective stories are of no benefit to anyone and often prove to be the cause of a great deal of crime." "C.R. Wright," MG 28, I 124, vol. 122, "Registers, 1926," FC-LAC.

120 Bradwin, *The Bunkhouse Man*, 165.
121 Ibid., 164.
122 "Anson Stokes," MG 28, I 124, vol. 124, "Registers, 1928," FC-LAC.
123 "James Stewart Daly," MG 28, I 124, vol. 120, "Registers, 1923," FC-LAC. He estimated that of the sixty men in his camp, 80 percent were British- or Canadian-born.

CHAPTER FOUR

1 Palmer, *Working-Class Experience*, 241; Horn, *The Great Depression*, 10.
2 Cassidy, "Relief and Other Social Services," 174–80; Brown, "Unemployment Relief Camps," 523.
3 Makahonuk, "The Saskatoon Relief Camp," 55; Sefton MacDowell, "Canada's Gulag," n.p.; Struthers, *"No Fault of Their Own,"* 47–51. For a discussion of the regional variations in the definition of the non-resident or "transient" during the 1930s, see Cassidy, "Relief and Other Social Services," 173–4.
4 As Michael Ekers notes in his excellent article "'The Dirty Scruff,'" studies of the demonization of the unemployed abound but fewer scholars have attended to "how representations of the jobless are historically established." "'The Dirty Scruff,'" 1121. See also McCallum, "Vancouver"; and "The Great Depression's First History?"
5 Struthers, *"No Fault of Their Own,"* 6–8.
6 Qtd. in ibid., 53; qtd. in Horn, *The Dirty Thirties*, 457–8. For examples of Vancouver media coverage of "alien" agitators, see Ekers, "'The Dirty Scruff,'" 1124.

7 These details are taken from Chapter 2 of Struthers, *"No Fault of Their Own."* For a brief history of municipal and provincial solutions to unemployment in Ontario prior to 1932, see Sefton MacDowell, "Relief Camp Workers."
8 The scholarship on DND camps tends to focus on British Columbia or on the events of the 1935 On-to-Ottawa Trek, where radicalism and strike activity were greater. See Ekers, "'The Dirty Scruff'"; and Hak, "The Communists and the Unemployed"; as well as Brown, *When Freedom Was Lost*; Hewitt, "'We Are Sitting'"; Howard, *"We Were the Salt of the Earth"*; and Liversedge, *Recollections*. Cassidy points out that the DND relief camps in British Columbia held almost one third of the total DND camp population. "Relief and Other Social Services," 189. On DND relief camps in other regions of the country, see Brown, "Unemployment Relief Camps"; Sefton MacDowell, "Canada's Gulag" and "Relief Camp Workers"; and St. Denis, "The Great Depression."
9 Qtd. in Sefton MacDowell, "Relief Camp Workers," 209.
10 Qtd. in Ekers, "'The Dirty Scruff,'" 1131.
11 Waiser, "Relief Camps," n.p; Cassidy, "Relief and Other Social Services," 183.
12 Brown, *When Freedom Was Lost*, 50; Makahonuk, "The Saskatoon Relief Camp," 66. In his account of the Depression, D.H. Bocking notes that in July of 1933 he "was finally cut off relief for refusing to go to camp." Bocking, "Experiences of a Depression Hobo," 65.
13 Brown, "Unemployment Relief Camps," 532; Cassidy, "Relief and Other Social Services," 186.
14 Sefton MacDowell, "Relief Camp Workers," 214–15; Brown, "Unemployment Relief Camps," 531–2. At Lac Seul, for instance, each worker cleared 0.5 cords of wood per day, which was only one tenth of the DND's estimated output (and which had already accounted for the fact that men would work at fifty percent efficiency). Sefton MacDowell, "Canada's Gulag," n.p. In their 1936 report on relief camps for the Department of Labour, R.A. Rigg, Humphrey Mitchell, and Bradwin estimated the efficiency of relief camps workers at "not more than 35% of the normal standards." Rigg et al. to Hon. Norman McL. Rogers, 31 January 1936, MG 28, I 124, vol. 164, "Questionnaire, 1935," FC-LAC.
15 Sefton MacDowell, "Relief Camp Workers," 220–3.
16 Brown, "Unemployment Relief Camps," 534. Brown cites a different figure (12,601 men expelled for disciplinary reasons up to the end of June 1935) in his later publication *When Freedom Was Lost*, but there he is quoting a 1935 speech in the House of Commons given by R.B. Bennett rather than McNaughton's papers.

17 Sefton MacDowell, "Canada's Gulag," n.p.
18 Qtd. in ibid., n.p.
19 Brown, "Unemployment Relief Camps," 536–7.
20 Ibid., 538. For the original list of demands, see "Our Seven Demands," 3.
21 Qtd. in Brown, *When Freedom Was Lost*, 51–52. Brown points out that the British Columbia relief camps that preceded the DND scheme often permitted "camp committees" de facto recognition in negotiations with camp supervisors. The shift in policy under the DND scheme was therefore doubly unpalatable because it reversed a customary arrangement. *When Freedom Was Lost*, 58. As Makahonuk points out, military personnel were also employed in the administration of municipal relief camps prior to the DND scheme. In Saskatoon, for instance, P.J. Philpott, an ex-army officer and president of the local Canadian Legion, was appointed superintendent of the municipal camp established in 1930 because of his purported ability to maintain a "disciplined and orderly camp free from radicals and agitators." "The Saskatoon Relief Camp," 56.
22 Liversedge, *Recollections*, 38–9.
23 Heron, *The Canadian Labour Movement*, 70–1; Avery, "Dangerous Foreigners," 128; Howard, "We Were the Salt of the Earth," 7. On the CPC's work organizing the unemployed during the 1930s, see Chapter 15 of Angus, *Canadian Bolsheviks*; Avakumovic, *The Communist Party*, Chapters 3 and 4; Howard, "We Were the Salt of the Earth"; and Manley, "'Starve, Be Damned!'" Avakumovic points out that the CPC had few competitors in their attempts to organize the unemployed: provincial labour parties were weak outside of Winnipeg; the CCF was not a player until after 1933; craft unions such as the TLC were working to protect their employed (and dues-paying) members; and the fledgling IWW continued to insist on the need to organize in the workplace. *The Communist Party*, 74.
24 Manley, "'Starve, Be Damned!'" 471–2, 480; Avakumovic, *The Communist Party*, 74–78; Avery, "Dangerous Foreigners," 126–33. The figure for participation in the 1932 International Day of Struggle comes from Manley; Avakumovic puts the number higher, at 76,150. *The Communist Party*, 77. On the WUL's and NUWA's receptivity to Asian workers during the 1930s, see Creese, "Exclusion or Solidarity?"
25 Manley, "'Starve, Be Damned!,'" 473.
26 Ibid., 473; Howard, "We Were the Salt of the Earth," 18.
27 Manley, "'Starve, Be Damned!'" 485–7; Howard, "We Were the Salt of the Earth," 38.

28 Regional councils of the NUWA published their own versions of the *Unemployed Worker* during the early 1930s. Amicus lists holdings in Canadian libraries for the Ottawa, Vancouver, and Manitoba papers, as well as a periodical of the same name published by the Vancouver WUL. For information about *The Agitator* and its role in the Dundurn relief camp strike of December 1935–January 1936, see Brown, "Unemployment Relief Camps," 543.
29 "Our Seven Demands," 3. Howard estimates that at the time of the 1935 Kamloops conference, the British Columbia contingent of the RCWU was about one thousand members strong. *"We Were the Salt of the Earth,"* 24. The RCWU was succeeded in the wake of the trek by the Relief Project Workers' Union, which organized the 1938 Vancouver Sit-Down Strike.
30 Avakumovic, *The Communist Party*, 80–1. See also Brown, *When Freedom Was Lost*; Hewitt, "'We Are Sitting'"; Howard, *"We Were the Salt of the Earth"*; and Liversedge, *Recollections*.
31 Howard, *"We Were the Salt of the Earth,"* 16.
32 The 1 September 1934 issue of the *Relief Camp Worker* describes the Literature and Press Agents jobs accordingly: the first was meant to "procure working-class literature for distribution to all camp literature agents. To be responsible for the sending of all monies for the sale of literature to the district literature agent W.U.L. from whom literature must be ordered"; the second was meant to "gather all news, write articles, etc., for the working-class press on matters pertaining to the class struggle." "Amended Draft," 3.
33 Brown, *When Freedom Was Lost*, 63.
34 Howard, *"We Were the Salt of the Earth,"* 16–17; 27; 29; Liversedge, *Recollections*, 47–8.
35 Hasenbank, "Assembly Lines," 132.
36 An Act Respecting the Criminal Law, 1927 R.S., ch. 36, s. 98.
37 Molinaro, *An Exceptional Law*, 78–85.
38 Indeed, many have argued for the meaningful relationship between the rise of the workers' movements in the latter half of the nineteenth and the beginning of the twentieth century and this period's tremendous expansion of cheap print, in particular. For the case of western Europe (and especially France), see Debray, "Socialism: A Life Cycle"; and for the United States, see Martinek, *Socialism and Print Culture*. The literature on leftist periodicals is vast, but publications dealing with the North American context include Denning, *The Cultural Front*; Doyle, *Progressive Heritage*; Irr, *The Suburb of Dissent*; Irvine, *Editing Modernity*; Martinek, *Socialism*

and Print Culture; Mason, *Writing Unemployment* and "'Rebel Woman,' 'Little Woman'"; Nelson, *Revolutionary Memory*; Rifkind, *Comrades and Critics*; and Watt, "The Literature of Protest."
39 Thoburn, *Anti-Book*, 61–2.
40 "Mimeograph," *Encyclopedia Britannica*, accessed 11 January 2017, https://www.britannica.com/technology/mimeograph. By the early twentieth century, large newspapers employed linotype (machine-cast type) technology and were produced on large rotary presses that could print, by the beginning of the century, 96,000 twelve-page papers (in black ink) in an hour. Hoe, *A Short History of the Printing Press*, 85.
41 Adorno, *Minima Moralia*, 51.
42 Debray, "Socialism: A Life Cycle," 17.
43 Howard, *"We Were the Salt of the Earth,"* 16; Liversedge, *Recollections*, 47.
44 Between 1917 and 1938, the *Toronto Evening Star* was priced at two cents per copy. "History of the Toronto Star," thestar.com, accessed 19 Jan. 2018, https://www.thestar.com/about/history-of-the-toronto-star.html.
45 Liversedge, *Recollections*, 52.
46 "Camp Reports – Revelstoke District," 2.
47 "Workers' Education: Working-Class History No. 1," 7.
48 "According to the Yellow Press," 5.
49 "Police Attack Camp Strikers," 6.
50 Howard, *"We Were the Salt of the Earth,"* 16; Liversedge, *Recollections*, 47.
51 Nelson, *Revolutionary Memory*, 145, 159.
52 "In Regina City on Dominion Day," 4; "Grafting at Oyama Camp Exposed," 1, 6–7.
53 "Workers in the Slave Camps," 7.
54 "The Camp Striker," 4. On the "revolutionary chorus," see Nelson, *Revolutionary Memory*, 165–79.
55 See, for example, the call for "work and wage," the critique of military control, and the use of the figure of "slave" in the following poems: "Rhymes by the Batty Bard," 3; "The Truth," 5; "The Camp Striker," 4; and "Workers in the Slave Camps," 7.
56 See "Our Seven Demands," 3.
57 "Stand Solid Behind Your Delegation," 1.
58 As John Manley notes, imperialist discourse clashed with interests of the left frequently during the Depression. For example, veterans' groups such as the Canadian Legion "used 'Britishness' to undermine class identity by lodging claims for privileged treatment of their unemployed members over foreigners, who had never served the empire." Claims to limited resources were thus shaped by residual colonial ideologies. This contest over

resources frequently assumed the form of an opposition that pitted "citizens" against "foreign" "reds" or "radicals." Manley, "'Starve, Be Damned!'" 481–2.

59 On the introduction of social welfare legislation in Canada, including the 1940 Unemployment Insurance Act, see Guest, *The Emergence of Social Security*. On the Unemployment Insurance Act in particular, see Struthers, *"No Fault of Their Own."* On the history of workers' compensation legislation in BC, see Anjan Chaklader, "History of Workers' Compensation in B.C.," *Royal Commission on Workers' Compensation in British Columbia*, accessed 8 February 2018, http://www.qp.gov.bc.ca/rcwc/research/index.htm.

60 Marshall, *Social Policy*. As I discuss in *Writing Unemployment*, social democrats and Communists employed different rhetorical styles in this period, but they shared not only a general critique of the failure of governments to address the suffering caused by the Depression, but also a *solution*: the conviction that insurance for the unemployed – what would later be known as one of the social rights of citizenship – was necessary to ameliorate the crisis was common across the left in the early 1930s. See Chapter 2 of Mason, *Writing Unemployment*.

61 Struthers, *"No Fault of Their Own,"* 97.

62 Manley, "'Starve, Be Damned!'" 480. In his 1933 register, instructor Charles R. Welch noted that the men in his Bonfield, Ontario, camp were very grateful for a radio donated by the local IODE. "Charles R. Welch," MG 28, I 124, vol. 126, "Registers, 1933," FC-LAC.

63 Selman, *Adult Education in Canada*, 419; Tippett, *Making Culture*, 60. For more information on the BC Department of Education's extension work in provincial relief camps during the 1930s, see Selman's essay "Adult Education in British Columbia During the Depression" in *Adult Education in Canada*, 417–36.

64 Sacouman, "Underdevelopment and the Structural Origins," 68; Selman, *Adult Education in Canada*, 95–99, 119–49; Bradwin to Morse A. Cartwright, 30 July 1935, MG 28, I 124, vol. 155, "Canadian Association of Adult Education, 1935," FC-LAC. By the late 1920s Fitzpatrick had joined the American Association for Adult Education (founded by the president of the Carnegie Corporation of New York, Frederick P. Keppel, and his assistant, Morse A. Cartwright). Bradwin remained active in this association, as well, attending the 1935 Convention on Adult Education in Montreal that led to the founding of the CAAE with funding provided by them. Morse A. Cartwright to Fitzpatrick, 18 March 1927, MG 28, I 124, vol. 155,

"Correspondence–A. Fitzpatrick, 1927"; Bradwin to Morse A. Cartwright, 30 July 1935, MG 28, I 124, vol. 155, "Canadian Association of Adult Education, 1935," FC-LAC.

65 For correspondence regarding the Department of Northern Development and its Trans-Canada Highway camps, see the government correspondence in MG 28, I 124, vol. 46, "Federal Government," and vol. 47, "Ontario Government," FC-LAC. By the end of 1932, Bradwin (now principal) received word from a federal official that McNaughton intended to contact Frontier College regarding its collaboration in the new relief camp scheme. See Office of the Under-Secretary of State for External Affairs to Bradwin, 13 December 1932, MG 28, I 124, vol. 47, "Dominion Government," FC-LAC.

66 Bradwin to Major VandenBerg, 11 January 1934, MG 28, I 124, vol. 164, "Correspondence Re: Relief Camps, 1934," FC-LAC. See also "Reports, 1933," MG 28, I 124, vol. 109, FC-LAC. Correspondence from 1935 indicates the rate of pay established slightly later for instructors in camps with fewer than 250 men: in March 1935, the DND agreed to give instructors in the larger camps twenty dollars per month; instructors in smaller camps would receive fifteen dollars, which Frontier College agreed to supplement to the amount of twenty-five dollars. Bradwin to Secretary of the DND, 26 June 1935, MG 28, I 124, vol. 165, "Correspondence with Dept. of National Defence, 1935," FC-LAC.

67 DND to Bradwin, 24 May 1933, MG 28, I 124, vol. 50, "Dominion Government," FC-LAC. Bradwin insisted in his correspondence to camp superintendents that Frontier College men were to labour alongside the unemployed in the relief camps. See, for example, Bradwin to "The Superintendent," 4 June 1935, MG 28, I 124, vol. 164, "Reay, Ontario," FC-LAC. For Bradwin's insistence on the labourer-teacher's duty to uphold the authority of the DND, see Bradwin to The Foreman, 3 July 1935, MG 28, I 124, vol. 164, "Questionnaires," FC-LAC.

68 For 1934 and 1935 instructor placements, see "Reports, 1934," MG 28, I 124, vol. 109, FC-LAC. For 1936, see "Reports, 1936," MG 28, I 124, vol. 109, FC-LAC. Of the forty instructors who have registers for 1933, twenty-seven were in Ontario camps; of the eighty-three instructors counted in the reports for 1933, sixty-three (or 76 percent) were in Ontario camps. See "Field Staff of the Frontier College in the Camps of Canada," MG 28, I 124, vol. 108, "Reports, 1933," FC-LAC. For 1935 data on camp locations visited, see "Field Staff Frontier College Season 1935," MG 28, I 124, vol. 108, "Reports, 1935," FC-LAC. For McNaughton's concerns regarding the Department of Education's work

in British Columbia, see Bradwin to the Secretary of the DND, 2 April 1935, MG 28, I 124, vol. 165, "Correspondence with Dept. of National Defence, 1935," FC-LAC.

69 Broughton to Bradwin, 5 February 1934, MG 28, I 124, vol. 165, "Correspondence with Dept. of National Defence, 1934," FC-LAC.

70 However, the relief camp commitment was costly for Frontier College: the association accumulated a two-thousand-dollar debt to meet its commitment to relief camps in 1933, for example. Bradwin to Major H.L. Sherwood, 26 February 1934, MG 28, I 124, vol. 164, "Correspondence Re: Relief Camps, 1934," FC-LAC.

71 Menzies, Adamoski, and Chunn, "Rethinking the Citizen," 28; Ekers, "'The Dirty Scruff,'" 1125. Denyse Baillargeon points out that relief provisions for women during the 1930s operated to "support the prerogatives of the male heads of the household"; married women, cast as the economic dependents of their husbands, were generally ineligible for relief. "Indispensable But Not a Citizen," 180. See also Campbell, *Respectable Citizens*. On the distinction between the deserving and the undeserving poor and its influence on relief policy, see Chapter 1 of Struthers, *"No Fault of Their Own."*

72 "Survey Frontier College Work–1933," MG 28, I 124, vol. 109, "Reports, 1933," FC-LAC. The reference to "healthy and sound Canadianism" can be found in "Education for Men in Unemployment Camps," MG 28, I 124, vol. 109, "Reports, 1933," FC-LAC.

73 Bradwin to Col. G.E.A. Dupuis, 10 September 1934, MG 28, I 124, vol. 164 "Correspondence Re: Relief Camps, 1934"; Bradwin to W.B. Swanton, 4 June 1935, MG 28, I 124, vol. 165, "Questionnaire re: Conditions 1934," FC-LAC. For an example of the arguments used to discourage non-white applicants, see the 14 June 1936 letter from Western Representative G.H. Cockburn to applicant James H. Yonemura, in which Cockburn attributes his inability to hire Yonemura to his "ignorant fellow racials" who "would prove inept pupils, and their foolishness would come between you and them." Krotz, Martin, and Fernandez, *Frontier College Letters*, 50.

74 "Frontier College Report to Hon. N. McL Rogers-February 1936," MG 28, I 124, vol. 109, "Reports, 1936," FC-LAC.

75 "Give Teacher and Worker More in Common," MG 28, I 124, vol. 109, "Reports, 1939," FC-LAC.

76 "Resume of Work of Frontier College," MG 28, I 124, vol. 109, "Reports, 1935," FC-LAC.

77 Fitzpatrick, *Handbook for New Canadians*, 161; Brown, "Unemployment Relief Camps," 539.

78 "Some Results During 1936," MG 28, I 124, vol. 108, "Reports, 1936," FC-LAC.
79 "Memorandum re: Recreation Facilities in Unemployment Relief Camps," MG 28, I 124, vol. 164, "Clippings on the Committee to Make Survey of Relief Camps, 1935–36"; Rigg et al. to Hon. Norman McL. Rogers, 31 Jan. 1936, MG 28, I 124, vol. 164, "Questionnaire, 1935," FC-LAC.
80 G.R. Chetwynd to Bradwin, 29 January 1935, MG 28, I 124, vol. 164, "Hudson, Ont.," FC-LAC.
81 "Allen, H.W." MG 28, I 124, vol. 127, "Registers, 1935," FC-LAC.
82 "Baker, Clarence P." MG 28, I 124, vol. 127, "Registers, 1935," FC-LAC. Many of the registers in this period also note the preference for popular fiction magazines. Jack McGowan noted in his final report for 1935 that the men in his Ontario relief camp went to town to purchase their own copies of *The Argosy* – the first American pulp magazine and actually named *Argosy All-Story Weekly* during the 1930s – and *Detective Story Magazine* – one of the first pulps to devote itself entirely to the genre of crime fiction. See Nathan Vernon Madison, "The Argosy," *The Pulp Magazines Project*, accessed 9 April 2018, https://www.pulpmags.org/content/info/argosy.html; and Travis Kurowski, "Detective Story Magazine," *The Pulp Magazines Project*, accessed 9 April 2018, https://www.pulpmags.org/content/info/detective-story-magazine.html. Gordon Bennett's register for a Salmo, British Columbia, camp indicates that he sent away to Calgary for a "bundle of popular fiction magazines" that the men desired. Stephen H. Gibson wrote that men in his Lake of Two Rivers, Ontario, camp liked fictional and pictorial magazines best. From Killaloe, Ontario, Edward A. Reid observed that men preferred magazines of the "Digest" type, western- and detective-story magazines, and sports magazines. "Jack McGowan," "L. Gordon Bennett," and "Stephen H. Gibbon," MG 28, I 124, vol. 127, "Registers, 1935," FC-LAC; "Edward A. Reid," MG 28, I 124, vol. 128, "Registers, 1935," FC-LAC. For a history of the American pulp industry that notes its interwar peak, see Mike Ashley, "The Golden Age of Pulp Fiction," *The Pulp Magazines Project*, accessed 9 April 2018, https://www.pulpmags.org/contexts/essays/golden-age-of-pulps.html. For a study of working-class readers and pulp magazines in the American interwar context, see Smith, *Hard-Boiled*. Mary Vipond notes that the Canadian periodical market was "swamped with American publications" by the end of the First World War, leading Canadian periodical publishers to lobby throughout the 1920s and 30s for state protections for the domestic industry (in addition to a long-established postal subsidy for domestic newspapers and periodicals). Vipond, "Major Trends," 244.

83 "S.J. Taylor," MG 28, I 124, vol. 128, "Registers, 1935"; "W. Newby," MG 28, I 124, vol. 127, "Registers, 1934"; "George H. Cockburn," MG 28, I 124, vol. 126, "Registers, 1933," FC-LAC.
84 "The University in Overalls," by M.G. Rhodes, MG 28, I 124, vol. 109, "Reports, 1933," FC-LAC.
85 Bradwin to G.E. Richardson, 14 July 1929, MG 28, I 124, vol. 109, "Reports, 1936"; "Reginald Perry," MG 28, I 124, vol. 128, "Registers, 1935," FC-LAC.
86 For examples of such charges against labourer-teachers, see Bradwin to Foreman MacGregor, 3 February 1934, and Bradwin to Rycroft, 5 July 1934, MG 28, I 124, vol. 164, "Correspondence Re: Relief Camps, 1934"; and Bradwin to the Foreman, 3 July 1935, MG 28, I 124, vol. 164, "Questionnaires," FC-LAC.
87 Bradwin to A. Grant Bucknell, 21 December 1932, MG 28, I 124, vol. 109, "Reports, 1936"; "Letter Accompanying Item on Goethe and His Maxims," MG 28, I 124, vol. 109, "Reports, 1937," FC-LAC.
88 "Helps to Men on the Field," MG 28, I 124, vol. 109, "Reports, 1936," FC-LAC; "Henry Wadsworth Longfellow." Bradwin's "help" is quoted in a 1933 talk given by instructor M.G. Rhodes, who was stationed at the Dundurn, Saskatchewan, relief camp. It was therefore in circulation by 1933 and possibly earlier; the file in the 1936 folder is undated. See "The University in Overalls," by M.G. Rhodes, MG 28, I 124, vol. 109, "Reports, 1933," FC-LAC. On the decline of Longfellow's literary reputation in the wake of his death in 1882, which the author attributes largely to the modernist view of Victorian literature and culture, see Morton, "Longfellow, Tennyson," 6–7.
89 "Letter Accompanying Item on Goethe and His Maxims," MG 28, I 124, vol. 109, "Reports, 1937," FC-LAC. The information about the name of the poem "The Bridge" comes from Longfellow, *The Poetical Works*, 217.
90 Section 353 of the DND policy, which includes this regulation, is quoted in Brown, "Unemployment Relief Camps," 535.
91 "Helps to Men on the Field," MG 28, I 124, vol. 109, "Reports, 1936," FC-LAC.
92 Hubert, *Harmonious Perfection*, 83. The introduction to *The Bunkhouse Man* notes that Bradwin completed his undergraduate studies in history and economics at Queen's between 1907 and 1915; he studied extramurally, while completing stints in work camps as a labourer-teacher and, later, a supervisor. Bradwin, *The Bunkhouse Man*, 16. On the shift from imperialist to nationalist thinking in the wake of the First World War, see the conclusion of Berger, *The Sense of Power*. On the development of

romantic nationalist ideals in the literary discourse of the 1920s and 30s, see chapter 3 of Lecker, *Keepers of the Code*.

93 "Labourer-Teacher: A Constructive Factor in the Camp," MG 28, I 124, vol. 109, "Reports, 1936," FC-LAC. Although undated, this "help" is grouped among others from 1933 and 1934. "Suggestions to Men in the Field: Unemployment Insurance, 18 Jan. 1935" MG 28, I 124, vol. 109, "Reports, 1936," FC-LAC. Many of Bradwin's "helps" appear in the folder "Reports, 1936" (collected in the 1936 "Frontier College Report to Hon. N. McL Rogers").

94 Cohen, "Sentimental Communities," 112, 114–15. Berlant devotes much of *The Female Complaint* to examining what she calls the "*Uncle Tom* genealogy"—texts that, in the wake of Harriet Beecher Stowe's tremendously popular novel *Uncle Tom's Cabin* (1852), are linked by the "centrality of affective intensity and emotional bargaining amidst structural inequality." Cohen's and Berlant's readings of sentimental community and the intimate public sphere of "women's culture" diverge in significant ways, but both want to take seriously the ways that sentimentality operates rather than viewing it simply as, in Berlant's words, a "failure to be politics." *The Female Complaint*, 20, 25.

95 "Extract from Final Report," MG 28, I 124, vol. 109, "Reports, 1934"; "The University in Overalls," by H.G.E. Rhodes, MG 28, I 124, vol. 109, "Reports, 1933," FC-LAC.

96 Berlant, *Cruel Optimism*, 224–5, 227.

97 "Inculcating Savings, 7 March 1935," "Story of the Morris Car," "Government Not a Panacea for All Ills," MG 28, I 124, vol. 109, "Reports, 1937," FC-LAC.

98 Berlant, *The Queen of America*, 5–6.

99 Weir, "Unemployed Youth," 139–40, 141–8; Bradwin to Carl Welty, 16 December 1935, MG 28, I 124, vol. 109, "Reports, 1936"; "Frontier College," MG 28, I 124, vol. 109, "Reports, 1933," FC-LAC.

100 I take this information from the forty-one (Barnes to Zimmerman) instructors' registers found in MG 28, I 124, vol. 126, "Registers, 1933," LAC.

101 See this book's chapter 3, 162.

102 "James E.R. Shaver," MG 28, I 124, vol. 126, "Registers, 1933," FC-LAC.

103 "A.J.H. MacDonald," MG 28, I 124, vol. 127, "Registers, 1935"; "Robert McRae," MG 28, I 124, vol. 127, "Registers, 1935," FC-LAC.

104 Brown, "Unemployment Relief Camps," 530–31, 537–38, 543.

105 "H.G.E. Rhodes," MG 28, I 124, vol. 126, "Registers, 1933"; "The University in Overalls," by H.G.E. Rhodes, MG 28, I 124, vol. 109, "Reports, 1933," FC-LAC.

106 "W.E. Trott," MG 28, I 124, vol. 126, "Registers, 1933," FC-LAC. Trott's 1933 discussions attracted the following numbers of men: "economics" (14 August, ten men); "government" (12 September, four men); "economics" (16 September, nine men); "behaviour" (21 September, six men). To calculate the percentage of men in the camp these numbers represent, I took the mean of 200 and 450 (Trott estimated that there were 200 to 450 men in the camp).
107 Bradwin to W.B. Swanton, 28 November 1934, MG 28, I 124, vol. 164, "Correspondence Re: Relief Camps, 1934," FC-LAC.
108 Rigg et al. to Hon. Norman McL. Rogers, 31 January 1936, MG 28, I 124, vol. 164, "Questionnaire, 1935," FC-LAC.
109 Rigg et al. to Hon. Norman McL. Rogers, 31 January 1936, MG 28, I 124, Vol. 164, "Questionnaire, 1935," FC-LAC; Struthers, *"No Fault,"* 146–47. The questionnaires the commission distributed to labourer-teachers can be found in MG 28, I 124, vol. 164, "Questionnaire, 1935," FC-LAC.
110 Rigg et al. to Hon. Norman McL. Rogers, 31 January 1936, MG 28, I 124, vol. 164, "Questionnaire, 1935," FC-LAC; Struthers, *"No Fault,"* 19–21, 39–41, 197–204.
111 Bradwin to Frontier College Instructors, 30 November 1935, MG 28, I 124, vol. 109, "Annual Reports, 1935," FC-LAC.
112 Rigg et al. to Hon. Norman McL. Rogers, 31 January 1936, MG 28, I 124, vol. 164, "Questionnaire, 1935," FC-LAC.
113 In his appeals to private donors such as the Carnegie Foundation during the 1930s, Bradwin clearly stated that federal funding for the association's educational work was not possible: "Unfortunately, Frontier College is confronted with the fact that education at Confederation was left as a prerogative of the provinces. This right has been jealously guarded, especially by the Province of Quebec in its desire to maintain its entity in the matter of Language and its Creed." In this particular letter, he notes that General McNaughton stated unequivocally that financial help from Ottawa in the form of stable funding for Frontier College education work was impossible. Bradwin to Dr. F.P. Keppel, 13 November 1933, MG 28, I 124, vol. 164, "C-Miscellaneous, 1933," FC-LAC.
114 Strong-Boag, "Who Counts?" See also Chapter 12 of Giddens, *Profiles and Critiques*. It is also crucial to note that Québécois and Indigenous contestations of citizenship are crucial sites of struggle over the meanings of citizenship in Canada. See, for example, Coleman, "Imposing sub-Citizenship"; Denis, "Indigenous Citizenship"; and Rudin, "From the Nation to the Citizen."
115 Balibar, *Citizenship*, 55–6.

CONCLUSION

1 Bradwin to H.M. Cassidy, 19 March 1934, MG 28, I 124, vol. 51, "C-Miscellaneous, 1934," FC-LAC.
2 See Bradwin to Major-General LaFleche, 18 April 1941, MG 28, I 124, vol. 71, "Dominion Government-1941"; and Mackenzie King to Bradwin, 14 August 1940, MG 28, I 124, vol. 71, "Dominion Government–1941," FC-LAC; as well as the correspondence in the folders "Dominion Government–1945," "Federal Government-1948," and "Federal-1950," MG 28, I 124, vols. 80, 87, and 91, FC-LAC.
3 Selman, Cooke, and Dampier, *The Foundations*, 48–50; Selman, *Adult Education in Canada*, 119–49. On the National Farm Radio Forum and Citizens' Forum, see also Kuffert, "'Stabbing Our Spirits Broad Awake'"; Romanow, "'The Picture of Democracy We Are Seeking'"; and Sandwell, "'Read, Listen, Discuss, Act.'" This scholarship makes clear that of these two programs, the former was more progressive and connected to grassroots social change. Selman's essay on the early years of the CAAE in *Adult Education in Canada* argues that its more social-democratic orientation to "particular social policy" in the 1940s gave way to a less politicized view of adult education for citizenship in the 1950s. For documents from 1950 that demonstrate Bradwin's ongoing role in the CAAE, see MG 28, I 124, vol. 91, "Canadian Association for Adult Education," FC-LAC.
4 Citizens' Forum pamphlets can be consulted in "Citizens' Forum Pamphlets Accompanying Broadcasts, 1943–1958," MG 28, I 103, vol. 335, CF-CAAE-LAC.
5 Friesen, "Adult Education," 175; Romanow, "'The Picture of Democracy We Are Seeking,'" 117. See also McInnis, "Teamwork for Harmony."
6 "The Organizations of Functions of the Canadian Citizenship Branch," MG 28, I 103, vol. 335, "Citizenship, General 1945–51," CF-CAAE-LAC; Joshee, "The Federal Government," 110–13. In 1966, with the dissolution of the Department of Citizenship and Immigration, the Citizenship Branch (later, the Multiculturalism Directorate) went back to the Department of the Secretary of State, where it remained until 1999, when it was transferred to the new Department of Canadian Heritage.
7 See Bradwin to W.C. Davis, 19 August 1947, MG 28, I 124, vol. 85, "Federal Government-1947"; Bradwin to Frank Foulds, 20 September 1948, MG 28, I 124, vol. 87, "Federal Government-1948"; and Frank Foulds to Bradwin, 8 June 1950, MG 28, I 124, vol. 91, "Federal-1950," FC-LAC. There is a good deal of correspondence with citizenship-related

departments of the federal government from this period that shows that the work of Frontier College was known to them. See, for example, R.L. Elliott to Bradwin, 19 November 1947, MG 28, I 124, vol. 85, "Federal Government-1947," FC-LAC. Elliott, an editor with the Citizenship Branch of the Department of the Secretary of State, wrote to Bradwin to inquire about the history of Frontier College, noting that he intended to write articles about all agencies concerned with the "education of the newcomer to Canada."

8 Joshee, "The Federal Government," 117.
9 Ibid., 116–18. Joshee quotes Martin, then Minister of National Health and Welfare, on p. 117 from an address delivered in the House of Commons in 1946; he also quotes Department of Citizenship and Immigration officials from a 1956 policy document titled *The Integration of Immigrants in Canada*, prepared by E. Bussière (director of the Citizenship Branch).
10 Draper and Carere, "Selected Chronology," 51–58; Druick, *Projecting Canada*, chapter 5. This chapter in *Projecting Canada* draws attention to the ways that, during the early 1950s, NFB films were used in the service of Cold War foreign policy – to promote democratic processes and government abroad, for example. During the sixteen years between 1946 and 1962, immigration almost reached the heights it had achieved in the early 1910s: an average of 126,559 people arrived each year (for comparison, in the fifteen years between 1899 and 1914, an average of 195,671.25 people arrived each year). Kelley and Trebilcock, *The Making of the Mosaic*, 318; Avery, *Reluctant Host*, 11.
11 Druick, *Projecting Canada*, 5, 114.
12 Iacovettta, *Gatekeepers*, 51, 55, 58–9. Frontier College continued to work in frontier camps in the postwar period, although this was a diminishing component of its efforts. Bradwin represented this work to the federal government as citizenship education among the "D.P.'s" (displaced persons) who were arriving in Canada in this period. See Bradwin to Humprey Mitchell, 27 September 1948; and Bradwin to Paul Martin, 8 December 1948, MG 28, I 124, vol. 87, "Federal Government-1948," FC-LAC.
13 Fuld, *The Book of World-Famous Music*, 309.
14 Gabilliet, *Of Comics and Men*, 31, 39–40. Similar legislation in Canada was a significant factor in the decline of the Canadian pulp industry after 1949. The Canadian pulp industry boomed during the 1940s as a result of the War Exchange Conservation Act, which prohibited the importation of leisure and luxury items, as well as pulp (detective, sex, western, true crime) magazines. Strange and Loo, "Canadian Pulp Magazines," 255–8.

15 Druick, "International Cultural Relations," 186. Kevin Dowler uses Maurice Chartrand's concept of the "absent nation" to analyze how postwar cultural policy was linked to what were essentially security concerns stemming from the fact that Canada had built a communications infrastructure but had not filled it with national content, leaving the nation open to the influence of American mass culture. "The Cultural Industries." See also Berland, "Nationalism and the Modernist Legacy"; and Litt, *The Muses*.
16 Canada, *Report. Royal Commission on the Arts, Letters, and Sciences*, 226.
17 Druick, "International Cultural Relations," 186, 188–9.
18 "Distribution Reviewing Committee–Report," 52-119-1960; and "A Frontier College Report on the Use of Films and Filmstrips as Educational Aids for Frontier College Instructors in Isolated Camps of Canada," 52-119-1955, Frontier College, NFB Archives.
19 A.D.P. Heaney (Under-Secretary of State) to Bradwin, 28 December 1948, MG 28, I 124, vol. 90, "Dominion-1949"; Information Division, Department of External Affairs to Bradwin, 1 March 1950, MG 28, I 124, vol. 91, "Federal-1950," FC-LAC.
20 Selman, *The Foundations of Adult Education*, 42; Selman, *Adult Education in Canada*, 186–88. Kidd's son, Ross Kidd, worked as a Frontier College labourer-teacher in 1964 and 1965, went on to write his master's thesis on Frontier College at the University of Toronto (1975), and later became president of Frontier College. On the 1977 UNESCO prize, see http://www.unesco.org/new/en/education/themes/education-building-blocks/literacy/literacy-prizes.
21 Russell, "Bridging the Boundaries," 138–9; Slaughter, *Human Rights, Inc.*, 276. Joshee highlights the ways that language training, which has often been cast as a literacy initiative, and other forms of citizenship education tended to be linked, particularly after 1967, to labour force participation and skill development for employability. "The Federal Government," 119–22.
22 Munro, "Literacy for Citizenship," 102–3, 104.
23 Goar, "Pall Hangs Over Literacy Day," A14; Matthew Pearson, "Literacy Organizations Say Federal Government Abandoning Them," *Ottawa Citizen*, 20 May 2014, accessed 20 February 2016, http://ottawacitizen.com/news/local-news/literacy-organizations-say-federal-government-abandoning-them.
24 Many scholars have pointed to the influence of neoliberalism on the definition of literacy found in the OECD literacy surveys. See Atkinson, "Grade

12 or Die"; Hamilton and Barton, "The International Adult Literacy Survey"; and Judith Walker, "The Needy and Competent Citizen."
25 "Programs for Adults," Frontier College, accessed 20 January 2019, https://www.frontiercollege.ca/Programs/Programs-Offered/Programs-for-Adults.
26 Martin, "Action and Advocacy," 2 (see Welton, "Introduction," for a similar argument regarding the tensions that have characterized adult education in Canada); Fernandez and Thompson, "Frontier College: A Century of Lifelong Learning Outside the Boxes," 12–13.
27 Jenson, "Fated to Live," 641–44; Turner, "We Are All Denizens Now"; Brodie, "Citizenship and Solidarity." For a widely cited source on the emergence of neoliberalism, see Harvey, *A Brief History of Neoliberalism*.
28 Turner, "We Are All Denizens Now," 684; Brodie, "Citizenship and Solidarity," 390; Tonon and Raney, "Building a Conservative Nation," 216. For a similarly critical but differently oriented critique of *Discover Canada*, see Findlay, "'The Toil and Spoil of Translation.'"
29 McKay, "The Liberal Order Framework," 643; Brodie, "Citizenship and Solidarity," 384–7. On the introduction of the social rights of citizenship in Canada, see Brodie, "Citizenship and Solidarity," 382–6. See also Guest, *The Emergence of Social Security*, 104–45, whose analysis of the Liberal Party's compromises with the social-democratic left in the latter half of the 1940s offers a particularly useful view of the "reluctance" I am identifying. See also Menzies, Adamoski, and Chunn, "Rethinking the Citizen," for an overview of critiques of the social rights of citizenship; and Brodie, "The Social in Social Citizenship," for a more fully elaborated critique. For Gramsci's concept "passive revolution," see Gramsci, *Selections from the Prison Notebooks*, 106–14.
30 Henderson, "*Sui Generis*," 416. See also Borrows, *Recovering Canada* (especially for his conception of "landed" citizenship); and Coleman, "Imposing subCitizenship."
31 Brodie, "The Social," 22; Brouillette, "Neoliberalism," 277.
32 Cooper, *Family Values*, 9; Procacci, "Governmentality and Citizenship," 49–50. In his 1843 essay "On the Jewish Question," Marx distinguished between the "political emancipation" offered by the liberal-democratic state and "human emancipation." The former is limited because it depends on the idea that "egoistic man" and his "natural rights" form the precondition for the political state. The citizen, who is only ever an abstraction of "egoistic man," has not "recognized and organized his own powers (*forces propres*) as *social* powers so that he no longer separates this social power from himself as *political* power." "On the Jewish Question," 31. In *Family*

Values, Cooper points out that neoliberals in the United States have been making common cause with the new social conservatives since the early 1970s, when both rejected not the Keynesian welfare state itself (which they were willing to tolerate) but the demands of the liberation movements of the 1960s, 1970s, and 1980s, which called for greater income redistribution while "refusing the normative constraints of the Fordist family wage." What neoliberals and new social conservatives alike proposed in response "was not a return to the Fordist family wage ... but rather the strategic reinvention of a much older, poor-law tradition of private family responsibility, using the combined instruments of welfare reform, changes to taxation, and monetary policy." *Family Values*, 21.

Bibliography

ARCHIVES

AP-LAC: Aberdeen Papers, Library and Archives Canada
CF-CAAE-LAC: Citizens' Forum, Canadian Association for Adult Education, Library and Archives Canada
CGP-UM: Charles W. Gordon Papers, Elizabeth Dafoe Library Department of Archives and Special Collections, University of Manitoba
DELC-AO: Department of Education Library Correspondence Files, Archives of Ontario
FC-LAC: Frontier College Fonds, Library and Archives Canada
FC [multiple media], LAC: Frontier College Fonds [multiple media], Library and Archives Canada
MTL-MLMU: McLennan Travelling Library 1901–1968, Rare Books and Special Collections, McLennan Library, McGill University
NFB Archives: National Film Board Archives
PLB-AO: Public Libraries Branch Files, Archives of Ontario

PUBLISHED SOURCES

Abella, Irving. *A Coat of Many Colours: Two Centuries of Jewish Life in Canada*. Toronto: Lester & Orpen Dennys, 1990.
"According to the Yellow Press." *Relief Camp Worker*, 1 October 1934, 5.
Adamoski, Robert, Dorothy E. Chunn, and Robert Menzies, eds. *Contesting Canadian Citizenship: Historical Readings*. Peterborough: Broadview Press, 2002.
Adorno, Theodor. *Minima Moralia*. Translated by E.F.N. Jephcott. London: Verso, 2005.

"To Aid the Immigrant." *The Globe*, 2 June 1913, 6. *ProQuest Historical Newspapers*.

Alexander, Anne McDonald. *The Antigonish Movement: Moses Coady and Adult Education Today*. Toronto: Thomson Educational, 1997.

Allen, Richard. *The Social Passion: Religion and Social Reform in Canada, 1914–1928*. Toronto: University of Toronto Press, 1971.

Altick, Richard. *The English Common Reader: A Social History of the Mass Reading Public, 1800–1900*. Columbus: Ohio State University Press, [1957]1998.

"Amended Draft of Relief Camp Workers Union." *Relief Camp Worker*, 1 September 1934, 3–4, 7.

Anderson, Benedict. *Imagined Communities: Reflections on the Origin and Spread of Nationalism*, rev. ed. London: Verso, 2006.

Anderson, J.T.M. *The Education of the New Canadian*. Toronto: Dent, 1918.

Angus, Ian. *Canadian Bolsheviks: An Early History of the Communist Party of Canada*. Montreal: Vanguard, 1981.

Ashworth, Mary. *Immigrant Children in Canadian Schools*. Toronto: McClelland and Stewart, 1975.

Atkinson, Tannis. "Grade 12 or Die: Literacy Screening as a Tactic of Bio-Power." In *Canadian Education: Governing Practices and Producing Subjects*, edited by Brenda L. Spencer, Kenneth D. Gregory, Kari Delhi, and James Ryan, 7–21. Rotterdam: Sense, 2012.

Austin, O.D. "The Y.M.C.A. in the Camps of B.C." *Pacific Coast Lumberman*, October 1919, 42, 56.

Avakumovic, Ivan. *The Communist Party in Canada: A History*. Toronto: McClelland and Stewart, 1975.

Avery, Donald. "*Dangerous Foreigners*": *European Immigrant Workers and Labour Radicalism in Canada, 1896–1932*. Toronto: McClelland and Stewart, 1979.

– *Reluctant Host: Canada's Response to Immigrant Workers, 1896–1994*. Toronto: McClelland and Stewart, 1995.

Baillargeon, Denyse. "Indispensable But Not a Citizen: The Housewife in the Great Depression." Translated by Yvonne M. Klein. In Adamoski, Chunn, and Menzies, eds., *Contesting Canadian Citizenship*, 179–98.

Baldick, Chris. *The Social Mission of English Criticism, 1848–1932*. Oxford: Clarendon Press, 1983.

Balibar, Étienne. *Citizenship*. Translated by Thomas Scott-Railton. Cambridge: Polity Press, 2015.

Bannister, Jerry. "Canada as Counter-Revolution: The Loyalist Order Framework in Canadian History, 1750–1840." In Constant and Ducharme, eds., *Liberalism and Hegemony*, 98–146.

Bausenhart, W. "The Ontario German Language Press and Its Suppression by Order-in-Council 1918." *Canadian Ethnic Studies* 4, no. 1 (1972): 35–48.

Baylen, Joseph O. "Stead's Penny 'Masterpiece Library.'" *Journal of Popular Culture* 9, no. 3 (1975): 710–25. ProQuest.

Beaulieu, Michel S. *Labour at the Lakehead: Ethnicity, Socialism, and Politics, 1900–35*. Vancouver: UBC Press, 2011.

Bercuson, D.J. *Fools and Wise Men: The Rise and Fall of the One Big Union*. Toronto: McGraw-Hill Ryerson, 1978.

Berger, Carl. *The Sense of Power: Studies in the Ideas of Canadian Imperialism, 1867–1914*. Toronto: University of Toronto Press, 1970.

Berland, Jody. "Nationalism and the Modernist Legacy: Dialogues with Innis." In *Capital Culture: A Reader on Modernist Legacies, State Institutions, and the Value(s) of Art*, edited by Shelley Hornstein and Jody Berland, 14–38. Montreal and Kingston: McGill-Queen's University Press, 2000.

Berlant, Lauren. *Cruel Optimism*. Durham: Duke University Press, 2011.

– *The Female Complaint: On the Unfinished Business of Sentimentality in American Culture*. Durham: Duke University Press, 2008.

– *The Queen of America Goes to Washington City: Essays on Sex and Citizenship*. Durham: Duke University Press, 1997.

Biggs, Julian, dir. *Frontier College*. 1954. Canada: National Film Board, 2009. DVD, 20 min, 51s.

Blanchard, James. "Anatomy of Failure: Ontario Mechanics' Institutes, 1835–1895." *Canadian Library Journal* 38, no. 6 (1981): 393–8.

Bocking, D.H. "Experiences of a Depression Hobo." *Saskatchewan History* 22, no. 2 (1969): 60–5.

"Books for Michipicoten: First Travelling Library Starts on its Round." *The Globe*, 24 May 1901, 10. *ProQuest Historical Newspapers*.

Borrows, John. *Recovering Canada: The Resurgence of Indigenous Law*. Toronto: University of Toronto Press, 2002.

Bothwell, Robert. "Something of Value? Subjects and Citizens in Canadian History." In Kaplan, ed., *Belonging*, 25–35.

Bourdieu, Pierre. *Distinction: A Social Critique of the Judgment of Taste*. Translated by Richard Nice. London: Routledge, 2010.

- "The Field of Cultural Production, or: The Economic World Reversed." In *The Field of Cultural Production*, edited by Randal Johnson, 29–73. New York: Columbia University Press, 1993.
Bourdieu, Pierre, and J.C. Passeron. *Reproduction in Education, Society, and Culture*. Translated by Richard Nice. London: Sage, 1990.
Bradbury, Bettina. *Working Families: Age, Gender, and Daily Survival in Industrializing Montreal*. Toronto: University of Toronto Press, 2007.
Bradwin, Edmund. *The Bunkhouse Man: A Study of Work and Pay in the Camps of Canada, 1903–1914*. Toronto: University of Toronto Press, [1928]1972.
- "Frontier College." *Journal of Adult Education* XI (3 June 1939): 268–70.
Brodie, Janine. "Citizenship and Solidarity: Reflections on the Canadian Way." *Citizenship Studies* 6, no. 4 (2002): 377–94.
- "The Social in Social Citizenship." In *Recasting the Social in Citizenship*, edited by Engin F. Isin, 20–43. Toronto: University of Toronto Press, 2008.
- "White Settlers and the Biopolitics of State Building in Canada." In *Shifting the Ground of Canadian Literary Studies*, edited by Smaro Kamboureli and Robert Zacharias, 87–108. Waterloo: Wilfrid Laurier University Press, 2012.
Brouillette, Sarah. "Neoliberalism and the Demise of the Literary." In *Neoliberalism and Contemporary Literary Culture*, edited by Mitchum Huehls and Rachel Greenwald Smith, 277–90. Baltimore: Johns Hopkins University Press, 2017.
Brown, Lorne A. "Unemployment Relief Camps in Saskatchewan, 1933–1936." In Sefton MacDowell and Radforth, eds., *Canadian Working-Class History*, 523–46.
- *When Freedom Was Lost: The Unemployed, the Agitator, and the State*. Montreal: Black Rose Books, 1986.
Brown, Robert Craig, and Ramsay Cook. *Canada, 1896–1921: A Nation Transformed*. Toronto: McClelland and Stewart, 1974.
Bruce, Lorne. "Reading Camps and Travelling Libraries in New Ontario, 1900–1905." *Historical Studies in Education / Revue d'histoire de l'éducation* 26, no. 2 (2014): 71–97.
Bruno-Jofré, Rose. "Citizenship and Schooling in Manitoba between the End of the First World War and the End of the Second World War." In Hébert, ed., *Citizenship Transformation in Canada*, 112–33.
Brydon, Diana. "Metamorphoses of a Discipline: Rethinking Canadian Literature within Institutional Contexts." In Kamboureli and Miki, eds., *Trans.Can.Lit*, 1–16.

Burnet, Jean. "An Introduction." In Bradwin, *The Bunkhouse Man*, vi–xv.
"Camp Reports – Revelstoke District." *Relief Camp Worker*, 1 October 1934, 2–3.
"The Camp Striker." *Relief Camp Worker*, 13 April 1935, 4.
Campbell, Lara. *Respectable Citizens: Gender, Family, and Unemployment in Ontario's Great Depression*. Toronto: University of Toronto Press, 2009.
Canada. Citizenship and Immigration Canada. *Discover Canada: The Rights and Responsibilities of Citizenship*. Ottawa: 2012.
– *Fifth Census of Canada 1911*, vol. II. Ottawa: C.H. Parmelee, 1913.
– "Fifth Census of Canada, 1911, Instructions to Officers, Commissioners and Enumerators." Supplement to *The Canada Gazette*, 22 April 1911, 6–68.
– *Report of the Royal Commission on National Development in the Arts, Letters, and Sciences, 1949–51*. Ottawa: Edmond Cloutier, 1951.
– *Special Report on the Foreign-Born Population*. Ottawa: Government Printing Bureau, 1915.
Canada, Department of Immigration and Colonization. *A Manual of Citizenship*. Ottawa: 1923.
– *A Manual of Citizenship*. Ottawa: 1925.
"Canadianizing Foreigners." *Toronto Daily Star*, 1 November 1920, 6. ProQuest Historical Newspapers.
Candy, Philip C. "From Homo Canadiannus Colonialus to Homo Canadiannus Nationalus: Adult Education and Nation-Building in Late Nineteenth Century Canada." In *Proceedings of the Fourth Annual Conference of the Canadian Association for the Study of Adult Education*, edited by Marcel Savaria, 427–50. Montréal: Université de Montréal, 1985.
Cassidy, H.M. "Relief and Other Social Services for Transients." In Richter, ed., *Canada's Unemployment Problem*, 172–221.
Catalogue of Books in the Library of the Mechanics' Institute of Montreal with the Rules of the Library and Reading Room. Montreal: A.A. Stevenson, 1869. Microform. Canadian Institute for Historical Microreproductions, no. 91888.
Cavallo, Guglielmo, and Roger Chartier, eds. *A History of Reading in the West*. Translated by Lydia G. Cochrane. Amherst: University of Massachusetts Press, 1999.
Chan, Anthony. "Bachelor Workers." In Iacovetta, ed., *A Nation of Immigrants*, 231–50.

- *Gold Mountain: The Chinese in the New World.* Vancouver: New Star, 1983.
Chartier, Roger. *The Order of Books: Readers, Authors, and Libraries in Europe between the Fourteenth and the Eighteenth Centuries.* Cambridge: Polity Press, 1994.
Chen, Xiaobei. *Tending the Gardens of Citizenship: Child-Saving in Toronto, 1880s–1920s.* Toronto: University of Toronto Press, 2005.
Cho, Lily. "Diasporic Citizenship: Contradictions and Possibilities for Canadian Literature." In Kamboureli and Miki, eds., *Trans.Can.Lit.*, 93–110.
- "Diasporic Citizenship and the De-Formation of Citizenship." In *The Oxford Handbook of Canadian Literature*, edited by Cynthia Sugars, 527–38. New York: Oxford University Press, 2016.
Christie, Nancy. *Engendering the State: Family, Work, and Welfare in Canada.* Toronto: University of Toronto Press, 2000.
Christie, Nancy, and Michael Gauvreau. *A Full-Orbed Christianity: The Protestant Churches and Social Welfare in Canada, 1900–1940.* Montreal and Kingston: McGill-Queen's University Press, 1996.
Clark, Penney. "'Great Chorus of Protest': A Case Study of Conflict over the 1909 Eaton's Readers." *History of Education* 38, no. 5 (2009): 681–703.
- "The Publishing of School Books in English." In Lamonde, Fleming, and Black, *History of the Book*, 335–40.
Cohen, Margaret. "Sentimental Communities." In *The Literary Channel: The Inter-National Invention of the Novel*, edited by Margaret Cohen and Carolyn Dever, 106–32. Princeton: Princeton University Press, 2002.
Colclough, Stephen, and David Vincent. "Reading." In *The Cambridge History of the Book in Britain*, edited by David McKitterick, vol. 6 (1830–1914), 281–323. Cambridge: Cambridge University Press, 2014.
Coleman, Daniel. "Imposing subCitizenship: Canadian White Civility and the Two Row Wampum of the Six Nations." In Fleischmann, Styvendale, and McCarroll, eds., *Narratives of Citizenship*, 177–212.
- *White Civility: The Literary Project of English Canada.* Toronto: University of Toronto Press, 2006.
Connor, Ralph. *Black Rock: A Tale of the Selkirks.* London: Hodder and Stoughton, [1897]1918.
- *The Foreigner: A Tale of the Saskatchewan.* Toronto: The Westminster Co., 1909.
- *To Him That Hath.* New York: George H. Doran, 1921.

- *The Man from Glengarry: A Tale of the Ottawa*. Toronto: McClelland and Stewart, [1901]1993.
Constant, Jean François, and Michel Ducharme. "Introduction: A Project of Rule Called Canada
- The Liberal Order Framework and Historical Practice." In Constant and Ducharme, eds., *Liberalism and Hegemony*, 3–31.
Constant, Jean-François, and Michel Ducharme, eds. *Liberalism and Hegemony: Debating the Canadian Liberal Revolution*. Toronto: University of Toronto Press, 2009.
Cook, George L. "Alfred Fitzpatrick and the Foundation of Frontier College (1899–1922)." *Canada: An Historical Magazine* 4, no. 3 (1976): 15–39.
- "Educational Justice for the Campmen: Alfred Fitzpatrick and the Foundation of Frontier College." In Welton, ed., *Knowledge for the People*, 35–51.
Cook, George L., and Marjorie Robinson. "'The Fight of My Life': Alfred Fitzpatrick's Struggle for the Frontier Charter, 1902–1933." *Histoire Sociale / Social History* 23, no. 45 (1990): 81–112.
Cook, Ramsay. *The Regenerators: Social Criticism in Late Victorian English Canada*. Toronto: University of Toronto Press, 1985.
Cooper, Melinda. *Family Values: Between Neoliberalism and the New Social Conservatism*. Cambridge, MA: MIT Press, 2017.
Creese, Gillian. "Exclusion or Solidarity? Vancouver Workers Confront the 'Oriental Problem.'" In Sefton MacDowell and Radforth, *Canadian Working-Class History*, 312–32.
Crerar, Duff. "'Crackling Sounds from the Burning Bush': The Evangelical Impulse in Canadian Presbyterianism before 1875." In *Aspects of the Canadian Evangelical Experience*, edited by G. Rawlyk, 123–36. Montreal and Kingston: McGill-Queen's University Press, 1997.
Crowley, Terry. "The Origins of Continuing Education for Women: The Ontario Women's Institutes." *Woman Studies/Les cahiers de la femme* 7, no.3 (1986): 79–81.
Curtis, Bruce. "'After Canada': Liberalisms, Social Theory, and Historical Analysis." In Constant and Ducharme, *Liberalism and Hegemony*, 176–200.
- "Beyond Signature Literacy: New Research Directions." *Historical Studies in Education / Revue d'histoire de l'éducation* (Fall 2007): 1–12.
- *Building the Educational State: Canada West, 1836–1871*. London: Falmer Press, 1988.

- "'Littery Merit,' 'Useful Knowledge,' and the Organization of Township Libraries in Canada West, 1840–1860." *Ontario History* 78, no. 4 (1986): 285–311.
- *Ruling by Schooling Quebec: Conquest to Liberal Governmentality. A Historical Sociology.* Toronto: University of Toronto Press, 2012.

Curtis, Susan. "The Son of Man and God the Father: The Social Gospel and Victorian Masculinity." In *Meanings for Manhood: Constructions of Masculinity in Victorian America*, edited by Mark C. Carnes and Clyde Griffen, 67–78. Chicago: University of Chicago Press, 1990.

Dandurand, Madame. "William H. Drummond." *La Presse*, 12 April 1907, 4. Microfilm.

Darnton, Robert. *The Case for Books: Past, Present, and Future.* New York: Public Affairs, 2009.
- "First Steps Toward a History of Reading." In Towheed, Crone, and Halsey, *The History of Reading*, 23–35.
- *The Forbidden Best-Sellers of Pre-Revolutionary France.* New York: W.W. Norton, 1995.
- *The Great Cat Massacre: And Other Episodes in French Cultural History.* New York: Basic Books, 2009.
- "What Is the History of Books?" *Daedalus* 111, no. 3 (Summer 1982): 65–83.

Dawson, Gowan. "Stead, William Thomas (1899–1912)." In *DNJC: Dictionary of Nineteenth-Century Journalism*, edited by Laurel Brake and Marisa Demoor, n.p. London: British Library, 2009. *C19 The Nineteenth-Century Index*.

Debray, Régis. "Socialism: A Life Cycle." *New Left Review* 46 (July–August 2007): 5–28.

Denis, Claude. "Indigenous Citizenship and History in Canada: Between Denial and Imposition." In Adamoski, Chunn, and Menzies, *Contesting Canadian Citizenship*, 114–26.

Denning, Michael. *The Cultural Front: The Laboring of American Culture in the Twentieth Century.* New York: Verso, 1996.

Dennison, Carol J. "'Housekeepers of the Community': The British Columbia Women's Institutes, 1909–46." In Welton, ed., *Knowledge for the People*, 52–72.

Derrida, Jacques. *Mal d'archive: une impression freudienne.* Paris: Galilée, 1995.

Devereux, Cecily. *Growing A Race: Nellie McClung and the Fiction of Eugenic Feminism.* Montreal and Kingston: McGill-Queen's University Press, 2005.

Distad, Merrill. "Newspapers and Magazines." In Lamonde, Fleming, and Black, eds., *History of the Book*, 293–303.
Donzelot, Jacques. "The Promotion of the Social." *Economy and Society* 17, no. 3 (1988): 395–427. doi:10.1080/03085148800000016.
Dowler, Kevin. "The Cultural Industries Policy Apparatus." In *The Cultural Industries in Canada*, edited by Michael Dorland, 328–46. Toronto: James Lorimer, 1996.
Doyle, James. *Progressive Heritage: The Evolution of a Politically Radical Literary Tradition in Canada*. Waterloo: Wilfrid Laurier University Press, 2002.
Draper, James A. "Introduction to the Canadian Chronology." *Canadian Journal for the Study of Adult Education* 12, no. 2 (1998): 33–43.
Draper, James, and James Carere. "Selected Chronology of Adult Education in Canada." *Canadian Journal for the Study of Adult Education* 12, no. 2 (1998): 44–76.
Druick, Zoe. "International Cultural Relations as a Factor in Cold War Cultural Policy: The Relevance of UNESCO for the Massey Commission." *Canadian Journal of Communications* 31, no. 1 (2006): 177–95. doi:https://doi.org/10.22230/cjc.2006v31n1a1742.
– *Projecting Canada: Government Policy and Documentary Film at the National Film Board*. Montreal and Kingston: McGill-Queen's University Press, 1994.
Drummond, W.H. *The Habitant and Other French-Canadian Poems*. New York: G.P. Putnam's Sons, 1897.
– *Johnnie Courteau and Other Poems*. New York: G.P. Putnam's Sons, 1901.
Durham, Nancy. "Beside the Campfire: A Great Book." *The Globe*, August 21, 1920, 12. *ProQuest Historical Newspapers*.
– "Rules for Membership." *The Globe*, 4 September 1920, 32. *ProQuest Historical Newspapers*.
Eadie, James A. "The Napanee Mechanics' Institutes." *Ontario History* 68, no. 4 (1976): 209–21.
Eagleton, Terry. "The Rise of English." In *Literary Theory: An Introduction*, 15–46. Minneapolis: University of Minnesota Press, 2008.
Edwards, Brendan Frederick R. *Paper Talk: A History of Libraries, Print Culture, and Aboriginal Peoples in Canada Before 1960*. Lanham: Scarecrow Press, 2005.
Ekers, Michael. "'The Dirty Scruff': Relief and the Production of the Unemployed in Depression-Era British Columbia." *Antipode* 44, no. 4 (2012): 1119–42. doi:10:1111/j.1467-8330.2011.00979.x.

English, James. "Everywhere and Nowhere: The Sociology of Literature after 'the Sociology of Literature.'" *New Literary History* 41, no. 2 (2010): v–xxiii. doi:10.1353/nlh.2010.0005.

Fee, Margery. "Canadian Literature and English Studies in the Canadian University." *Essays on Canadian Writing* 48 (1993): 20–40.

Feola, Michael. "Fear and Loathing in Democratic Times: Affect, Citizenship, and Agency." *Political Studies* 64, supp. 1 (2016): 53–69. doi:10.1111/1467-9248.12197.

Ferguson, Barry. *Remaking Liberalism: The Intellectual Legacy of Adam Shortt, O.D. Skelton, W.C. Clark, and W.A. Mackintosh, 1890–1925*. Montreal and Kingston: McGill-Queen's University Press, 1993.

Fergusson, C. Bruce. *Mechanics' Institutes in Nova Scotia*. Halifax: Public Archives of Nova Scotia, 1960.

Fernandez, Philip, and Sarah Thompson. "Frontier College: A Century of Lifelong Learning outside the Boxes." *Education Canada* 40, no. 2 (Summer 2000): 12–14.

Ferry, Darren. *Uniting in Measures of Common Good: The Construction of Liberal Identities in Central Canada*. Montreal and Kingston: McGill-Queen's University Press, 2008.

"Financial Help Is Needed to Citizenize Our Foreign Workmen." *Toronto Daily Star*, 8 November 1920, 4. *ProQuest Historical Newspapers*.

Findlay, Len. "Always Indigenize! The Radical Humanities in the Postcolonial University." *ARIEL* 31, nos. 1–2 (2000): 307–26.

– "'The Toil and Spoil of Translation': A Godardian Reading of the *Study Guide: Discover Canada / Guide d'étude: Découvrir le Canada* (2010)." In *Trans/Acting Culture, Writing, and Memory: Essays in Honour of Barbara Godard*, edited by Eva C. Karpinski, Jennifer Henderson, Ian Sowton, and Ray Ellenwood, 149–66. Waterloo: Wilfrid Laurier University Press, 2013.

Fitzpatrick, Alfred. "The Frontier College." *The Globe*, 14 March 1923, 4. *ProQuest Historical Newspapers*.

– *Handbook for New Canadians*. Toronto: Ryerson Press, 1919.

– "Life in Lumbering and Mining Camps – A Plea for Reform." *The Canadian Magazine*, May 1901, 49–52. *Early Canadiana Online*.

– "The Neglected Citizen in the Camps." *The Canadian Magazine*, May 1905, 43–8. *Early Canadiana Online*.

– "Social Amelioration in the Lumbering Camps." *The Canada Lumberman*, May 1904, 15–16. *Early Canadiana Online*.

– *The University in Overalls: A Plea for Part-Time Study*. 1920. Toronto: Frontier College Press, 1923.
Fleischmann, Aloys N.M., Nancy Van Styvendale, and Cody McCarroll, eds. *Narratives of Citizenship: Indigenous and Diasporic Peoples Unsettle the Modern State*. Edmonton: University of Alberta Press, 2011.
Forest, Marsha, and James Morrison. "The Women of Frontier College." *Canadian Women's Studies* 9, nos. 3–4 (Fall/Winter 1988): 21–23.
Forestell, Nancy M. "Bachelors, Boarding Houses, and Blind Pigs: Gender Construction in a Multi-Ethnic Mining Camp, 1909–1920." In Iacovetta, ed, *A Nation of Immigrants*, 251–90.
Foucault, Michel. *"Society Must Be Defended": Lectures at the Collège de France, 1975–1976*. Edited by Mario Bertani and Alessandro Fontana. Translated by David Macey. New York: Picador, 2003.
Frank, David. "Class Conflict in the Coal Industry, Cape Breton, 1922." In Sefton MacDowell and Radforth, *Canadian Working-Class History*, 459–80.
Fraser, Brian. *The Social Uplifters: Presbyterian Progressives and the Social Gospel in Canada, 1875–1915*. Waterloo: Wilfrid Laurier University Press, 1988.
Fréchette, Louis. Introduction. In Drummond, *The Habitant and Other French-Canadian Poems*, v–x.
"Free Reading Camps to Benefit Workmen in Isolated Northern Districts." *The Globe*, 26 August 1901, 10. ProQuest Historical Newspapers.
Friesen, Gerald. "Adult Education and Union Education: Aspects of English-Canadian Cultural History in the Twentieth Century." *Labour/Le Travail* 34 (Fall 1994): 163–88.
Friesen, Gerald, and Lucy Taksa. "Workers' Education in Australia and Canada: A Comparative Approach to Labour's Cultural History." *Labour/Le Travail* 38 (Fall 1996): 170–97.
Frontier College. *A Primer for Adults: Elementary English for Foreign-Born Workers in Camps*. Toronto: Frontier College, 1926.
Fuld, James J. *The Book of World-Famous Music: Classical, Popular, Folk*. New York: Crown, 1971.
Fuller, Danielle. "Listening to the Readers of 'Canada Reads.'" *Canadian Literature* 193 (Summer 2007): 11–34.
Fuller, Danielle, and DeNel Rehberg Sedo. *Reading Beyond the Book: The Social Practices of Contemporary Literary Culture*. New York: Routledge, 2013.

- "A Reading Spectacle for the Nation: The CBC and 'Canada Reads.'"
  Journal of Canadian Studies 40, no. 1 (Winter 2006): 5–36.
Gabilliet, Jean-Paul. *Of Comics and Men: A Cultural History of American Comic Books*. Oxford: University Press of Mississippi, 2009.
Gauvreau, Michael. *The Evangelical Century: College and Creed in English Canada from the Great Revival to the Great Depression*. Montreal and Kingston: McGill-Queen's University Press, 1991.
Gauvreau, Michael, and Nancy Christie. *Cultures of Citizenship in Postwar Canada, 1940–1955*. Montreal and Kingston: McGill-Queen's University Press, 2003.
Gerson, Carole. *A Purer Taste: The Writing and Reading of Fiction in English in Nineteenth-Century Canada*. Toronto: University of Toronto Press, 1989.
Gerson, Carole, and Jacques Michon, eds. *History of the Book in Canada*, vol. 3. Toronto: University of Toronto Press, 2007.
Giddens, Anthony. *Profiles and Critiques in Social Theory*. London: Palgrave, 1982.
Gidney, R.D., and W.P.J. Millar. "How to Teach English to Immigrant Children: Canadian Pedagogical Theory and Practice, 1910–1960." *Historical Studies in Education / Revue d'histoire de l'éducation* 26, no. 2 (2014): 98–115.
Goar, Carole. "Pall Hangs Over Literacy Day." *Toronto Star*, 26 January 2007, A14. ProQuest: CBCA Complete.
Gorham, Eric. "Social Citizenship and Its Fetters." *Polity* 28, no. 1 (1995): 25–47.
Graff, Gerald. *Professing Literature: An Institutional History*. Chicago: University of Chicago Press, 1989.
Graff, Harvey J. *The Literacy Myth: Cultural Integration and Social Structure in the Nineteenth Century*. 1979. London: Routledge, 2017.
- *Literacy and Social Development in the West: A Reader*. Cambridge: Cambridge University Press, 1981.
- "Respected and Profitable Labour: Literacy, Jobs, and the Working Class in the Nineteenth Century." In *Essays in Canadian Working-Class History*, edited by Gregory S. Kealey and Peter Warrian, 58–82. Toronto: McClelland and Stewart, 1976.
"Grafting at Oyama Camp Exposed." *Relief Camp Worker*, 14 March 1935, 1, 6–7.
Gramsci, Antonio. *Selections from the Prison Notebooks*. Edited and translated by Quintin Hoare and Geoffrey Nowell Smith. New York: International, 2008.

Grant, George. *Lament for a Nation: The Defeat of Canadian Nationalism.* Toronto: McClelland and Stewart, 1965.
Greer, Allan. "1837–38: Rebellion Reconsidered." *Canadian Historical Review* 76, no. 1 (1995): 1–18.
Guest, Dennis. *The Emergence of Social Security in Canada.* Vancouver: UBC Press, 1997.
Habermas, Jürgen. *The Structural Transformation of the Public Sphere: An Inquiry into a Category of Bourgeois Society.* Translated by Thomas Burger and Frederick Lawrence. Cambridge, MA: MIT Press, 1989.
Hak, Gordon. "British Columbia Loggers and the Lumber Workers Industrial Union, 1919–1922." *Labour / Le Travail* 23 (Spring 1989): 67–90.
– "The Communists and the Unemployed in the Prince George District, 1930–1935." *BC Studies* 68 (Winter 1985–86): 45–61.
Hamilton, Mary, and David Barton. "The International Adult Literacy Survey: What Does It Really Measure?" *International Review of Education* 46, no. 5 (2000): 377–89.
Hardy, Edwin Austin. *The Public Library: Its Place in Our Educational System.* Toronto: William Briggs, 1912.
Harney, Robert. "Men Without Women: Italian Migrants in Canada, 1885–1930." In Iacovetta, ed., *A Nation of Immigrants*, 206–30.
Harrol, Corrinne, and Mark Simpson. "Introduction: Toward a Literary History for the Twenty-First Century." In *Literary/Liberal Entanglements: Toward a Literary History for the Twenty-First Century*, edited by Harrol and Simpson, 3–28. Toronto: University of Toronto Press, 2017.
Harvey, David. *A Brief History of Neoliberalism.* Oxford: Oxford University Press, 2005.
Hasenbank, Andrea. "Assembly Lines: Researching Radical Print Networks." *English Studies in Canada* 41, no. 1 (2015): 129–53. doi:https://doi.org/10.1353/esc.2015.0005.
Heathorn, Stephen. *For Home, Country, and Race: Constructing Gender, Class, and Englishness in the Elementary School, 1880–1914.* Toronto: University of Toronto Press, 2000.
Hébert, Yvonne M., ed. *Citizenship Transformation in Canada.* Toronto: University of Toronto Press, 2002.
Hébert, Yvonne M., and Lori Wilkinson. "The Citizenship Debates: Conceptual, Policy, Experiential, and Educational Issues." In Hébert, *Citizenship Transformation in Canada*, 3–36.
Henderson, James (Sákéj) Youngblood. "*Sui Generis* and Treaty Citizenship." *Citizenship Studies* 6, no. 4 (2002): 415–40.

Henderson, Jennifer. *Settler Feminism and Race Making in Canada.* Toronto: University of Toronto Press, 2003.
"Henry Wadsworth Longfellow." In *Gale Online Encyclopedia.* Detroit, MI: Gale, 2019. *Literature Resource Centre.*
Heron, Craig. *The Canadian Labour Movement: A Short History.* Toronto: James Lorimer, 1989.
Hewitt, S.R. "We Are Sitting at the Edge of a Volcano." *Prairie Forum* 19, no. 1 (1994): 51–64.
Hjartarson, Paul. "Print Culture, Ethnicity, and Identity." In Lamonde, Fleming, and Black, eds., *History of the Book*, 43–53.
Hoe, Robert. *A Short History of the Printing Press and of the Improvements in Printing Machinery From the Time of Gutenberg Up to the Present Day.* New York: 1902.
Hoggart, Richard. *The Uses of Literacy.* London: Transaction, [1957]2008.
Holmes, Stephen. "Liberal Guilt: Some Theoretical Origins of the Welfare State." In *Responsibility, Rights, and Welfare: The Theory of the Welfare State*, edited by J. Donald Moon, 77–106. London: Westview Press, 1988.
Horn, Michiel, ed. *The Dirty Thirties.* Toronto: Copp Clark, 1972.
– *The Great Depression of the 1930s in Canada.* Ottawa: Canadian Historical Association, 1984.
Horowitz, Gad. "Conservatism, Liberalism, and Socialism in Canada: An Interpretation." *Canadian Journal of Economics and Political Science* 32, no. 2 (1966): 143–71.
Howard, Victor. *"We Were the Salt of the Earth": A Narrative of the On-to-Ottawa Trek and the Regina Riot.* Regina: Canadian Plains Research Center, 1985.
Hubert, Henry A. *Harmonious Perfection: The Development of English Studies in Nineteenth-Century Anglo-Canadian Colleges.* East Lansing: Michigan State University Press, 1994.
Hunter, Ian. *Culture and Government: The Emergence of Literary Education.* London: Palgrave Macmillan, 1988.
Iacovetta, Franca. *Gatekeepers: Reshaping Immigrant Lives in Cold War Canada.* Toronto: Between the Lines, 2006.
– "Making 'New' Canadians: Social Workers, Women, and the Reshaping of Immigrant Families." In *Gender Conflicts: New Essays in Women's History*, edited by Franca Iacovetta and Mariana Valverde, 261–303. Toronto: University of Toronto Press, 1992.
Iacovetta, Franca, ed., with Paula Draper and Robert Ventresca. *A Nation of Immigrants: Women, Workers, and Communities in Canadian History, 1840s–1960s.* Toronto: University of Toronto Press, 1998.

Irr, Caren. *The Suburb of Dissent: Cultural Politics in the United States and Canada during the 1930s*. Durham: Duke University Press, 1998.

Irvine, Dean. *Editing Modernity: Women and Little Magazine Cultures in Canada, 1916–1956*. Toronto: University of Toronto Press, 2008.

Jansen, Clifford J. *Italians in Multicultural Canada*. Lewiston: Edwin Mellen Press, 1988.

Jenson, Jane. "Fated to Live in Interesting Times: Canada's Changing Citizenship Regimes." *Canadian Journal of Political Science* 30, no. 4 (1997): 627–44.

Johnson, Brian. "National Species: Ecology, Allegory, and Indigeneity in the Wolf Stories of Roberts, Seton, and Mowat." In *In Other Selves: Animals in the Canadian Literary Imagination*, edited by Janice Fiamengo, 333–52. Ottawa: University of Ottawa Press, 2007.

Johnson, Carol. "The Politics of Affective Citizenship: From Blair to Obama." *Citizenship Studies* 14, no. 5 (2010): 495–509. doi:10.1080/13 621025.2010.506702.

Johnston, Anna, and Alan Lawson. "Settler Colonies." In *A Companion to Postcolonial Studies*, edited by Henry Schwarz and Sangeeta Ray, 360–76. Malden: Blackwell, 2000.

Jones, Manina. "Wildlifewriting?: Animal Stories and Indigenous Claims in Ernest Thompson Seton's *Wild Animals I Have Known*." *Journal of Canadian Studies* 42, no. 3 (2008): 133–49.

Joshee, Reva. "The Federal Government and Citizenship Education for Newcomers." *Canadian and International Education* 25, no. 2 (1996): 108–27.

Kalar, Joseph. "Review of *The Bunkhouse Man*." *New Masses*, November 1929, 16.

Kamboureli, Smaro. *Scandalous Bodies: Diasporic Literature in English Canada*. Toronto: Oxford University Press, 2000.

Kamboureli, Smaro, and Roy Miki, eds. *Trans.Can.Lit.: Resituating the Study of Canadian Literature*. Waterloo: Wilfrid Laurier University Press, 2007.

Kaplan, William, ed. *Belonging: The Meaning and Future of Canadian Citizenship*. Montreal and Kingston: McGill-Queen's University Press, 1993.

Karr, Clarence. *Authors and Audiences: Popular Canadian Fiction in the Early Twentieth Century*. Montreal and Kingston: McGill-Queen's University Press, 2000.

– "Popular and Bestselling Fiction." In Gerson and Michon, eds., *History of the Book*, 396–401.

Kealey, Gregory. "1919: The Canadian Labour Revolt." *Labour/Le Travail* 13 (Spring 1984): 11–44.
- "The Early Years of State Surveillance of Labour and the Left in Canada: The Institutional Framework of the Royal Canadian Mounted Police Security and Intelligence Apparatus, 1918–26." *Intelligence and National Security* 8, no. 3 (1993): 129–48. doi:10.1080/0268452 9308432218.
- "State Repression of Labour and the Left in Canada, 1914–1920: The Impact of the First World War." *Canadian Historical Review* 7, no. 3 (1992): 179–210.
- "The Surveillance State: The Origins of Domestic Intelligence and Counter Subversion in Canada, 1914–21." *Intelligence and National Security* 7, no. 3 (1992): 179–210. doi:10.1080/0268452920 8432165.
Kealey, Gregory, and Reg Whitaker, eds. *R.C.M.P. Security Bulletins: The Early Years, 1919–1929.* St. John's: Canadian Committee on Labour History, 1994.
Keane, Patrick. "A Study in Early Problems and Policies in Adult Education: The Halifax Mechanics' Institute." *Social History / Histoire sociale* 8, no. 16 (1975): 254–74.
Kelley, Ninette, and Michael Trebilcock. *The Making of the Mosaic: A History of Canadian Immigration Policy.* Toronto: University of Toronto Press, 2010.
Kertzer, Jonathan. *Worrying the Nation: Imagining a National Literature in English Canada.* Toronto: University of Toronto Press, 2000.
Keshen, Jeffrey A. *Propaganda and Censorship During Canada's Great War.* Edmonton: University of Alberta Press, 1996.
Kidd, Ross. "The Frontier College Labourer-Teacher: A Study of His Role, Reception, and Performance." Master's thesis, University of Toronto, 1975.
Knight, Lorna. "Reaching Out to Isolated Readers." In Gerson and Michon, eds., *History of the Book,* 491–96.
Krawchuk, Peter. *The Ukrainian Socialist Movement in Canada (1907–1918).* Toronto: Progress Books, 1979.
Krotz, Larry, with Erica Martin and Philip Fernandez. *Frontier College Letters: One Hundred Years of Teaching, Learning, and Nation Building.* Toronto: Frontier College Press, 1999.
Kuffert, Leonard. "'Stabbing Our Spirits Broad Awake': Reconstructing Canadian Culture, 1940–1948." In Gauvreau and Christie, *Cultures of Citizenship,* 27–62.

Kulba, Tracy. "Citizens, Consumers, Critique-al Subjects: Rethinking the 'Statue Controversy' and Emily Murphy's *Black Candle* (1922)." *Tessera* 31 (Winter 2002): 74–89.
Lamonde, Yvan, Peter F. McNally, and Andrea Rotundo. "Public Libraries and the Emergence of a Public Culture." In *History of the Book in Canada*, vol. 2, edited by Yvan Lamonde, Patricia Lockhart Fleming, and Fiona A. Black, 250–71. Toronto: University of Toronto Press, 2005.
Leacock, Stephen. "Frontier College Is Making Foreigners into Canadians." *Toronto Star Weekly*, 27 September 1919, 9. Microfilm.
Lecker, Robert. *Keepers of the Code: English-Canadian Literary Anthologies and Representations of Nation.* Toronto: University of Toronto Press, 2013.
Lewis, Paul E. "The Goderich Mechanics' Institute, 1852–1870." *Western Ontario Historical Notes* 26 (1972): 19–24.
Lindström, Varpu. *Defiant Sisters: A Social History of Finnish Immigrant Women in Canada.* Beaverton: Aspasia Books, 2003.
Litt, Paul. *The Muses, the Masses, and the Massey Commission.* Toronto: University of Toronto Press, 1992.
Liversedge, Ron. *Recollections of the On-to-Ottawa Trek.* Montreal and Kingston: McGill-Queen's University Press, 1973.
Loewen, Royden. *Family, Church, and Market: A Mennonite Community in the Old and New Worlds, 1850–1930.* Toronto: University of Toronto Press, 1993.
Long, Elizabeth. *Book Clubs: Women and the Uses of Reading in Everyday Life.* Chicago: University of Chicago Press, 2003.
Longfellow, Henry Wadsworth. *The Poetical Works of Henry Wadsworth Longfellow*, vol. 1. Boston: Houghton Mifflin and Company, 1886.
Loo, Tina, and Carolyn Strange. *Making Good: Law and Moral Regulation, 1867–1939.* Toronto: University of Toronto Press, 1997.
Lotz, Jim, and Michael R. Welton. "'Knowledge for the People': The Origins and Development of the Antigonish Movement." In Welton, ed., *Knowledge for the People*, 97–111.
"Lumber Camp Libraries." *The Canada Lumberman*, December 1904, 17. *Early Canadiana Online.*
Lyons, Martyn. "New Readers in the Nineteenth Century: Women, Children, Workers." In Cavallo and Chartier, eds., *A History of Reading in the West*, 313–42.
– *Readers and Society in Nineteenth-Century France: Workers, Women, Peasants.* New York: Palgrave, 2001.

Macdonald, J.F. *William Henry Drummond.* Toronto: Ryerson Press, n.d.
Mack, Barry D. "Modernity without Tears: The Mythic World of Ralph Connor." In *The Burning Bush and a Few Acres of Snow*, edited by William Klempa, 139–57. Ottawa: Carleton University Press, 1994.
Mackey, Eva. *The House of Difference: Cultural Politics and National Identity in Canada.* Toronto: University of Toronto Press, 2002.
MacPherson, Ian. *Each for All: A History of the Co-operative Movement in English Canada, 1900–1945.* Toronto: Macmillan, 1979.
Makahonuk, Glen. "The Saskatoon Relief Camp Workers' Riot of May 8, 1933: An Expression of Class Conflict." *Saskatchewan History* 37, no. 2 (1984): 55–72.
"Making Good Canadian Citizens Out of Our Foreign Workmen." *Toronto Daily Star*, 25 October 1920, 6. ProQuest Historical Newspapers.
Mangan, J.A., and James Walvin, eds. *Manliness and Morality: Middle-Class Masculinity in Britain and America, 1800–1940.* Manchester: Manchester University Press, 1987.
– Introduction. In Mangan and Walvin, eds., *Manliness and Morality*, 1–6.
Manley, John. "'Starve, Be Damned!': Communists and Canada's Urban Unemployed, 1929–39." *Canadian Historical Review* 79, no. 3 (1998): 466–91.
Marks, Lynne. *Revivals and Roller Rinks: Religion, Leisure, and Identity in Late-Nineteenth-Century Small-Town Ontario.* Toronto: University of Toronto Press, 1996.
Marshall, David. "'A Canoe, and a Tent and God's Great Out-of-Doors': Muscular Christianity and the Flight from Domesticity, 1880s–1930s." In *Masculinity and the Other: Historical Perspectives*, edited by Heather Ellis and Jessica Meyer, 23–42. Newcastle upon Tyne: Cambridge Scholars' Press, 2009.
Marshall, T.H. *Social Policy.* London: Hutchinson, 1975.
Martin, Erica. "Action and Advocacy: Alfred Fitzpatrick and the Early History of Frontier College." Master's thesis, University of Toronto, 2000.
Martinek, Jason D. *Socialism and Print Culture in America, 1897–1920.* London: Pickering and Chatto, 2012.
Martynowych, Orest T. "'Canadianizing the Foreigner': Presbyterian Missionaries and Ukrainian Immigrants." In *New Soil – Old Roots: The Ukrainian Experience in Canada*, edited by Jaroslav Rozumnyj, 33–57. Winnipeg: Ukrainian Academy of Arts and Sciences in Canada, 1983.

- *Ukrainians in Canada: The Formative Period, 1891–1924*. Edmonton: Canadian Institute of Ukrainian Studies, 1991.
Marx, Karl. *Grundrisse: Foundations of the Critique of Political Economy*. Translated by Martin Nicolaus. New York: Vintage Books, 1973.
- "On the Jewish Question." *Early Writings*. Translated and edited by T.B. Bottomore, 1–40. London: C.A. Watts, 1963.
Marx, Karl, with Friedrich Engels. *The German Ideology: Including Theses on Feuerbach and Introduction to the Critique of Political Economy*. Amherst: Prometheus Books, 1998.
Mason, Jody. "Creating a 'Home Feeling': The Canadian Reading Camp Association and the Uses of Fiction, 1900–1905." *Labour/Le Travail* 76 (Fall 2015): 109–31.
- "'Rebel Woman,' 'Little Woman,' and the Eclectic Print Culture of Protest in *The Woman Worker*, 1926–1929." *Canadian Literature* 220 (Spring 2014): 17–35.
- *Writing Unemployment: Worklessness, Mobility, and Citizenship in Twentieth-Century Canadian Literatures*. Toronto: University of Toronto Press, 2013.
Matthews, Geoffrey J., and Donald P. Kerr. *Historical Atlas of Canada*, vol. 3: *Addressing the Twentieth Century, 1891–1961*. Toronto: University of Toronto Press, 1990.
McCallum, Todd. "The Great Depression's First History? The Vancouver Archives of Major J.S. Matthews and the Writing of Hobo History." *The Canadian Historical Review* 87, no. 1 (2006): 79–107.
- "Vancouver Through the Eyes of a Hobo: Experience, Identity, and Value in the Writing of Canada's Depression-Era Tramps." *Labour/Le Travail* 59 (2007): 43–68.
McCullough, Thomas. *The Nature and Uses of a Liberal Education Illustrated: Being a Lecture Delivered at the Opening of the Building, Erected for the Accommodation of the Classes of the Pictou Academical Institution*. Halifax: A.H. Holland, 1819. Microform. Canadian Institute for Historical Microreproductions, no. 63419.
McHenry, Elizabeth. *Forgotten Readers: Recovering the Lost History of African American Literary Societies*. Durham: Duke University Press, 2002.
McInnis, Peter. "Teamwork for Harmony: Labour–Management Production Committees and the Post-War Settlement in Canada." In Gauvreau and Christie, *Cultures of Citizenship*, 95–132.

McKay, Ian. "The Liberal Order Framework: A Prospectus for a Reconnaissance of Canadian History." *Canadian Historical Review* 81, no. 4 (2000): 616–45.
- "For a New Kind of History: A Reconnaissance of 100 Years of Canadian Socialism." *Labour / Le Travail* 46 (Fall 2000): 69–125.
- *Reasoning Otherwise: Leftists and the People's Enlightenment in Canada, 1890–1920.* Toronto: Between the Lines, 2008.

McKillop, Brian. *A Disciplined Intelligence: Critical Inquiry and Canadian Thought in the Victorian Era.* Montreal and Kingston: McGill-Queen's University Press, 2001.

McLaren, John. "Creating 'Slaves of Satan' or 'New Canadians'? The Law, Education, and the Socialization of Doukhobor Children, 1911–1935." In *Essays in the History of Canadian Law*, vol. 7: *British Columbia and the Yukon*, edited by Hamar Foster and John McLaren, 352–85. Toronto: University of Toronto Press, 1995.

McLean, Lorna R. "Education, Identity, and Citizenship in Early Modern Canada." *Journal of Canadian Studies* 41, no. 1 (Winter 2007): 5–30.
- "'The good citizen': Masculinity and Citizenship at Frontier College, 1899–1933." In Adamoski, Chunn, and Menzies, *Contesting Canadian Citizenship*, 225–45.

McLeod, K.A. "A Short History of the Immigrant Student as 'New Canadian.'" In *Education of Immigrant Students: Issues and Answers*, edited by Aaron Wolfgang, 19–31. Toronto: Ontario Institute for Studies in Education, 1975.

M.C.M. [Untitled.] *Catholic World*, June 1905, 428–29.

Mehta, Uday S. "Liberal Strategies of Exclusion." In *Tensions of Empire: Colonial Cultures in a Bourgeois World*, edited by Frederick Cooper and Ann Laura Stoler, 59–86. Berkeley: University of California Press, 1997.

Mein, Stewart G. "The Aberdeen Association: An Early Attempt to Provide Library Services to Settlers in Saskatchewan." *Saskatchewan History* 38, no. 1 (1985): 2–19.

Menzies, Robert, Robert Adamoski, and Dorothy E. Chunn. "Rethinking the Citizen in Canadian Social History." In Adamoski, Chunn, and Menzies, *Contesting Canadian Citizenship*, 11–41.

Metsaranta, Marc, ed. *Project Bay Street: Activities of Finnish-Canadians in Thunder Bay Before 1915.* Thunder Bay: Finnish-Canadian Historical Society, 1989.

Mills, Allen. *Fool for Christ: The Political Thought of J.S. Woodsworth.* Toronto: University of Toronto Press, 1991.

Mitchell, Tom. "'The Manufacture of Souls of Good Quality': Winnipeg's 1919 National Conference on Canadian Citizenship, English-Canadian Nationalism, and the New Order after the Great War." *Journal of Canadian Studies* 31, no. 4 (Winter 1996/1997): n.p. *Proquest Literature Online*.

Mitchison, Wendy. "Early Women's Organizations and Social Reform: Prelude to the Welfare State." In Moscovitch and Albert, eds., *The "Benevolent" State*, 77–92.

Molinaro, Dennis G. *An Exceptional Law: Section 98 and the Emergency State*. Toronto: University of Toronto Press, 2017.

Montreal Mechanics' Institute. *Catalogue of Books in the Library of the Mechanics' Institute of Montreal, with the Rules of the Library and Reading Room*. Montreal: A.A. Stevenson, 1860. Microform. Canadian Institute for Historical Microreproduction: fiche 91888.

Moore, Wallace. "The Frontier College Instructor." *The Globe*, 4 September 1920, 32. *ProQuest Historical Newspapers*.

Morris, Paul. "From 'Stalwart Peasant' to Canadian Citizen: Immigrant Identity in Early Twentieth-Century Canadian Fiction." In *The Canadian Alternative*, edited by Klaus Martens, 52–64. Wurzburg: Verlag Königshausen & Neuman, 2003.

Morrison, James H. *Alfred Fitzpatrick: Founder of Frontier College*. Tantallon: Four East, 1995.

– "Black Flies, Hard Work, Low Pay: A Century of Frontier College." *The Beaver* 79, no. 5 (November 1999): 33–8.

– *Camps and Classrooms: A Pictorial History of Frontier College*. Toronto: Frontier College Press, 1989.

Morton, Desmond. "Divided Loyalties? Divided Country?" In Kaplan, ed., *Belonging*, 50–63.

Morton, John. "Longfellow, Tennyson, and Transatlantic Celebrity." *Critical Survey* 27, no. 3 (September. 2013): 6–23. doi:10.3167/cs.2015.270302.

Moscovitch, Allan, and Jim Albert, eds. *The "Benevolent" State: The Growth of Welfare in Canada*. Toronto: Garamond Press, 1987.

Moscovitch, Allan, and Glenn Drover. "Social Expenditures and the Welfare State: The Canadian Experience in Historical Perspective." In Moscovitch and Albert, eds., *The "Benevolent" State*, 13–43.

Mouffe, Chantal. "Democratic Citizenship and the Political Community." In *Dimensions of Radical Democracy: Pluralism, Citizenship, Community*, edited by Mouffe, 225–39. London: Verso, 1992.

Munro, Brad. "Literacy for Citizenship: The Literacy Role of the Secretary of State Department." In *Canada and Citizenship Education*, edited by

Keith A. McLeod, 101–5. Toronto: Canadian Education Association, 1989.

Murray, Heather. *"Come, bright Improvement!": The Literary Societies of Nineteenth-Century Ontario.* Toronto: University of Toronto Press, 2002.

– "Teachers Must Read: Imagining and Instructing the Teacher-as-Reader in Nineteenth-Century English Canada." *Papers of the Bibliographical Society of Canada* 53, no. 1 (2015): 7–48.

– *Working in English: History, Institution, Resources.* Toronto: University of Toronto Press, 1996.

Murray, Heather, and Andrea Rotundo. "Surveying the Habit of Reading." In Gerson and Michon, eds., *History of the Book*, 455–9.

Nelson, Cary. *Revolutionary Memory: Recovering the Poetry of the American Left.* New York: Routledge, 2003.

New, W.H. "Service, Robert." In *Encyclopedia of Literature in Canada*, edited by W.H. New, 1033–34. Toronto: University of Toronto Press, 2002.

Noonan, Gerald. "Drummond – The Legend and the Legacy." *Canadian Literature* 90 (1981): 179–87.

Ontario. Ministry of Education. *Special Report of the Minister of Education on the Mechanics' Institutes (Ontario).* Toronto: C. Blackett Robinson, 1881.

"The Ontario Library Association, Toronto, March 31, April 1 1902." *The Library Journal* 27 (January–December 1902): 271–3.

The Ontario Readers. First Book. Toronto: T. Eaton Co., 1909.

Osborne, Ken. "Education Is the Best National Insurance: Citizenship Education in Canadian Schools, Past and Present." *Canadian and International Education* 25, no. 2 (1996): 31–59.

"Our Seven Demands." *Relief Camp Worker*, 19 March 1935, 3, 8.

Palmer, Bryan D. *A Culture in Conflict: Skilled Workers and Industrial Capitalism in Hamilton, Ontario, 1860–1914.* Montreal and Kingston: McGill-Queen's University Press, 1979.

– *Working-Class Experience: Rethinking the History of Canadian Labour, 1800–1991*, rev. ed. Toronto: McClelland and Stewart, 1992.

Pawley, Christine. *Reading on the Middle Border: The Culture of Print in Late Nineteenth-Century Osage, Iowa.* Amherst: University of Massachusetts Press, 2001.

Pennee, Donna Palmateer. "Literary Citizenship: Culture (Un)Bounded, Culture (Re)Distributed." In *Home-work: Postcolonialism, Pedagogy, and Canadian Literature*, edited by Cynthia Sugars, 75–86. Ottawa: University of Ottawa Press.

Perry, Adele. *On the Edge of Empire: Gender, Race, and the Making of British Columbia, 1849–1871*. Toronto: University of Toronto Press, 2001.
- "Women, Racialized People, and Making of the Liberal Order in Northern North America." In Constant and Ducharme, eds., *Liberalism and Hegemony*, 274–97.
Petryshyn, Jaroslav. *Peasants in the Promised Land: Canada and the Ukrainians, 1891–1914*. Toronto: James Lorimer, 1985.
Phillips Casteel, Sarah. "The Dream of Empire: The Scottish Roots of English Studies in Canada." *Ariel* 31, nos. 1–2 (2000): 127–52.
Pictured Words for New Canadians. Toronto: Council for Social Service of the Church of England of Canada, 1927.
"Police Attack Camp Strikers." *Relief Camp Worker*, 30 April 1935, 1, 6.
Pollock, Grace. "William Henry Drummond's True 'Canayen': Dialect Poetry and the Politics of Canadian Imperialism." *Essays on Canadian Writing* 79 (Spring 2003): 103–31.
Povinelli, E.A. *The Empire of Love: Toward a Theory of Intimacy, Genealogy, and Carnality*. Durham: Duke University Press, 2006.
Price, Leah. "Reading: The State of the Discipline." *Book History* 7 (2004): 303–20.
Prinsloo, Mastin. "Literacy and the New Literacy Studies." In *The Encyclopedia of Educational Theory and Philosophy*, edited by D.C. Phillips, 487–90. Thousand Oaks: Sage, 2014.
Procacci, Giovanna. *Gouverner le misère: La question sociale en France (1789–1848)*. Paris: Éditions du Seuil, 1993.
- "Governmentality and Citizenship." In *The Blackwell Companion to Political Sociology*, edited by Kate Nash and Alan Scott, 342–51. Oxford: Blackwell University Press, 2004.
Prokop, Manfred. "Canadianization of Immigrant Children: Role of the Rural Elementary School in Alberta, 1900–1930." *Alberta History* 37, no. 2 (1989): 1–10.
Purdy, Sean. "Building Homes, Building Citizens: Housing Reform and Nation Formation in Canada, 1900–1920." *Canadian Historical Review* 79, no. 3 (1998): 492–517.
Putman, J.H., and G.M. Weir. *Survey of the School System*. Victoria: Charles F. Banfield, 1925.
Quayson, Ato. "Paracolonialism, Delirious Sovereignty, and Affronted Ethno-nationalisms: Concerning Cosmopolitanism and National Identities." Plenary paper presented at Mikinaakominis/TransCanadas: Literature, Justice, Relation, Toronto, ON, May 2017.

Radforth, Ian. *Bushworkers and Bosses: Logging in Northern Ontario, 1900–1980*. Toronto: University of Toronto Press, 1987.
Radforth, Ian, and Joan Sangster. "A Link between Labour and Learning: The Workers' Educational Association in Ontario, 1917–1951." *Labour/Le Travail* 8/9 (1981/82): 41–78.
Radway, Janice. *Reading the Romance: Women, Patriarchy, and Popular Literature*. Chapel Hill: University of North Carolina Press, [1984]1992.
Ramirez, Bruno. "Brief Encounters: Italian Immigrant Workers and the CPR, 1900–30." *Labour / Le travail* 17 (Spring 1986): 9–27.
– *On the Move: French-Canadians and Italian Migrants in the North Atlantic Economy, 1860–1914*. Toronto: McClelland and Stewart, 1991.
– *Les premiers Italiens de Montréal*. Montreal: Boréal, 1984.
Ramsay, Ellen L. "Art and Industrial Society: The Role of the Toronto Mechanics' Institute in the Promotion of Art, 1831–1883." *Labour/Le travail* 43 (Spring 1999): 71–103.
Reaman, George Elmore. *English for New Canadians*. Toronto: National Council Y.M.C.A., 1919.
"In Regina City on Dominion Day." *Relief Camp Worker*, 29 July 1935, 4.
"Rhymes by the Batty Bard." *Relief Camp Worker*, 9 May 1935, 3.
Richter, L., ed. *Canada's Unemployment Problem*. Toronto: The Macmillan Co. of Canada, 1939.
Rifkind, Candida. *Comrades and Critics: Women, Literature, and the Left in 1930s Canada*. Toronto: University of Toronto Press, 2009.
Robert, Lucie, Christl Verduyn, and Janet B. Friskney. "Canadianization of the Curriculum." In Gerson and Michon, eds., *History of the Book*, 56–63.
Roberts, Barbara. *Whence They Came: Deportation from Canada, 1900–1935*. Ottawa: University of Ottawa Press, 1988.
Roberts, Peter. *English for Coming Americans. First Reader*. New York: Association Press, 1911.
– *English for Coming Canadians. First Reader*. New York: Association Press, 1913.
– *English for Coming Americans. A Rational System for Teaching English to Foreigners*. New York: Young Men's Christian Association Press, 1910.
– *English for Coming Canadians: Teacher's Manual. A Rational System for Teaching English to Foreigners*. New York: Association Press, c. 1912.

Robins, Nora. "'Useful Education for the Workingman': The Montreal Mechanics' Institute, 1828–70." In Welton, ed., *Knowledge for the People*, 20–34.
Robinson, Eric. "The History of Frontier College." Master's thesis, McGill University, 1960.
Robinson, Sydney W. *Muckraker: The Scandalous Life and Times of W.T. Stead*. London: Robson Press, 2012.
Romanow, Paula. "'The Picture of Democracy We Are Seeking': CBC Radio Forums and the Search for Canadian Identity, 1930–1950." *Journal of Radio Studies* 12, no. 1 (2005): 104–19.
Rose, Jonathan. *The Intellectual Life of the British Working Classes*. New Haven: Yale University Press, 2001.
Ross, Murray G. *The Y.M.C.A. in Canada: The Chronicle of a Century*. Toronto: Ryerson Press, 1951.
Rubin, Joan Shelley. "'They Flash Upon That Inward Eye': Poetry Recitation and American Readers." In *Reading Acts: US Readers' Interaction with Literature 1800–1950*, edited by Barbara Ryan and Amy Thomas, 258–80. Knoxville: University of Tennessee Press, 2002.
Rudin, Ronald. "From the Nation to the Citizen: Québec Historical Writing and the Shaping of Identity." In Adamoski, Chunn, and Menzies, eds., *Contesting Canadian Citizenship*, 95–112.
"Rural School Reading." *The Globe*, 14 December 1901, 7. ProQuest Historical Newspapers.
Russell, Roberta. "Bridging the Boundaries for a More Inclusive Citizenship Education." In Hébert, ed., *Citizenship Transformation in Canada*, 134–49.
Sacouman, James R. "Underdevelopment and the Structural Origins of Antigonish Movement Co-Operatives in Eastern Nova Scotia." *Acadiensis* 7, no. 1 (1977): 66–85.
Sandwell, R.W. "The Limits of Liberalism: The Liberal Reconnaissance and the History of the Family in Canada." *Canadian Historical Review* 84, no. 3 (2003): 423–53.
– "Missing Canadians: Reclaiming the A-Liberal Past." In Constant and Ducharme, eds., *Liberalism and Hegemony*, 246–73.
– "Notes Towards a History of Rural Canada, 1870–1940." In *Social Transformation in Rural Canada: Community, Cultures, and Collective Action*, edited by John R. Parkins and Maureen G. Reed, 21–42. Vancouver: UBC Press, 2013.

- "'Read, Listen, Discuss, Act': Adult Education, Rural Citizenship, and the Canadian National Farm Radio Forum, 1941–1965." *Historical Studies in Education* 71 (2012): 170–94.
- "Rural Reconstruction: Toward a New Synthesis in Canadian History." *Histoire Sociale/Social History* 27, no. 53 (1994): 1–32.

Schueller, Malini Johar. "Colonial Management, Collaborative Dissent: English Readers in the Philippines and Camilo Osias, 1905–1932." *Journal of Asian American Studies* 17, no. 2 (June 2014): 161–98. doi:10.1353/jaas.2014.0018.

Schuessler, Karl, and Mary Schuessler. *School on Wheels: Reaching and Teaching the Isolated Children of the North*. Erin: Boston Mills Press, 1986.

Schugurensky, Daniel. "Adult Citizenship Education: An Overview of the Field." In *Contexts of Adult Education: Canadian Perspectives*, edited by Tara Fenwick, Tom Nesbit, and Bruce Spencer, 68–80. Toronto: Thompson Educational, 2006.

Sefton MacDowell, Laurel. "Canada's Gulag: Project #51 Lac Seul (A Tale from the Great Depression)." *Journal of Canadian Studies* 28, no. 2 (1993): n.p. *Proquest Literature Online.*
- "Relief Camp Workers in Ontario During the Great Depression of the 1930s." *Canadian Historical Review* 76, no. 2 (1995): 205–28.

Sefton MacDowell, Laurel, and Ian Radforth, eds. *Canadian Working-Class History*. Toronto: Canadian Scholars' Press, 1992.

Selman, Gordon. *Adult Education in Canada: Historical Essays*. Toronto: Thompson Educational, 1995.
- *Citizenship and the Adult Education Movement in Canada*. Vancouver: Centre for Continuing Education, 1991.

Selman, Mark, Michael Cooke, and Paul Dampier. *The Foundations of Adult Education in Canada*, 2nd ed. Toronto: Thompson Educational, 1998.

Service, Robert W. *Songs of a Sourdough*. Toronto: William Briggs, 1909.

Seton, Ernest Thompson. *Wild Animals I Have Known*. Toronto: McClelland & Stewart, [1998]1991.

Sharpe, Robert J. "Citizenship, the Constitution Act, 1867, and the Charter." In Kaplan, *Belonging*, 221–44.

Sheehan, Nancy M. "Women's Organizations and Educational Issues, 1900–1930." *Woman Studies / Les cahiers de la femme* 7, no. 3 (1986): 90–94.

Sheffer, Jolie A. "'Citizen Sure Thing' or 'Jus' Foreigner'? Half-Caste Citizenship and the Family Romance in Onoto Wantanna's Orientalist Fiction." *Journal of Asian American Studies* 13, no. 1 (2010): 81–105.
Sher, Richard. *The Enlightenment and the Book: Scottish Authors and Their Publishers in Eighteenth-Century Britain, Ireland, and America.* Chicago: University of Chicago Press, 2006.
Slaughter, Joseph. *Human Rights, Inc.: The World Novel, Narrative Form, and International Law.* New York: Fordham University Press, 2007.
Smith, Adam. *An Inquiry into the Nature and Causes of the Wealth of Nations.* London: Printed for A. Strahan and T. Cadell, in the Strand, 1789. Eighteenth Century Collections Online.
Smith, Erin. *Hard-Boiled: Working-Class Readers and Pulp Magazines.* Philadelphia: Temple University Press, 2000.
Smith, Michelle. "Fiction and the Nation: The Construction of Canadian Identity in *Chatelaine* and *Canadian Home Journal* during the 1930s and 1940s." *British Journal of Canadian Studies* 27, no. 1 (2014): 37–53.
Somers, Margaret R. "Citizenship and the Place of the Public Sphere: Law, Community, and Political Culture in the Transition to Democracy." *American Sociological Review* 58, no. 5 (1993): 587–620.
Somerville, John. *The News Revolution in England: Cultural Dynamics of Daily Information.* Oxford: Oxford University Press, 1996.
Springhall, John. "Building Character in the British Boy: The Attempt to Extend Christian Manliness to Working-Class Adolescents, 1880–1914." In Mangan and Walvin, eds., *Manliness and Morality*, 52–74.
"Stand Solid Behind Your Delegation." *Relief Camp Worker*, 8 November 1934, 1, 6.
St. Denis, Michael. "The Great Depression: Letters from the Relief Camps of Prince Albert National Park." *Prairie Forum* 28, no. 2 (2003): 235–38.
Stoler, Ann Laura. *Carnal Knowledge and Imperial Power: Race and the Intimate in Colonial Rule.* Berkeley: University of California Press, 2002.
Storey, John. *Cultural Consumption and Everyday Life.* New York: Oxford University Press, 1999.
Strange, Carolyn, and Tina Loo. "Canadian Pulp Magazines and Second World War Regulations." In Gerson and Michon, eds., *History of the Book*, 255–8.
Street, Brian. *Literacy in Theory and Practice.* Cambridge: Cambridge University Press, 1984.

- "What 'New' in New Literacy Studies? Critical Approaches to Literacy in Theory and Practice." *Current Issues in Comparative Education* 5, no. 2 (2003): 77–91.
Stringer, Arthur. *The Prairie Wife*. New York: A.L. Burt, 1915.
Strong-Boag, Veronica. "Claiming a Place in the Nation: Citizenship Education and the Challenge of Feminists, Natives, and Workers in Post-Confederation Canada." *Canadian and International Education* 25, no. 2 (1996): 128–45.
- "Who Counts? Late Nineteenth- and Early Twentieth-Century Struggles about Gender, Race, and Class in Canada." In Hébert, ed., *Citizenship Transformation in Canada*, 37–56.
Struthers, James. *"No Fault of Their Own": Unemployment and the Canadian Welfare State, 1914–1941*. Toronto: University of Toronto Press, 1983.
Sugars, Cynthia, and Laura Moss, eds. *Canadian Literature in English: Texts and Contexts*, vol. 1. Toronto: Pearson Longman, 2008.
Sutherland, Neil. *Children in English-Canadian Society: Framing the Twentieth-Century Consensus*. Waterloo: Wilfrid Laurier University Press, 2000.
Swyripa, Frances, and John Thompson, eds. *Loyalties in Conflict: Ukrainians in Canada during the Great War*. Edmonton: Canadian Institute of Ukrainian Studies, 1983.
Taylor, Peter A. "Seton, Ernest Thompson." In *Encyclopedia of Literature in Canada*, edited by W.H. New, 1034–36. Toronto: University of Toronto Press, 2002.
Thoburn, Nicholas. *Anti-Book: On the Art and Politics of Radical Publishing*. Minneapolis: University of Minnesota Press, 2016.
Thompson, E.P. *The Making of the English Working Class*. New York: Pantheon, [1963]1964.
Tippett, Maria. *Making Culture: English-Canadian Institutions and the Arts before the Massey Commission*. Toronto: University of Toronto Press, 1990.
"Toil and Teaching Effective Mixture in Frontier Work." *The Globe*, 5 October 1929, 20. *ProQuest Historical Newspapers*.
Tonon, Laura, and Tracey Raney. "Building a Conservative Nation: An Examination of Canada's New Citizenship Guide, *Discover Canada*." *International Journal of Canadian Studies* 47 (2013): 201–19.
Tosh, John. *A Man's Place: Masculinity and the Middle-Class Home in Victorian England*. New Haven: Yale University Press, 1999.

"Touching Tributes to Teachers by Pupils of Frontier College." *The Globe*, 21 February 1925, 13. ProQuest Historical Newspapers.

Towheed, Shafquat, Rosalind Crone, and Katie Halsey, eds. *The History of Reading: A Reader*. London: Routledge, 2011.

Tough, David. "'Civilization Had Given Him the Vote': Citizenship and the Ballot in Sara Jeannette Duncan's *The Imperialist.*" *Journal of Canadian Studies* 40, no. 3 (2006): 120–34.

"Travelling Libraries." *The Globe*, 24 January 1901, 8. ProQuest Historical Newspapers.

"The Truth." *Relief Camp Worker*, 22 April, 1935, 5.

Tulchinsky, Gerald. *Taking Root: The Origins of the Canadian Jewish Community*. Toronto: Lester, 1992.

Turner, Bryan S. "Contemporary Problems in the Theory of Citizenship." In *Citizenship and Social Theory*, edited by Bryan S. Turner, 1–18. London: Sage, 1993.

– "We Are All Denizens Now: On the Erosion of Citizenship." *Citizenship Studies* 20, nos. 6–7 (2016): 679–92. doi:10.1080/13621025.2016.1191432.

Turner, Mark W. "Periodical Time in the Nineteenth Century." *Media History* 8, no. 2 (2002): 183–96.

Valverde, Mariana. *The Age of Light, Soap, and Water: Moral Reform in English Canada, 1885–1925*. Toronto: McClelland and Stewart, 1991.

Veracini, Lorenzo. *Settler Colonialism: A Theoretical Overview*. New York: Palgrave Macmillan, 2010.

Verrette, Michel. *L'alphabétisation au Québec, 1660–1900*. Sillery: Les éditions du Septentrion, 2002.

– "Measuring Literacy." In Gerson and Michon, eds., *History of the Book*, 453–5.

Verrette, Michel, and Yvan Lamonde. "Literacy and Print Culture." In Lamonde, Fleming, and Black, eds., *History of the Book*, 452–8.

Vincent, David. *Literacy and Popular Culture: England, 1750–1914*. Cambridge: Cambridge University Press, 1989.

Vipond, Mary. "Major Trends in Canada's Print Mass Media." In Gerson and Michon, eds., *History of the Book*, 242–7.

Viswanathan, Gauri. *Masks of Conquest: Literary Study and British Rule in India*. New York: Columbia University Press, [1989]2014.

Wadland, John H., and Margaret Hobbs. "The Printed Word." In *Historical Atlas of Canada*, vol. 2, edited by R. Louis Gentilcore, 136–7. Toronto: University of Toronto Press, 1993.

Waiser, Bill. "Relief Camps." In *The Oxford Companion to Canadian History*, edited by Gerald Hallowell, n.p. Toronto: Oxford University Press, 2004. *Oxford Reference Online*.

Walker, Judith. "The Needy and Competent Citizen in OECD Policy Documents." In *The State, Civil Society, and the Citizen: Exploring Relationships in the Field of Education in Europe*, edited by Michal Bron Jr., Paula Guimarães, and Rui Viera de Castro, 97–112. Frankfurt am Main: Peter Lang, 2009.

Walter, Pierre. "Adult Literacy Education on the Canadian Frontier." *Adult Basic Education* 13, no. 1 (Spring 2003): 3–18.

– "Literacy, Imagined Nations, and Imperialism: Frontier College and the Construction of British Canada, 1899–1933." *Adult Education Quarterly* 54, no. 1 (2003): 42–58.

Wan, Amy J. *Producing Good Citizens: Literacy Training in Anxious Times*. Pittsburgh: University of Pittsburgh Press, 2014.

Warner, Michael. *The Letters of the Republic: Publication and the Public Sphere in Eighteenth-Century America*. Cambridge, MA: Harvard University Press, 1992.

Watt, F.W. "Literature of Protest." In *Literary History of Canada*, vol. 1: *Canadian Literature in English*, edited by Carl F. Klinck, 473–89. Toronto: University of Toronto Press, 1976.

Weir, H.A. "Unemployed Youth." In Richter, ed., *Canada's Unemployment Problem*, 111–71.

Welton, Michael R., ed. "Introduction: Reclaiming Our Past: Memory, Traditions, Kindling Hope." In Welton, *Knowledge for the People*, 1–19.

– *Knowledge for the People: The Struggle for Adult Learning in English-Speaking Canada, 1828–1973*. Toronto: OISE Press, 1987.

Wigmore, Shirley K. "Mining the Frontier College Archives: Labourer-Teachers at the Castle-Tretheway Mine, Northern Ontario, 1925–1930." In *Proceedings of the Tenth Annual Conference of the Canadian Association for the Study of Adult Education*, edited by H.K. Baskett and Morris H.K. Baskett, 268–81. Kingston: Queen's University Faculty of Education, 1991.

Wilde, Terry. "Literacy at the Resource Frontier: A Matter of Life and Death." *Historical Studies in Education / Revue d'histoire de l'éducation* 24, no. 1 (2012): 130–49.

Williams, Raymond. *Keywords: A Vocabulary of Culture and Society*. Oxford: Oxford University Press, [1976]2015.

– *Marxism and Literature*. Oxford: Oxford University Press, [1977]2009.

- *The Sociology of Culture.* 1981. Chicago: University of Chicago Press, 1995.
Willinsky, John. *Learning to Divide the World: Education at Empire's End.* Minneapolis: University of Minnesota Press, 1998.
Willmott, Glenn. *Unreal Country: Modernity in the Canadian Novel in English.* Montreal and Kingston: McGill-Queen's University Press, 2002.
Wilson, J.D., R.M. Stamp, and L.P. Audet, eds. *Canadian Education: A History.* Scarborough: Prentice Hall, 1970.
Wiseman, John. A. "Phoenix in Flight: Ontario Mechanics' Institutes, 1880–1920." *Canadian Library Journal* 38, no. 6 (1981): 401–5.
Woodsworth, J.S. "Nation-Building." *University Magazine* 16, no. 1 (February 1917): 85–99.
- *Strangers Within Our Gates; Or, Coming Canadians.* Toronto: F.C. Stephenson, 1909.
"Workers' Education: Working-Class History No. 1." *Relief Camp Worker*, 8 November 1934, 7.
"Workers in the Slave Camps." *Relief Camp Worker*, 28 February 1935, 7.
Worton, David A. *The Dominion Bureau of Statistics: A History of Canada's Central Statistical Office and Its Antecedents, 1841–1972.* Montreal and Kingston: McGill-Queen's University Press, 1998.
"'Y' Work Among Lumbermen." *Pacific Coast Lumberman*, June 1919, 34.
Zaslow, Morris. *Opening of the Canadian North, 1870–1914.* Toronto: McClelland and Stewart, 1971.
Zavitz [Robinson], Marjorie Elizabeth. "The Frontier College and 'Bolshevism' in the Camps of Canada, 1919–1925." Master's thesis, University of Windsor, 1974.

Index

Aberdeen Association, xviii–xxi, 34; and Stead, William Thomas, xix–xx
American Federation of Labor, 110, 261n8
Anderson, J.T.M., 271n91; and *The Education of the New Canadian*, 80, 90, 92–3, 98–9, 151, 236n5, 270n84
Antigonish Movement, xxi, 190

bildungsroman, 42, 48–57
Bradwin, Edmund, 20, 86, 91, 93, 120, 125–6, 132, 171–2, 190–4, 199–207, 270n86, 297n92, 299n113; and *The Bunkhouse Man*, 71, 117–18, 139–41, 169; and the Canadian Association for Adult Education, 220, 293n64. *See also* Rigg Commission

Canadian Association for Adult Education, 190, 293n64; and CBC's National Farm Radio Forum and Citizens' Forum, 220, 300n3. *See also* Bradwin, Edmund; Corbett, E.A. ("Ned")

Canadian Citizenship Act, 97–8
Canadianization: federal government and responsibility for, 94–5, 128–31; growing concern for, 70, 80, 86–7, 99, 121–2, 133–4, 153, 269n79; and the "higher type," 87–9; and the teaching of adults, 90; as tool to fight socialism and communism, 109, 141–2; versus Americanization, 129–30. *See also* Anderson, J.T.M.; *Handbook for New Canadians*
Canadian Pacific Railway and Canadian National Railway: contributions to Frontier College, 141; and "schools on wheels,' xxii–iii
citizenship: affective, 5–6, 11–12, 29, 52–5, 105, 206–7; liberal, 7–12, 18–19, 54–5, 99–108, 125–36, 138–50, 160–2, 194–6; limits of liberal citizenship, 12–14, 88–9, 112–18; and Naturalization Act 1914, 95, 98, 102. *See also* Canadian Citizenship Act; social rights of citizenship

Communist Party of Canada, 139, 181, 283n70; and organization of unemployed workers, 177–8, 181, 290n23. See also Relief Camp Workers' Union; Section 98 of the Criminal Code
Connor, Ralph: See Gordon, Charles
Corbett, E.A. ("Ned"), 190. See also Canadian Association for Adult Education
cultural idealism: influence on late nineteenth-century Anglo-Canadian universities, 32, 39, 41–2, 202

Department of National Defence: and relief camps, 172–7, 188, 191–217
Drummond, W.H.: Alfred Fitzpatrick's preference for his poetry, 44–5, 57–8; imperialism in *The Habitant* and *Johnnie Courteau*, 57–63; reception of his poetry in camps, 63–4. See also Ontario Travelling Libraries; sentimentality

English as a second language, 89–90; and early teaching materials, 91–2, 96, 155–6, 269n79; primary school readers as resource for, 83–6

Fitzpatrick, Alfred: attitude toward bilingualism in education, 90; attitude toward foreign-language periodicals, 77–83, 146–7; conviction regarding state responsibility for the education of adults, 30–1, 33–4, 94, 126–35; development of materials for education of non-British immigrants, 91–4; and Dominion Charter for Frontier College, 125–6, 135–6; educational background of, 31–2; and fear of the "Red," 109–12, 140, 148–50; and founding of Canadian Reading Camp Association, 23–6, 33; idealism and utilitarianism as influences, 34–6, 39–42; and preference for Canadian authors, 64–5; and preference for popular fiction, 42–5; and Social Gospel movement, 10–11, 27–30, 32–3; and use of music in camps, 72–4. See also Drummond, W.H.; Gordon, Charles; Seton, Ernest Thompson
Fraser, William Alexander: Alfred Fitzpatrick's preference for his fiction, 41, 43–4. See also Ontario Travelling Libraries
Frontier College Act, 1922, 125–6, 131, 135–6

Gordon, Charles (Ralph Connor): 65; and *The Foreigner*, 106; and *To Him That Hath*, 111; influence on Alfred Fitzpatrick, 48–9, 53–5, 255n85; influence of Henry Drummond on, 53; and *The Man from Glengarry*, 50–3. See also National Conference on Character Education in Relation to Canadian Citizenship; Ontario Travelling Libraries
Gramsci, Antonio: and hegemony, 9–10, 14–15, 17–18; and passive revolution, 232–3

Grant, George Monro, 32–3, 58–9, 102–3

Habermasian public sphere, 6, 112–13
Hamilton, Charles Frederick. *See* Royal Canadian Mounted Police
Handbook for New Canadians: Alfred Fitzpatrick's attempt to secure contributions for, 94–5; as citizenship guide, 96–108, 273n101; and "enemy languages," 82–3, 95; and hierarchies of "race," 112–18, 139; and imperialism, 59; inception of, 91, 93, 270n86; lack of relevance in relief camps, 194–6; as language primer, 96, 273n100; relation to pre–Second World War federal citizenship materials, 128–9; as tool to fight socialism and communism, 109–12, 147–8; use of in the camps, 136–7, 150–65, 284n86
Hardy, Edward Austin, 38–9, 42–3

immigration to Canada: and Chinese Immigration Act 1923, 3–4, 160, 278n12, 286n105; early twentieth-century increase of, 68–9, 106–7, 121–2. *See also* Section 41 of the Immigration Act
imperialism: and conceptions of French Canadian culture, 58–63; declining influence on ideas about citizenship education, 97; and ideas of George Munro Grant, 33; and renewal of urban masculinity, 40

International Workers of the World, 68, 87, 109–10, 139, 141, 149, 261n8, 281n44, 290n23
intimate public, 11–12, 205–6

liberal order framework, 9–11, 14, 113, 258n120, 278n11
literacy: and literacy myth, xv–vi; rates in British North America and Canada, xvi–ii
Longfellow, Henry Wadsworth: and "The Bridge," 200–5

Macdonald-Robertson movement, 39, 41. *See also* utilitarianism
McLennan Travelling Libraries, 34, 249n9, 251n34
Mechanics' Institute Movement, xviii, 36–8, 249n13, 252n51, 256n103. *See also* utilitarianism

National Conference on Character Education in Relation to Canadian Citizenship, 111, 121, 134
National Film Board: and citizenship education, 220, 223, 228; and Cold War foreign policy, 301n10; and documentary film *Frontier College*, 223–8

One Big Union, 68, 139–41, 149, 261n8, 281n44
Ontario Travelling Libraries, 33–4, 40–4, 74–6, 166–8, 249n9, 253n71, 255n84; Ralph Connor's fiction in, 49; W.A. Fraser's fiction in, 44, 76; W.H. Drummond's poetry in, 57–8
On-to-Ottawa Trek, 175–6, 178–9, 185

Presbyterianism: and evangelical liberalism, 32–3, 36, 73; and ideas about education, 31–2. *See also* Fitzpatrick, Alfred

Relief Camp Workers' Union, 175; and *Relief Camp Worker*, 178–89
Rigg Commission, 212–16
Royal Canadian Mounted Police: and Charles Frederick Hamilton, 132–3, 148–50; and relief camps, 173, 175, 179, 209

Section 41 of the Immigration Act, 102, 127–8, 187, 273n112
Section 98 of the Criminal Code, 82–3, 180–1, 187, 267n58
sentimentality, 11–12, 74, 200–1; in the poems of Robert Service, 167; in the poems of W.H. Drummond, 57–8; and "sentimental community," 204–5
Service, Robert: and *Songs of a Sourdough*, 166–8, 287n116; workers' preference for the poems of, 168–9, 287n119. *See also* sentimentality
Seton, Ernest Thompson: Alfred Fitzpatrick's preference for his animal stories, 42, 44–6, 64; animal stories and early twentieth-century "practical education," 41, 255n78; and *Wild Animals I Have Known*, 46–8
Social Democratic Party of Canada, 82, 110

Social Gospel movement, 10–11, 27–8, 32–3. *See also* Gordon, Charles (Ralph Connor)
social rights of citizenship, 7–12, 187–8, 216–17, 231–4. *See also* citizenship

Trades and Labor Congress of Canada, 68, 110, 139–40, 261n8, 290n23

United Nations Education, Scientific, and Cultural Organization, 227–9, 302n20
utilitarianism: and ideas about literacy, xv, 37, 39–40. *See also* Macdonald-Robertson Movement; Mechanics' Institute Movement

Winnipeg General Strike, 68, 70, 95, 109–11, 132–3. *See also* Section 98 of the Criminal Code
Winnipeg People's Forum, xxiii. *See also* J.S. Woodsworth
Women's Christian Temperance Union, 28–9
Woodsworth, J.S., xxiii, 87–8, 268n75
Wordsworth, William: and "The Solitary Reaper," 103–4
Workers' Educational Association, xxi, 125, 136, 238n20

Young Men's Christian Association, xxiii, 84; and English as a second language materials, 91–2, 96